Work Options for Older Americans

WORK OPTIONS FOR
OLDER AMERICANS

EDITED BY

Teresa Ghilarducci & John Turner

University of Notre Dame Press
Notre Dame, Indiana

81150309

Library of Congress Cataloging-in-Publication Data

Work options for older Americans / edited by Teresa Ghilarducci and John Turner.
    p.   cm.
  Includes bibliographical references and index.
  ISBN-13: 978-0-268-02970-8 (pbk. : alk. paper)
  ISBN-10: 0-268-02970-9 (pbk. : alk. paper)
1. Older people—Employment—United States.   2. Age and employment—
United States.   3. Retirees—Employment—United States.   I. Ghilarducci, Teresa.
II. Turner, John A. (John Andrew), 1949 July 9–
  HD6280.W683   2007
  331.3'980973—dc22
                                                                          2007003382

Contents

Preface

KATHLEEN CHRISTENSEN

The Alfred P. Sloan Foundation is committed to designing research strategies that will help ordinary workers navigate their way through the changing needs of employers and the changing demands at the workplace. Though there is great need for concern about the working poor and intermittent workers, this volume focuses on the 70 percent of families in the middle of the income distribution—the third to ninth deciles—whose members are most likely to be strongly attached to the labor market.

The Alfred P. Sloan Foundation supported this volume, with distributional assistance from AARP, in order to examine some key questions:

- Do older workers who want to postpone retirement have the work options they need in order to find the work schedules they want? Though family-life issues (vital unpaid duties that constrain work scheduling) concern workers at all ages, this book explores whether older workers have special issues that affect their relationships with their employers. Perhaps, employers have identified issues particular to older workers. Much has been said about the sandwich generation—older workers taking care of adults and children. Human resource experts are identifying new challenges in the wake of older men forming new families.
- Another obvious concern is the degree to which aging causes health conditions that affect work. Has the general health improvement of the population affected the labor force participation and work effort of older Americans?
- It is important for economists and other social scientists to investigate whether working older Americans are more satisfied with their lives than were older

people who were working in the past. Are the healthiest, happiest older people working? If so, what is the causation? Are they healthier and happier than older people not working because they have more income and are finding meaning in their work? Or do healthier, more satisfied people tend to continue working? Economists are interested (as are others) in the distinction between "voluntary" and "involuntary" part-time work. Answering these questions may help economists characterize the nature of older worker labor force participation.

- This issue of voluntary versus involuntary work raises the question of whether a sudden and substantial fall in financial pension wealth induces older Americans to work more. Does uncertainty about healthcare coverage and the status of their savings, pension, and Social Security plan cause older people to work more? Do the size and source of a wealth decline matter?

- We must turn to the employer side of the issue. What attitudes do employers have that may impede accommodating older workers? Age discrimination claims have increased by 31 percent since the recession started in 2001. Did the economic expansion of the 1990s hide latent prejudices that older workers are too expensive because they are not sufficiently trained in modern skills and techniques? Is the relatively high cost of health insurance for the older work force a deterrent to older worker employment?

- Furthermore, do certain kinds of employer characteristics predict more accommodation and demand for older workers than others? An issue in the 1997 United Parcel Service (UPS) and Teamsters strike was whether the UPS pension system's provisions would remain varied by region or become one large company plan. An argument for regional plans was that each region displayed a very different set of tradeoffs between money and time. In the east, workers and employers tend to agree to early retirement ages and reduced benefits. In the west, there were fewer early retirement options, but higher benefits.

- Labor economists have described seniority systems as ways employers and workers handle an aging workforce and aging in general as one works throughout a lifetime. For instance, in the coal mines under contract with the United Mine Workers of America, the oldest workers are able to bid for the job running the controls that guide the "man trips"—the actual name of the carts that take miners underground a mile or two, and out again. He (or, theoretically, she) works on a mountaintop in a warm shack with a tiny TV.

- We also need to investigate special barriers older workers may face due to racial or ethnic discrimination in occupations where skills atrophy especially quickly.

- External constraints also affect the optimal relationship older workers and employers want. Those external constraints could include regulatory treatment of pension benefits that restrict phased or partial retirement arrangements. In particular, does the Employee Retirement Income Security Act (ERISA, pension law) pose particular constraints compared to other tax and state regulations?
- In short, we focus on how workplaces have, and might yet, adapt to and accommodate an aging work force. These questions are especially important because between 2000 and 2020 the number of workers between 55 and 64 years old will grow by 17.8 million, while there will be no growth in workers between 24 and 54.

This volume brings innovations in measurement as well as original perspectives, including contributions by economist Robert Hutchens and psychologist Patricia Raskin. Hutchens surveys employers and checks their responses against a national sample of workers to find out what employers are doing to respond to workers' stated desire to gradually retire from their career jobs. Raskin and Gregory Gettas's opinion about who retires and why comes from their survey of older individuals and actual clinical work with patients.

The volume is the result of a conference that brought together researchers, mostly economists, working on aspects of the macroeconomic and labor-relations aspects of an aging workforce. The result is a highly focused look at government policies and the desires of workers and employers.

Most of the authors address Alfred P. Sloan Foundation president Ralph Gomery's call for scientists to identify what is known in scientific research, what is unknown and pertinent to discover, and what is unknowable and will have to be stipulated. This process winnows out ideology and is an efficient way to plot needed research.

Introduction

Determining the Quality of Work Options for Older Americans

TERESA GHILARDUCCI *&* JOHN TURNER

This book lays out bold analyses and sharp proposals for the future of work in America as the work force ages. The scholars writing here address the pressing concerns, the red herrings, and what economists, lawyers, sociologists, and psychologists, know, don't know, and consider unknowable concerning what the options to work will be like for older Americans. Each author addresses the best ways to prepare for the gigantic growth in older workers and does not judge them for their political feasibility. We take the view that all good ideas are politically feasible.

Though individual scholars prepared the chapters and each chapter pertains to the author's own interests, focus, and areas of expertise, the editors identified one particular theme throughout. As each of us looked in our crystal balls and saw the labor market changing dramatically as workers age, we explicitly or implicitly addressed how the changes would affect the ongoing bargaining between employers and workers. One can easily articulate this overall theme: labor market outcomes, such as work arrangements and pay for older workers, are a result of a bargaining process between workers and firms, where each side weighs the costs and benefits of working longer at older ages and hiring older workers. Therefore, in the United States, which bans mandatory retirement, work is always an option; the question is, are the options that workers want the same as those that employers offer?

One way to envision how a government policy affects the quality of the work options that older Americans will be offered is by considering the effects of the level of Social Security benefits. The amount of pension security a worker has affects the terms of employment an older worker will accept and an employer will offer. An employee with a generous Social Security benefit will demand, and perhaps be able to receive higher pay and better working conditions, than an employee with no pension income. Because employment contracts are constructed privately, the only way the state can affect outcomes is with guidelines, regulations, and mandates. Therefore each chapter in this book assesses how its proposals might affect the balance of power between workers and firms.

For example, Rudoph Penner, Pamela Perun, and Eugene Steuerle suggest a provocative proposal in chapter 5: making Medicare the first medical insurance payer instead of the secondary payer, which would lower the cost of hiring older workers. In turn, as a result of taxpayers subsidizing the health insurance of older workers, employers could raise wages and provide attractive work schedules to older workers—or not. The outcome depends on older workers' reservation wages, which depend on pension and Social Security trends.

All of the authors took special pains to assess their article's contribution to what we might guess will be the working conditions and labor market environment for older working Americans in the near future. The authors also reviewed what is not known in their area but should be. There is a careful call for research that will answer particularly poignant questions. Even more importantly, the authors and commentators perform good science, honestly and forthrightly noting uncertainties, so that policy makers won't predict policy outcomes with unwarranted confidence.

AN OVERVIEW OF THE CHAPTERS

Alicia Munnell presents the motivation for the book concisely. She describes several converging forces that are likely to increase the labor force participation of older people in the near future. She assumes that having work as an option is good for Americans since their pensions are diminishing in generosity. Chapter 3, by Patricia M. Raskin and Gregory Gettas, is a refreshing analysis of the meaning of work and determinants of work satisfaction. Their database shows that for some, work can be highly beneficial, and that there are many ways people can increase their employment in some occupations going through restructuring and technological change. For others, however, work is likely to be harsh and depressing, and phased retirement could be cause for a diminution of job status.

Edward Wolff in chapter 6 provides one of the few chapters that look at distributional issues between workers with different wealth levels and different work histories. How each proposal and vision for the future affects people from different socioeconomic backgrounds is an essential feature of any policy debate. He reminds us, as does the paper by Sharon Hermes and Teresa Ghilarducci (chapter 8), what the advantages of defined benefit plans are for workers. Wolff acknowledges that while defined contribution plans have advantages in terms of transparency and portability, defined benefit plans have historically been a reliable source of income to many low- and middle-income retirees.

Rudoph Penner, Pamela Perun, and Eugene Steuerle argue in chapter 5 that employers and workers are going to face some key constraints in establishing the best deals for older workers and employers. They are especially concerned that because it is difficult for workers to collect a pension while phasing out work, people may retire when they really don't want to. They propose that the government take a proactive stance and provide guidance to employers who are chary of experimenting under threat of losing all their pension tax deductions, and they issue guidelines based on the progressive and effective experiments in the public sector and for university faculty covered by TIAA-CREF. They explore possible reasons for these partial-pension/partial-retirement arrangements. These arrangements may be intended to induce employees to declare when they will actually retire. From this perspective, they are a succession-planning tool. Penner and coauthors also establish criteria for good legislation regarding formal phased retirement plans. The legislation should (a) clearly say what a legal plan would look like, and (b) provide a safe harbor for plans that look like that.

Chapter 4, by Robert Hutchens and Jennjou Chen, considers both sides of the market—workers and employers—concerning the options to retire and work at advanced ages. Though in principle hardly anyone is against phased retirement, it seems workers haven't found that employers' offers for phased retirement have been very attractive. Hutchens and Chen add institutional sophistication by acknowledging the legal issues associated with their proposal for extending health insurance to phased retirees in special circumstances where employers especially want a full-time worker to stay. An example of special circumstances might be a worker who moves from full-time to part-time employment after attaining a minimum of, say, 10 years of job tenure. Since the main barrier to this proposal is the nondiscrimination rules promulgated by the Internal Revenue Service, the main issue is whether this enhanced health insurance for phased retirees favors high-wage workers. Joseph Quinn, in his comments on chapter 4, relates his earlier work on phased retirement and the prevalence of bridge jobs to what Hutchens found.

The chapter by Dana Muir and John Turner (7) cleverly, and for the first time, analyzes the urgent issue of how improving longevity causes the increasing pension costs for employer-provided plans. Many nations are facing this problem, which is illustrated well in chapter 10 on international trends in private defined benefit plans. They pose a classic economic question: what are employers doing to reduce this cost that they face, which is increasing at about 1 percent per year. As Hutchens comments, economists love this kind of paper. Muir and Turner show that employers have a number of options for dealing with this problem, though some good ones are prevented by law: they could ignore the problem by choosing to not update mortality tables; use conservative funding assumptions to offset the misrepresentation of costs that an outdated mortality table will yield; cut future benefit accruals; or encourage their employees to take a lump-sum option (though this won't matter if the appropriate mortality table is used). More likely, firms are switching to defined contribution plans, which are immune to the glacial inevitability of improved longevity. Muir and Turner think that defined benefit plans have beneficial effects on pension retirement security. If the Employee Retirement Income Security Act were changed so that benefits could be expressed in terms of accrued present value (in a way liabilities are expressed), then firms could be more encouraged to maintain, and perhaps even adopt, defined benefit plans.

The Government Accountability Office review by Charles Jeszeck and others (chapter 10) and Sara Rix's discussion of the international trends, imply that a third party, the state, has an interest in giving more options to older citizens to work, and each nation reviewed does so with incentives and disincentives—carrots and sticks. The state is key in determining if older workers will stay in the labor force with a great deal of bargaining power or next to none. The Swedish social security system was turned into a massive cash balance plan, which lowered the generosity of early-retirement benefits. The Swedish government implemented a number of highly specialized job and training initiatives designed to make work more attractive to the elderly at the same time that it decreased pensions. In that nation, the state induced an altering of work patterns in such a way as to even out the distribution of bargaining power between employers and employees. In the Netherlands, workers can require accommodation for their old age in much the same way that disabled workers can require an accommodation in work schedules. These kinds of protection clearly help the worker's side in the balance of power.

Christian Weller and Jeffrey Wenger (chapter 9) echo Joseph Piacentini's argument (see his comments on chapter 7) that retirement policy is health policy. Any effort to raise the retirement age and have workers voluntarily remain employed will require an ability to have them get health insurance without making their employers pay for it, given the extraordinary expense of older workers' health insurance coverage.

Todd Elder agrees with Weller and Wenger that an increased labor-force participation of Americans aged 55–64, which was caused by cutbacks in retiree health insurance that were primarily the result of shifting the costs of increased premiums onto retirees a decade ago, may be evident now. In addition, Weller and Wenger's findings that retirees have less private health insurance suggests that the cost of this insurance has increased so much that workers delay retirement in order to keep their employers' health insurance. Elder connects Weller and Wenger's findings on health insurance and work incentives with Hutchens' findings that employers do not accommodate many older workers' desires to keep their health insurance and work part-time. Both findings suggest that older Americans are working more because they don't have adequate health insurance coverage when they retire, even under Medicare. Increased reliance on Supplemental Security Insurance and other disability programs may also reflect the diminishment of health insurance for retirees.

Elder's comprehensive review notes that researchers know that access to retiree health insurance affects retirement behavior, but we just don't know how much. We also know medical costs are increasing (though it is unknowable whether technological changes will actually reduce costs someday), but it will remain to be seen how much shifting costs to retirees can continue. If it does, we can expect that retirement decisions will be affected by the cost of retiree health insurance and, importantly, the uncertainty about future health insurance costs.

Sharon Hermes and Teresa Ghilarducci (chapter 8) contribute to the existing knowledge about older workers by showing that older-worker participation in the labor force during the most recent recession is a reverse of past trends. Men and women have stayed in and entered the labor force in proportions never seen before. The wealth shock, due to the combination of workers' pensions being exposed by the financial markets in ways they never have been before, and the financial markets' plunging suggest that losing pension wealth played a major role in the increased labor-force participation in ways that support Munnell's predictions.

In his comments, Stephen Woodbury reminds us that economists have exceedingly narrow views of work, by evoking Thorstein Veblen's notion that "workmanship" is part of human nature. Economic models include nonmonetary aspects of a job as a part of compensation, attempting to account for the vitality, meaning, and desire to be useful in a community that people want from their jobs. But economists don't do this very well. Psychologists Raskin and Gettas (chapter 3) provide a fascinating review of what hundreds of older workers say about their jobs and their lives after their career jobs. Older people consider work and retirement in very individual ways, but gender and class strongly affect attachment to work. Middle-class jobs may give adults meaning and autonomy, but most jobs aren't professional jobs where one can obtain self-expression. Some men find freedom from "the bonds of earning a wage" in retirement while other men may feel incompetent because they are not working. Women evaluate their self-efficacy in terms of home life and work life, but women with strong work identities are more fearful and skeptical of retirement.

If employers want greater numbers of older workers, then they will have to make older workers feel welcomed; judge competency objectively, not by stereotypical age norms; and accommodate older workers' desires for flexibility and autonomy. From the workers' points of view, the most important determinant of work and retirement satisfaction is whether each activity is done by choice and not driven by severe income needs, an obvious but salient point that well-being is associated with a sense of control over one's life.

WHAT IS TO BE DONE?

Possible policy options raised by various authors that may facilitate or encourage work at older ages include the following:

- Address the need of older workers to have meaningful training opportunities
- Expand the Americans with Disabilities Act to include accommodations for limitations caused by age
- Permit reduced work hours and partial pension payments
- Permit defined benefit plans to adjust to increased life expectancy with more flexibility
- Adjust Social Security early and normal retirement ages to take into account increased life expectancy and the improved health of some older workers
- Base full retirement benefits on the number of years worked, rather than age
- Have Medicare be the primary insurer for workers age 65 and older
- Address ways to reduce the costs of health benefits for older workers
- Mitigate the effect defined contribution plans have on making the wealth and income distribution more unequal by implementing saver's credits for lower income workers or mandating a defined contribution supplement to Social Security

FURTHER RESEARCH

The contributions here suggest another look at an important policy idea— raising the Social Security early retirement age. The arguments mustered by opponents are the disparate impacts resulting from race and socioeconomic class and the fact that 30 percent of all people age 60–64 cannot work because of physical or mental limitations. Raising the retirement age for the collection of full benefits may reduce the pressure on pension plans and keep them stronger, but such a move entails a large cut in benefits for those who still retire at "younger" ages. In a roundtable discussion among all the participants, many expressed concern for the individuals in poor health who can't work, especially those who started work early because they didn't attend college.

Wenger proposed a possible alternative to that controversial proposal—the Italian model! Instead of using age to establish eligibility for early retirement benefits, Social Security could use the number of covered quarters. College-educated workers tend to be in better health, have higher salaries, and find work later in life to be more rewarding. College-educated workers start work at much older ages than blue-collar and lower-income individuals do. One of the reasons educated workers want to work longer may be that eagerness to work at older ages is related to the number of years one has been working. Another fact that may support the idea that normal retirement ages be linked to total years of full-time work is that older women are increasing their labor-force participation rates faster than older men, and faster than younger women. Women may be adjusting their retirement ages to get forty years of work in.

The problem with basing the eligibility for retirement benefits on how long one has been working is that unemployment spells, child-rearing, and family care could be reasons people have fewer years in the workforce. The new rule could actually hurt low-income workers and women if they are likely the groups to be affected by these life events. However, the adverse distributional issues that this would cause could be taken care of by granting work credits for periods of dependent care and unemployment.

PART 1

LIVING LONGER,
WORKING LONGER

CHAPTER ONE

Working Longer

A Potential Win-Win Proposition

ALICIA H. MUNNELL

If people continue to retire in their early 60s, they will not have enough money to comfortably support themselves in retirement. Social Security, the backbone of the retirement system, will not replace as much preretirement income in the future as it does today. Employer-sponsored pensions also involve considerably more uncertainty given the shift from defined benefit (DB) to defined contribution (DC) plans, such as 401(k)s. With institutional savings arrangements on the decline, one might have thought that people would be saving more on their own. But the personal saving rate remains very low. Combine the retirement income crunch with the dramatic increase in life expectancy, and continued employment in later life appears like a promising option for ensuring the financial security of older Americans.

At the same time, employers are likely to face a labor shortage going forward. Because of the decline in the fertility rate, they will no longer be able to tap into a rapidly growing pool of younger workers. Increased reliance on women, immigrants, and capital, as well as relocation to low-wage areas may relieve some of the pressure. But many employers will find these responses inadequate to make up for the shortfall.

Thus, continued employment of older workers could be a win-win situation for employers and employees. Staying in the labor force longer will ease the crunch on retirement income faced by older Americans, and the hiring of older workers will ease the labor shortage faced by employers. There are some signs of hope that things will work out. Older workers will be better educated and healthier than in the past, they will have a lifetime of experience, and they will be well suited to a job market that has become much less physically demanding. On the other hand, companies generally resist employing part-time workers, and most older people do not want to work full time. Older workers are also expensive in terms of health insurance and defined benefit–plan pension costs. And while employers value the reliability and experience of older workers, they generally view them as inflexible and not worth training. Increasing the employment of older workers, therefore, will require increased flexibility on the part of both employers and employees.

The first section of this chapter explores the declining prospects for traditional sources of retirement income and documents how continued employment could help. The second section identifies possible ways that employers could fill the upcoming labor market shortfall, and suggests reasons why older workers might be an attractive option. The third section explores impediments to employing older workers. The final section draws several conclusions.

RETIREMENT INCOME TRENDS AND THE NEED FOR CONTINUED EMPLOYMENT

The relative importance of the various sources of retirement income for those aged 65 and over is shown in Figure 1. Social Security is dominant even for the household in the middle of the income distribution. Pensions are second, fol-

Figure 1. Retirement Income by Source, Households Aged 65 and Older, Middle Income Quintile

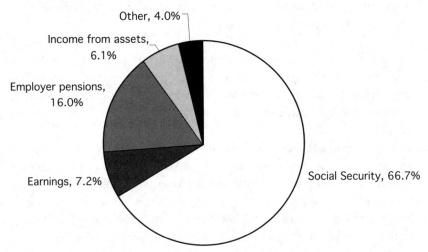

Source: U.S. Social Security Administration. 2006. *Income of the Population Aged 55 and Older, 2000.* Washington, DC, (February). http://www.ssa.gov/policy/docs/statcomps/income_pop55/2004/incpop04.pdf.

lowed by individual savings and earnings. The important issue is what these retirement income sources will look like going forward.

The Outlook for Social Security

Even under current law, Social Security will provide less retirement income relative to previous earnings than it does today. Combine the already legislated reductions with potential cuts to close the financing gap, and Social Security might
no longer be the mainstay of the retirement system for many people.

Normal retirement age is rising.   First, under current law, the normal retirement
age (NRA) is scheduled to increase from 65, for those who reached 62 before
2000, to 67 for people reaching age 62 in or after 2022. The increase in the NRA
is equivalent to an across-the-board benefit cut. For those who do retire at age 65,
this cut takes the form of lower monthly benefits; for those who continue to work
to the NRA, it takes the form of fewer years of benefits. The replacement rate for
the medium earner who retires at age 65, for example, will drop from 40.8 percent in 2002 to 36.3 percent in 2030 (Figure 2).

Medicare will take bigger bite.   The second development that will affect future
replacement rates is the rising cost of Medicare. Premiums for Medicare Part B,
which are automatically deducted from Social Security benefits, are scheduled
to increase from 6.8 percent of benefits for someone who retired in 2000 to

Figure 2. Social Security Replacement Rate for Worker with a History of Average
Earnings, 2002 and 2030

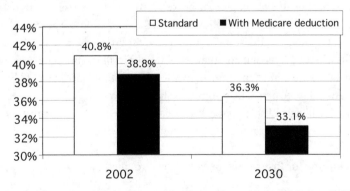

Source: U.S. Social Security Administration. 2006b. *The 2006 Annual Report of the Board of Trustees
of the Federal Old-Age and Survivors Insurance and Disability Insurance Trust Funds and Supplementary Medical Insurance Trust Fund.* http://www.ssa.gov/OACT/TR/TR06/tr06.pdf; http://cms.hhs.gov/
ReportsTrustsFunds/downloads/tr2006.pdf.

10.2 percent for someone retiring in 2030. Since premiums tend to rise rapidly after retirement, they will account for an even larger share of Social Security benefits as recipients age, potentially consuming all cost-of-living adjustments provided along the way.

More benefits will be taxed. The third factor that will reduce Social Security benefits is the extent to which they are taxed under the personal income tax. Under current law, individuals with less than $25,000 and married couples with less than $32,000 of "combined income" do not have to pay taxes on their Social Security benefits.[1] Above those thresholds, recipients must pay taxes on a portion of their benefits.

Today most beneficiaries with a history of medium earnings—and thus about $14,000 in Social Security benefits—pay no tax. But the thresholds are not indexed for growth in average wages or even for inflation. By 2030, the nominal Social Security benefit for the worker with a history of medium earnings is projected to nearly triple to about $38,000. If other nominal income increases similarly, many medium earners will pay tax on half of their benefits. (Note that the full Social Security benefit is considered for tax purposes, even though the Medicare Part B premium is deducted before payment.) A 15 percent personal income tax on half of the benefits will reduce replacement rates by another 7.5 percent as compared to today.[2]

The financing gap creates further pressure. The final development, unlike those discussed above, is by necessity speculative. Eliminating the entire 75-year deficit by reducing benefits alone would require a 13 percent cut in benefits right now. But that figure makes no allowance for protecting the benefits of those 55 and over and the benefits of people who are disabled. Holding these groups harmless, which seems politically likely, requires a benefit cut of about 20 percent to restore balance. If Congress closes the funding gap by splitting the difference—so that benefits are cut 10 percent and the rest of the shortfall is eliminated through additional revenue—the replacement rate for the medium earner would be cut by an additional three percentage points. In short, as shown in Table 1, forces already in place are likely to lead to a markedly reduced role for Social Security. This reduced role will have a profound effect on future retirees.

The Outlook for Private Sector Employer-Provided Pensions

With a diminished role for Social Security, retirees will be increasingly dependent on employer-sponsored pensions. One problem is that at any moment in

Table 1. Social Security Replacement Rate in 2030 for a Worker with a History of Average Earnings, Retiring at Age 65 and Age 62

Development	Percent of Earnings in 2030	
	Age 65	Age 62
Unadjusted	41.3	32.8
After extension of Normal Retirement Age	36.3	28.7
After Medicare Part B Premium	32.6	25.0*
After Personal Income Tax	29.9	22.8
After 10% benefit cut to eliminate financing gap	26.3	20.0

Source: U.S. Social Security Administration (2003a); (2003b); and author's estimate.
Note: For the individual retiring at age 62, the Medicare Part B premium will not begin until age 65.

time, less than half the private sector workforce aged 25–64 participates in an employer-sponsored plan of any type, and this fraction, which has remained virtually unchanged since the late-1970s, is unlikely to improve (Figure 3).[3] Since pension participation tends to increase with earnings, it is only middle- and upper-income individuals who will have an employer-provided pension to supplement their Social Security benefits.

Figure 3. Percent of the Private Workforce Participating in a Pension, 1979–2004

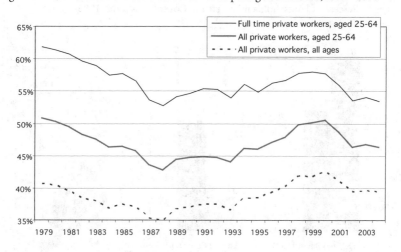

Source: Author's calculations using the March CPS, 1979–2004.

The other issue is that the nature of pension coverage has changed dramatically. Twenty years ago, most people with pension coverage had a traditional DB plan that paid a lifetime annuity at retirement.[4] Today the world looks very different. Most people with a pension have a DC plan—most often a 401(k) (see Figure 4). In contrast to DB plans, DC plans are like savings accounts. Generally the employee, and often the employer, contributes a specified percentage of earnings to the account. These contributions are invested, usually at the direction of the employee, mostly in mutual funds consisting of stocks and bonds. Upon retirement, the worker generally receives the balance in the account as a lump sum, albeit with the option to roll it over to an Individual Retirement Account (IRA).

The defining characteristics of 401(k) plans are that participation is voluntary and that the employee as well as the employer can make pre-tax contributions. These characteristics shift a substantial portion of the burden for providing for retirement to the employee; the employee decides whether or not to participate, how much to contribute, how to invest the assets, and how to use the assets at retirement. In addition, workers have some access to 401(k) plan funds before retirement, adding another element of individual responsibility.

Although 401(k) plans give individuals control of their investments and are much better than DB plans for the mobile employee, they come up short in a number of ways. *In theory,* workers could accumulate substantial pension wealth under 401(k) plans. But *in practice* they do not. For example, the average house-

Figure 4. Percent of Households with Pension Coverage by Type, 1983–2004

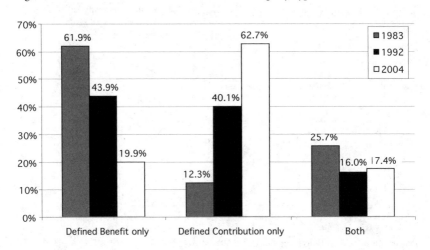

Source: Author's calculations from the Survey of Consumer Finances.

hold approaching retirement in 2001 had accumulated only $55,000—not much to support a couple for two decades (Aizcorbe, Kennickell, and Moore 2003). The reason for these relatively low balances appears to be that the entire burden is on employees, and many make mistakes at every step along the way. A quarter of those eligible to participate in a plan fail to do so; less than 10 percent of those that do participate contribute the maximum; more than half fail to diversify their investments; many overinvest in company stock; and almost none rebalance their portfolios in response to age or market returns. Most importantly, many cash out when they change jobs, and very few annuitize at retirement.

In addition to the shift in pension coverage from DB to 401(k) plans, many employers are converting their traditional DB plans to "cash balance" plans.[5] The key characteristic of these plans is that they define the benefit in terms of a lump sum rather than an annuity payment. Thus, many workers in these plans can cash out accumulations when they change jobs; and, at retirement, all workers face the daunting task of allocating fixed sums over their expected remaining lifetimes.

In short, workers with employer-sponsored pension coverage face an array of challenges. First, the majority now rely on 401(k) and similar plans, and 401(k)s are coming up short. Second, within the DB world, many employers have transformed their traditional plan to a hybrid that generally provides lump-sum benefits rather than a stream of payments. Still, people with 401(k) plans and hybrids are the lucky ones. At any time, about half the workforce aged 25–64 has no pension coverage at all.

The Outlook for Individual Saving

The personal saving rate, as a percentage of disposable personal income, has fallen steadily from 10 percent in 1980 to below zero in 2005, with a slight interruption during the previous recession in 1991 (Figure 5). In fact, the personal saving rate of 2005 was at its lowest point since the Great Depression.

The precipitous drop in the U.S. saving rate during the 1990s can be attributed in part to the "wealth effect" and the way savings are measured. The stock market boom and hot economy convinced many Americans that their retirement would be secure as they saw their investments, such as 401(k)s and IRAs, grow in value. Capital gains, however, are not included in the measurement of national income since they do not reflect increases in output. The increase in wealth nevertheless spurred a mass increase in consumption (Perozek and Reinsdorf 2002). As consumption rose, savings fell. This pattern was mirrored in contributions to traditional DB plans.

Because of the "wealth effect" and pension accounting conventions, one would expect the personal savings rate to rise significantly after the market crash. Yet it

Figure 5. Personal Saving in the United States as a Percentage of Disposable Personal Income, 1980–2005

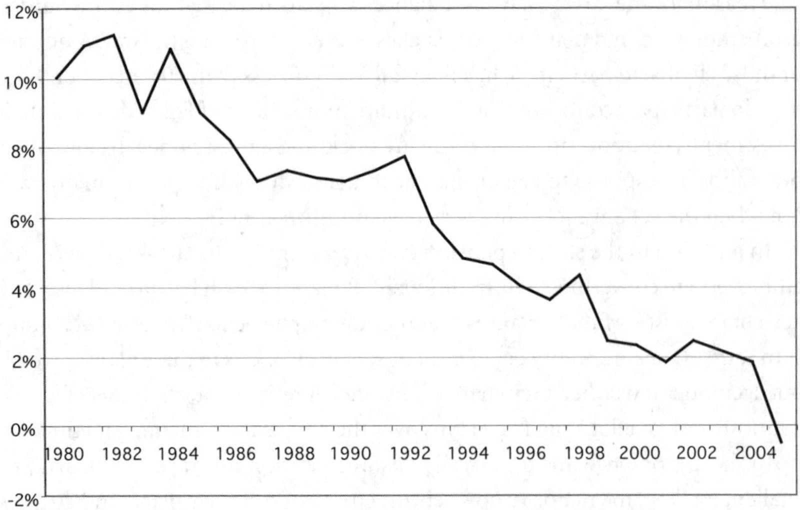

Source: Bureau of Economic Analysis. 2006. *National Income and Product Accounts (NIPA) Data.* U.S. Department of Commerce. http://www.bea.gov/bea/dn/nipaweb/SelectTable.asp?Selected=N#S2.

actually fell during the market rout of 2001, and rose just slightly to 2.4 percent in 2002. These numbers are a far cry from the average 8 to 10 percent savings rate the United States experienced between the Second World War and the 1980s.

This development does not bode well for the baby boomers about to retire. These soon-to-be retirees need some other form of income to ensure a good retirement—an assurance that Social Security and employer-sponsored pensions no longer provide. The future of personal savings remains uncertain, as Americans seem intent on continuing their high level of consumption. Lawmakers have enacted an array of tax incentives designed to spur saving, but these efforts have produced only limited results (Perozek and Reinsdorf 2002; Saxton 1999). In short, personal saving seems unlikely to compensate for the decline in Social Security and the increased uncertainty of pension income. Given the need for more income in retirement, working longer may be a good solution.

The Impact of Working Longer on Retirement Income

The financial implications of another year's work are striking. Table 2 shows how additional years of work can change the retirement finances of a typical married

Table 2. How Retirement Age Affects Assets Needed in Retirement, Married Couple
Earning $62,000 before Taxes, $48,943 after Taxes (in 2003 Dollars)

Retirement Age	Annual Social Security Payments*	Additional Retirement Income Needed to Achieve 80 Percent of After-Tax Pre-retirement Income ($39,154)	Assets Needed at Retirement to Produce that Additional Income*
62	17,735	21,419	330,170
63	19,279	19,875	295,680
64	20,958	18,196	260,630
65	22,770	16,384	225,330
66	24,591	14,563	191,740
67	26,517	12,637	158,740
68	28,593	10,561	126,080
69	30,832	8,322	94,010
70	31,908	7,246	77,060

Source: Congressional Budget Office.
Note: The table assumes a married couple earning $62,000 (roughly the median annual income of mar-
ried households aged 55 to 64) solely from wages, with one member of the couple earning twice as
much as the other. The couple pays annual federal income taxes of $6,260 (filing jointly), state income
taxes of $2,054, and Social Security taxes of $4,743, and has an after-tax income of $48,943. Taxes
(including average state income taxes) are calculated using 2003 rates specified in the National Bureau of
Economic Research's TAXSIM model (available at www.nber.org/~taxsim/taxsim-calc5/). For simplicity,
the example assumes that retirement income is not taxed, that people have typical life expectancies, and
that they die at predictable dates leaving no bequests.
* Taken from the Social Security Administration's "Social Security Quick Calculator" (available at www.
ssa.gov/OACT/quickcalc/index.html).
** Assuming a real rate return of 3 percent.

couple. Each additional year in the workforce increases income directly through
earnings, reduces the number of years over which retirement savings need to be
spread, and increases Social Security benefits by 5 to 10 percent.

In the example, if the couple retires at age 62, the two people will receive
$17,735 from Social Security and will need $21,419 from personal saving to
achieve the 80 percent replacement rate. To produce that additional income
requires assets of $330,170. However, if they work to age 65 they will receive a
higher annual Social Security benefit, and they will need a smaller amount of
supplementary income. Thus, they will require fewer assets for two reasons:
(1) their required supplementary income is lower and (2) they will spread their
accumulated resources over a shorter retirement. In the extreme, the couple that
works until age 70 would need one-third of the additional retirement income
of someone who retired at age 62, and thus less than one-fourth of the assets

at retirement. Clearly, continued employment is a powerful response to the projected decline in traditional sources of retirement income. The question is whether employers will want to retain or hire older workers.

Employers and the Coming Labor Shortage

The baby-boom generation is about to move from ages when most people work to ages when most people retire. The early baby boomers will turn 62 in 2008 and the late boomers, in 2026. With the retirement of the baby boomers, labor force growth will slow markedly, reflecting the drop in the fertility rate. Figure 6 shows the projected percentage change in the labor force between 2010 and 2025 for those aged 16–54 and those aged 55 and over. The number of younger workers will remain virtually constant over the fifteen-year period, while the number of older workers will grow by 24 percent. While older workers will still account for less than 20 percent of the labor force, total labor labor force growth will be determined by those under 55. The result is that total growth will average only 0.4 percent per year between 2010 and 2025—far below the 1.3 percent experienced between 1980 and 2000.

Figure 6. U.S. Labor Force, Percentage Change 2010–2025

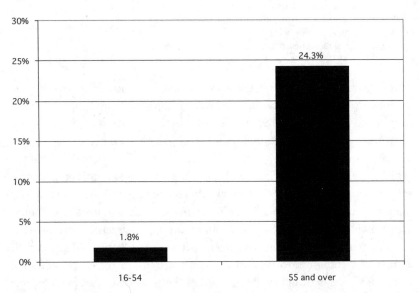

Source: Bureau of Labor Statistics. 2003. "Labor Force Data." ftp://ftp.bls.gov/pub/special.requests/ep/labor.force.

Possible Employer Responses to the Coming Labor Shortage

In theory, the nation could respond to the upcoming shortage of prime-age workers (defined as workers between the ages of 25 and 54) by supplying the existing workers with more capital, by tapping unconventional sources of labor, such as immigrants and women, by relocating, or by employing more older workers.

Use more capital.   Increasing the amount of capital per worker to raise the productivity of the labor force seems unlikely to solve the problem. The same demographic trends that lead to the aging of the population and slowing of labor force growth are likely to reduce both personal and government saving. Lower saving means lower investment and relatively less capital than would have occurred without the demographic shift.

According to the conventional economic model of life-cycle saving, people save when they are young and then draw down their accumulated assets when they reach retirement. The implication of this theory is that as the baby boomers leave the labor force, they will draw down their 401(k) plans and other assets to replace their foregone income from earnings. This dissaving will swamp the saving undertaken by incoming younger cohorts. Although economists have not been able to document a strong relationship between demographics and aggregate personal saving, less personal saving would be the expected outcome.

Government saving—the difference between revenues and expenditures—will also be under pressure in the face of an aging population. The large programs that support older Americans—Social Security and Medicare—are financed primarily on a pay-as-you-go basis. Currently, both programs have commitments far in excess of scheduled revenues. As retiring workers claim their Social Security and Medicare benefits, these programs will put increased strain on the rest of the budget. This strain is likely to reduce government saving.

With lower levels of personal and government saving, investment should also decline. The only way to avoid such a decline is to borrow from abroad. In the 1980s, also a period of large government deficits, such borrowing allowed the United States to avoid a major decline in investment spending. But the United States's current account deficit is now so large relative to GDP that further borrowing seems unlikely to offset the projected decline in national saving. As a result, lower national saving should produce less investment and limit the extent to which employers can substitute capital for the decline in the prime-age labor force.

Employers' alternative to adding more capital is to increase the labor force by turning to untapped sources. The two most often mentioned are immigrants and women.

Figure 7. Immigration to the United States, 1900–2000

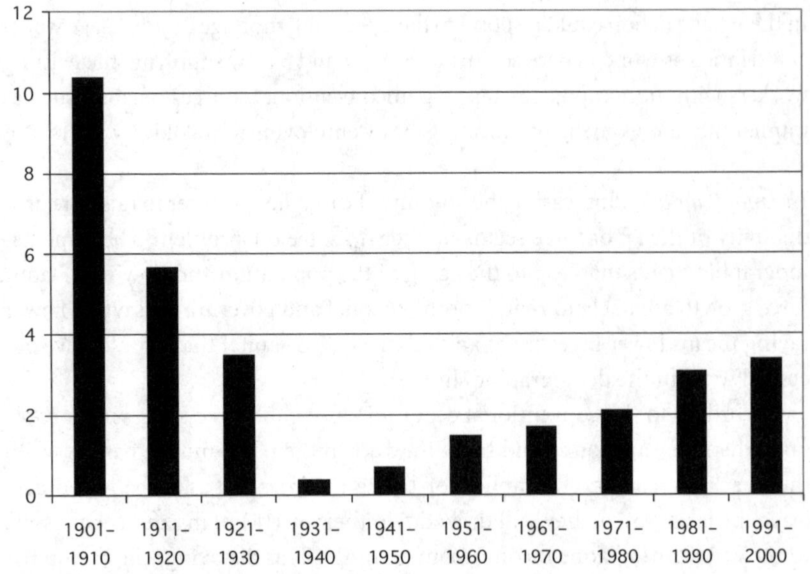

Source: Kyle N. Brown and Sylvester Schieber. 2003. "Structural Impediments to Phased Retirement." Watson Wyatt Worldwide. Mimeo, (March 27).

Hire more immigrants.   In considering the role that immigrants might play in alleviating the future labor shortage, it is important to keep the numbers in mind. First, current levels of immigration have been high from a historical perspective. As shown in Figure 7, the United States went from very high immigration rates in the early part of the century to extremely low rates during the Depression and World War II. Immigration then gradually picked up, and the rate in the 1990s returned to that of the 1920s.

Second, current labor force projections already assume that substantial numbers of new workers will continue to enter the country. The Census Bureau's middle assumption, which underlies the labor force projections reported in Figure 6, is net immigration of about 900,000 per year including both legal and those classified as "other than legal." This level would be in keeping with the pattern of the 1990s. Higher levels of immigration seem unlikely for the foreseeable future in the wake of September 11, 2001. Given today's much more restrictive environment, immigration is unlikely to solve the problems created by the projected national shortage of prime-age workers.

Figure 8. Labor Force Participation Rates for Men and Women, 1960–2004

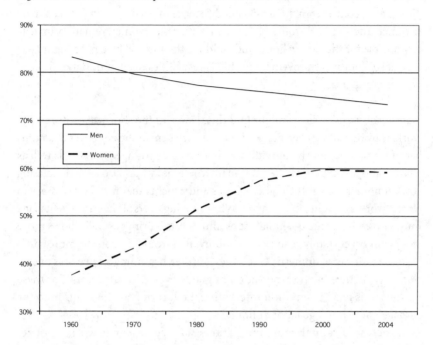

Source: U.S. Bureau of the Census. 2006. "Section 12: Labor Force, Employment, and Earnings." Statistical Abstract of the United States: 2006, Table 578. http://www.census.gov/compendia/statab/ labor_force_employment_earnings/labor.pdf; U.S. Bureau of the Census. 1996. "Section 13: Labor Force, Employment, and Earnings." Statistical Abstract of the United States: 1995, Table 628. http:// www.census.gov/prod/1/gen/95statab/labor.pdf.

Employ more women.   Women have contributed enormously to the growth in the labor force since 1960. Nationally, their labor force participation has increased from 37.7 percent in 1960 to 59.2 percent today (Figure 8). The question is whether further increases in labor force participation by women can close the gap.

Women born in 1940 and thereafter came into the labor force at ever increasing rates, and they stayed in the labor force at higher levels than those born before them. This pattern came to a halt, however, with those born around 1965, when labor force participation reached a plateau (Nyce and Schieber 2002). By the 1990s, the continued increase in female labor labor force participation reflected the retirement of older women, who had relatively low lifetime participation, and their replacement by younger women with higher labor force activity. The current gap in participation between men and women aged 35–44 has narrowed to 15 percentage points (92.6 percent versus 77.2 percent), and that discrepancy comes from the significant difference in participation between married men and married women (Figure 7). Given that women remain primarily responsible for the care of home and children, they are likely to need higher pay and/or substantial improvement in childcare facilities to enter the labor force in greater numbers.

Relocate overseas.   Firms might find the answer to the shortage of prime-age workers by relocating overseas. Such a move may benefit the employer in a number of ways, especially by providing a larger crop of younger workers as well as labor that is less expensive. Relocation internationally may also avoid increasing costs at home, such as the higher salaries and benefits that may be necessary to attract work in a tight labor market. While moving overseas has its benefits, one must also consider the potentially substantial costs it brings as well. Such a move would almost certainly require new training that would perhaps be more costly than the training of domestic employees. Further, beginning an overseas operation may require the transportation of goods over great distances. For these reasons, it is hard to envision international relocation as the solution to the shortage of prime-age labor at home.

If increased capital, more immigrants, a surge of female workers, or relocation are unlikely to fill the gap left by the lack of growth of the under-55 work force, will employers turn to older workers? In many ways, employing older workers seems like the logical response to the coming drop in labor force growth.

The Potential Demand for Older Workers

The population over age 55 will soon increase sharply and permanently, and a much larger portion of this population will likely be seeking to remain employed as the traditional sources of retirement income recede. Moreover, tomorrow's older workers will be well educated, they will have a lifetime of experience, they will be healthier than older workers in the past, and the jobs employers need filled have become much less physically demanding.

Older workers are well educated.   The U.S. population has become more educated over time. As shown in Figure 9, the share of the national adult population with at least a bachelor's degree has increased from 11 percent in 1970 to 24 percent in 2000. This overall gain in education should make older workers more desirable.

Figure 9. Percent of Persons 25 and Over with a Bachelor's Degree or More, 1970–2000

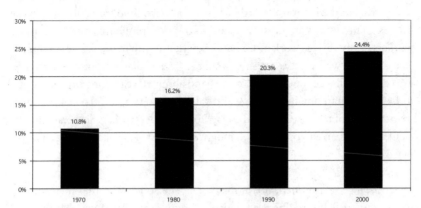

Source: Author's calculations using the Census one-percent file, 1970, 1980, 1990; U.S. Bureau of the Census. 2003. *United States: 2000—Summary Social, Economic, and Housing Characteristics.* PHC-2-1. Washington, DC. (July). http://www.census.gov/prod/cen2000.

Also, the educational discrepancy between older and younger workers is now a thing of the past. Individuals 65 and over have substantially less education than their younger counterparts (Table 3). But educational levels for men aged 45 to 64, which includes the bulk of the baby boomers, are better than levels for younger men. The picture for women is more complicated, given the enormous social change that has occurred in post–World War II America. The educational attainment of each succeeding cohort of women surpasses that of earlier cohorts. But even here, the gap between women aged 45 to 64 and younger groups is much less than with women 65 and over. In short, older workers will look much like younger workers in terms of their educational attainment.[6]

Table 3. Percent of U.S. Population with a Bachelor's Degree or More, 2004

Age	Men	Women
25–34	28.0	32.4
35–44	29.3	29.8
45–64	32.0	27.3
65 and over	25.4	13.7

Source: U.S. Bureau of the Census. 2004. "Educational Attainment of the Population 15 Years and Over, by Age, Sex, Race, and Hispanic Origin: 2004." *Current Population Survey.* http://www.census. gov/population/www/socdemo/education/cps2004.html.

Older workers have a lifetime of experience.   Older workers have logged a great many years in the labor force and have generally acquired valuable skills in the process. These skills are not just useful to their current employer. Most older workers have a diverse work history and experience with many different employers, as the U.S. workforce is extremely mobile.[7] The median job tenure is currently 4.7 years for all wage and salary workers and about 10 years for workers aged 55 to 64; fewer than one in five wage and salary workers aged 60 to 64 has more than 25 years of tenure (Copeland 2003). Today's older workers are generally efficient, versatile, able to display good judgment, and capable of adjusting to workplace changes.

Older people are healthier than in the past.   The conclusion that the health of older workers is improving is a relatively new finding (Freedman, Martin, and Schoeni 2002). Demographers who examined the issue in the 1970s concluded that the elderly were increasingly less healthy (Cutler 2002). But these early conclusions may have been based on less than ideal data that allowed multiple interpretations. A new survey of those 65 and older, designed in part to solve these data problems—the National Long-Term Care Survey—was first conducted in 1982 and now challenges this view. It asks detailed questions about disability in a consistent manner over time and now provides almost twenty years of information.[8]

Between 1982 and 1999, the share of the elderly with severe disabilities, measured roughly in terms of lack of ability to function independently with ease, declined from 26.2 percent to 19.7 percent (Figure 10) (Manton and Gu 2001). This is a 25 percent cumulative reduction in the disability rate, or 1.7 percent per year. Moreover, the rate of reduction is increasing over time. Between 1982 and 1989, disability rates fell by 1.0 percent per year; between 1989 and 1994, by 1.6 percent per year; and between 1994 and 1999, by 2.6 percent per year. The elderly are increasingly healthy, and getting healthier at a faster rate. The dramatic improvement in the health status of those 65 and over suggests that those in their late 50s and early 60s must also be healthier.

The outlook for the future depends on the cause of these health improvements (Cutler 2002). If largely due to public-health changes at the beginning of the twentieth century, they will fade over time as people born well after these improvements were instituted enter old age. If primarily due to new medical treatments, such as drugs for arthritis or cataract surgery for eye problems, they are likely to persist over time. Similarly, if people are healthier mainly because of behavioral changes, such as a reduction in smoking or fat consumption, or improved education and thus better access to medical care and greater understanding about appropriate behavior, the trend of continued improvement is likely to persist.

Figure 10. Share of the Elderly with Chronic Disabilities

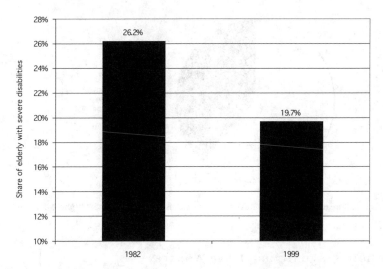

Source: K.G. Manton and X. Gu. 2001. "Changes in the Prevalence of Chronic Disability in the United States: Black and Non-Black Population above Age 65 from 1982 to 1999." *Proceedings of the National Academy of Sciences of the United States of America 98*, no. 12 (June): 6354–6359.

For the purpose of assessing employers' willingness to hire older workers, the improved health of older people is definitely positive. Healthy older workers are more productive than those with infirmities and will appear more similar to younger workers in terms of physical and mental capabilities than in the past.

Jobs are no longer physically demanding.   The nature of employment has changed dramatically since 1980. As manufacturing declined, the service sector exploded. This has reduced the number of workers in jobs requiring physical work (Figure 11). This expansion reflects the growth in jobs at places such as universities, hospitals, software development companies, and management consulting firms. Even within manufacturing the nature of jobs has changed, as firms have automated or outsourced production and now employ more managers, engineers, and technicians (Massachusetts Office of the Governor 2001). This has led to an overall shift to more knowledge-based activities. Employers looking to fill less physically demanding, knowledge-based jobs should be more willing to hire older workers who offer a wealth of skills and experience.

In summary, employers will need to find another input since they will no longer have an influx of young workers. Increasing the amount of capital and greater reliance on women and immigrants may help, but such answers are unlikely to fill the gap. Hiring older workers seems like a natural solution.

Figure 11. Job Status of Workers in the U.S., 2000

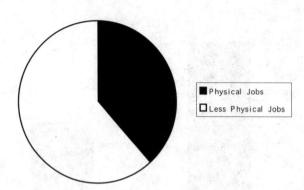

Source: U.S. Bureau of the Census. 2003. http://www.census.gov/prod/cen2000/phc-2-1-pt1.pdf.

IMPEDIMENTS TO HIRING OLDER WORKERS

Although the stage appears set for hiring older workers—alleviating the problems of workers and employers alike—a number of impediments stand in the way. First, older workers are expensive. Second, employers resist part-time employment, which older workers disproportionately favor. Third, personnel considerations and legal impediments preclude employers from offering phased retirement. Finally, age discrimination, while illegal, probably continues to exist at least to some extent.

Older Workers Are Expensive

Older workers are expensive for a number of reasons. First, their earnings tend to be higher than those of comparable younger workers. One would expect rising salaries as workers become more productive with increased experience. But the issue here is increases in salary that exceed what can be attributed to productivity gains. Economists explain this phenomenon in terms of implicit contracts between employers and workers whereby younger workers are underpaid and older workers are overpaid (Lazear 1979). The idea is that the promise of future high salaries encourages the worker with firm-specific skills to remain with the company, and that compensation reflects the value of the workers' contributions over their lifetimes. This pattern may be less prevalent than in the past with the onset of tight labor markets, the pressure of global competition, and the flattening of corporate personnel systems. Nevertheless, older workers tend to be paid somewhat more than younger workers on a quality-adjusted basis.

Figure 12. Annual Aggregate Medical Claim Costs for Employees and Dependents, by Age of Employee

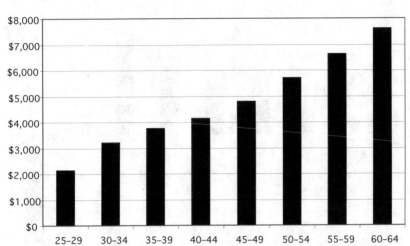

Source: "The Business Case for Workers Age 50+: Planning for Tomorrow's Talent Needs in Today's Competitive Environment." A Report for AARP Prepared by Towers Perrin. December 2005.

In addition to cash earnings, the cost of fringe benefits—health insurance and pensions—also rises with age. Health insurance costs increase for two reasons. First, the percentage of workers covered rises with age, suggesting that older workers demand such coverage as part of their compensation package. Thus, 82 percent of full-time workers aged 55 to 64 have employer-provided health insurance, compared to 55 percent of 16 to 24 year olds and 76 percent of 25 to 44 year olds (Committee for Economic Development 1999).[9] Second, the cost of fringe benefits increases with age. Private health insurance costs for full-time year-round workers and their covered dependents are between $2,000 and $3,800 for those aged 25 to 39, compared to more than $5,000 for workers 50 to 54, and to $6,000 for workers 55 to 64 (see Figure 12). If the employer self-insures, hiring an older worker—all else equal—will drive up healthcare costs. If the employer purchases insurance from a carrier, hiring older workers will raise the cost of the policy.

In the case of pension costs, the impact of hiring older workers depends on the type of plan provided. With 401(k)s, the employer's contribution is generally a fixed percentage of salary and therefore rises in line with pay increases. If the older worker's salary simply reflects greater productivity, then 401(k) contributions raise no cost issue. To the extent that older workers' salaries are higher because of implicit contracts, the 401(k) contribution adds to the extra expense.

Figure 13. Average Accruals in Private-Sector Defined Benefit Plans, for Workers
Starting at Age 25

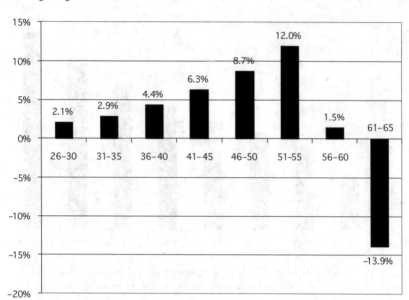

Source: Rudolph G. Penner, Pamela Perun, and Eugene Steuerle. 2002. "Legal and Institutional Impediments to Partial Retirement and Part-Time Work by Older Workers." The Urban Institute, (November 20). http://www.urban.org/UploadedPDF/410587_SloanFinal.pdf.
Note: The analysis is based on a sample of 340 salary-based DB plans in the private sector. Accrual estimates assume that workers join the firm at age 25 and leave at the age that maximizes the present discounted value of pension benefits (or age 70). The analysis assumes that wages grow at the average age-specific rate for college-educated male workers with DB plans. The real interest rate is set at 3 percent and the inflation rate at 3.3 percent. Estimates are weighted by firm size.

On the whole, however, 401(k) plans are not a major factor in the hiring of older workers. Neither are the new cash balance plans that some employers have adopted to replace their traditional DB plans.

The real pension issue with regard to older workers arises in traditional DB plans. Figure 13 shows the average accrual rate in a sample of traditional private-sector DB plans by age—that is, the increase in the present discounted value of pension benefits as a percent of earnings for each age group. The accrual rate rises sharply from 2.1 percent for those aged 26–30 to 12 percent for those aged 51–55. The reason for this increase is the multiplier effect inherent in the traditional DB formula. Assume that the formula provides 1.5 percent of final salary for each year of service and a 54-year-old with 20 years of service works for another year. That worker's replacement rate will increase from 30 to 31.5 percent.

Figure 14. Average Pension Accruals in Private-Sector Defined Benefit Plans during the First Five Years of Service, by Start Age

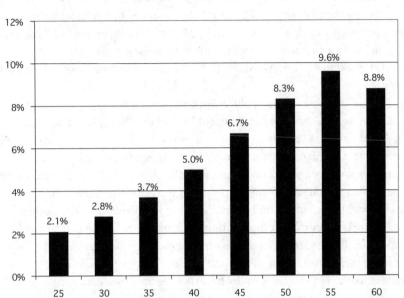

Source: Rudolph G. Penner, Pamela Perun, and Eugene Steuerle. 2002. "Legal and Institutional Impediments to Partial Retirement and Part-Time Work by Older Workers." The Urban Institute, (November 20). http://www.urban.org/UploadedPDF/410587_SloanFinal.pdf.
Note: The analysis is based on a sample of 340 salary-based DB plans in the private sector. Accrual estimates assume that workers leave the firm at the age that maximizes the present discounted value of pension benefits, or age 70, whichever comes first. The analysis also assumes that all workers receive a starting annual salary of $35,000 that grows at 5 percent per year. The real interest rate is set at 3 percent and the inflation rate at 3.3 percent. Estimates are weighted by firm size.

In addition, the entire 31.5 percent will apply to the salary earned in that twenty-first year of service, increasing the value of all the previously earned pension credits. For this reason, DB pension accruals rise much faster than salaries, making the retention of older workers very expensive.

DB plans also make *hiring* older workers costly. Figure 14 shows the present discounted value of pensions earned during the first 5 years for workers starting at different ages. A person who starts with a plan at age 25 accrues very little— 2.1 percent of pay; whereas someone who starts at age 55 accrues benefits equal to 9.6 percent of pay. Again, suppose the plan provides 1.5 percent of final salary and that the employee earns $35,000 during the first year of employment. Both the older and younger worker will be entitled to benefits of $525 per year (1.5 percent of $35,000) when they retire. The older worker, however, can retire in five years at age 60 and claim the benefit, while the younger worker has to wait 35 years. That means in terms of calculating the present value of the accrued pension benefit at age 60, the $525 for the older worker is discounted by 5 years while the $525 for the younger worker is discounted by 35 years. The fewer years of discounting means a much larger required contribution to the pension plan for the older worker, making the hiring of older workers in firms with traditional DB plans very expensive.

Several other items make older workers more expensive to retain or hire (Committee for Economic Development 1999). One is paid leave. Both vacation days and sick leave tend to increase with tenure, so older workers are generally entitled to more days off than younger ones. The second is life insurance costs. Many employers provide term life insurance for their employees, and the cost of these policies is directly related to the age of the workforce. Finally, the cost associated with work injury and disability tends to be higher for older workers.

In short, the current compensation structure tends to make older workers expensive. To the extent that they are more productive because they have spent years on the job, some of the disadvantage to retaining older workers disappears. But for workers in jobs that require little training, the cost disadvantage of older workers is a serious problem. Similarly, the compensation structure discourages the hiring of older workers since their healthcare and benefit costs are higher; and they cost firms with traditional DB plans significantly more, yet they do not have the past experience on the job to mitigate these costs.

More flexible compensation structures would benefit older workers. For example, the movement to 401(k) and cash balance plans in the pension area will make older workers more attractive to employers (though these plans, as discussed earlier, raise a number of other issues). In terms of health insurance, eliminating the requirement that Medicare serve as the secondary payer would reduce costs for workers over 65, but would further burden a program already facing enormous long-term deficits (Penner, Perun, and Steuerle 2002; Committee on Ways and Means 2000). In summary, the cost of older workers remains a major hurdle to their retention and hiring.

Employers Resist Part-Time Employment

Another hurdle is that older people tend to want to work part-time. For example, a study based on the Health and Retirement Study reports that 56 percent of respondents aged 55 to 65 in 1996 said they would prefer to gradually reduce their hours as they age (U.S. General Accounting Office 2001). And older self-employed people tend to reduce hours worked as they approach retirement.

Figure 15. Percent of Workers Employed Part Time, 1980–2004

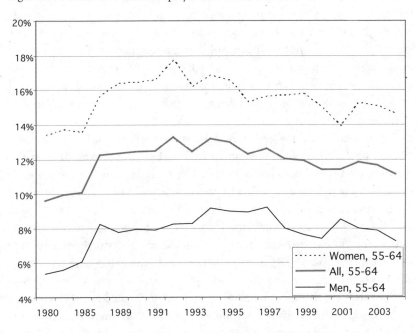

Source: Author's calculations of the Current Population Survey, 1980–2004.

The problem is that the percent of workers employed part-time appears to have been on the decline since the early 1990s (Figure 15). Some of that decline may have been due to the strong economy of the 1990s, which pulled some part-time workers into full-time employment. It could also be attributable to the fact that the large cohort of baby boomers was in its prime earning years, during which both men and women tend to work full time. In any event, part-time employment appears to be less, rather than more, prevalent.

The question is whether employers will increase part-time job opportunities.[10] Economic theory suggests that employers will hire more part-time workers only when their cost relative to other inputs (including full-time workers) declines. Currently, part-time employment is concentrated in small establishments and in establishments in the service sector (Montgomery 1988). This is true even after controlling for other factors that would affect demand, such as wages, fringe benefits, seasonal fluctuations in demand, and hiring costs. It is not exactly clear why this is the case. Large firms might avoid part-time workers because they tend to have higher turnover rates than full-time employees (Tilly 1991). Part-time work might be more common in the service sector because it is labor intensive and faces fluctuations in demand, and because employers find it is easier to meet these fluctuations with part-time workers. Employers in general might resist part-time employment because a number of costs, such as supervising and record keeping, hiring and training new workers, and fringe benefits like health insurance, are unrelated to hours worked and make two part-time people more expensive than one full time person. While all these theories are plausible, they have not been supported by rigorous empirical studies (Hutchens 2001).

Not only do large firms tend to shun part-time employment, but the demand for part-time work could increase in the future for one of two reasons. First, the price of part-time workers could decline. This should happen if large numbers of older workers wanted to work on a part-time basis and were willing to accept lower wages in order to attain a part-time slot. Economists do not have a good idea, however, how much compensation would have to decrease relative to full-time workers to spur demand. That is, it is unclear whether part-time compensation would have to fall by 5 percent or 20 percent relative to full-time to persuade employers to hire more part-time workers.

The other way that the demand for part-time work could increase is if some of the impediments declined over time. For example, if the quasi-fixed costs discussed above could be reduced, part-time employees would look more attractive. However, it is difficult to conceive of how hiring and training costs will decrease; they simply do not vary with hours worked. Similarly, health insurance tends to be an all-or-nothing proposition that does not depend on whether the employee is full- or part-time. Some advocate that health insurance costs for older workers could be reduced if Medicare became the primary payer. But as discussed above, such a change seems unlikely given the extraordinary shortfalls facing the Medicare program.

In short, older workers consistently report that they would like to reduce their hours as they age, and this preference is clearly evident in the behavior of the self-employed, who cut back gradually as they approach retirement. But employers outside of the service sector and small firms appear reluctant to hire part-time workers. Unless structural changes make the hiring of part-time workers more attractive, employer demand for older workers will fall short of the supply, except at very low wages.

Legal Impediments to Flexible Retirement Provisions

One way to reduce the cost to employers of part-time work at older ages is phased retirement, with employees supplementing their reduced earnings by drawing on their pensions. Phased retirement offers employers a way to keep employees who have specialized skills and institutional knowledge and to avoid the costs of hiring and training new employees.

Despite the apparent appeal of phased retirement, few private-sector firms offer such an option. Watson Wyatt Worldwide undertook a survey of nearly 600 employers in 1999: although more than 60 percent responded that they were currently having problems attracting workers, only 16 percent offered any form of phased retirement (Graig and Paganelli 2000). Most of these firms said that they rehired workers after they retired on either a part-time or temporary basis. Slightly less than half said that they contracted with retired workers as consultants.

The question is why so few firms offer phased retirement. One answer may be personnel considerations. For instance, it is difficult to think how a manager could function effectively coming in three days a week. Similarly, activities requiring teamwork would not lend themselves to one person working part-time. That the two most popular phased retirement arrangements require the employee to separate from the firm (rehiring retired employees on a part-time or temporary basis and hiring retirees as contractors) also suggests that personnel policies play a role. The rehiring approach allows employers to pick and choose those older workers with whom they want a continuing relationship—something otherwise difficult to accomplish.

More than personnel considerations are at play, however. Allowing employees to remain with their employer and reduce their work effort as they approach retirement also faces a number of legal impediments. First, benefits in DB plans are generally based on final earnings, so cutting back on hours could reduce the base for benefit computation. Although current law explicitly precludes pension reduction due to increased age or service, no law specifically prohibits a reduction due to a decline in final average pay. The Internal Revenue Service has asserted that pensions cannot be reduced because final pay goes down, but others report that benefits have been reduced and that the courts have upheld these reductions (ERISA Advisory Council 2000). The uncertainty surrounding the treatment of retirement benefits thus is one factor that inhibits phased retirement.

A second factor is that employees covered by a DB plan cannot receive any pension benefits as they move to part-time employment until they have reached the plan's normal retirement age. A plan that pays benefits to an active employee before the normal retirement age could lose its tax-qualified status since it is permitted to pay benefits only in the event of death, disability, termination of employment, or at the normal retirement age. To the extent that workers who reduce their hours need to supplement their earnings with pension benefits, existing regulations regarding DB plans make continued employment with the same firm difficult.

The rules for in-service distributions from 401(k) plans are different. Participants who reach age 59.5 can continue to work for their employer and receive distributions from their account. Before age 59.5, any distribution—in service or not—is subject to a 10 percent excise tax in addition to ordinary income taxes. The law provides two exceptions. First, distributions may begin as early as 55 if the employee separates from his employer under an early retirement plan. Second, if benefits are paid as a lifelong annuity, they can begin at any age. Thus, these plans do not preclude part-time work and pension receipt. To the extent that coverage has shifted in the private sector, the pension issue will become less important.

The above discussion highlights only a few of the legal impediments to phased retirement and innovative retirement provisions. In 2000, the ERISA Advisory Council identified a host of other ERISA and Internal Revenue Code restrictions that constrain employers in implementing flexible employment arrangements. The Council, for example, recommended relaxing rules on in-service distributions and the rules governing nondiscrimination. These are complicated issues, and none of the Council's recommendations have been adopted to date. If these regulatory issues are not addressed, however, they will remain an impediment to workers staying in the workforce longer.

Age Discrimination

Age discrimination is one barrier that should have been removed with the passage of the Age Discrimination in Employment Act. But evidence suggests that age discrimination still exists, at least to some extent, and it will become an increasingly important barrier as the population ages by influencing hiring practices and shaping workplace culture. Secondary effects are also likely since workers' perceptions of employers' practices are likely to influence their workforce decisions.

One problem in gauging the importance of age discrimination is the lack of definitive measures. Age discrimination is, thus, difficult to detect. Studies on race and gender discrimination proceed on the assumption that, all else equal, minorities and women are as productive as white and male workers, respectively. Any remaining differences in earnings can therefore be attributed to discrimination. This approach is not suitable to age discrimination since the very process of aging affects productivity, both positively and negatively.

Furthermore, as noted earlier, firms may have legitimate concerns about the cost of employing older workers. As earnings increase over a worker's lifetime, they can reach a point where they exceed productivity. Health and life insurance, often provided by the employer, are more costly for older than younger workers.

Other benefits whose cost is related to tenure, such as paid leave, may also be higher for older workers. In addition, older workers are more likely than younger workers to experience an extended injury or disability. Each of these factors provides employers with a legitimate reason to view older and younger workers differently (Committee for Economic Development 1999).

Because of the difficulty of testing for discrimination with conventional techniques, researchers rely primarily on self-reported information. The findings suggest that managers value older workers. Managers indicate that older workers often work harder and are more reliable and motivated than their younger counterparts. They also state that older workers display good judgment, quality control, and attendance, and have lower turnover (Sterns and McDaniel 1994). On the other hand, employers express concern that older workers are less willing to adapt to changing technologies or workplace practices and are more likely to have difficulty learning new skills.

These negative perceptions of older workers appear to be reflected in hiring and training decisions. In one study, résumés for an older and younger worker with equal qualifications were mailed to nearly 800 firms in the United States. When a position appeared vacant, the older worker received a less favorable response about 25 percent of the time (Figure 16) (Bendick, Jackson, and Romero 1996). Another study based on a nationally representative sample of nearly 1,500 employers with 50 or more employees found that about 70 percent of younger employees received formal training in the previous year, compared to only about 50 percent of employees aged 55 years and older. Of those who were trained, older employees also had many fewer hours of training compared to employees aged 25 to 54 (Figure 17) (Frazis et al. 1998).

Beyond the direct effects of age discrimination by employers on recruitment and training, age discrimination creates an additional, more subtle, barrier to work through the perceptions of older workers. According to data from the Health and Retirement Study, between 10 and 20 percent of older workers indicate that younger workers are given preference over older workers and that their employers exert pressure on them to retire. This perception of discrimination on the part of workers significantly increases the likelihood that they will leave their jobs and the workforce.

CONCLUSION

Current sources of retirement income will likely be inadequate for low- and middle-income individuals. The Social Security program will be significantly less

Figure 16. Percent with Favorable Employer Responses, by Age, to Paired Résumés

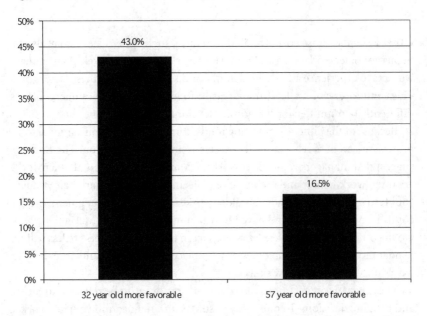

Source: Marc Bendick, Jr., et al. 1996. "Employment Discrimination against Older Workers: An Experimental Study of Hiring Practices." *Journal of Aging & Social Policy* 8 (4): 25–46.

Figure 17. Hours of Formal Training per Employee, by Age, May–October 1995

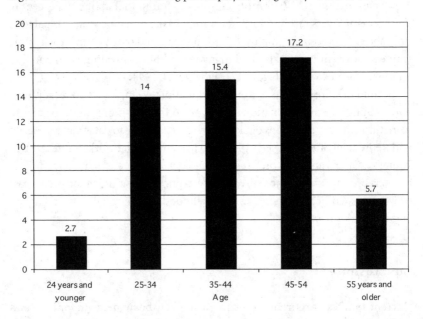

Source: Harley Frazis et al. 1998. "Results from the 1995 Survey of Employer-Provided Training." *Monthly Labor Review* (June).

generous relative to preretirement income in the future than it is today; and employer-sponsored pensions, where coverage has moved from traditional plans to 401(k)s, will provide less reliable retirement income. Because of these impending shortcomings in traditional sources of retirement income, many people will seek employment later in life as a way to provide a more secure retirement.

The same demographic shifts that will cause Social Security to be less generous will put employers in a tight situation as well. They will no longer be able to rely on a rapidly growing group of younger workers in the future. So how will employers respond to a stagnating supply of labor? They will expand their use of women, immigrants, and capital, and some firms may relocate. But these responses will not be enough to make up for the labor shortfall. Older workers are well educated and healthier than in the past and have a lifetime of experience.

Although the stage appears set for hiring older workers, a number of impediments exist. First, older workers are expensive. They are paid more, sometimes in excess of their greater productivity. They involve expensive healthcare costs and rapidly rising pension costs under traditional DB plans. Second, most existing employment policies have been geared to encouraging early retirement. Incentives to retire early rather than later are the hallmark of traditional DB plans. Although these plans are less important in the private sector than they were in 1980, they are still the dominant plan for states and localities. Third, employers resist part-time employment, which is the preferred mode for older workers, and it is unclear that employer preferences will change in the future. Fourth, legal impediments preclude employers from offering flexible retirement arrangements. Finally, age discrimination, while technically illegal, probably exists.

In sum, increased employment of older workers is clearly in the interest of both workers and employers. But mutual interest is not enough. It will require massive social change, legal and regulatory reform, and increased flexibility on the part of both employers and employees for these employment options to materialize. The speed at which we make these social, legal, personal, and personnel-policy changes could well be the most important factor in assuring the future retirement income of the elderly.

NOTES

The author would like to thank Kevin Meme for his excellent research assistance and Jerilyn Libby for updating all the figures and tables.

1. Combined income is adjusted gross income as reported on tax forms plus nontaxable interest income plus one half of Social Security benefits.

Review." *Journal of the American Medical Association.* 288, no. 24 (December): 3137–3146.

Friedberg, Leora. 2001. "The Impact of Technological Change on Older Workers: Evidence from Data on Computer Use." Working Paper 8297. Cambridge, MA: National Bureau of Economic Research.

Graig, Laurene A., and Valerie Paganelli. 2000. "Phased Retirement: Reshaping the End of Work." *Compensation and Benefits Management.* 16, no. 2 (Spring).

Hutchens, Robert. 2001. "Employer Surveys, Employer Policies, and Future Demand for Older Workers." Prepared for the "Roundtable on the Demand for Older Workers," sponsored by the Retirement Research Consortium, The Brookings Institution, (March 23). [Available at: http://www.bc.edu/centers/crr/special_pubs/hutchens_ld.pdf].

Lazear, Edward P. 1979. "Why Is There Mandatory Retirement?" *Journal of Political Economy.* 87, no. 6 (December): 1261–1284.

Manton, K.G., and X. Gu. 2001. "Changes in the Prevalence of Chronic Disability in the United States: Black and Non-Black Population above Age 65 from 1982 to 1999." *Proceedings of the National Academy of Sciences of the United States of America.* 98, no. 12 (June): 6354–6359.

Massachusetts Office of the Governor. 2001. *Massachusetts toward a New Prosperity: Building Regional Competitiveness.* [Available at: http://www.massachusetts.gov/econ/newprosperity].

Montgomery, Mark. 1988. "On the Determinants of Employer Demand for Part-Time Workers." *Review of Economics and Statistics.* 70, no. 1 (February): 112–117.

Munnell, Alicia H. 2003. "The Declining Role of Social Security" *Just the Facts.* No. 6 (February). Chestnut Hill, MA: Center for Retirement Research at Boston College.

Munnell, Alicia, and Annika Sundén. 2004. *Coming Up Short: The Challenge of 401(k) Plans.* Brookings Institution Press.

Munnell, Alicia H., Annika Sundén, and Elizabeth Lidstone. 2002. "How Important Are Private Pensions?" *Issue in Brief.* No. 8 (February). Chestnut Hill, MA: Center for Retirement Research at Boston College.

Nyce, Steven A., and Sylvester J. Schieber. 2002. "The Decade of the Employee: The Workforce Environment in the Coming Decade." *Benefits Quarterly.* 1: 60–79.

Penner, Rudolph G., Pamela Perun, and Eugene Steuerle. 2002. "Legal and Institutional Impediments to Partial Retirement and Part-Time Work by Older Workers." Washington, D.C.: The Urban Institute. (November 20) [Available at: http://www.urban.org/UploadedPDF/410587_SloanFinal.pdf].

Perozek, Maria, and Marshall Reinsdorf. 2002. "Alternative Measures of Personal Saving." *Survey of Current Business.* (April). Washington, DC: Bureau of Economic Analysis.

Saxton, Jim. 1999. "Negative Personal Savings Rate Shows Need For Saving Incentives." Press Release from the Congress of the United States Joint Economic Committee (May 3).

Sterns, H. L., and M. A. McDaniel. 1994. "Job Performance and Older Workers." In *Older Workers: How Do They Measure Up?* edited by Sara E. Rix. American Association of Retired Persons.

Survey of Consumer Finances. Federal Reserve Board of Governors. http://www.federal reserve.gov/pubs/oss/oss2/scfindex.html.

Tilly, Chris. 1991. "Reasons for the Continuing Growth of Part-time Employment." *Monthly Labor Review.* 114, no. 3 (March): 10–18.

U.S. Bureau of the Census. 1996. "Section 13: Labor Force, Employment and Earnings." *Statistical Abstract of the United States: 1995.* Table 628. http://www.census.gov/prod/1/gen/95statab/labor.pdf.

U.S. Bureau of the Census. 2002. "Employment-Based Health Insurance: 1997." *Current Population Reports,* 70–81.

U.S. Bureau of the Census. 2006. "Section 12: Labor Force, Employment, and Earnings." *Statistical Abstract of the United States: 2006.* Table 578. http://www.census.gov/compendia/statab/labor_force_employment_earnings/labor.pdf.

U.S. Bureau of the Census. 2003. *United States: 2000—Summary Social, Economic, and Housing Characteristics.* PHC-2-1. Washington, DC (July). http://www.census.gov/prod/cen2000.

U.S. Bureau of the Census. 2004. "Educational Attainment of the Population 15 Years and Over, by Age, Sex, Race, and Hispanic Origin: 2004." *Current Population Survey.* http://www.census.gov/population/www/socdemo/education/cps2004.html.

U.S. General Accounting Office. 2001. *Older Workers: Demographic Trends Pose Challenges for Employers and Workers.* Report GAO-02-85.

U.S. Social Security Administration. 2003a. *The 2003 Annual Report of the Board of Trustees of the Federal Old-Age and Survivors Insurance and Disability Insurance Trust Funds.* Washington, DC: U.S. Government Printing Office (March 17).

U.S. Social Security Administration. 2006a. Income of the Population Aged 55 and Older, 2004. Washington, DC (February). http://www.ssa.gov/policy/docs/statcomps/inc_pop55/2004/incpop04.pdf.

U.S. Social Security Administration. 2006b. *The 2006 Annual Report of the Board of Trustees of the Federal Hospital Insurance and Survivors Insurance and the Disability Insurance Trust Funds.* Washington, DC: U.S. Government Printing Office (March 17).

Comments on "Working Longer: A Potential Win-Win Proposition"

JOHN TURNER

Alicia Munnell develops the hypothesis that it would be good public policy to encourage Americans to work longer and retire at older ages. She argues that it would be good policy both for many workers and for many employers. For workers, it would help solve the problem of not having sufficient savings to support a long retirement, due in part to increased life expectancy, as well as due to the poor savings habits of many Americans. Some widows may fall into poverty as a result of their husbands having taken early retirement, which results in their receiving reduced Social Security benefits. This problem might be ameliorated by people working longer. For employers, having employees work longer would help solve the problem of an anticipated labor shortage when the baby-boom generation (born between 1946 and 1964) begins to retire.

Increases in life expectancy have led to large increases in the expected years in retirement, placing a heavy burden on defined benefit (DB) pension systems, both employer-provided DB pensions and Social Security. Thus, her article title could add a third "win" for the positive effects working longer could have on Social Security and DB pensions.

Working longer appears to be a feasible option for many people. As Munnell documents, older workers are better educated and healthier than in the past. However, the labor supply effect of the increased lifetime wealth of workers suggests that they will want to have more lifetime hours of leisure, which may translate into opposition to working longer.

Working longer would be facilitated by the large increases in life expectancy, which could permit both more lifetime hours of leisure and more hours of work. Life expectancy at birth rose from 47.7 years in 1900 to 76.6 in 2000, a 60 percent increase. Most of this change (72 percent) occurred before 1950. At age 65, life expectancy rose from 11.7 years in 1900 to 21.2 years in 2000, an 81 percent increase. Most of this increase (75 percent) occurred since 1950 (Technical Panel on Assumptions and Methods 2003). Life expectancy is projected to continue increasing. Because mortality rates are already low at ages younger than age 65 (Board of Trustees 2003), future increases in life expectancy are expected to result mainly from mortality reductions at older ages. Unless retirement ages increase, future retirees may spend substantially more years retired than do current retirees.

Working longer would be facilitated by the decline in the number of jobs that are physically demanding. Farm workers were among the occupations with the largest job declines over the period 1988–2000. Technology gains and new labor-saving machinery were the main reasons for the decline, along with increased farm consolidation. Over that period, other physically demanding occupations that experienced a decline in the number of workers included highway maintenance workers (7 percent), butchers and meat cutters (15 percent), fishers (22 percent), and cannery workers (32 percent) (Alpert and Auyer 2003). Between 2001 and 2002, employment in mining declined from 531,000 to 458,000 (U.S. Department of Labor 2003). While these occupations are frequently mentioned as ones where it would be difficult to work longer, a serious policy to encourage most groups of workers to work longer may encounter resistance from unexpected groups. For example, there is some international evidence that classical musicians are one such group, due to the physical demands of practice and performance (Tomes 2005; Turner and Guenther 2005).

The best solution for retirement for occupational groups unable to continue working into old age because of the physical demands of their work may be occupational pension plans that permit early retirement. For example, police, fire fighters, the military, and miners—occupations with physically demanding jobs—all have occupational pension plans that permit early retirement.

If working longer makes sense for both workers and employers, can we expect it to naturally happen? Changes in employer-provided pensions suggest that to some extent employers will make adjustments that will encourage later retirement ages. In the past, many employers offered incentives for early retirement through their DB pension plans. In fact, early-retirement subsidies are common in DB plans. For most large employers that offer DB plans, a typical worker's lifetime value of benefits is larger if the worker retires before the normal retirement age than if the worker postpones retirement to the normal retirement age. While annual benefits increase with postponed retirement, the increase is insufficient to offset the loss of benefits that occurs with postponement of retirement (McGill et al. 1996, 453, 462). The shift to 401(k) plans and the decline in DB plans has reduced the number of workers who are facing pension-based incentives to retire. Further, the shift toward cash balance plans, which are categorized in pension law as a type of DB plan, and away from traditional DB plans, is also reducing the pension-based incentives to retire. Cash balance plans are hybrid plans that to employees operate in many ways like defined contribution plans, and by design do not have incentives for early retirement.

The eligibility age in pensions may affect the ages at which some people retire. Age 62 is the minimum age at which Social Security benefits can be received. In 401(k) plans, workers can take their benefits starting at age 59 1/2 even if they are still working for the sponsoring employer. At age 59 1/2, workers can receive benefits from an Individual Retirement Account (IRA) or a Roth IRA without penalty. The majority of workers in private DB pension plans are in plans with an early retirement age of 55. Changes in eligibility ages may be an avenue for policy affecting retirement ages.

The primary criticism of policies that encourage working longer is that doing so places an unfair burden on certain vulnerable groups who have shorter life expectancies, who are unable to work at older ages because of physical limitations, or who become unemployed at older ages and are unable to find other jobs. Raising the eligibility ages may pose problems for workers forced to take early retirement, or who are fired in the few years before the pensionable age, because of the greater difficulty older workers have in leaving unemployment and finding a job.

Policies that encourage later work have a differential effect by race because of the racial disparity in life expectancy. Life expectancies at birth in 2001 were 75.0 and 68.6 for white and black males respectively, and 80.2 and 75.5 for white and black females (Centers for Disease Control and Prevention 2003).

Workers who retire before age 62 tend to be healthier, wealthier, and better educated than other workers. By contrast, workers that expect to retire at age 62 are in relatively poor health, more often in physically demanding jobs, and less financially well off (Panis et al. 2002). Workers who have high discount rates will place little value on the increase in benefits with postponed retirement and will tend to retire at the earliest date possible. Gustman and Steinmeier (2002) estimate that about three-fifths of those workers in the United States retiring at age 62 would postpone their retirement to age 64 if that were the new pensionable age.

A higher retirement age in pension and Social Security benefits may increase the demand by workers for disability benefits and poverty benefits, which would reduce the savings in benefit expense to the government. One study estimated that 22 percent of U.S. Old Age and Survivors Insurance (OASI) beneficiaries aged 62–64 have health problems that substantially impair their ability to work, and that 12 percent would qualify medically for disability insurance benefits were the OASI benefits not available to them at that age (Leonesio, Vaughan, and Wixon 2000). The majority of those workers who would qualify medically for disability benefits, however, would not actually qualify for disability benefits because they lack either the requisite quarters of coverage or fail the recent-work criterion for eligibility. Because more workers at older ages would need to withdraw from labor force activity due to increases in disability rates with age, an increase in the pensionable age would increase the demand for disability benefits. If the pensionable age is raised, it may be desirable to reduce the stringency of requirements to qualify for disability benefits, providing an alternative pathway for some workers to early retirement. This change would better integrate and coordinate disability- and retirement-income policy.

Measuring the extent to which raising the retirement age would hurt vulnerable groups, one study found that fewer than 10 percent of men who take Social Security benefits at age 62 in the United States are both in poor health and have no source of pension income other than Social Security. For women, the figure is 20 percent (Burkhauser, Couch, and Philips 1996).

CONCLUSION

Alicia Munnell has made an important contribution by exploring some of the issues involved in policies intended to encourage workers to retire at later ages. Policies that removed barriers to work at older ages would expand the opportunities for older workers. Policies that ended incentives to retire early may also have positive effects for both workers and employers. Some groups of workers may have difficulty working at older ages. To the extent possible, it may be desirable for employer-provided pensions to continue to facilitate early retirement for those groups.

NOTE

The views, opinions and judgments expressed here are solely the responsibility of the author and do not necessarily represent the position of AARP.

REFERENCES

Alpert, Andrew, and Jill Auyer. 2003. "The 1988–2000 Employment Projections: How Accurate Were They?" *Occupational Outlook Quarterly.* (Spring): 2–21.

Board of Trustees, Federal Old-Age and Survivors Insurance and Disability Insurance Trust Funds. 2003. *The 2003 Annual Report of the Board of Trustees of the Federal Old-Age and Survivors Insurance and Disability Insurance Trust Funds.* Washington, DC: U.S. Government Printing Office.

Burkhauser, Richard V., Kenneth A. Couch, and John W. Philips. 1996. "Who Takes Early Social Security Benefits? The Economic and Health Characteristics of Early Beneficiaries." *The Gerontologist.* Vol. 36, no. 6: 789–99.

Centers for Disease Control and Prevention (CDC). 2003. "Trends in Aging—United States and Worldwide." *Morbidity and Mortality Weekly Report.* Vol. 52 (February): 101–09.

Gustman, Alan L., and Thomas L. Steinmeier. 2002. "The Social Security Early Entitlement Age in a Structural Model of Retirement and Wealth." NBER Working Paper 9183.

Leonesio, Michael V., Denton R. Vaughn, and Bernard Wixon. 2000. "Early Retirees under Social Security: Health Status and Retirement Resources." *Social Security Bulletin.* Vol. 63, no. 4: 1–16.

McGill, Dan M., Kyle N. Brown, John J. Haley, and Syvester J. Schieber. 1996. *Fundamentals of Private Pensions.* 7th ed., Philadelphia: University of Pennsylvania Press.

Panis, Constantijn, Michael Hurd, David Loughran, Julie Zissimopoulos, Steve Haider, and Patricia St. Clair. 2002. "The Effects of Changing Social Security Administration's Early Entitlement Age and the Normal Retirement Age." Report prepared for the Social Security Administration. Rand: Santa Monica, CA. (June).

Technical Panel on Assumptions and Methods. 2003. *Report to the Social Security Advisory Board.* Washington, DC. (October).

Tomes, Susan. 2005. "From Here to Eternity: If the Retirement Age is Raised, It Will Cause Untold Misery for Huge Numbers of Classical Musicians." *The Guardian.* (July). http://www.guardian.co.uk/arts/fridayreview/story/0,,1518036,00.html. Downloaded July 1, 2005.

Turner, John, and Roy Guenther. Forthcoming in 2005. "A Comparison of Early Retirement Pensions in the U.S. and Russia: The Pensions of Musicians." *Journal of Aging and Social Policy.* Vol. 17, no. 4.

U.S. Department of Labor, Bureau of Labor Statistics. 2005. "Union Affiliation of Employed Wage and Salary Workers by Occupation and Industry." http://www.bls.gov/news.release/union2.t03.htm.

CHAPTER TWO

Older Workers

Employment and Retirement Trends

PATRICK J. PURCELL

As the members of the baby-boom generation—people born between 1946 and 1964—approach retirement, the demographic profile of the U.S. workforce will undergo a substantial shift: a large number of older workers will be joined by relatively few new entrants to the labor force. According to the U.S. Bureau of the Census, while the number of people between the ages of 55 and 64 will grow by about 17.5 million between 2000 and 2020, the number of people who are 25 to 54 years old will not grow at all. This trend could have important effects on wage rates and economic growth because the labor force participation rate (the percentage of people either employed or unemployed but looking for work) begins to fall steadily after age 55.

Recent employment trends among older Americans vary by age and sex. Census Bureau data indicate that from 1995 to 2003 employment remained steady among men 55 to 61 years old and rose among women in this age group. Of men ages 55 to 61, 71 percent were employed in 2003, compared with 72 percent in 1995. Employment among women ages 55 to 61 rose from 54 percent in 1995 to 61 percent in 2003. Among both men and women ages 62 to 64, employment rose throughout the period. About 47 percent of men ages 62 to 64 were employed in 2003, compared with 42 percent in 1995. Among women 62 to 64, employment increased from 31 percent in 1995 to 37 percent in 2003.

Factors influencing the rate of employment among persons aged 55 years and older, include the rate of economic growth, eligibility for Social Security benefits, and the prevalence and design of employer-sponsored pensions. The Senior Citizens' Right to Work Act (Public Law 106-182), enacted on April 7, 2000, eliminated the Social Security earnings test for people at or above the "full retirement age" (currently 65 years and 2 months), effective January 1, 2000. Labor force participation among people 55 and older might also be affected by the trend away from defined benefit (DB) pension plans, which often include early-retirement subsidies and pay a guaranteed benefit for life, toward defined contribution (DC) plans, which are age neutral and often pay a lump sum at retirement.

As more workers reach retirement age over the next several years, employers may try to induce some to remain on the job, perhaps on a part-time schedule. This is known as "phased retirement." Several approaches to phased retirement—job sharing, reduced work schedules, and rehiring retired workers on a part-time or temporary basis—are accommodated under current law. Some of these approaches, however, require the individual to separate from the firm before returning under an alternative work arrangement. Under current law, a pension plan cannot pay benefits unless the recipient has either separated from the employer or reached the pension plan's normal retirement age. Some employers would like to pay partial pension distributions to workers at the plan's early retirement age and to limit participation to workers in particular occupational categories. However, targeted participation could cause a pension plan to violate the provisions of the tax code that prohibit retirement plans from discriminating in favor of highly compensated employees.

Deciding when to retire is a choice that will affect an individual's economic circumstances for the rest of his or her life. Retirement is most often defined with reference to two characteristics: (1) nonparticipation in the paid labor force and (2) receipt of income from pensions, Social Security, and other retirement plans. An individual who does not work for compensation and who receives income only from pensions, Social Security, and financial assets would meet this definition of retirement. An individual who works for compensation and receives no income from pensions or Social Security would not be retired according to this definition.

Between these two extremes, however, are those individuals, for example, who have retired from careers in law enforcement or the military—both of which typically provide pensions after 20 years of service—who often work for many years at other jobs, while also receiving a pension from prior employment. On the other hand, many people who retire from full-time employment continue to work part time to supplement the income they receive from pensions and Social Security. If the majority of their income is provided by Social Security, pensions, and savings, economists typically classify them as retired, even though they continue to engage in paid employment. As these examples suggest, not everyone who receives pension income is retired, and some people who work for pay actually are retired.

This chapter starts with an analysis of data from the Census Bureau's Current Population Survey on employment and receipt of pension income in recent years among persons age 55 and older. Employment trends among older workers are then discussed in the context of data from the Social Security Administration on the proportion of workers who claim retired-worker benefits before the full retirement age. The final section discusses recent proposals to promote phased retirement through amendments to the sections of the Internal Revenue Code that govern the taxation of pension income.

THE AGING OF THE LABOR FORCE

The number of people between the ages of 25 and 64 is projected to increase by about 17.5 million between 2000 and 2020. The *entire* increase is projected to occur among people between the ages of 55 and 64.

The labor force participation rate varies by age and sex. Men aged 55 and older are less likely to participate in the labor force today than were their counterparts a half-century ago. According to data from the Current Population Survey (CPS), a monthly survey conducted by the U.S. Bureau of the Census, in the 1950s, five out of six men ages 55 to 64 participated in the labor force; that is, they were either working or actively looking for work (see Table 1).[1] By 2000, only two in three men in that age group participated in the labor force. Most of the historical decline occurred over a relatively brief period, from about 1970 to the mid-1980s. Among men 65 and older, the decline in labor force participation began earlier, but it also appears to have ended around 1985. Between 1950 and 1985, the labor force participation rate among men 65 and older fell from 46 percent to about 16 percent. Since the mid-1980s, the labor force participation rate among men ages 55 to 64 years has remained in the range of 66–68 percent, while the rate for those ages 65 and older has increased modestly, from 16 percent to 18 percent (see chapters 1 and 4, including the comments to chapter 4).

From 1950 to the present, women's labor force participation has steadily increased. Among women ages 55 to 64, the rate rose from 27 percent in 1950 to 45 percent in 1990 and to 55 percent in 2002. Among women 65 and older, however, the labor force participation rate has changed very little over the last 50 years, remaining between 8 and 10 percent over most of the 1950–2002 period. The stability of labor force participation rates among men ages 55 and older since the mid-1980s is likely attributable to several factors. First, Social Security now covers virtually all private-sector nonfarm workers in the United States. The earliest age of eligibility for Social Security retired-worker benefits was set at 62—for women in 1956 and for men in 1961—and has not changed since. Second, in the private sector, the expansion in pension coverage that occurred in the 1950s and 1960s had ended by 1980.[2]

Table 1. Labor Force Participation Rates, 1950–2010

Men	Age Groups		
Year	25 to 54	55 to 64	65 and up
1950	96.5%	86.9%	45.8%
1955	97.4%	87.9%	39.6%
1960	97.0%	86.8%	33.1%
1965	96.7%	84.6%	27.9%
1970	95.8%	83.0%	26.8%
1975	94.4%	75.6%	21.6%
1980	94.2%	72.1%	19.0%
1985	93.9%	67.9%	15.8%
1990	93.4%	67.8%	16.3%
1995	91.6%	66.0%	16.8%
1996	91.8%	67.0%	16.9%
1997	91.8%	67.6%	17.1%
1998	91.8%	68.1%	16.5%
1999	91.7%	67.9%	16.9%
2000	91.6%	67.3%	17.5%
2001	91.3%	68.1%	17.7%
2002	91.0%	69.2%	17.8%
*2010	90.9%	67.0%	19.5%

Women	Age Groups		
Year	25 to 54	55 to 64	65 and up
1950	36.8%	27.0%	9.7%
1955	39.8%	32.5%	10.6%
1960	42.9%	37.2%	10.8%
1965	45.2%	41.1%	10.0%
1970	50.1%	43.0%	9.7%
1975	55.1%	40.9%	8.2%
1980	64.0%	41.3%	8.1%
1985	69.6%	42.0%	7.3%
1990	74.0%	45.2%	8.6%
1995	75.6%	49.2%	8.8%
1996	76.1%	49.6%	8.6%
1997	76.7%	50.9%	8.6%
1998	76.5%	51.2%	8.6%
1999	76.8%	51.5%	8.9%
2000	76.8%	51.8%	9.4%
2001	76.4%	53.0%	9.7%
2002	76.0%	55.1%	9.9%
*2010	80.4%	55.2%	11.1%

Source: U.S. Department of Labor, Bureau of Labor Statistics.
*Estimated by the Bureau of Labor Statistics.

Data collected by the Census Bureau indicate that from 1995 to 2003 employment remained generally steady among men 55 to 61 years old and rose among women in this age group (see Table 2 and Table 3).[3] Of men ages 55 to 61, 71 percent were employed in 2003, compared with 72 percent in 1995. Employment among women ages 55 to 61 rose from 54 percent in 1995 to 61 percent in 2003. Among both men and women ages 62 to 64, employment rose steadily throughout the period. About 47 percent of men were employed in 2003, compared with 42 percent in 1995. Among women, employment increased from 31 percent in 1995 to 37 percent in 2003.

Among men 65 to 69 years old, an average of 26.4 percent were employed each year from 1995 through 1999. From 2000 to 2003, an average of 30.7 percent of men in this age group were employed. Among women in the same age group, the increase in employment since 1995 has been smaller. An average of 17.9 percent of women were employed in each year from 1995 through 1999. From 2000 through 2003, the average rate of employment among women was 20.1 percent. Among both men and women age 70 and older, rates of employment changed little from 1995 through 2002. During this period, the employment rate averaged 11.5 percent among men 70 and older and 5.6 percent among women age 70 and older.

EMPLOYMENT TRENDS AMONG OLDER WORKERS

Retirement Income among Older Workers

Table 4 shows the proportion of men and women age 55 and older who reported on the CPS that they received pension income of some kind during the calendar year prior to the survey. In this table, "pension income" includes employer-sponsored pensions (including military retirement); veterans' pensions; and periodic payments from annuities, insurance policies, individual retirement accounts, 401(k) accounts, and Keogh plans for the self-employed. In 2002, only 18 percent of men ages 55 to 64 received income from a pension or other retirement plan; among those 65 years and older, however, 44 percent had income from pensions or retirement savings plans. The patterns among women are similar: only 11 percent received income from pensions or retirement savings plans in 2002, while 27 percent of those aged 65 years and older received such income.

The 18 percent of men ages 55 to 64 who were receiving pension income represents a decline from 23 percent in 1994. Over the same period, the proportion of men ages 65 and older receiving pension income fell from 47 percent to

Table 2. Employment of Men Age 55 and Older, 1995–2003

Age in March	Population (000s)	Number Employed (000s)	Percent Employed	Employment	
				Full-time	Part-time
55 to 61					
1995	6,993	5,035	72.0%	91.5%	8.5%
2001	8,479	6,138	72.4%	91.6%	8.4%
2002	9,307	6,608	71.0%	91.9%	8.1%
2003	9,870	7,050	71.4%	92.0%	8.0%
62 to 64					
1995	2,879	1,206	41.9%	79.0%	21.0%
2001	2,771	1,284	46.3%	77.2%	22.8%
2002	3,059	1,491	48.7%	78.1%	21.9%
2003	3,279	1,539	46.9%	79.7%	20.3%
65 to 69					
1995	4,395	1,169	26.6%	54.7%	45.3%
2001	4,449	1,328	29.9%	63.2%	36.8%
2002	4,451	1,358	30.5%	60.0%	40.0%
2003	4,318	1,385	32.1%	63.2%	36.8%
70 and older					
1995	8,607	970	11.3%	44.9%	55.1%
2001	9,730	1,198	12.3%	48.1%	51.9%
2002	9,785	1,141	11.7%	51.1%	48.9%
2003	10,210	1,209	11.8%	54.2%	45.8%

Source: CRS analysis of the annual March supplement to the *Current Population Survey.*

44 percent. The proportion of women ages 55 to 64 with pension income was more stable, at 11–12 percent throughout the 1994–2001 period. Among women 65 and older, 27 percent received income from pensions and retirement savings plans in 2002, about one percentage point less than in 1994.

To study the relationship between the employment rates shown in Tables 2 and 3 and the data on receipt of pension distributions shown in Table 4, I grouped

Table 3. Employment of Women Age 55 and Older, 1995–2003

Age in March	Population (000s)	Number Employed (000s)	Percent Employed	Employment	
				Full-time	Part-time
55 to 61					
1995	7,716	4,196	54.4%	74.1%	25.9%
2001	9,296	5,365	57.7%	77.3%	22.7%
2002	10,023	5,881	58.7%	76.7%	23.3%
2003	10,677	6,529	61.2%	78.2%	21.8%
62 to 64					
1995	3,162	975	30.8%	58.3%	41.7%
2001	3,236	1,185	36.6%	62.6%	37.4%
2002	3,479	1,306	37.6%	61.9%	38.1%
2003	3,552	1,307	36.8%	62.1%	37.9%
65 to 69					
1995	5,263	919	17.5%	36.3%	63.7%
2001	4,933	947	19.2%	42.3%	57.7%
2002	5,146	982	19.1%	49.6%	50.4%
2003	5,121	1,152	22.5%	51.7%	48.3%
70 and older					
1995	13,001	650	5.0%	30.4%	69.6%
2001	13,866	840	6.1%	39.3%	60.7%
2002	14,388	850	5.9%	38.0%	62.0%
2003	14,585	896	6.1%	40.7%	59.3%

Source: CRS analysis of the annual March supplement to the Current Population Survey.

the men and women into two age groups, 55 to 64, and 65 and older and calculated the correlation coefficient between employment and receipt of pension income. Among men, there is a strong negative correlation between receipt of pension income and employment. Over the period from 1995 to 2003, the correlation between receipt of pension income and current employment was −0.75 for men 55 to 64 years old and −0.74 for men 65 and older.

Among women, employment rates and the receipt of pension income are not strongly correlated (0.16 for women 55–64 and 0.20 for women 65 and older). This is partly due to the fact that the rate of labor force participation among women under age 65 has been rising steadily over many years. Thus, one reason that the percentage of *all* women 55 and older who receive pension income has not fallen along with that of men is that an increasing percentage of women have earned retirement benefits through their own employment. This could mask a decline in the percentage of working women who are (or will be) eligible to receive pension distributions.

Work by Recipients of Retirement Income

The data displayed in Table 4 show the number and percentage of people 55 and older who received pensions or distributions from retirement accounts. The data in Table 5 show that among men ages 55 to 64 who received income from a pension or retirement savings plan during 2002, 34.9 percent were employed either full or part time in March 2003—a decrease of 3.4 percentage points from the 38.3 percent who were employed in 2002. Relatively few men age 65 or older who receive income from pensions or retirement savings plans also engage in paid employment: only 10–12 percent were employed, on average, over the 1995–2003 period. Women who receive pension income are less likely than men to be employed. Among 55- to 64-year-old women who received income from a pension or retirement savings plan in 2002, 33.7 percent were employed in March 2003, an increase of 4.9 percentage points from the level of March 2002. The average rate of employment for these women from 1995 to 2003 was 30.3 percent. Among women age 65 or older who received income from a pension or retirement savings plan, only 6–8 percent, on average, were employed during the 1995–2003 period.

Older Workers and Phased Retirement

In the traditional view of retirement, a worker moves from full-time employment to complete withdrawal from the labor force in a single step. In fact, however, some workers choose to continue working after they have retired from their "career" jobs. The process of retiring often occurs gradually, over several years, with many workers retiring from year-round, full-time employment and moving to part-time or part-year work at another firm, often in a different occupation. The data in Table 5, for example, show that 35 percent of men and 34 percent of women ages 55 to 64 who received income from private pension plans in 2002 were employed in March 2003.

Table 4. Receipt of Income from Employer Pensions and Retirement Savings Plans for All Individuals, Age 55 and Older

Men	Individuals 55 to 64 years old			Individuals age 65 and older		
	Number of people (000s)	Number of recipients (000s)	% age	Number of people (000s)	Number of recipients (000s)	% age
1995	9,872	2,303	23.3%	13,001	6,108	47.0%
1996	10,090	2,279	22.6%	13,260	6,206	46.8%
1997	10,256	2,177	21.2%	13,404	6,316	47.1%
1998	10,667	2,152	20.2%	13,524	6,317	46.7%
1999	10,959	2,195	20.0%	13,727	6,457	47.0%
2000	11,131	2,174	19.5%	13,886	6,358	45.8%
2001	11,249	2,124	18.9%	14,179	6,099	43.0%
2002	12,366	2,371	19.2%	14,235	6,276	44.1%
2003	13,149	2,372	18.0%	14,527	6,414	44.2%
Women						
1995	10,878	1,316	12.1%	18,264	5,252	28.8%
1996	10,991	1,164	10.6%	18,398	5,025	27.3%
1997	11,210	1,287	11.5%	18,474	4,933	26.7%
1998	11,580	1,253	10.8%	18,559	5,114	27.6%
1999	11,943	1,403	11.7%	18,668	5,186	27.8%
2000	12,250	1,439	11.7%	18,735	5,513	29.4%
2001	12,532	1,475	11.8%	18,799	5,426	28.9%
2002	13,501	1,525	11.3%	19,535	5,412	27.7%
2003	14,229	1,572	11.0%	19,706	5,379	27.3%

Source: CRS analysis of the March supplement to the *Current Population Survey.*
Notes: Retirement plans may include a traditional pension, a retirement savings plan, or both. The income year is the year when the income was received, which is the calendar year preceding the March CPS interview.

As members of the baby-boom generation begin to retire, millions of skilled and experienced workers will exit the labor force. As this occurs, employers may find it necessary to alter their employment practices and pension plans, offering phased retirement in order to induce some of those who would otherwise retire to remain on the job, perhaps on a part-time or part-year schedule. No statutory definition of "phased retirement" exists, but one analyst has described it as "the situation in which an older individual is actively working for an employer part time or [on] an otherwise reduced schedule as a transition into full retirement.

Table 5. Employment of Recipients of Employer Pensions and Retirement Savings Plans, Age 55 and Older

Men	Recipients, 55 to 64 years old			Recipients, age 65 and older		
	Number of recipients (000s)	Number employed (000s)	% age	Number of recipients (000s)	Number employed (000s)	% age
1995	2,303	864	37.5%	6,108	727	11.9%
1996	2,279	831	36.5%	6,206	726	11.7%
1997	2,177	832	38.2%	6,316	724	11.5%
1998	2,152	778	36.2%	6,317	648	10.3%
1999	2,195	870	39.7%	6,457	706	10.9%
2000	2,174	799	36.7%	6,358	739	11.6%
2001	2,124	797	37.5%	6,099	721	11.8%
2002	2,371	907	38.3%	6,276	739	11.8%
2003	2,372	827	34.9%	6,414	745	11.6%
Women						
1995	1,316	410	31.2%	5,252	326	6.2%
1996	1,164	324	27.9%	5,025	281	5.6%
1997	1,287	416	32.3%	4,933	277	5.6%
1998	1,253	363	29.0%	5,114	404	7.9%
1999	1,403	370	26.3%	5,186	426	8.2%
2000	1,439	442	30.7%	5,513	401	7.3%
2001	1,475	488	33.1%	5,426	436	8.0%
2002	1,525	439	28.8%	5,412	393	7.3%
2003	1,572	530	33.7%	5,379	425	8.0%

Source: CRS analysis of the March income supplement to the *Current Population Survey*.
Note: Retirement plans may include a traditional pension, a retirement savings plan, or both. The income year is the year prior to the survey. Employment is in current year.

[It] may also include situations in which older employees receive some or all of their retirement benefits while still employed" (Schopp 2000).

Advocates of phased retirement contend that many people would choose to continue working if employers could offer them the opportunity to collect pension benefits while still on the employer's payroll. Under current law, this option can be offered only to employees who have reached a pension plan's normal retirement age. Some employers have suggested that phased retirement would be embraced by more firms if this option could be offered to employees at the plan's early retirement age. Employers generally would prefer to offer the option of receiving these "in-service" distributions only to selected categories or classifications of plan participants.[4] In order for either of these actions to be taken, however, the Internal Revenue Code and the Employee Retirement Income Security Act (ERISA) would need to be amended.

Phased Retirement and Pension Distributions

Unless an employee has reached the pension plan's normal retirement age, the plan cannot pay retirement benefits to the individual while he or she remains employed by the firm, even if only on a part-time basis. A plan that pays benefits to an employee that has not yet reached the plan's normal retirement age could lose its tax-qualified status.[5] In order to qualify for the favorable tax status granted to tax-qualified pension plans, the plan must pay benefits only on condition of death, disability, termination of employment, plan termination, or at the normal retirement age (*Code of Federal Regulations*, § 1.401–1[b][1][i]). An employee who has reached the pension plan's normal retirement age can begin to receive distributions from the plan, even if he or she continues to be employed by the firm.[6] Likewise, an employee who has reached the plan's early retirement age can begin to receive distributions from the plan upon separation from the firm, provided that he or she has met the required number of years of service stipulated by the plan. If a participant has separated from the employer and has begun to receive distributions from the plan at the early retirement age, he or she can continue to receive these distributions, even if at some future date the participant becomes re-employed by the plan sponsor. In order to retain the plan's tax-qualified status, however, the employer may be required to demonstrate to the Internal Revenue Service that "both a bona fide retirement (or other termination of employment) and a legitimate rehire have occurred" (Fields and Hutchens 2002).

POLICY ISSUES

Some employers see the statutory prohibition on making in-service pension distributions to employees who have not yet reached normal retirement age as an obstacle to establishing phased retirement plans. Some older workers would find it financially impractical to cut back to a part-time or part-year work schedule if they were unable to supplement their earnings with pension income. One way for a firm to offer phased retirement to these workers under current law, without jeopardizing the tax-qualified status of its pension plan, would be to lower the normal retirement age. For example, if the normal retirement age under the plan were 62 years and the early retirement age were 55 years, the firm could reduce the normal retirement age to some age between 55 and 61. From the employer's point of view, there would be at least two potential drawbacks to such an approach. First, it could result in an unintended exodus of workers into retirement because all eligible plan participants would be able to receive full pension benefits at an earlier age than previously. Second, it could result in a dramatic increase in the cost of funding the plan because full benefits would be payable at a younger age.

An amendment to the tax code to permit in-service distributions at the early retirement age would alter incentives to work or retire, as well as how much to work and for whom to work. Consequently, it would affect both labor force participation and hours worked among older employees. The net effect of these changes in labor force participation and hours worked would be almost impossible to predict. Some workers who otherwise would have fully retired before the plan's normal retirement age would choose instead to continue working for their current employer on a reduced schedule because they would be able to take partial pension distributions while still employed. This would tend to increase labor force participation. Other workers who would have taken early retirement and then sought other employment might choose instead to remain with their current employer on a reduced schedule. The effect of this change in behavior on hours worked might be close to neutral, depending on the wages available from alternative employment and the income received from pension distributions. Finally, some employees who otherwise would have chosen to continue working until reaching the plan's normal retirement age might instead reduce their work schedule and supplement their earnings with partial distributions from the retirement plan. This would tend to reduce total hours worked.

Distributions from 401(k) Plans

Coverage under DC plans, such as those authorized under section 401(k) of the Internal Revenue Code, grew rapidly during the 1990s. Between 1991 and 1997, the proportion of workers in medium and large private-sector establishments (those with 100 or more employees) who participated in DC retirement plans increased from 49 percent to 57 percent (Bureau of Labor Statistics 1993, and Bureau of Labor Statistics 1999). The trend among small establishments (those with fewer than 100 employees) was similar. In 1996, 38 percent of employees in small private establishments participated in DC retirement plans, compared with

28 percent in 1990 (Bureau of Labor Statistics 1991, 5, table 1; and Bureau of Labor Statistics 1999, 5, table 1).

In-service distributions from DC plans that occur before the participant reaches age 59$\frac{1}{2}$ are subject to a 10 percent excise tax in addition to ordinary income taxes. Distributions may begin as early as age 55, however, if the employee separates from his employer under an early-retirement plan. Some advocates of phased retirement arrangements have suggested that the minimum age for in-service distributions from DC plans should be lowered to age 55 from 59$\frac{1}{2}$.[7] The effect on labor force participation of such a change in tax policy would likely be very similar to the effect of allowing in-service distributions from a DB plan at the plan's early retirement age. Some workers who might have fully retired from the labor force earlier than age 59$\frac{1}{2}$ so that they could begin taking distributions from the plan would be induced to work longer. Others who would have taken early retirement and then sought work elsewhere would remain with their current employers because they would be able to combine wages from part-time work with distributions from the retirement plan. Finally, some employees who otherwise would have chosen to continue working until age 59$\frac{1}{2}$ or later would reduce their work schedules and supplement their earnings with distributions from the retirement plan.

Flexibility versus Nondiscrimination

Pension plans that provide benefits mainly to the owners of a firm or to highly paid employees do not qualify for favorable tax treatment under the Internal Revenue Code.[8] The tax code defines specific tests that must be applied to a pension plan to determine whether or not it discriminates in favor of highly compensated employees in terms of either benefits or employer contributions (26 U.S.C. § 410[b]). These tests consist mainly of mathematical computations of the percentage of plan participants who are highly compensated employees and the percentage of contributions to the plan or benefits paid by the plan that are made on behalf of highly compensated employees.

In general, employers would prefer the flexibility to offer phased retirement to some—but not all—pension plan participants. Some analysts have suggested that even if Congress were to amend the Internal Revenue Code to allow in-service distributions from pension plans before the normal retirement age, it would do little to spur the growth of phased retirement unless employers also were permitted to limit eligibility for this benefit to employees with particular skills or abilities. However, a phased retirement option that offered in-service distributions only to managerial or professional employees could result in the plan failing to meet the nondiscrimination requirements of the Internal Revenue Code by altering the distribution of benefits among plan participants in a way that favored the highly compensated group.

Section 410(b) of the Internal Revenue Code prescribes specific tests for determining if a pension plan's coverage or benefits discriminate in favor of highly compensated employees. These tests are mathematical calculations that reveal the proportion of plan participants who are highly compensated employees and the proportion of contributions or benefits that are made on behalf of highly compensated employees. Some plan sponsors who would like to implement phased retirement programs would prefer to have these tests for nondiscrimination replaced by the more subjective method of testing that was in effect until 1994, which was based on the "facts and circumstances" surrounding the operation of the plan. In some cases, a phased retirement option that fails the mathematical tests for nondiscrimination that are required under current law might not fail if it could be tested under the earlier (pre-1994) approach.

Policy Responses to an Aging Population

The rules that govern eligibility for Social Security benefits can have a substantial influence on workers' decisions about when to retire. Empirical evidence indicates that more retirements occur at age 62—the earliest age at which reduced retired-worker benefits are available—and age 65—the earliest age at which full retired-worker benefits are available—than at other ages. The "earnings test," which reduces benefits for some Social Security beneficiaries who work, and the delayed retirement credit (DRC), which increases benefits for workers who defer their benefits until after age 65, also may influence one's decision to work (and how much to work) after becoming eligible for Social Security. At times, each of these provisions has been amended to provide greater incentives for individuals who are eligible for Social Security to continue working.

The Social Security amendments of 1983 mandated a gradual increase in the age at which individuals are eligible for full retirement benefits from 65 to 67 years old in 2022. As a result, the actuarial reduction in Social Security benefits for those who retire at 62 will increase from 20 percent to 30 percent, creating a financial incentive to delay receipt of Social Security and continue working. The 1983 amendments also provided for an increase in the DRC for workers who defer their application for Social Security benefits until after age 65. In 1977, Congress set the DRC at 3 percent, meaning that benefits were permanently increased by 3 percent for each year that a worker delayed receipt of Social Security beyond age 65. The 1983 amendments provided for a gradual increase in the DRC beginning in 1990. When fully phased in, the DRC will be 8 percent per year for people who turn age 65 in 2008 or later, which will result in a DRC that is close to being "actuarially fair" for the average worker.

In April 2000, the Social Security Act was amended to repeal the earnings test for beneficiaries who are 65 or older. As a result of P. L. 106-182, the earnings test was eliminated for people at the full retirement age (currently 65 years) or older, effective January 1, 2000. The earnings test remains in effect, however, for beneficiaries who are under the full retirement age. In 2003, Social Security recipients under age 65 have their benefits reduced by $1 for each $2 of earnings in excess of $11,520.

Allowing in-service pension distributions to begin when a participant has reached the earliest of a plan's normal retirement age, 59 $^1/_2$, or the completion of 30 years of service might promote continued employment among older workers who—if given the choice between working full time and taking early retirement—would otherwise have chosen to retire. A more complicated issue is whether employers should be permitted to offer such an option only to specific categories of workers.

NOTES

This essay is an excerpt from a report by Congressional Research Service Library of Congress economist Patrick Purcell on "Older Workers: Employment and Retirement Trends" updated October 8, 2003 (Order Code RL30629).

1. Labor force participation rates are annual averages from the monthly CPS data. For more information on the CPS, see Bureau of Labor 1997, 4–14.

2. Approximately one-quarter of the employees of state and local governments—about 5 million people—work for governments that have elected not to participate in Social Security. This is the only remaining large group of workers not covered by Social Security.

3. The labor force participation rates discussed in the previous section were based on annual averages of monthly data. The employment data in this section are from the March supplement to the CPS, and show employment in the week prior to the CPS interview. The March CPS files were used for this analysis because they include detailed data about sources of income in the previous year. CRS used information about current labor force status rather than information about labor force status in the previous year because an individual who reported that he or she both worked and received pension income during the previous year might have worked and received pension income consecutively rather than concurrently.

4. This discussion refers to in-service distributions under DB pension plans. In-service distributions under DC plans are discussed later in this report.

5. In a "tax-qualified" plan, employer contributions to the plan are deductible business expenses for the firm and neither the employer contributions nor investment

earnings on those contributions are counted as income to the employee in the years that they occur; instead, pensions are taxed as income when the benefits are paid to plan participants in retirement. Usually, retirees are taxed at a lower marginal tax rate than when they worked.

6. If a plan participant continues to work for an employer beyond the plan's normal retirement age, the plan must meet the statutory requirements for continued benefit accruals. See 26 U.S.C. § 411(b)(1)(H).

7. It might also seem reasonable that if legislation were passed to allow in-service distributions from an employer's DB plan at the plan's early retirement age, then distributions from the employer's DC plan should be permitted at the same age (perhaps with a lower limit of age 55). However, such a policy would suffer from at least two drawbacks. First, the minimum age for in-service distributions from DC plans, which is now the same for all such plans, would differ from firm to firm, thus making the retirement planning process even more confusing for workers and their families. Second, it would be administratively difficult—and in some cases, perhaps, impossible—to tie the minimum age for in-service distributions in the DC plan to the early retirement age specified in the employer's DB plan.

8. 26 U.S.C. § 401(a)(4) states that a qualified pension trust is one in which "the contributions or benefits provided under the plan do not discriminate in favor of highly compensated employees (within the meaning of section 414[q])." The term "highly-compensated employee" is defined at 26 U.S.C. § 414(q) as a person who is at least a 5-percent owner of the firm or is paid compensation of at least $85,000 and is among the top 20 percent of employees in the firm with respect to compensation.

REFERENCES

Fields, Vivian, and Robert Hutchens. 2002. "Regulatory Obstacles to Phased Retirement in the For-Profit Sector." *Benefits Quarterly*. Vol. 18 no. 3.

Schopp, Wilma K. 2000. "Testimony on Behalf of the Association of Private Pension and Welfare Plans before the U.S. Senate Special Committee on Aging." (April 3).

U.S. Bureau of Labor Statistics. 1998. *BLS Handbook of Methods*. Washington, DC: Bulletin 2490 (April).

U.S. Bureau of Labor Statistics. 1993. "Employee Benefits in Medium and Large Private Establishments." Washington, DC: Bulletin 2422 (May).

U.S. Bureau of Labor Statistics. 1999. "Employee Benefits in Medium and Large Private Establishments." Washington, DC: Bulletin 2517 (September).

U.S. Bureau of Labor Statistics. 1991. "Employee Benefits in Small Private Establishments." Washington, DC: Bulletin 2388 (September).

U.S. Bureau of Labor Statistics. 1999. "Employee Benefits in Small Private Establishments." Washington, DC: Bulletin 2507 (April).

CHAPTER THREE

Continued Labor Force Participation

Individual Differences

PATRICIA M. RASKIN *&* GREGORY GETTAS

As Americans live and stay healthy longer, the idea of retirement no longer means that they have just a few years left. Rather, as 55-year-olds in our society look forward to decades of health and energy, the issue of when or whether to retire becomes a different question than it used to be. Over the past century, the average number of years lived in retirement prior to death has increased from 3 to almost 15 (Vaillant 2002). More than 16 million Americans over 55 are working or seeking work, and older workers currently make up 13 percent of the workforce (Montenegro et al. 2002). This number is likely to increase (Hall and Mirvis 1994). Moreover, if older workers do not continue in the labor force, there will be a severe labor shortage by 2010 (Knechtel 2003; Montenegro et al. 2002; Pine 2003).

Although labor force participation and retirement are defined in many arenas and are increasingly the focus of study, we know little about career development and work attitudes in later life. Most of the research on older workers' attitudes is done from the employer's perspective and is centered on how these workers behave at work, continue to contribute to organizations, and think about leaving the labor force.

The question about whether continued labor force participation is good for individuals is a complicated one. Although we are learning more and more about their psychological and physical health, and their adjustment at this stage of life, almost nothing is known about how they make individual career decisions at this stage, and what factors may contribute to the decisions they make to retire or not (Greller and Simpson 1999; London 1990).

The Meaning of Work

Work is not just about work. Work is about a meaningful existence, our communities, and our society as a whole. "Most of us, even those of us who work at routine jobs, don't dislike work as much as we say we do. Not too rebelliously, we accept the fact that work is what we build our lives around, and many of us discover it to be a satisfaction, even a pleasure. It not only gets us what we need and want, it proves to us that we are grown up" (Stegner 1978, 229).

Sigmund Freud suggested that the hallmarks of a psychologically healthy life were the capacities to love and to work. For many of us, who we are in the world of work is a central feature of our self-concept (Montenegro et al. 2002; Schlossberg 2004). Indeed, adult developmental theorists assume that how one engages in the world of work is central to successful progression through the life course (Erikson et al. 1986; Levinson 1978; Vaillant 2002). Work often gives our lives meaning and is the "ultimate measure of adulthood . . . the scaffolding that holds up the adult life" (Stegner 1978, 230). This can be especially true when we work in middle-class environments, with some degree of autonomy. The more education or training we have, the more likely we are to identify with our professions. Further, as workers mature in their jobs, they develop intrinsic satisfaction based on their success in achieving challenging goals (Schein 1978). Montenegro and her colleagues have called the 45-year-olds who hold these attitudes and values "contributors" (Montenegro et al. 2002, 4).

Initial attitudes toward work are developed late in adolescence (Fannin 1979; Greenhaus 1973) and play a continuing role in overall career attitudes. Although career salience or work involvement may increase or decrease somewhat, depending on the work environment, career salience is usually a deeply held value and may be predictive of attitudes about how long to work (Harpaz 2002; Harpaz and Fu 2002). It is also tied to identity (Thoits 1983) and mastery (Erikson et al. 1986; Pearlin et al. 1981). These early career attitudes are also associated with psychological well being: the more involved one is, the more social roles one occupies, the better one's adjustment. This finding has been borne out in a number of longitudinal studies on both men and women (Roberts and Friend 1998; Vaillant 2002). As we move through career stages, our attitudes towards work may mature. Ginn (1994) suggests that as individuals approach later life, they have learned the limits of their self-created roles, the value of cooperation, that working is a form of self-expression, and that external reward systems do not matter as much as internal values and generativity.

If work is a source of identity and mastery, then the age bias, or "gray ceiling," one encounters as one ages is potentially devastating, making it difficult to think about continuing to work. As Imel suggests, "Older workers don't fear change, they fear discrimination" (1996, 2). Further, because of the concern that older workers may have about negative evaluation (Hall 1986), the intrinsic satisfaction obtained from a sense of mastery earlier in one's career may change to a much more conservative posture—taking fewer risks, establishing safer routines. The lack of respect accorded older workers and the sometimes indirect suggestion that it is "time to leave" may have the effect of pushing people out of the workforce—what appears to be voluntary retirement may not be so voluntary from a psychological perspective. The decision to retire, however, is potentially risky, a decision that may result in a loss of identity, a departure from the roles and responsibilities of "true" adulthood. This departure from the labor force may make an individual vulnerable to the dangers of living in a world where there are few opportunities for mastery in domains that signal meaning, and where there is the risk of becoming "invisible" is high (Thompson 1994). Nevertheless, retirement has been constructed as a culturally transmitted right, concomitant with economic support and autonomy, especially in the management of time. Individuals now in the labor force who are approaching retirement age have "paid their dues," devoting most of their waking hours to labor force participation. As a cohort, they have been loyal to their companies and their professions, and have sacrificed personal time in order to earn a living and provide for their families. The prospect of retirement, then, is one of letting go of their previous commitments: of time constraints, of financial responsibility for family, of work obligations.

Gender Differences

"Work and career dominate a man's identity" (Gradman 1994, 104). For many men, work is associated with masculinity as well as with other aspects of adulthood (Drost 2003; Gradman 1994). Many men believe that being the breadwinner is a prerequisite for being a man in our society. Unemployment of any kind puts that self-conception in danger.

Based on twenty-eight interviews with the 80-year-old parents of the Berkeley Guidance Study participants (an original 1928 sample of 248 mostly white, protestant, and middle-class infants, resulting in a total longitudinal cohort of 214; the most recent data were collected in 1969 [Huffine and Aerts 1998]), Erikson et al. (1986) found that among men in their sample, a sense of competency in old age was correlated with a sense of mastery derived from earlier experiences in the workplace. With their retirement and the subsequent suspension of the extrinsic, monetary rewards that accompanied work, however, many noted a diminished sense of primary competence and accomplishment once derived from their ritualized bringing home of a paycheck. Nevertheless, retirement, for some of these men, also brought positive exposure to new tasks—some welcomed, as in the development of new skills or hobbies, and some not welcomed, as in the need to care for a seriously disabled spouse. This exposure created a newly discovered sense of intrinsic motivation. For the first time in their lives, freed from the bonds of earning a wage and supporting their families, some men were able to channel their talents in wholly new directions and thus derived "satisfaction from the experience of competence as integral to activity itself" (160). For other men, however, the opposite seemed to be true; no longer working, they sensed a loss of competence and, as a result, appeared to cling to past business achievements or, worse, began to denigrate their own lifelong accomplishments in light of a current perceived sense of inadequacy.

Work may have different meanings for women. Erikson and his colleagues found that for most of the women they studied, home-based effectiveness mattered more than the world of work, although many of the interviewees both worked and liked work (Erikson et al. 1986). The number of women who are remaining in the workforce and about to retire is just beginning to increase (Moen 1996). Furthermore, even though women's labor force participation has been on the rise for many years, that participation may be more fragmented than men's; women are more likely to enter the labor force late (Prentis 1980), move in and out of the labor force, and occupy part-time or part-year jobs, even when they are highly educated (Fannin 1981; Moen 1996).

Caring for children has historically been a woman's role, and having children is one of the strongest predictors of occupational interruption and impediments (Choi 2002; Roberts and Friend 1998). We know less about women's attitudes toward work and retirement than we know about men's, but we do know that being invested in a career is related to high self-esteem in women as well as in men. Erdner and Guy (1990) found that, as expected, female schoolteachers with stronger work identities had significantly more negative attitudes toward retirement than female teachers who had weaker work identities. This finding suggests that when women are career salient (and more and more women are in this category), their attitudes toward work and retirement are not very different from men's (Talaga and Beehr 1995; Walshok 1981). Price (2002) made a similar observation and found that women who were not career salient adjusted to retirement more easily than women who were invested in their work.

Just as men and women differ in terms of their labor force participation, and the meaning that participation has, so do men and women differ in terms of the decision to retire. Men are more likely to decide to retire based on their relationship to the world of work, whereas women are more likely to take relationships and family obligations into account (Hatch and Thompson 1992; Price 2002; Szinovacz and Ekerdt 1995). In some cases, women are more reluctant to leave the labor force because of late entry—they are just getting started as their husbands are thinking about winding down (Moen 1996). Further, women are not particularly accurate in anticipating what factors to consider as they plan for retirement. Zimmerman and her colleagues found that although the actual timing of retirement was affected by family care-giving responsibilities and by health or stress factors, women did not perceive these issues to be important in their pre-retirement planning. Finally, a word must be said about financial resources. Most women earn less than men do throughout their lives and have lower-paying jobs that do not provide pensions. When women do have pensions, they receive only half the average benefits that men do. Even when women work in better jobs, they continue to earn $.73 for every $1 men earn. This represents a lifetime loss of over $300,000, and plays a part in retirement decision-making (Zimmerman et al. 2000).

Deciding About Retirement

A number of factors affect the decision to retire.

Work Involvement

Older full-time workers tend to be satisfied and committed to their jobs (London 1990; Montenegro et al. 2002), although these positive attitudes can decline with the experience of prejudice. Intrinsic satisfaction can be influenced by context, specifically by how welcome workers feel in their current environment. When stress increases as a result of negative bias and other uncontrollable factors (e.g., the continuing need to adapt and compensate for age-related changes), these positive attitudes can change and motivate workers to retire (Remondet and Hansson 1991). The importance of self-assessment cannot be underestimated; individuals' attitudes toward their own aging can create self-fulfilling prophecies (Hansson et al. 1997). Individuals who are aware of coworker attitudes may begin to feel awkward if their age exceeds traditional age norms, and they may avoid job change if they believe they will be stereotyped. The most difficult job changes individuals can make, however, are ones that devalue prior experiences (Bailey and Hansson 1995). The belief that one is perceived to be too old, taken together with the belief that one's contributions to the organization no longer have meaning, can create a desire to leave the organization even if one is highly career salient (Barnes-Farrell 2003).

Many individuals remain in the workforce for extrinsic reasons (e.g., salary, health benefits), although there is some evidence to suggest that the psychosocial components of work play a part as well, for example, the provision of structure, work friendships, or "social embeddedness" (Henkens and Tazelaar 1997). Montenegro described a group of 45-year-old workers as "connectors" (Montenegro et al. 2002, 3). We have no way of knowing whether the rewards obtained from these motivators predict remaining at work or wanting to retire. It is conceivable that when the extrinsic rewards of retirement balance the extrinsic rewards one earns while working, the wish to retire will increase, if other factors are held constant (e.g., health, ageism).

Employer Attitudes

There is no doubt that bias against older workers occurs, and that this bias is even greater in industries that are inclined to hire young workers, or to brand themselves as youthful (Weinberg 1998). Older workers are stereotyped as indecisive, slow, dissatisfied, and less adaptable (Rosen and Jerdee 1988), and not worth the cost of training because they will "retire soon" (Pine 2003), even when there is little data to support that stereotype (Greller and Simpson 1999). Employers also believe that older workers are expensive, in terms of earnings and health insurance costs (Pine 2003). At the same time, however, employers believe that older workers have lower absenteeism and lower turnover rates, as well as better work attitudes, motivation, job skills, and loyalty than younger workers (Barth et al. 1993). On balance, the research seems to show that managers almost always underestimate the productivity of older workers (Mcnaught 1994) and that employers are currently ambivalent about those older workers. Since age discrimination in the workplace is associated with increased stress symptoms and depression (Abraham and Hansson 1994), employers' ambivalence may create a self-fulfilling prophecy: the less valued an employee feels, the more likely he or she is to exhibit the behaviors the employer believes to be true. Indeed, Montenegro and her colleagues found that 67 percent of the workers they studied who were 45 and older believed that age discrimination exists (Montenegro et al. 2002).

Health Issues

Poor health is predictive of early retirement or other involuntary labor force exits, and there is some evidence to suggest that functional difficulties may be even stronger predictors of leaving the work force than illness itself (Wray 2003). Mental health may be an even more important predictor (Mitchell and Anderson 1989; Wray 2003). We do know that older workers do not diminish in their work performance, and when they are less effective, organizational demography or stereotyping are often the source of that diminished effectiveness (Greller and Simpson 1999, 334).

In addition, choice matters. The more control people who are employed have over their schedules, the better their health and well being (Herzog et al. 1991). Having the sense of control about when and how to retire may also affect attitudes about leaving the labor force. Unanticipated retirement is much more likely to cause stress and its sequelae than planned retirement. In a cohort analysis, however, based on the Study of Adult Development at Harvard University (N = 824 sample, consisting of three separate cohorts), Vaillant (2002) found retirement "highly overrated as a major life problem" (220) even though stress may have resulted when a retiree's previous job masked an unhappy home life or when retirement had been precipitated by failing health. Such problems, however, were present among only a fraction of Vaillant's sample, and the results appear consistent with the work of Ekerdt et al. (1983), who found that retirement didn't seem to contribute to the deterioration of health at all. On the contrary, Streib and Schneider (1971) found that retirees claimed that retirement *improved* their health, especially, according to Vaillant (2002), in cases when retirement was made less stressful by celebrating it as one of an individual's developmental milestones, or part of a progression.

Psychological and Birth Cohorts

As Moen suggests (1996), large-scale social shifts in opportunity mean that individuals from different cohorts are born into vastly different worlds. Moreover, they enter the workplace with vastly different attitudes: toward work itself, toward their employers, and towards their peers, subordinates, and leaders, who represent both younger and older generations. Generational differences in respect for authority, company loyalty, and organizational and team structure can create discomfort in older workers, who may feel undervalued and not respected for their experience and longevity in the company. This set of difficulties is somewhat different from age discrimination; that is, it is not the issue of age that is at play, rather it is a question of values. Each cohort has been raised with a different set of expectations, and younger employees (generations X and Y) are not as likely as older silent-generation or baby-boom cohort members to respect hierarchy, be loyal to a particular company (Strauss and Howe 1991), or value experience over immediately necessary skill sets.

The differences among generations may superficially look like age discrimination, but they go much deeper and can be nearly intractable. Bennis and Thomas (2002) write that "the era into which we are born has a profound impact on our lives" (29), and this cohort perspective is reflected in attitudes about both jobs and careers. Their work specifically focuses on the influence cohort era has on the development of leadership skills—an influence, they feel, that has profound life-long ramifications with respect to, among other things, the qualities individuals bring to their work world. They studied 43 leaders, half under the age of 35 ("geeks") and half over the age of 70 ("geezers"), with a total male and female sample range between the ages of 21 and 93.

Bennis and Thomas found three primary attitudinal differences between these two generations when their aspirations were compared at roughly the same chronological age (when both groups were in their mid to late 20s). First, members of today's digital geek cohort were much more ambitious than were the analogue geezers at the same age; the geeks aspired to change the world's course, whereas the geezers were more interested in making a steady income (causing their careers, the methodology by which to achieve such financial security, to become central to their social identities). Second, geeks were less likely than geezers to have been influenced by heroes, especially heroes who might have influenced their leadership skills. Third, by a substantial margin, geeks were far more committed to achieving a work-life balance. The authors attributed that commitment to the intensity inherent in the geeks' new-economy work; the fact that women in organizations have, in recent times, been forcing the work-life balance issue; and that the competitive demand for market talent was creating compensation packages that included time off for training, sabbaticals, and family schedules. The fact that today more and more women are not only in the workforce but occupying seats at policy-making tables, suggests that their influence may soon be felt on the entire retirement process, just as Bennis and Thomas's geeks, anxious to shake up the status quo and to define their careers as "acts of imagination" (158), will undoubtedly influence it in the future.

"Second Acts," or, "Rewiring, not Retiring"

At least 84 percent of workers who are 45 and older (an AIG poll reported 95 percent of their N = 1000 sample of 55-year-olds) indicate that they want to continue to work, but they want to work in a different way than they previously have. They want more flexibility and autonomy, and they want less stress, more pleasure, and a sense of purpose (Brown 2003; Montenegro et al. 2002). They are more likely to want to consult or to be self-employed (DBM 2001). In addition, there may be a number of reasons why professionals who originally planned to retire decide to change jobs or occupations instead of leaving the labor force altogether. First, they may have no control over leaving their career jobs (Brandstrader 2003). Second, they may need the money; the downturn in the stock market has changed the financial picture for many people who thought they would be able to retire when they wanted (Brown 2003). Third, as some people contemplate decades of life without work, they can't imagine a life based purely on leisure; they have no passion other than work.

Choi (2002) has summarized much of the research on exits from the labor force and suggests that "a sizable proportion of both male and female workers stretch their retirement process by engaging in partial retirement or 'bridge jobs' before completely withdrawing from the labor force or by rejoining the labor force, usually at reduced hours, following their retirement" (44–45). Three key benefits of such employment have been identified: continued activity and daily structure (Atchley 1989), less work and stress than full-time employment (Feldman 1994), and a sense of generativity—being able to give guidance to the next generation (Brown 2003; Levinson 1978).

These jobs, however, are often part time and not well compensated. Haider and Loughram (2001) indicate that the employees who take these jobs are "buying" flexible schedules, that is, taking low-wage jobs not out of financial necessity, but because they enjoy work and it contributes to their sense of well being. Indeed, fewer than 20 percent of preretirees indicate that they will seek professional jobs in retirement (Brown 2003).

How Do Retirees Feel about Retirement?

As we consider remaining in the labor force or retiring, it makes sense to find out how current retirees feel about having left employment and how attitudes vary. To some degree, these attitudes are associated with the locus of the decision. If retirees were forced out of their jobs, they are less likely to be satisfied (Herzog et al. 1991). Quick and Moen (1998) found that men were more likely to be satisfied with retirement than women, although the differences were small.

Retirement quality was associated with good health for both men and women. Men were more likely to be satisfied with retirement if they had enjoyed their preretirement work, had planned for retirement, were not career salient, and were intrinsically motivated to do things other than work. Women were more likely to be satisfied if they had retired early from full-time work and had sufficient income. In a report for AIG, Harris Interactive (2003) defined retirees as "ageless explorers," "comfortably contents," "live for todays," and "sick and tireds." These groups were differentiated by attitudes toward retirement, years of savings, and financial assets. The researchers found that although financial resources were clearly the most important component of individual attitudes, almost 40 percent of the preretirees in this sample thought that retirement would look a lot like their lives look now, or would present exciting opportunities.

Community Involvement

There is some data to suggest that not only does volunteering benefit the community, it benefits retirees as well (Shmotkin et al. 2003). Community provides a sense of place and of membership in a valued collectivity (Weiss 1990), and it may protect individuals from the invisibility, sense of marginality, and exile (Moen 1996) that can be associated with the loss of primary roles. Community involvement, however, rarely starts at the moment of retirement. Instead, one can see a history of involvement throughout life and that it increases when one has the time. Maggie Kuhn, the founder of the Gray Panthers, said that "Old age is an excellent time for outrage" (Bernikow 2004); there is some evidence that the more passionately one is involved in community issues (local, national, or international), the more alive one feels.

Beyond the pleasure derived from accomplishment through activism, community involvement and volunteerism also provide retirees with an important vehicle to develop and maintain social relationships. According to the McArthur Foundation Study of Successful Aging (Rowe and Kahn 1998), social relationships have long been recognized as important for well-being and, indeed, have served as a dependable predictor of longevity. This is especially important for men who, if cut off from new friends, cohorts, or family, are "more likely to become ill and less likely to live long lives" (46). The authors of the McArthur study—conducted over ten years and involving dozens of research projects and more than 1,200 subjects in several countries—consider "active engagement with life" to be one of three key behaviors or characteristics that define successful aging (the other two being low risk of disease and disease-related disability, and high mental and physical function) (38).

Passion

At every stage of life, the capacity for passion enhances existence. Passion can be the cornerstone of work or the cornerstone of retirement planning. Passion for an activity can structure life, foster community, be an enduring aspect of identity, and it is probably associated with self-efficacy and agency. There is, however, no research on passion about work, or about leisure. Often, passion is sacrificed for earning power, for example, a musician who takes a "straight" job because he cannot earn enough doing what he is passionate about. We would predict that looking forward to the freedom to pursue long-held interests could influence the decision about working longer. In fact, although passion itself is not the object of study, when retirees are asked about their psychological adjustment, "having something to get up for in the morning" is associated with greater well-being.

Late-Stage Career Choice: The Pilot Study

In preparation for a study on late-stage career choice, a pilot study was conducted to elicit attitudes about retirement in individuals who were either working or retired. The convenience sample consisted of 20 men and women ranging in age from late 50s to mid 90s. It was equally divided between the wealthy and those who have to think about money. It was politically homogeneous: somewhat left of center. The data were collected through interviews and focus groups alone, but individuals in the sample wanted to tell their stories their way, often with an audience, so the data collection method was both compromised and informed by participants' behavior.

Although a number of areas of inquiry were planned in advance, the participants preferred autobiography, often starting from the earliest days of their careers. Of course, no generalizations can be made to any other sample or population, but it is clear from the above review that most of the findings with this sample have been corroborated in prior research. In order to corroborate the research described earlier in the chapter, some biography or case material is in order.

L (age 63) worked for a telecommunications company for more than 30 years. He retired when he felt like it but quickly got bored "doing nothing." He took a job as a school-bus driver because he loves kids. He loves that job, and now he needs the money. His wife, who could be considered a "trailing spouse" (that is, she followed him after he retired), stayed in the career she had prior to his retirement. She was a legal secretary, and now she works part time as a legal secretary at a new firm, in their new community. They have been working at these jobs for the past five years. In recent months, however, both L and his wife, B (age 65), have been rethinking their decisions. They are now tired of working and tired of working to pay the mortgage on the big house they live in, and B's arthritis makes it difficult for her to negotiate the many stairs. Disappointed that their grown children do not visit their leisure community more often, they want to scale back, sell the house, move into a small condominium that requires little upkeep and is nearer to their children's families, and then travel when they can, especially to get away from the cold in the winter. Time feels very finite to them: "If we're lucky, we have another 10 years."

D, on the other hand, was a career endodontist. His mother was a concert pianist. His brother was the principal dancer of a world-famous dance company. He was forced to leave the United States during the McCarthy era, and he opened his endodontistry practice in Mexico, a country both he and his wife (an artist) fell in love with on their honeymoon. He never thought he was a natural at his practice, but he values excellence and worked very hard to be good. As he got older and the Mexican economy took a downturn, he moved back to Florida so that his wife could open a gallery there. They bought their apartment before they left Mexico, becoming active in the artistic community in Florida. D now is a musicologist. At the age of 87, he frequently gives six lectures a week before concerts. His wife continued to paint, collect, and promote Mexican art in the United States until she died at the age of 90 within the year before D's interview.

B is D's son. An acupuncturist, he retired at 56 from the professoriate. He was forced out for political reasons, and very shortly after, he retired from independent practice due to health problems. He consults 15 to 20 hours a week for his wife's mid-sized, international, home-based consulting business. He is also heavily involved with his godchildren's education and has become politically active in the education community, focusing on learning disabilities.

J is a professor. She has not retired, only because of the downturn in the stock market. She doesn't know what she wants to do next, but she has recently bought a house in the Southwest, near her brother's family. She is not married. Next year, she will teach during the fall and summer semesters and spend January through May in her new community.

Lo is in his 90s. He has worked in real estate his entire life. He can't imagine stopping. He has no other interests.

Among these people who look, on the face of it, quite different, there were some personal and developmental similarities. They all liked their jobs (for different reasons) and acquired a sense of identity from their occupations and work communities. They also had relatively high self-esteem. (It is entirely possible that those who had lower self-esteem chose not to be interviewed, so there may be some systematic bias here.) In addition, all the participants in the sample had similar health issues, chronic problems that were observable but not mentioned. None of them experienced their disabilities as stopping them. B said,

"If I wasn't satisfied with what I was doing, my health would bother me a lot more." At the end of an interview with a woman who had been the owner of a fairly large business, she admitted that she has been legally blind her entire life. She acquired the business after her husband dropped dead one day, although she had been a housewife until that moment. She took over the business, increased its profit, and never told anyone she was visually impaired.

There were, however, meaningful differences, for instance, socioeconomic status. Income levels varied enormously, from about median income to great wealth. Some of these individuals had supportive mates, while some did not. Some had no mates. They also differed in the degree to which they wanted to give back to the community. There were some participants who said, "It is our role as retirees to engage in political action because no one else has the time." The degree to which they engaged in volunteerism varied in intensity. Some were so passionate about their views that their actions verged on civil disobedience, while others became active because they had been drawn in by friends or through religious institutions. People also differed in the degree to which they had had organizational ties in their lifetime.

From preretirement to postretirement, there were continuities among all of the participants. Activity levels did not change. If they were busy before they left the workforce, they were busy after. Self-esteem also did not change, neither increasing nor decreasing. Loneliness did not change. People who had been lonely when they were at work were still lonely, and people who were not lonely, even if they were widowed and living alone, were not lonely. Personality, of course, is remarkably stable and hard to change. The presence or absence of a driving internal force also remained the same. There were some genuine extroverts, and there were some genuine introverts, and in interviews it became apparent that people were the same this way pre- and postretirement.

There were, of course, discontinuities as well. The increase in the sense of freedom was quite powerful, experienced almost as an aphrodisiac for a time. It was why people wanted to leave the labor force. It was what they felt best about when they jettisoned their burdens. They also had less sense of obligation to their families. They had grown children, but they didn't talk about them much, and when they did it was matter-of-factly, with the understanding that those children were living their own lives.

Climate mattered. Whether in the north or in Florida, all of the participants talked about being somewhere physically comfortable. This variable may also be about mobility needs, although they were not specifically mentioned. Ambulatory and respiratory difficulties, more prominent in later life, can make local travel daunting, and good weather makes it easier to get around.

For these individuals, retirement was not just retirement. It had intrinsic meaning. It connoted the right to economic support: I worked all my life; I have earned it and saved enough. In many cases, the participants in the study had saved enough, and they believed that they had earned the right to decide how they were going to spend their days.

Retirement was also defined idiosyncratically. Although F, who is a lawyer and a judge, takes only pro bono work, what she called "small matters," she defines herself as still working. That work, however, is not immediately apparent to others. People in her community question her self-definition, since she lives in Florida and practices law in New York. Lo defined retirement as the moment he could control his day. Specifically, he said, "I wanted the time to come when I would get up when my eyes opened by themselves." That happened when he was 40. He is now in his mid 90s, and he is still doing what he did then—buying properties, renovating them, and reselling. For many, retirement is a process that occurs over time. It is not a finite event. Lo, F, and G continued to do what they did, although at a much reduced level. M and B retired and then unretired, going back into the labor force for economic reasons.

Their involvement in the new communities they joined increased gradually and took on more meaning, completely unrelated to age. Individuals felt and thought the way they always had. There were very few dramatic shifts in behavior. The more continuities people took into retirement, the more satisfied they were. As they aged, the more their work identity actually faded, and, importantly, all of them felt the need to share what they had learned throughout their journeys. They had advice for those who are considering retirement in the near future: "You can't just do something completely new. You have to enter that realm before you retire. You can't show up on the doorstep of a civic agency and say I'm here, use me. You have to do something before then to get known, to get valued and respected."

CONCLUSION

It is clear that retirement is defined individually: one size does not fit all, and we do not know enough about individuals' late-stage career attitudes to know which individual differences should contribute to policy recommendations. Remaining in the labor force can be satisfying for some, stressful for others. The same can be said for retiring, and the relationship between attitudes toward continued work and attitudes toward retirement is not orthogonal (Barnes-Farrell 2003). The rewards and anxieties associated with each domain are unique and cannot be assumed to be complementary. Until we know more about how the meaning of work changes as we age, the issue of whether and when to retire will be largely idiosyncratic. Our common sense informs us as well: the degree to which individuals are passionately attached to their work or other activities plays a large part in their attitudes toward work and retirement.

What we do know is that past behavior and attitudes are likely to be stable, that is, personality does not change much (Costa and McCrae 1980), and neither does resilience or self-esteem (Reitzes et al. 1996). Activity levels are stable, as is community involvement. We also know that throughout the lifespan, a sense of control over one's life is associated with well-being. Thus, self-awareness can mitigate some of the adjustment issues in retirement, and it can motivate individuals to plan. The question, then, about the value of continued labor force participation should reside in the individual, in partnership with families, organizations, and government. That would be a true win-win proposition.

References

Abraham, J. D., and R. O. Hansson. 1994. "Perceived Age Discriminations in the Workplace: Implications for Occupational Well-Being and Performance." Groningen, Netherlands: International Conference Personal Relationships.

Atchley, R. 1989. "A Continuity Theory of Aging." *Gerontologist.* Vol. 29: 183–90.

Bailey, L. L. I., and R. O. Hansson. 1995. "Psychological Obstacles to Job or Career Change in Late Life." *Journal of Gerontology: Psychological Sciences.* B(6):280.

Barnes-Farrell, J. L. 2003. "Beyond Health and Wealth: Attitudinal and Other Influences on Retirement Decision Making." In *Retirement: Reasons, Processes, and Results.* G. A. Adams and T. A. Beehr, eds. New York: Springer. 19–87.

Barth, M. C., et al. 1993. "Corporations and the Aging Workforce." In *Building the Competitive Workforce: Investing in Human Capital for Corporate Success.* P. H. Mirvis, ed. New York: Wiley.

Bennis, W. G., and R. J. Thomas. 2002. *Geeks and Geezers: How Era, Values, and Defining Moments Shape Leaders.* Boston: Harvard Business School Press.

Bernikow, L. 2004. "Maggie Kuhn Invents Activism Against 'Ageism.'" *Women's e-news.*

Brandstrader, J. R. 2003. "Retirees Are Jumping Back into the Labor Pool, for Fun and Profit." *Barron's.* 22.

Brown, S. K. 2003. *Staying Ahead of the Curve 2003: The AARP Working in Retirement Study.* Washington, DC: AARP.

Choi, N. G. 2002. "Self-Defined Retirement Status and Engagement in Paid Work among Older Working-Age Women: Comparison between Childless Women and Mothers." *Sociological Inquiry.* Vol. 72, no. 1: 43–71.

Costa, P. T., and R. R. McCrae. 1980. "Still Stable after all These Years: Personality as a Key to Some Issues in Adulthood and Old Age." In *Life Span Development and Behavior.* P. B. Baltes and O. G. Brim, eds. New York: Academic Press.

DBM. 2001. *Career Choices and Challenges of Younger and Older Workers.* Philadelphia: DBM.

Drost, C.M. 2003. "Male Gender Role Conflict in Older Men." *Counseling and Clinical Psychology.* New York: Teachers College, Columbia University: 138.

Ekerdt, D.J., L. Baden, R. Bossé, and E. Dibbs. 1983. "The Effect of Retirement on Physical Health." *American Journal of Public Health.* Vol. 73: 779–83.

Erdner, R.A. and R.F. Guy. 1990. "Career Identification and Women's Attitudes toward Retirement." *International Journal of Aging and Human Development.* Vol. 30, no. 2.

Erikson, E.H., et al. 1986. *Vital Involvement in Old Age.* New York: Norton.

Fannin, P.M. 1979. "The Relation between Ego Identity Status and Sex-Role Attitude, Work-Role Salience, Atypicality of Major, and Self-Esteem in College Women." *Journal of Vocational Behavior.* Vol. 14: 12–22.

Fannin, P.M. 1981. "Essay Review: The Careers of Professional Women." *Teachers College Record.* Vol. 82, no. 4.

Feldman, D.C. 1994. "The Decision to Retire Early: A Review and Reconceptualization." *Academy of Management Review.* Vol. 19: 285–311.

Ginn, R.J., Jr. 1994. *Discovering Your Career Life Cycle.* Cambridge, MA: Radcliffe College.

Gradman, T.J. 1994. "Masculine Identity from Work to Retirement." In *Older Men's Lives.* J. Thompson, ed. Thousand Oaks, CA: Sage. 104–21.

Greenhaus, J.H. 1973. "A Factorial Investigation of Career Salience." *Journal of Vocational Behavior.* Vol. 3: 95–98.

Greller, M.M., and P. Simpson. 1999. "In Search of Late Career: A Review of Contemporary Social Science Research Applicable to the Understanding of Late Career." *Human Resource Management Review.* Vol. 9, no. 3: 309–47.

Haider, S., and D. Loughram. 2001. *Elderly Labor Supply: Work or Play?* Santa Monica, CA: Rand.

Hall, D.T., ed. 1986. *Breaking Career Routines: Midcareer Choice and Identity Development.* San Francisco: Jossey-Bass.

Hall, D.T., and P.H. Mirvis. 1994. "The New Workplace and Older Workers." In *Aging and Competition: Rebuilding the U.S. Workforce.* J.A. Auerbach and J.C. Welsh, eds. Washington, DC: National Council on the Aging and National Planning Associates.

Hansson, R.O., et al. 1997. "Successful Aging at Work: Annual Review, 1992–1996: The Older Worker and Transitions to Retirement." *Journal of Vocational Behavior.* Vol. 51: 202–33.

Harpaz, I. 2002. "Expressing a Wish to Continue or Stop Working as Related to the Meaning of Work." *European Journal of Work and Organizational Psychology.* Vol. 11: 177–98.

Harpaz, I., and X. Fu. 2002. "The Structure of the Meaning of Work: A Relative Stability amidst Change." *Human Relations.* Vol. 55: 639–67.

Harris Interactive. 2003. "Traditional Perception of Retirement Is Obsolete." Los Angeles. notyetretired.com.

Hatch, L.R., and A. Thompson. 1992. "Family Responsibilities and Women's Retirement." In *Families and Retirement.* M. Szinovacz, D.J. Ekerdt, and B.H. Vinick, eds. Newbury Park, CA: Sage. 99–113.

Henkens, K., and F. Tazelaar. 1997. "Explaining Retirement Decisions of Civil Servants in the Netherlands: Intentions, Behavior, and the Discrepancy between the Two." *Research on Aging*. Vol. 19: 139–73.

Herzog, A. R., et al. 1991. "Relation of Work and Retirement to Health and Well-Being in Older Age." *Psychology and Aging*. Vol. 6, no. 2: 202–11.

Huffine, C. L., and E. Aerts. 1998. the Intergenerational Studies at the Institute of Human Development, University of California, Berkeley: Longitudinal Studies of Children and Families, 1928–Present: A Guide to the Data Archives. Berkeley, CA: University of California.

Imel, S. 1996. "Older Workers." ERIC Clearinghouse: Adult, career and vocational education.

Knechtel, R. 2003. *Productive Aging in the 21st Century*. http://www.go60.com/go60 work.htm.

Levinson, D. J. 1978. *Seasons of a Man's Life*. New York: Knopf.

———. 1986. "A Conception of Adult Development." *American Psychologist*. Vol. 41: 3–13.

London, M. 1990. "Enhancing Career Motivation in Late Career." *Journal of Organizational Change Management*. Vol. 3, no. 2: 58–71.

Mcnaught, W. 1994. "Realizing the Potential: Some Examples." In *Age and Structural Lag*. M. W. Riley, R. L. Hahn, and A. Foner, eds. New York: Wiley.

Mitchell, J. M., and K. H. Anderson. 1989. "Mental Health and the Labor Force Participation of Older Workers." *Inquiry*. Vol. 26: 262–71.

Moen, P. 1996. "A Life Course Perspective on Retirement, Gender, and Well-Being." *Journal of Occupational Health Psychology*. Vol. 1, no. 2: 131–44.

Montenegro, X., et al. 2002. *Staying Ahead of the Curve: The AARP Work and Career Study*. Washington, DC: AARP.

Pearlin, L. I., et al. 1981. "The Stress Process." *Journal of Health and Social Behavior*. Vol. 34: 363–80.

Pine, P. P. 2003. *Older Workers: Retirement or Continued Work?* New York State Office for the Aging.

Prentis, R. S. 1980. "White-Collar Working Women's Perception of Retirement." *Gerontologist*. Vol. 20: 90–95.

Price, C. A. 2002. "Retirement for Women: The Impact of Employment." *Journal of Women and Aging*. Vol. 14, no. 3: 41–57.

Quick, H. E., and P. Moen. 1998. "Gender, Employment, and Retirement Quality: A Life Course Approach to the Differential Experiences of Men and Women." *Journal of Occupational Health Psychology*. Vol. 3, no. 1: 44–64.

Reitzes, D. C., et al. 1996. "Preretirement Influences on Postretirement Self-Esteem." *Journal of Gerontology: Series B: Psychological sciences and social sciences*. Vol. 51B(5): S242–50.

Remondet, J. H., and R. O. Hansson. 1991. "Job-Related Threats to Control among Older Employees." *Journal of Social Issues*. Vol. 47, no. 4: 129–41.

Roberts, B. W., and W. Friend. 1998. "Career Momentum in Midlife Women: Life Context, Identity, and Personality Correlates." *Journal of Occupational Health Psychology*. Vol. 3, no. 3: 195–208.

Rosen, B., and T. Jerdee. 1988. "Managing Older Workers' Careers." *Research in Personnel and Human Resources Management*. Vol. 6: 37–74.

Rowe, J.W., and R.L. Kahn. 1998. *Successful Aging*. New York: Dell.

Schein, E. 1978. *Career Dynamics: Matching Individual and Organizational Needs*. Reading, MA: Addison-Wesley.

Schlossberg, N. 2004. *Retire Smart, Retire Happy: Finding Your True Path in Life*. Washington, DC: American Psychological Association.

Shmotkin, D., et al. 2003. "Beyond Keeping Active: Concomitants of Being a Volunteer in Old-Old Age." *Psychology and Aging*. Vol. 18: 602–7.

Stegner, W. 1978. "The Writer and Adulthood." In *Adulthood*. E.H. Erikson, ed. New York: Norton. 227–36.

Strauss, W., and N. Howe. 1991. *Generations: The History of America's Future, 1584 to 2069*. New York: William Morrow.

Streib, G.F, and C.J. Schneider. 1971. *Retirement in American Society: Impact and Process*. Ithaca, NY: Cornell University Press.

Szinovacz, M., and D.J. Ekerdt. 1995. "Families and Retirement." In *Handbook on Aging and the Family*. R. Blieszner and V.H. Beford, eds. Westport, CT: Greenwood. 375–400

Talaga, J., and T.A. Beehr. 1995. "Are There Gender Differences in Predicting Retirement Decisions?" *Journal of Applied Psychology*. Vol. 80: 16–28.

Thoits, P.A. 1983. "Multiple Identities and Psychological Well-Being: A Reformation and Test of the Social Isolation Hypothesis." *American Sociological Review*. Vol. 48: 174–87.

Thompson, E.H., ed. 1994. *Older Men's Lives: Research on Men and Masculinity*. Thousand Oaks, CA: Sage.

Vaillant, G. 2002. *Aging Well*. Boston: Little Brown.

Walshok, M. 1981. *Blue Collar Women: Pioneers on the Male Frontier*. New York: Anchor.

Weinberg, N. 1998. "Help Wanted: Older Workers Need Not Apply." CNN.com.

Weiss, R. 1990. "Losses Associated with Mobility." In *On the Move: The Psychology of Change and Transition*. S. Fisher and C.L. Cooper, eds. Chichester, England: Wiley. 3–12.

Wray, L.A. 2003. *Mental Health and Labor Force Exits in Older Workers: The Mediating or Moderating Roles of Physical Health and Job Factors*. Ann Arbor, MI: University of Michigan Retirement Research Center.

Zimmerman, L., et al. 2000. "Unanticipated Consequences: A Comparison of Expected and Actual Retirement Timing among Older Women." *Journal of Women and Aging*. Vol. 12(1/2): 109–28.

Comments on "Continued Labor Force Participation: Individual Differences"

KEVIN NEUMAN

While studies examining demographic trends for the aging population, pension incentives for employees, and public policy restrictions on employer behavior are extremely important for understanding the work options faced by older workers, the studies tend to underemphasize one very important consideration: what do older workers actually want? For example, do older workers want "work options," or does retirement dominate all other labor force states? While the answers to these kinds of questions are complex, Patricia Raskin and Greg Gettas's study does an excellent job of highlighting, from a psychological perspective, the most important nonfinancial motivations people have for continuing or returning to work, as well as their psychological motivations for retiring.

Drawing primarily from firsthand interviews with older individuals about their jobs and their attitudes about work and leisure, Raskin and Gettas find that individuals have quite distinct later-life labor force patterns. Some of their interviewees returned to paid work in jobs outside their careers. Others began new "careers" after retirement, which often looked like full-time employment even though these situations many times were unpaid. Still others had not retired at all, either due to financial concerns or because their jobs occupied the primary role in their lives.

Despite the differences in personal characteristics of all of these individuals, Raskin and Gettas find that two characteristics remain as the most important predictors of later-life labor force activity: career salience and prior passions. Simply defined, career salience is the importance of one's job in one's identity formation. For example, if an individual's view of herself is derived primarily from the duties performed and status obtained in her occupation, the individual displays a high level of career salience. Prior passions are generally related to activities outside of work, activities that the individual enjoyed earlier in life that were maintained in later life, but were superseded in importance by career. If later in life an older worker begins to rekindle interest in the activities and hobbies that she had enjoyed prior to the establishment of her career, the individual is being influenced by their prior passions. As Raskin and Gettas discovered, the more salient the individual's career is in identity formation, the less likely is retirement, since work occupies a more important role for the individual. Alternatively, the more one's identity is tied to one's nonwork, outside interests—one's prior passions—the more likely one is to retire, since the individual is being pulled into the leisure state by activities that he enjoys.

Perhaps the most significant contribution made by this interesting research, especially in the context of the current dialogue, is a reminder from scholars outside of economics that retirement is not just retirement. Deciding whether or when to withdraw from the labor force entails more for an individual than simply choosing the source and magnitude of monthly income. Although retirement means different things for different people, as shown by the interviews, most individuals reported an increased sense of freedom and a reduced sense of obligation to family. Along with financial considerations such as pensions and health insurance, the desire for time autonomy may play quite a strong role in the retirement decision. Often these intangible factors are neglected in economic analyses of the retirement transition, either because they are deemed unimportant or because they are quite difficult to quantify, particularly in large survey data.

In addition, as Raskin and Gettas point out, work can be beneficial for many individuals by providing a source of identity and status, as well as time structure and a sense of accomplishment. Other researchers have found that the beneficial aspects of work may transfer to physical health as well (Ross and Mirowsky 1995). However, Raskin and Gettas's analysis suggests that the work experience may be changing for many older workers as organizations shift toward flatter hierarchies with less loyalty and respect for workers. Members of the silent and baby-boom generation psychological cohorts, who became accustomed to an atmosphere of authority at work, may have difficulty adjusting to the new corporate structure, reducing the relative benefits of continuing to work.

The changing work environment for these generations introduces the question of whether continued work is beneficial to older workers or whether retirement and the freedom it brings makes older workers better off. This question is important because it has largely been unexamined by economists, although the other social sciences have examined it more extensively. It is important also because much retirement research seems to imply that working longer may make many workers better off, a somewhat paternalistic notion providing an unintended bonus from pension reforms. If the rewards for continued work are eroding, as implied by Raskin and Gettas's research, there may be additional costs to pension reform previously unaccounted for. Alternatively, if there are rewards in retirement, this bolsters the case for retirement preservation.

My own research attempts to answer a related question: does retirement improve the physical health of retirees? The study examines the change in health reported by an individual in the period after he or she retires in order to see whether retirees are more likely to experience health improvements or health preservation relative to workers. By using physical health changes, the study looks at one important mechanism through which the well-being of individuals may be affected by retirement.

The question of whether retirement improves the health of individuals may seem misdirected because many theories of retirement, as well as anecdotal evidence, suggest that retirement actually harms health. (For summaries of these theories, refer to Minkler 1981; Mein et al. 1998; and Palmore, Fillenbaum, and George 1984.) The observation that retirees tend to be in worse health than workers seems to add support to this negative view of retirement. Early sociological theories attempted to explain the negative correlation between health and retirement, proposing that individuals were negatively affected by retirement due to disengagement from society and the loss of the productive work role. However, as retirement has become an accepted stage of life in society, it seems that these effects may no longer exist.

Another theory proposes that it is the stress of the retirement transition that drives negative health changes. Because retirement is a major life event that requires significant adjustment for many retirees, the theory posits that the adjustment stress causes the observed poor health. Once again, the mechanisms of this theory are called into doubt by research showing that retirement is not actually stressful for most individuals (Bossé et al. 1991; Gall, Evans, and Howard 1997; Kremer 1985; Ekerdt et al. 1983; and Gillanders et al. 1991). One study actually finds that for men working in jobs with substantial chronic stress caused by unpredictable hours, excessive monitoring, and other negative factors, the "stress" of retirement was actually positive, improving the mental health of the retiree (Wheaton 1990). The lack of stress in the retirement transition may again be the result of the fact that retirement has become an accepted, even expected, part of life for many individuals.

Even though the theories of negative health effects of retirement seem to be losing support, if they were ever accurate, it does not necessarily mean that retirement would improve health. However, there is a theoretical basis for health improvements after retirement. If health is considered to be a durable good that depreciates over time and can be increased through investment behavior, health can be treated much like human capital. If we assume that individuals can invest in health by combining medical goods and services, such as prescription drugs and doctor visits, with leisure time, retirement could improve health in two ways. First, if aspects of an individual's job—such as hazardous working conditions, heavy lifting, or high stress—elevate the level of health depreciation, removing these health-detrimental aspects through retirement would allow health investment to improve health rather than simply maintain it. The individual no longer must take care of himself simply to be healthy enough to work; he can actually make himself better off. Second, retirement increases the amount of time that an individual is able to use in health investment. The individual no longer must spend forty or more hours a week at work; she can use some of this free time in health investment behaviors such as exercising. Retirement does not mean that individuals will use all of their time in health investment. If individuals remain active, as many of the people in Raskin and Gettas's study did, they are not constrained by work time requirements as they were previously and can allocate more time to health investment if they feel it is necessary.

While there exist theoretical reasons for improvements in health due to retirement, identifying the effects is not as straightforward as it would seem. The difficulty in an empirical analysis of the health effects of retirement is disentangling what is actually caused by retirement and what is caused by unobservable elements correlated with retirement behavior, making the retirement decision endogenous. By using the Health and Retirement Study, which interviewed over 20,000 individuals during the 1990s about a wide array of topics, I was able to isolate retirement's effect on health by controlling for a number of issues affecting both health and retirement, and by removing the effect of endogenous retirement status using exogenous variation in Social Security and private pension benefits.

My study includes demographic and descriptive information such as the individual's age, race, marital status, and education; financial information about the individual's overall and pension wealth; proxies for genetic and early-life characteristics; and information about the individual's career industry and occupation. Also included is detailed information about the initial health of the individual. Through the detailed health information in the HRS, this model was capable of including a self-rating of the individual's health, as well as information about the incidence of specific chronic conditions such as diabetes, cancer, and heart problems. All of these factors could influence both health and retirement behavior, potentially biasing the results if not included.

Using samples of 6,748 men and 9,174 women, I found that retirement does seem to affect the health of both men and women by a significant amount. Increasing the probability of retirement by fifty percent at the mean decreases the probability of a health improvement by over 11 percent for men, but actually increases the probability of a health improvement by about 19 percent for women. Interestingly, this difference in the effects is not driven by shorter work histories of women, regardless of generation or other specifications, suggesting that retirement truly affects the health of men and women differently.

Despite the differences in the likelihood of a health improvement, retirement does preserve health for both sexes, reducing the likelihood of health deterioration. A fifty percent increase in retirement probability decreases the probability of a health decline by about 3.5 percent for men and by about 4.5 percent for women. Another significant finding is that the effects of reduced labor force participation are similar using a continuous measure of annual hours. Reductions in annual hours for men and women result in similar magnitude changes in health, with the same pattern of differences across sex as the retirement variables.

A potential concern with the results is that the model is not capturing changes in actual health but changes in how individuals answer questions about their health. If individuals are justifying their retirement status by reporting poor health, then the results may reflect fewer health improvements than are actually occurring. The fact that male retirees are less likely to experience a health improvement while female retirees are more likely, suggests that this type of behavior may be present in the estimates. Additionally, if retirees simply feel better after leaving their jobs because they are less active, and thus less constrained by health in their retiree role, the results may be more positive than actual health changes.

One way to test whether this type of reporting bias is present in the estimates is to estimate the model using more objective health change measures as outcomes. If the results for the two types of health questions match, it would suggest that there are real health changes behind the previous results. To test for this type of bias, a summary index of chronic conditions was constructed that included high blood pressure, diabetes, cancer, lung disease, heart problems, stroke, psychiatric problems, and arthritis. A few measures of functional ability were also constructed, which include questions about whether the individual had difficulty performing activities such as walking several blocks, climbing stairs, bathing, sitting for two hours, pushing heavy objects, and other activities. The objective health index results suggest that the original results did not seem to be driven by retirees neglecting to report health improvements after retirement. There was some evidence using the objective measures that men were truly less likely to have health improvements after retirement. The test was not able to definitively rule out that retirees were less active than workers and therefore simply felt healthier after retirement because they were not limited by health. This bias could account for some of the preservative health effects found previously. However, it is not clear that retirees are less active than workers. Raskin and Gettas's interviews show that many individuals are quite active after retirement even though they are not being paid. Therefore, it seems that the results obtained do likely represent actual health improvements and preservation.

Overall, the results suggest that while retirement may not improve health for men, withdrawing from work is not detrimental to health either. For women, retirement has unambiguously positive health effects, both increasing the likelihood of a health improvement and decreasing the likelihood of a health decline. In addition, the similar result using measures of annual hours suggests that it may not be retirement per se that affects health but reductions in labor force participation at any level, although this conclusion should be restricted to this age category. The results for reductions in hours implies that partial retirement schemes such as those described by Robert Hutchens and Jennjou Chen in this volume may boost the health of individuals while still encouraging labor force participation among older workers. However, Hutchens's findings that attractive partial retirement options are rare in actuality, suggests that incentives are needed for employers to improve these work options for workers.

There are a few other economic studies examining the issue of retirement's effects on physical or mental health that can be used for comparison, but the results are conflicting. Charles (1999) finds that retirement increases well-being as measured by levels of depression and loneliness. Two other studies from the Netherlands (Kerkhofs and Lindeboom 1997; Kerkhofs, Lindeboom, and Theeuwes 1999) find that being in a non–labor force state later in life seems to improve physical health. Jewell (1992) finds the opposite, that retirement leads to worse health for retirees, although Jewell may not do as good of a job controlling for the endogeneity of the retirement decision and is likely picking up the negative correlation between health and retirement rather than a causal relationship. In general, my study agrees with the studies from the Netherlands, and extends the positive results of Charles to overall physical health.

There are interesting connections between the results from the HRS and those from Raskin and Gettas's study. First, the results imply, as emphasized by Raskin and Gettas, that work may not be as rewarding relative to retirement for older workers, at least with respect to physical health. However, one drawback of using the HRS, as opposed to smaller studies with personal interviews, is that it is unable to identify the mechanisms through which health changes. Other researchers have touched upon the issue using this different methodology. One study examining twenty-five retired British civil servants commonly cited reductions in work-related stress as a mechanism of health improvements, as well as an increase in free time to exercise and cook healthy meals (Mein et al. 1998). A Danish study cited the removal from detrimental work conditions such as dust from machines and lifting heavy loads, as well as less physical aspects such as the drudgery of work (Moller 1987). While Raskin and Gettas did not investigate health changes specifically, the British and Danish interview responses are similar to those from individuals in their study who reported a sense of freedom and greater autonomy over their time. The increase in leisure time associated with retirement may be the driving factor behind health improvements.

Another significant observation by Raskin and Gettas is that retirement behavior may differ significantly for men and women. If retirement behavior differs by sex, it seems logical that the effects of retirement may be different by sex as well. My analysis does find different health effects for men and women, possibly because men's identity is attached more closely to their occupation, as highlighted by Raskin and Gettas. The conclusions drawn by Raskin and Gettas as well as by the present study, strongly suggest that retirement policies should be evaluated separately for men and women, with the expectation that the effects may be quite different.

Finally, the study by Raskin and Gettas suggests that certain groups may be disproportionately affected by retirement reforms designed to delay retirement. Their interviews found that individuals view the retirement decision quite differently due to variations in career salience and prior passions. Individuals who are closely tied to their occupations may be less inclined to retire in general, making this group largely unaffected by reforms delaying retirement.

Similar implications can be drawn from the present analysis, although the groups affected may be different. Reforms delaying retirement will likely only do so for the low-income portion of the population, which is unable to retire by private means. If retirement does improve or preserve health, as indicated by my results, this segment of the population will disproportionately be denied the health benefits of retirement. Given that the low-income group also tends to be in worse health, retirement reform may harm the group most in need of the health improvements. If these types of reforms are unavoidable, they should at least be accompanied by relaxation of disability eligibility requirements so that individuals in very poor health can still exit the labor force.

Raskin and Gettas's study does an excellent job of highlighting personal differences in the retirement transition and emphasizing that work may not be as rewarding for some older workers as it once was. For some older workers, the only "work option" truly desired is retirement.

References

Bossé, Raymond, Carolyn M. Aldwin, Michael R. Levenson, and Kathryn Workman-Daniels. 1991. "How Stressful Is Retirement? Findings from the Normative Aging Study." *Journal of Gerontology: Psychological Sciences.* Vol. 46, no. 1: 9–14.

Charles, Kerwin K. 1999. "Is Retirement Depressing? Labor Force Inactivity and Psychological Well-Being in Later Life." *Ford School of Public Policy Working Paper.* University of Michigan #00-015.

Ekerdt, David J., Lynn Baden, Raymond Bossé, and Elaine Dibbs. 1983. "The Effect of Retirement on Physical Health." *American Journal of Public Health.* Vol. 73, no. 7: 779–83.

Gall, Terry L., David R. Evans, and John Howard. 1997. "The Retirement Adjustment Process: Changes in the Well-Being of Male Retirees across Time." *Journal of Gerontology: Psychological & Social Sciences.* Vol. 52, no. 3: 110–17.

Gillanders, William R., Terry F. Buss, Evelynn Wingard, and David Gemmel. 1991. "Long-Term Health Impacts of Forced Early Retirement among Steelworkers." *Journal of Family Practice.* Vol. 32, no. 4: 401–6.

Jewell, Robert T. 1992. "The Effect of Retirement on Health as Reported in the Retirement History Survey." University of California, Santa Barbara.

Kerkhofs, Marcel, and Maarten Lindeboom. 1997. "Age-Related Health Dynamics and Changes in Labour Market Status." *Health Economics.* Vol. 6, no. 4: 407–23.

Kerkhofs, Marcel, Maarten Lindeboom, and Jules Theeuwes. 1999. "Retirement, Financial Incentives and Health." *Labour Economics.* Vol. 6, no. 2: 203–27.

Kremer, Yael. 1985. "The Association between Health and Retirement: Self-Health Assessment of Israeli Retirees." *Social Science & Medicine.* Vol. 20, no. 1: 61–66.

Mein, G., P. Higgs, J. Ferrie, and S. A. Stansfeld. 1998. "Paradigms of Retirement: The Importance of Health and Ageing in the Whitehall II Study." *Social Science & Medicine.* Vol. 47, no. 4: 535–45.

Minkler, Meredith. 1981. "Research on the Health Effects of Retirement: An Uncertain Legacy." *Journal of Health and Social Behavior.* Vol. 22, no. 2: 117–30.

Moller, Iver H. 1987. "Early Retirement in Denmark." *Ageing and Society.* Vol. 7: 427–43.

Palmore, Erdman B., Gerda G. Fillenbaum, and Linda K. George. 1984. "Consequences of Retirement." *Journal of Gerontology.* Vol. 39, no. 1: 109–16.

Ross, Catherine E., and John Mirowsky. 1995. "Does Employment Affect Health?" *Journal of Health and Social Behavior.* Vol. 36, no. 3: 230–43.

Wheaton, Blair. 1990. "Life Transitions, Role Histories, and Mental Health." *American Sociological Review.* Vol. 55, no. 2: 209–23.

Comments on "Continued Labor Force Participation: Individual Differences"

STEPHEN A. WOODBURY

Heterodox economists and other critics of economics have long complained that economic models treat work in an exceedingly narrow way. In the simple income-leisure model, an individual gives up leisure to work, and work brings disutility. So individuals work only because the disutility of work is offset by the reward of earnings.

Thorstein Veblen (1914) argued that individuals work not for the reward of earnings but because they have an "instinct of workmanship"—a deep drive to solve problems, create, and be useful. Because he wrote almost a century ago, it is not surprising that Veblen couched his argument in Darwinian (and sometimes social Darwinist) terms: like other human drives, the instinct for workmanship is an evolutionary outcome—humans have the instinct for workmanship because workmanship is how we survived as a species. Veblen's insight is that the consumer model of William Stanley Jevons and Alfred Marshall (which was the target of his criticism) misses much or all of what really drives us. And by missing the basic human drives, that model leads to faulty and misleading conclusions.

Veblen's argument is echoed in the field of organization behavior, which has its roots in psychology, and in some of the industrial relations literature that flourished in the 1950s, 1960s, and 1970s. Occasionally, mainstream economists have raised concerns that echo Veblen's. For example, Scitovsky noted that "modern economists have nothing to say on whether work is pleasant or unpleasant. . . . Work which produces market goods may be an economic activity, but the satisfaction the worker himself gets out of his work is not an economic good because it does not go through the market and its value is not measurable" (1976, 90–91). In spite of recent efforts to infuse economics with insights from psychology, little if any recent work by economists has taken such criticisms to heart.

The reason may well be that economists do not see a problem that needs to be addressed. A mainstream labor economist might respond to the above complaints by saying that the income-leisure model can be adapted easily to include job characteristics as part of the choice that workers make when they decide whether and how much to work. Indeed, Rosen's hedonic model (1974) spawned a large literature that examines tradeoffs among various job characteristics and wages (see Rosen 1986 for an early review).

But this counterargument misses the point. The issue is not that some jobs are more pleasant than others, or that some jobs come with nonpecuniary rewards that others lack. Rather, the issue is that work itself is central to the physical and mental health of an individual because work makes a person feel useful. Raskin and Gettas's chapter is a reminder of this essential point and flags one of the continuing gaps in the economic model. If that gap could be closed, economics would be considerably enriched.

REFERENCES

Rosen, Sherwin. 1974. "Hedonic Prices and Implicit Markets: Product Differentiation in Pure Competition." *Journal of Political Economy.* Vol. 82, no. 1: 34–55.
Rosen, Sherwin. 1986. "The Theory of Equalizing Differences." In *Handbook of Labor Economics,* Volume I. Orley Ashenfelter and Richard Layard, eds. Amsterdam: North-Holland. 641–92.
Scitovsky, Tibor. 1976. *The Joyless Economy.* Oxford: Oxford University Press.
Veblen, Thorstein. 1914. *The Instinct of Workmanship, and the State of the Industrial Arts.* New York: A. M. Kelley.

PART 2

THE TRANSITION
TO RETIREMENT

CHAPTER FOUR

The Role of Employers in Phased Retirement

Opportunities for Phased Retirement among White-Collar Workers

ROBERT M. HUTCHENS & JENNJOU CHEN

While the labor market for older workers has many puzzling features, the small number of phased retirements is certainly one of the more curious. The basic idea of phased retirement is that an older worker remains with his or her employer while gradually shifting from full-time work to full retirement. For decades, experts have proclaimed the advantages of this type of retirement. Moreover, employees often express an interest in taking a phased retirement. In a recent national survey of the older population, more than half of the respondents ages 55 to 65 said they would prefer to reduce their hours of work gradually as they age rather than to fully retire abruptly (U.S. General Accounting Office 2001, 27). Yet, all indications are that phased retirements are rather rare. Past studies indicate that within a cohort of older workers, less than 10 percent took phased retirement; most people simply moved from full-time work to full retirement (see Quinn, Burkhauser and Meyers 1990 and Ruhm 1990). Nothing in the more recent data indicates that this has changed greatly (see Chen 2003).

One possible explanation for the low levels of phased retirement is limited opportunities provided by employers. Despite workers' interest in phased retirement, few are actually able to work out a suitable arrangement with their employers.

Little is known about opportunities for phased retirement, but, at least in principle, such opportunities are knowable. Take a randomly selected older worker and ask her employer whether there are conditions under which she would be permitted to do so if she proposed a phased retirement today. If there were, then we would know an opportunity exists. Of course, the worker may not view that opportunity as particularly attractive. It may involve a change of tasks or a change in pay and fringe benefits that the worker would find unacceptable. Indeed, the worker may look at the employer's conditions and decide that either full retirement or full-time work would be preferable. Regardless of such preferences, the point is that both the worker and an outside observer can know that an opportunity exists.

This chapter examines opportunities for phased retirement. It is built on a survey, funded by the Sloan Foundation, of 950 establishments that investigated how employers would react to a worker's request for phased retirement. It first asked employers whether a "generic" older white-collar worker would be permitted to take phased retirement. At a later point in the survey, a similar question was posed for an actual older worker. Using these data, it is possible to examine how opportunities for phased retirement vary across types of establishments as well as types of workers. More specifically, using these data in combination with the Health and Retirement Study (HRS), this chapter seeks to address three questions:

1. What fraction of older white-collar workers have good opportunities for phased retirement?
2. To what extent does an older white-collar worker's opportunity for phased retirement depend upon the characteristics of his or her establishment (e.g., industry, size, type of pension)?
3. To what extent does an older white-collar worker's opportunity for phased retirement depend upon his or her demographic characteristics (e.g., age, gender, education)?

The last two sections describe the establishment survey, presenting key results on establishment level policies and discuss establishment survey data on a specific older worker, the HRS data, model estimation, and predicted opportunities.

Assessing Opportunities for Phased Retirement

The Survey

The survey obtained data on 950 establishments between June 2001 and November 2002. An establishment was defined as a single physical location at which business was conducted or services or industrial operations were performed. An establishment may or may not be part of a larger organization; for example, some grocery stores are owner operated, while others are part of a large corporation. For purposes of studying phased retirement, establishment-level data are arguably better than data collected from a parent organization. In contrast to a survey of upper-level executives at corporate headquarters, establishment-level respondents are more likely to know how policy is implemented in practice. In order to obtain detailed information in a relatively brief interview, the survey focused on white-collar workers.[1] The sample was restricted to establishments not engaged in agriculture or mining, with twenty or more employees, and with at least two white-collar employees who were age 55 or older.[2] The latter restriction ensures that questions about phased retirement were relevant to the establishment's current situation.

The sample universe was the Dun and Bradstreet Strategic Marketing Record for December 2000. The main source of these data was credit inquiries, although information was also obtained from the U.S. Postal Service, banks, newspapers, yellow pages, and other public records. In order to insure adequate numbers of large establishments, the sample was stratified by establishment size. The results were weighted to provide representative results.

The survey was conducted over the telephone by the University of Massachusetts Center for Survey Research. After contacting the establishment, the interviewer asked for the person who was best able to answer questions about flexible work schedules and employee benefits, for example, a human resource manager or a benefits manager. Interviews were conducted with a CATI (Computer Assisted Telephone Interviewing) system, thereby permitting an interview to be completed over several phone calls. Although this technology simplified the interview process, new technologies on the respondent side (in particular AUDIX systems and answering machines) complicated matters. The median number of telephone calls to complete an interview was ten, with 10 percent of the interviews requiring thirty or more calls to complete.

The overall response rate was 61 percent. Most of the nonresponse occurred when screening establishments for eligibility, and before respondents knew the purpose of the survey. Interviews were completed in 89 percent of the establishments that were successfully screened. This is on a par with other establishment-level telephone surveys.[3]

Asking about Phased Retirement

After asking a series of question about the characteristics of the establishment and its human resource and pension policies, the interviewer posed the following question:

Q1: Think of a secure full-time white-collar employee who is age 55 or over. One day, that person comes to you and says that at some point in the next few years he/she may want to shift to a part-time work schedule at this establishment. Could this person's request to shift to part-time employment be worked out in a way that would be acceptable to your establishment?

If the response was "yes" or "in some cases," then the interviewer asked further questions about what form this hours reduction might take.[4]

It should be noted that whereas "phased retirement" usually means gradual reduction in hours, this question asks about a shift from working full-time to part-time. In designing the survey, it was decided to focus on a rather concrete form of phased retirement. If a respondent said such a shift was possible, the interviewer followed up with questions about what the respondent meant by "part time."

As indicated in Figure 1, the majority of establishments offer opportunities for some kind of phased retirement: fully 73 percent of the establishments indicated that "yes," something could be worked out, while another 14 percent said that something could be worked out "in some cases."[5]

Employers who said "in some cases" usually talked about possible scheduling difficulties or problems with getting the work done. For example,

Figure 1. Percentage of Establishments That Would Allow an Older White-Collar Employee to Reduce Hours

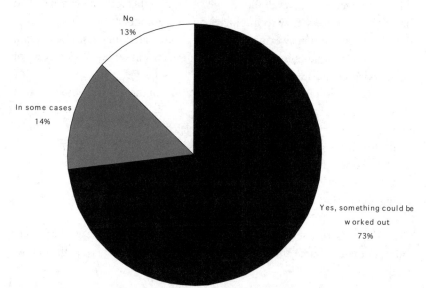

No
13%

In some cases
14%

Yes, something could be
worked out
73%

You'd have to find someone else to take up the slack.

[There are] issues with client deliverables and client contacts; [we need a person who is] easy to contact when not here; we need flexibility in an emergency; if they have Friday off and there's an emergency Friday, we would need them to come in.

[It] would require [us] to train someone else and hire another part-time person.

Saying that phased retirement can be worked out is not, of course, the same as saying that it is likely. An employer may take a hard look at both the employee and current business conditions before letting a specific employee take phased retirement. In addition, the terms under which the employer is willing to work out phased retirement may not be acceptable to the employee. How will health insurance be handled? Will it be possible to supplement salary with pension payments? Can an employee have a change of heart and return to full-time work? At the outset, however, it is important to emphasize that phased retirement can be defined in many ways, some of which imply very limited opportunities for its implementation.

Table 1 illustrates this point. The table begins with the 73 percent of establishments that gave an unambiguous "yes" to the question about whether some form of phased retirement could be worked out. Some of these employers were willing to work out phased retirement only if the employee were to retire officially and then return to the establishment as a rehire. If those establishments are excluded, the percentage that can work out phased retirement drops to 68 percent. Some employers will permit phased retirement if another person can be found to share the job. Of course, that can be difficult; indeed, in small establishments it may be impossible. Excluding establishments that require job sharing drops the percentage that can work out phased retirement to 59 percent. Continuing down the table, we see that if phased retirement is defined as permitting older workers to shift from full-time to part-time work before official retirement, without job sharing, with no change in health insurance, with pension payments that supplement salary,[6] and consent to return to full-time work if desired, then only 6 percent of the establishments permitted phased retirement.

In the initial section of the survey, phased retirement was defined in the broadest possible terms: whether something be worked out. The goal was to determine whether opportunities exist. If they did, then we probed deeper to understand the conditions under which phased retirement was possible. Since these

Table 1. Percentage of Establishments Allowing Various Forms of Phased Retirement

Case	Percentage
Employer says "yes," some form of phased retirement could be worked out	73 %
Employer permits phased retirement before official retirement	68 %
Employer permits phased retirement before official retirement and does not require job sharing	59 %
The phased retirement arrangement would include:	
Health insurance equivalent to that provided to full-time workers	16 %
Equivalent Health insurance with salary supplemented by pension payments	7 %
Equivalent Health insurance, pension payments, and—if desired —the person can return to full-time work	6 %

opportunities took a variety of forms, at least at the outset we wanted to consider all of those forms.

These opportunities are often real in the sense that employees have actually taken phased retirement. We know this because if a respondent told us that something could be worked out before official retirement, we asked whether in the last three years a white-collar worker age 55 or over had actually shifted from a full-time to a part-time work schedule; 36 percent said "yes."[7]

Phased retirement can occur either before or after official retirement.[8] This became clear during the design phase of the survey. In discussions with several managers, we learned that employers try to avoid reducing hours before official retirement, preferring instead that workers first retire and then come back as part-time or contract workers. The survey indicates that such preferences are not widespread. As indicated in Figure 2, most employers were willing to accommodate hours reductions regardless of whether they occur before or after official retirement. Indeed, only 7 percent indicated that the hours reduction should occur after official retirement.

Regardless of whether the hours reduction occurs before or after official retirement, most establishments handle phased retirement on an informal basis. About a third of the sample had any sort of formal written policy, and about a third of those indicate that the policy is flexible and tailored to individual cases.[9] These flexible formal policies usually permit hours reductions as long as certain

Figure 2. Percentage of Establishments Allowing Various Forms of Phased Retirement

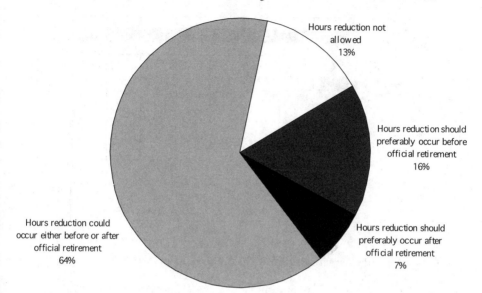

conditions are met. For example, one respondent spoke of the problem of finding another person to fill the other half of the job. "It depends on if it is difficult to recruit. For instance if it is a med tech, [it can be] difficult to find a part-time med tech in nursing . . . [we] probably cannot accommodate that schedule easily.

Figure 3 presents data on formal and informal policies for establishments that said some form of phased retirement was possible. As indicated here, informal policies are the rule in hours reductions before and after official retirement.

In most establishments, phased retirement was "conditional." While an establishment may permit phased retirement, a specific worker's opportunity for phased retirement depends on the employer's assessment of the situation. The opportunity can depend on the nature of the job, business conditions, or finding someone to cover the work. In these establishments, a request for phased retirement is like a request for a different job assignment; it may get a positive response in some situations and be turned down in others.

- "He would be able to continue the craft part of it, but not the supervision part of the job."
- "Depends on school's need—may change grade levels."
- "Probably not unless another person was hired to take up the slack."

Figure 3. Formal vs. Informal Policies When Phased Retirement Is Possible

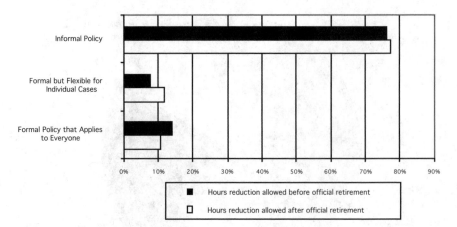

Establishment Characteristics and Phased Retirement

The survey also permits an assessment of how phased retirement policies vary with establishment characteristics. Since there are other papers that go into detail on that topic (see Hutchens and Grace-Martin 2006), it is sufficient to summarize results here.

1. Although establishment size is not closely linked to opportunities for phased retirement, the size of the parent organization does matter. Small organizations are more likely to permit phased retirement.
2. Industries differ in their opportunities for phased retirement. Opportunities tend to be greatest for establishments in the service sector. Opportunities tend to be most limited in public administration (excluding health, education, and social services).
3. Expanding and contracting establishments differ in their opportunities for phased retirement. Establishments that have increased their employment over the previous three years are more likely to report that phased retirement could be worked out.
4. An establishment is less likely to permit phased retirement when a large percentage of the white-collar workforce is unionized.
5. Establishments that employ part-time white-collar workers are more likely to permit phased retirement than those that do not.
6. Opportunities for phased retirement are most limited for managers and least limited for professionals.

Some of these results revise the earlier literature. For example, previous studies indicated that phased retirement is prevalent in health, education, and social services as well as public administration (for example, see Graig and Paganelli 2000). These results are different with regard to public administration, which pertains to local, state, and federal governments. Examples of establishments in this sector are police departments, fire departments, and prisons. Of the establishments in this sector, 29 percent indicated that phased retirement was not possible.

Other results are new but not especially surprising. For example, it is reasonable that phased retirement is more likely when the establishment has part-time workers (item 5). In this case, the employer does not have to create a new job for the phased retiree. Perhaps more noteworthy is the fact that this effect remains large and statistically significant in multivariate models. Similarly, it is no surprise that expanding establishments are more able to accommodate phased retirement than contracting establishments (item 3). Finally, managers are not good candidates for phased retirement because management is usually a full-time job (item 6). The phased retiree would presumably have to stop being a manager.

Still other results are surprising. In particular, it was a surprise to find that large organizations (and not large establishments) are associated with fewer opportunities for phased retirement (item 1) and that unionized establishments are less likely to permit phased retirement (item 4). Both results hold in multivariate models, and both could conceivably be due to employer preferences for handling phased retirement informally. For different reasons, large bureaucracies and unions often frown on informal arrangements. Large bureaucracies usually prefer the consistency imposed by a personnel policies handbook, and unions usually prefer the codification of a contract. The preference for policies and practices that are codified and consistent may have the effect of limiting opportunities for phased retirement.

OPPORTUNITIES FOR PHASED RETIREMENT AND INDIVIDUAL CHARACTERISTICS

Although the above establishment-level information is useful for understanding how opportunities for phased retirement differ across establishments, it does not address the question that motivates this paper: what fraction of older white-collar workers have good opportunities for phased retirement? It is quite possible that while 73 percent of the establishments permit some form of phased retirement, most of those establishments are small and employ few older workers. If older white-collar workers tend to be concentrated in the establishments that

Model 1: The selected worker is in an establishment where phased retirement is feasible.

Model 2: The selected worker is not only in an establishment where phased retirement is feasible but would be a good candidate for phased retirement (4 or 5 on Q2).

Model 3: The selected worker not only meets the criteria of model 2 but would not have to officially retire and could remain in the same job.

Model 4: The selected worker not only meets the criteria of model 3 but would have same health insurance as when working full-time.

The results are presented in Table 2.

To be used for prediction in the HRS, the explanatory variables (X and Z) in these models must be restricted to variables that are available in the HRS. As indicated in Table 2, the models were estimated on measures of establishment size, industry, region, occupation, age, years of education, job tenure, gender, union status, and pension type. By implication, some rather important explanatory variables are excluded from the models because they are not available in the HRS. Specifically, the models do not include variables indicating presence of part-time jobs in the establishment, the size of the parent organization, or the employer's assessment of the selected worker's job performance. As such, the estimated coefficients in Table 2 must be viewed with caution.

Still, the results are interesting. For purposes of exposition, we focus on Model 3, leaving it to readers to peruse the other models in Table 2. For Model 3, note that in terms of statistical significance, neither establishment size, nor industry, nor region are particularly important. In contrast, the coefficient on the selected worker's union status is large, negative, and statistically significant. This is, of course, thoroughly consistent with the establishment-level results summarized above. It is also interesting to note that the coefficient on the age of the selected worker is positive and statistically significant. Since the sample is restricted to workers over 55, this indicates that comparatively young older workers have fewer opportunities for phased retirement than their older counterparts. This result shows up again in the subsequent predictions. Finally, the results indicate that establishments with both a defined benefit (DB) and a defined contribution (DC) pension plan are less likely to permit phased retirement than those with just a DC pension plan.

Using the HRS for Prediction

The HRS provides a representative sample that can be used to predict an individual's opportunities of phased retirement. The HRS starts with a sample of

Table 2. Regression Coefficients from Establishment Survey

Variables	Model 1		Model 2		Model 3		Model 4	
	Coefficient	Standard Deviation	Coefficient	Standard Deviation	Coefficient	Standard Deviation	Coefficient	Standard Deviation
INDUSTRY								
Construction*	0.0000	0.0000	0.0000	0.0000	0.0000	0.0000	0.0000	0.0000
Manufacturing	-0.2691	0.1392	-0.0826	0.1026	-0.1807	0.1236	-0.0602	0.0807
Transportation, Communications and Utilities	-0.3871	0.1545	-0.1912	0.1138	-0.2405	0.1372	-0.0742	0.0896
Wholesale and Retail Trade	-0.2286	0.1429	-0.0952	0.1053	-0.1405	0.1270	-0.0694	0.0829
Finance	-0.2274	0.1527	-0.1162	0.1125	-0.2319	0.1356	-0.0321	0.0886
Other Services	-0.2245	0.1409	-0.0305	0.1038	-0.0842	0.1252	0.0159	0.0817
Health, Education, and Social Services	-0.1610	0.1374	0.0204	0.1012	-0.1522	0.1220	-0.0299	0.0797
Public Administration	-0.3822	0.1461	-0.2255	0.1077	-0.2211	0.1298	-0.0553	0.0848
ESTABLISHMENT SIZE								
Less than 49 employees*	0.0000	0.0000	0.0000	0.0000	0.0000	0.0000	0.0000	0.0000
50–99 employees	-0.0315	0.0554	0.0074	0.0408	-0.0122	0.0492	0.0540	0.0321
100–249 employees	-0.0296	0.0490	-0.0687	0.0361	-0.0363	0.0436	0.0155	0.0284
250–999 employees	-0.0016	0.0551	0.0044	0.0406	-0.0246	0.0489	0.0369	0.0320
more than 1000 employees	0.0742	0.0860	0.0768	0.0634	-0.0684	0.0764	0.0452	0.0499
YEARS OF EDUCATION								
Years of Education	-0.0085	0.0110	0.0018	0.0081	0.0064	0.0098	0.0007	0.0064
OCCUPATION								
Sales*	0.0000	0.0000	0.0000	0.0000	0.0000	0.0000	0.0000	0.0000
Professional	0.0665	0.0915	0.0569	0.0674	0.0144	0.0813	-0.0299	0.0531
Manager	-0.0147	0.0894	0.0746	0.0659	-0.1391	0.0794	-0.0637	0.0519
Clerical	0.0743	0.0986	0.1013	0.0727	0.0725	0.0876	0.0144	0.0572

Table 2. Regression Coefficients from Establishment Survey (*cont.*)

	Model 1		Model 2		Model 3		Model 4	
AGE								
Age	0.0131	0.0047	0.0036	0.0035	0.0157	0.0042	0.0071	0.0027
GENDER								
Female*	0.0000		0.0000		0.0000		0.0000	
Male	0.0094	0.0377	-0.0118	0.0278	0.0121	0.0335	-0.0022	0.0219
REGION								
Northeast*	0.0000		0.0000		0.0000		0.0000	
Midwest	-0.0036	0.0539	0.0840	0.0397	-0.0451	0.0479	-0.0601	0.0312
South	0.0033	0.0538	-0.0384	0.0397	-0.0326	0.0478	-0.0142	0.0312
West	0.0587	0.0571	0.0753	0.0421	0.0756	0.0507	0.0109	0.0331
PENSION TYPE								
DC*	0.0000		0.0000		0.0000		0.0000	
DB	-0.1273	0.0469	-0.0561	0.0346	-0.0271	0.0417	0.0325	0.0272
Both	-0.1722	0.0567	-0.0842	0.0418	-0.1131	0.0504	-0.0520	0.0329
Uncertain About Pension Type	-0.1138	0.0904	-0.1751	0.0666	-0.0728	0.0803	-0.0897	0.0524
None	0.0268	0.0652	0.0244	0.0480	0.0442	0.0579	-0.0516	0.0378
UNION STATUS								
No*	0.0000		0.0000		0.0000		0.0000	
Yes	-0.1443	0.0582	-0.1527	0.0429	-0.2197	0.0517	-0.0969	0.0338
YEARS OF JOB TENURE								
Years of Job Tenure	0.0026	0.0020	0.0007	0.0015	0.0028	0.0018	0.0003	0.0012
CONSTANT	-0.0123	0.3186	0.6350	0.2348	-0.4408	0.2830	-0.2498	0.1848
R-SQUARE	0.0824	.	0.1092	.	0.1074	.	0.0564	.

Note: *: are the excluded categories. Also, Model 1 is the predicted fraction of the HRS sample that is working in an establishment where the employer's response to Q1 is yes or in some cases, Model 2 is the predicted fraction of the HRS sample that is not only working in an establishment that permits phased retirement, but in the eyes of their employer would be a good candidate for phased retirement (4 or 5 on Q2), Model 3 is the prediction fraction of the HRS sample who would be likely to obtain phased retirement if asked, would not have to officially retire, and could remain in same job, and Model 4 is the predicted fraction of the HRS sample who would be likely to obtain phased retirement if asked, would not have to retire first, could remain in same job, and have same health insurance as when working full-time.

men and women who were ages 51 to 61 in 1992 and thereafter resamples these people every two years. Since the establishment survey focused on employees who were age 55 and over, the ideal wave for our purposes is the 1996 wave. In 1996, the HRS sample was 55 to 65. Since B_1 and B_2 were estimated in a sample of older full-time white-collar workers employed in establishments with more than twenty employees, we selected a similar sample in the HRS. After applying these conditions and using the sampling weights in the HRS, our HRS sample represents 3,252,671 white-collar workers.

For the purpose of comparison, the composition of both the establishment survey and the HRS sample are presented in Table 3. In general, the results in Table 2 indicate that both data sources have similar characteristics (see, for example, Industry, Occupation, and Region). There are, however, variables in which they differ. Although the establishment survey oversampled large establishments, it was not designed to replicate the distribution of workers across establishment sizes. Thus, this establishment survey has more people working in smaller establishments (41 percent) than does the HRS (24.8 percent). Related to this, since small firms often use DC pensions plans, unlike the HRS, most of the people in the establishment survey have a DC pension plan.

Who Has a Good Opportunity for Phased Retirement?

Using the estimated coefficients for the four models in Table 2 along with the HRS data, we computed four sets of predictions. These are presented in the top row of Table 4. For Model 1, a predicted 87 percent of the HRS sample is working in an establishment where the employer's response to Q1 is "yes" or "in some cases." That is, of course, quite similar to the number in the establishment data (see Figure 1). Thus, while the establishment data left open the question of whether older white-collar workers are concentrated in sectors where phased retirement is not permitted, this result resolves the matter. In fact, most older white-collar workers are in an establishment where the employer is willing to work out some form of phased retirement.

The results for Model 2 indicate the predicted fraction of the HRS sample that is not only working in an establishment that permits phased retirement but that would also be a good candidate for phased retirement (4 or 5 on Q2). The fraction is a surprising 50 percent. Thus, roughly half of all older white-collar workers who work in an establishment with twenty or more employees could approach their employer about phased retirement and get a positive response.

The results for Model 3 indicate the predicted fraction of the HRS sample who (a) would be a good candidate for phased retirement (4 or 5 on Q2), (b) would

Table 3. Composition of the Establishment Survey and HRS Sample

Variables	HRS	Establishment Survey
INDUSTRY		
Construction	2.7 %	1.8 %
Manufacturing	18.4 %	13.8 %
Transportation, Communications and Utilities	7.9 %	4.6 %
Wholesale and Retail Trade	12.0 %	12.6 %
Finance	7.1 %	6.1 %
Other Services	6.1 %	16.4 %
Health, Education, and Social Services	37.4 %	36.3 %
Public Administration	8.6 %	8.5 %
ESTABLISHMENT SIZE		
Less than 49 employees	24.8 %	41.1 %
50–99 employees	19.4 %	24.5 %
100–249 employees	19.7 %	20.1 %
250–999 employees	18.1 %	10.2 %
more than 1000 employees	18.0 %	4.2 %
YEARS OF EDUCATION		
less than 12 years	4.3 %	2.4 %
12 years	30.2 %	24.1 %
13–15 years	23.7 %	7.9 %
16 years	15.4 %	32.2 %
more than 16 years	26.4 %	25.1 %
OCCUPATION		
Manager	29.4 %	36.3 %
Professional	33.0 %	40.5 %
Sales	9.1 %	5.8 %
Clerical	28.5 %	17.3 %
AGE		
55–60 Years	74.6 %	79.8 %
61–65 Years	25.3 %	14.9 %
65 or more Years	0.1 %	5.2 %
GENDER		
Female	49.4 %	52.1 %
Male	50.6 %	47.9 %
REGION		
Northeast	21.3 %	17.0 %
Midwest	26.5 %	29.3 %
South	32.5 %	32.0 %
West	19.7 %	21.7 %
PENSION TYPE		
None	15.8 %	11.9 %
DB	45.8 %	25.1 %
DC	30.9 %	51.9 %
Both	7.6 %	11.1 %
UNION STATUS		
No	77.8 %	86.1 %
Yes	22.2 %	13.9 %
YEARS OF JOB TENURE		
less than 5 years	20.7 %	18.7 %
5–10 years	18.1 %	20.5 %
11–15 years	14.6 %	20.2 %
16–25 years	20.9 %	24.6 %
more than 25 years	25.8 %	14.9 %

not have to officially retire, and (c) could remain in same job. We expect a lower fraction in this model than in Model 2 since the conditions for phased retirement are more restrictive, and that is the case. The predicted fraction for this model is less than 30 percent.

Finally, the results for Model 4 indicate the fraction of the HRS sample who (a) would be a good candidate for phased retirement, (b) would not have to officially retire first, (c) could remain in same job, and (d) could have the same health insurance as when working full time. Thus, in addition to the conditions in Model 3, this model requires that an older employee be able to keep her health insurance benefits during phased retirement. Here the average probability drops to less than 10 percent. In the United States, health insurance complicates phased retirement.

Who has particularly good opportunities for phased retirement? For ease of exposition, we focus here on Model 3. Of course, readers who prefer alternative definitions of phased retirement will want to examine the other columns in Table 4. Consider the Industry category. Note that opportunities for phased retirement are highest in construction, wholesale and retail trade, and other services. There are two reasons for such differences across industries. First, the coefficients in Table 1 differ across industries. Second, the characteristics of white-collar workers differ across industries. For example, an industry may have more union workers or more workers under age 60 and in consequence have a lower probability of phased retirement.

Reading down the Model 3 column, it appears that opportunities for phased retirement are greatest when the older white-collar worker is employed in a small establishment (less than forty-nine employees). Managers are much less likely to have opportunities for phased retirement—at least while remaining in their current job. Opportunities do not appear to vary much with years of education or gender. Age is, however, important, with older workers enjoying greater opportunities. Region also appears to be important, with greater opportunities in the west than in other regions. Individuals who are not covered by a union contract have greater opportunity for phased retirement options, as do workers with less than five years of job tenure.

The pension results in Table 4 deserve special attention. Aspects of DB pensions can be incompatible with phased retirement. If benefits are based on salary in the final years prior to retirement, then a move to part-time work can result in a substantial reduction in future pension benefits. This is not an issue in a DC plan like a 401(k) because benefits are not based solely on salary in the final years prior to retirement. In addition, Internal Revenue Service regulations make it quite difficult for an employee with a DB plan to use pension benefits to

Table 4. Predicted Fraction of the Older White-Collar Population with an Opportunity for Phased Retirement

Characteristics	Model 1	Model 2	Model 3	Model 4
OVERALL	83.1 %	48.8 %	27.6 %	9.9 %
INDUSTRY				
Construction	91.7 %	76.3 %	43.2 %	12.2 %
Manufacturing	85.0 %	49.0 %	27.9 %	8.7 %
Transportation, Communications and Utilities	68.8 %	32.0 %	18.6 %	6.8 %
Wholesale and Retail Trade	78.6 %	51.6 %	33.4 %	7.6 %
Finance	80.4 %	49.8 %	22.7 %	12.0 %
Other Services	92.9 %	54.4 %	38.2 %	15.5 %
Health, Education, and Social Services	89.3 %	53.1 %	28.1 %	10.7 %
Public Administration	63.7 %	28.1 %	16.4 %	9.1 %
ESTABLISHMENT SIZE				
Less than 49 employees	84.2 %	50.9 %	30.7 %	6.7 %
50–99 employees	82.9 %	45.9 %	28.9 %	12.5 %
100–249 employees	75.2 %	44.8 %	25.5 %	8.4 %
250–999 employees	82.3 %	46.7 %	27.2 %	10.9 %
more than 1000 employees	91.0 %	55.3 %	24.3 %	12.4 %
YEARS OF EDUCATION				
less than 12 years	81.5 %	46.0 %	26.7 %	10.3 %
12 years	81.5 %	56.4 %	28.9 %	7.8 %
13–15 years	82.6 %	50.6 %	28.3 %	10.3 %
16 years	83.5 %	49.3 %	28.6 %	9.9 %
more than 16 years	84.4 %	46.6 %	26.0 %	9.8 %
OCCUPATION				
Manager	83.7 %	44.8 %	18.9 %	7.4 %
Professional	83.4 %	50.2 %	28.9 %	9.7 %
Sales	75.0 %	48.5 %	33.0 %	9.4 %
Clerical	84.6 %	51.4 %	33.4 %	13.0 %
Age				
55–60 Years	82.7 %	47.1 %	25.5 %	9.0 %
61–65 Years	83.7 %	53.2 %	33.1 %	12.7 %
65 or more Years	86.3 %	57.7 %	36.9 %	12.9 %
GENDER				
Female	85.0 %	50.2 %	29.0 %	11.1 %
Male	81.0 %	47.3 %	26.2 %	8.8 %
REGION				
Northeast	77.9 %	45.1 %	25.1 %	10.5 %
Midwest	89.7 %	48.7 %	25.1 %	6.1 %
South	77.8 %	49.2 %	27.5 %	11.4 %
West	88.4 %	52.1 %	33.6 %	12.0 %
PENSION TYPE				
None	89.4 %	58.7 %	43.6 %	7.4 %
DB	78.7 %	41.3 %	23.9 %	11.8 %
DC	87.8 %	57.3 %	31.0 %	10.7 %
Both	77.7 %	39.3 %	18.0 %	4.8 %

Table 4. Predicted Fraction of the Older White-Collar Population with an Opportunity for Phased Retirement (*cont.*)

Characteristics	Model 1	Model 2	Model 3	Model 4
UNION STATUS				
No	86.5 %	52.5 %	31.6 %	11.4 %
Yes	70.9 %	35.7 %	13.3 %	4.7 %
Years of Job Tenure				
less than 5 years	85.5 %	51.2 %	30.3 %	8.9 %
5–10 years	82.5 %	48.1 %	26.4 %	9.6 %
11–15 years	83.9 %	47.7 %	26.4 %	11.0 %
16–25 years	82.2 %	47.3 %	26.3 %	10.5 %
more than 25 years	81.8 %	49.2 %	28.0 %	10.0 %

Note: Model 1 is the predicted fraction of the HRS sample that is working in an establishment where the employer's response to Q1 is yes or in some cases, Model 2 is the predicted fraction of the HRS sample that is not only working in an establishment that permits phased retirement, but in the eyes of their employer would be a good candidate for phased retirement (4 or 5 on Q2), Model 3 is the prediction fraction of the HRS sample who would be likely to obtain phased retirement if asked, would not have to officially retire, and could remain in same job, and Model 4 is the predicted fraction of the HRS sample who would be likely to obtain phased retirement if asked, would not have to retire first, could remain in same job, and have same health insurance as when working full-time.

supplement salary when taking phased retirement with the employer who administers the pension. This is less of an issue for DC plans since these can be set up so that an active employee over age 59 1/2 can supplement earnings with pension benefits. As such, we would expect the prevalence of phased retirement to be lower at those establishments with DB pension plans (see Penner, Perun, and Steuerle 2002 and Fields and Hutchens 2002).

The pension results in Model 3 are consistent with this. Opportunities for phased retirement are greatest for workers with either no pension or a DC pension, and lowest for workers with a stand-alone DB plan or a DB plan combined with a DC plan. It is not surprising that the last category—DB combined with DC—provides no better opportunities than a simple DB pension. If shifting to half-time employment results in lower lifetime benefits from the DB plan, then regardless of the presence of a DC plan, phased retirement will be avoided.

It is important to sound a word of caution on these pension results. Workers with DB plans have other characteristics that reduce opportunities for phased retirement. In particular, DB plans are associated with large organizations and unions, and that association drives some of the pension differences in Table 4. In multivariate models that control for both organization size and presence of a union, pension variables tend to have small and statistically weak effects. One interpretation would be that a change in the pension law that made DB plans more compatible with phased retirement may have small and weak effects on actual opportunities for phased retirement. This is because workers covered by DB plans would continue to be in unions and in large organizations. They would have low probabilities of phased retirement even if there were changes in the law covering DB plans.

CONCLUSION

This chapter examines opportunities for phased retirement among older white-collar workers. A recent establishment survey funded by the Sloan Foundation asked about opportunities for phased retirement for older white-collar workers. The survey found that in most establishments employers are willing to work out some form of phased retirement. While that is a useful result, it leaves open a question about what fraction of the population of older white-collar workers are in establishments where phased retirement is feasible. It is conceivable that while most establishments permit phased retirement, a minority of older white-collar workers are employed in those establishments. To assess opportunities for phased retirement in the population, this chapter combines information from the establishment survey with data from the Health and Retirement Study. The results indicate that, in fact, more than 80 percent of white-collar workers are employed in an establishment that permits some form of phased retirement. Indeed, the results indicate that about 30 percent of older white-collar workers are employed in an establishment that would not only allow them to take phased retirement prior to official retirement, but would let them remain in their current job.

The results also indicate that opportunities depend on both establishment and worker characteristics. Although effects can depend on how phased retirement is defined, workers in public administration, under 60, with DB pension plans, and in a union tend to have more limited opportunities for phased retirement.

This chapter began with the observation that phased retirements are rare despite the fact that surveys of employees often indicate a strong interest in phased retirement among older workers. It conjectured that this scarcity of phased retirements is due to employer behavior, that is, employers constrain opportunities for workers to take phased retirement. The results of this paper indicate that that explanation is insufficient. It fails to capture the nuance of what is going on. In fact, employers are quite open to phased retirement.

There would seem to be two plausible explanations for why phased retirement is so rare. First, it is conceivable that although employers are open to phased retirement, workers are not aware of it. That seems unlikely. People usually seek to clarify what is possible in their workplace, and there tends to be a collective memory of precedent. One way to examine this is to compare our results with results from an HRS question that asked respondents whether they could reduce the number of hours in their regular work schedule. We would expect that the fraction answering "yes" to this question would be somewhat higher than the fraction in Model 3 in Table 4. Recall that Model 3 is the predicted fraction of the HRS older white-collar workers who would (a) be likely to obtain phased retirement, (b) not have to officially retire, and (c) remain in the same job. In fact, within our sample of older white-collar workers, 25 percent answered "yes" to the HRS question, while Model 3 in Table 4 predicts that 29 percent could take phased retirement. That difference could indicate that workers are not aware of their opportunities, but it could also be a consequence of statistical error.

We favor a second explanation for the scarcity of phased retirements: the terms of the employer's offer are frequently not attractive to older workers. Employers are primarily interested in informal arrangements where they maintain control over the how, when, and who of phased retirement. Moreover, the employer's phased retirement offer can often imply a change in health insurance as well as a different set of tasks. It could be that many older workers look at the terms of such an offer and decide that they would rather not take phased retirement. They would rather remain full-time workers or become full-time retirees, and phased retirement remains rare as a result.

NOTES

1. Blue-collar and white-collar workers often have different work arrangements and pensions. A thorough treatment of both groups would have required a longer survey and resulted in lower response rates.

2. The 1999 Census Bureau County Business Patterns indicates that excluding government, railroads, and the self-employed, approximately 15 percent of all establishments have twenty or more employees, and 75 percent of all employees work in establishments with twenty or more employees.

3. The response rate was 64 percent in the Educational Quality of the Workforce National Employers Survey, which was administered by the U.S. Bureau of the Census as a telephone survey in August and September 1994 to a nationally representative sample of private establishments with more than twenty employees (Lynch and Black 1998). The response rate was 65.5 percent in Osterman's 1992 telephone survey of establishments with more than fifty employees (1994). Holzer and Neumark (1999) report a response rate of 67 percent for establishments that were successfully screened in a telephone survey undertaken between June 1992 and May 1994.

4. Prior to this question, the interviewer clarified the meaning of "part-time," using the U.S. government's definition, which is less than thirty-five hours per week. To make sure we understood the respondent, however, this question was followed by a question that asked whether the respondent was referring to a part-week schedule, a part-year schedule, either schedule, or something else.

5. There were 96 establishments where information was missing or the respondent said "don't know." Since there is no way to know the establishment's policy toward phased retirement, these cases were excluded from this and subsequent tables.

6. Employers may not make defined benefit pension payments to current employees until they reach the normal retirement age stated in the pension plan document.

7. One would expect this percentage to be higher for large establishments. Small establishments may employ only a handful of people over 55. If none were interested in phased retirement, then regardless of the opportunity the right answer to our question would be "no." That is less likely in large establishments with larger numbers of people over 55. It turns out that the percentage is higher in large establishments. For establishments with five hundred or more employees, the comparable figure is 67 percent. The same thing applies to reduction of hours after official retirement. In establishments that reported that phased retirement could be worked out by employees who officially retire and then return as rehires, 22 percent reported that in the past three years they had rehired a retiree as a part-time or contract worker. In establishments with more than five hundred employees, that number jumps to 71 percent.

8. In some organizations, official retirement involves the bureaucratic process of submitting a letter declaring retirement and filling out appropriate forms. In others, it involves a break in service. While respondents may have given the phrase different meanings, they had no problem understanding how "official retirement" applied to their establishment.

9. This is consistent with other studies of phased retirement. For example, in a survey of over two hundred of its clients, the William M. Mercer consulting firm found that only 10 percent had a formal plan for reduced hours or schedules. However, another 45 percent of the respondents indicated that they prefer to handle such situations with individual arrangements.

10. Of course, if the respondent did not know of three older men or women in the establishment, then we accepted the other gender.

11. For reasons of exposition, this wording simplifies matters. In reality, we asked two questions: one regarding shifting to a part-time work schedule before official retirement and the other regarding a part-time work schedule after official retirement.

12. Consider a typical omitted variable bias case as follows:

$$y = X_1\beta_1 + X_2\beta_2 + \epsilon$$

where the observed variables are in X_1 ($N \times K_1$) and the unobserved variables are in X_2 ($N \times K_2$). N is the number of observations, K_1 is the number of observed variables, and K_2 is the number of unobserved variables. Also, assume that the relationship between X_1 and X_2 is linear for simplicity (i.e., let $X_2 = X_1\alpha + e$, where α is a matrix of coefficients ($K_1 \times K_2$) and e is a vector of disturbances with the usual properties). The expected y given X_1 is equal to

$$E(y|X_1) = E(X_1\beta_1 + X_2\beta_2 + \epsilon | X_1)$$
$$= X_1\beta_1 + E(X_1\alpha + e|X_1)\beta_2 + E(\epsilon|X_1)$$
$$= X_1\beta_1 + X_1\alpha\beta_2$$

where it is assumed that $E(\epsilon|X_1) = 0$. Now, suppose the Ordinary Least Squares method is used to estimate the above model (i.e., regress y on X_1), and obtain the following estimator for β_1:

$$b_1 = (X_1'X_1)^{-1}X_1'y$$
$$= (X_1'X_1)^{-1}X_1'(X_1\beta_1 + X_2\beta_2 + \epsilon)$$
$$= \beta_1 + (X_1'X_1)^{-1}X_1'X_2\beta_2 + (X_1'X_1)^{-1}X_1'\epsilon.$$

Note that the last term in the sum is zero by construction, and consequently drops out of what follows. When b_1 is used to predict y, the predictor of y is equal to

$$\hat{y} = X_1 b_1$$
$$= X_1[\beta_1 + (X_1'X_1)^{-1}X_1'X_2\beta_2]$$
$$= X_1\beta_1 + X_1(X_1'X_1)^{-1}X_1'X_2\beta_2$$

Thus, the expectation of the given X_1 is equal to:

$$E(\hat{y}|X_1) = E(X_1\beta_1 + X_1(X_1'X_1)^{-1}X_1'X_2\beta_2|X_1)$$
$$= X_1\beta_1 + X_1(X_1'X_1)^{-1}X_1'E(X_2|X_1)\beta_2$$
$$= X_1\beta_1 + X_1(X_1'X_1)^{-1}X_1'(X_1\alpha)\beta_2$$
$$= X_1\beta_1 + X_1\alpha\beta_2$$
$$= E(y|X_1)$$

So, $\hat{y}$ is an unbiased estimator for y given X_1. For our purposes, assuming that $E(X_2|X_1)$ is the same in the two samples, parameters estimated in the establishment survey yield unbiased predictions in the HRS.

References

Chen, Jennjou. 2003. "Part-Time Labor Market for Older Workers." Dissertation. Cornell University.

Fields, Vivian, and Robert Hutchens. 2002. "Regulatory Obstacles to Phased Retirement in the For-Profit Sector." *Benefits Quarterly*. Third Quarter.

Graig, Laurene A., and Valerie Paganelli. 2000. "Phased Retirement: Reshaping the End of Work." *Compensation and Benefits Management*. Vol. 16, no. 2 (Spring).

Holzer, Harry J., and David Neumark. 1999. "Are Affirmative Action Hires Less Qualified? Evidence from Employer-Employee Data on New Hires." *Journal of Labor Economics*. Vol. 17, no. 3 (July): 534–69.

Hutchens, Robert, and Karen Grace-Martin. 2006. "Employer Willingness to Permit Phased Retirement: Why Are Some More Willing Than Others?" *Industrial and Labor Relations Review*. Vol. 59, no. 4 (July): 525–46.

Lynch, Lisa M., and Sandra E. Black. 1998. "Beyond the Incidence of Employer-Provided Training." *Industrial and Labor Relations Review.* Vol. 52, no. 1 (October): 64–81.

Osterman, Paul. 1994. "How Common is Workplace Transformation and Who Adopts It?" *Industrial and Labor Relations Review.* Vol. 47, no. 2 (January): 173–88.

Penner, Rudolph G., Pamela Perun, and C. Eugene Steuerle. 2002. *Legal and Institutional Impediments to Partial Retirement and Part-Time Work by Older Workers.* Urban Institute.

Quinn, Joseph F., Richard V. Burkhauser, and Daniel A. Myers. 1990. *Passing the Torch: The Influence of Economic Incentives on Work and Retirement.* Kalamazoo, MI: W.E. Upjohn Institute for Employment Research.

Ruhm, Christopher J. 1990. "Bridge Jobs and Partial Retirement." *Journal of Labor Economics.* Vol. 8, no. 4 (October): 482–501.

U.S. General Accounting Office. 2001. *Older Workers: Demographic Trends Pose Challenges for Employers and Workers.* Report to the Ranking Minority Member, Subcommittee on Employer-Employee Relations, Committee on Education and the Workforce, House of Representatives. Washington, DC: GAO-02–85 (November).

William M. Mercer, Inc. 2001. *Phased Retirement and the Changing Face of Retirement.* William M. Mercer. (May).

Comments on "The Role of Employers in Phased Retirement: Opportunities for Phased Retirement among White-Collar Workers"

JOSEPH QUINN

Robert Hutchens and Jennjou Chen have written an outstanding paper that probes an area in which there has been relatively little study. It asks the right questions, it is well-written, and it suggests avenues for additional research to be done.

The paper asks why there is so little phased retirement *within* firms. Why do so few workers move to part-time status *on their career jobs* before leaving the firm and the labor force altogether? Were one to retire gradually, doing so on one's own career job would make great sense for a variety of reasons. The specific human capital accumulated over the years at this job would be utilized, no new training would be required, one could maintain personal contacts with colleagues, and uncertainty would be minimized. The firm knows the worker and the worker knows the firm. The employee also knows the specific job because he or she has already been doing it. Nonetheless, as the authors show, this type of gradual or partial retirement appears to be rare. The question is, why? Are these opportunities not available on career jobs, or are they available, but workers turn them down?

I would like to put these issues in a slightly broader context and then return to the specifics of this paper. I have worked on two related topics: *when* people retire (retirement trends, the timing of labor force withdrawal), and *how* people retire (retirement patterns, the nature of the withdrawal process). The latter, how people leave their career jobs, is of interest here. The bottom line from my research is that gradual or partial retirement is very common in America today. I estimate that between one-third and one-half of all older Americans utilize what economists call "bridge" jobs on the way out—a job between full-time work on a career job and complete labor force withdrawal (see Quinn 2002; Altman and Shactman 2002; or Clark et al. 2004). I am confident that this one-third to one-half estimate is in fact an underestimate. It may come as a surprise that this finding of extensive gradual retirement does not contradict Hutchens and Chen's results. It does not because most of this happens on new jobs, not on career jobs. Most workers take a bridge job with a new employer.

These findings emerge from two ways of analyzing data in the longitudinal Health and Retirement Study (HRS), which is following a large cohort of older Americans who were 51 to 61 years old in 1992 through the retirement process via extensive surveys every two years (see the *Journal of Human Resources* 1995). One methodology is to analyze the most current data, describe what the members of the sample were doing at that point in time, and then look back in time, via the HRS, to see how they got there. Did current retirees use a bridge job on the way out? Did those currently in a bridge job work at a career job beforehand? The second approach is to search back in time in the HRS to find people holding a career job and then follow them forward through time, utilizing the longitudinal nature of the data to study how they left those career jobs. How many career-job workers use bridge jobs on the way out? How many leave the career job and the labor force all at once? It turns out that these approaches yield similar results—there is considerable bridge-job activity among older Americans today.

The definition used here of a career job is a full-time job held for at least ten years. A bridge job, therefore, is either a part-time job of any duration or a full-time job of shorter duration than 10 years. Some colleagues have objected that ten years is too long; for example, perhaps an eight-year job should be viewed as another career job, rather than as a bridge job. The job tenure chosen in the definition is arbitrary, and I have experimented with other criteria: for example, eight years and five years. The lower the threshold for a career job, the less bridge-job activity because more of the transitional jobs are labeled new career rather than bridge jobs. But the qualitative results remain the same—considerable bridge job activity.[1]

Using the ten-year definition and the 4,300 men in the third wave of the HRS with some work experience at or after age 50, we find 23 percent of the men working at a bridge job in 1996. About two-thirds of that 23 percent are part-time workers and about one-third are working at a full-time job that we estimate will last less than ten years. In addition, 36 percent of the sample are already out of the labor force, and about one-third of these (another 12 percentage points, a third of 36 percent) last worked at a bridge job. If we add the 23 percent of the sample in a bridge job and the 12 percent who are out of the labor force but who last worked at a bridge job, we find about one-third of the men with a bridge job as part of the exit process. This counts none of the 40 percent of the sample who were still working in full-time career jobs in 1996. Some of these, of course, will move to bridge jobs in later waves of the HRS.

Among the women with job experience at or after age 50, the numbers are slightly higher. One-quarter were in a bridge job in 1996. Forty percent had already left the labor force, and half of them had last worked at a bridge job, so 45 percent exhibited bridge-job activity, a percentage that will increase over time as others leave full-time career employment.

The other approach is to go back in time, find career jobs, and then follow the respondents back to the present (in this case, 1996). This approach addresses a legitimate methodological concern. Some workers may have had whole careers of jobs that meet our definition of bridge employment (for example, a series of part-time positions). If so, why should we look at a particular bridge job and deduce retirement activity? When we observe part-time employment among 40 year olds, we do not conclude that these individuals have begun the retirement process. The same may be true for some 55 to 60 year olds. Using this approach, we concentrate only on those who did hold a full-time career job, for whom a bridge job would be a change.

When one goes back in the HRS, one can identify a career job for 84 percent of the men and 60 percent of the women in the 1996 sample. Of those who subsequently left their career jobs by 1996, half of the career men and half of the career women moved to bridge jobs rather than completely out of the labor force. Again, we find considerable bridge-job activity. What is particularly interesting is that the prevalence is the same for men and women who have held career jobs. This suggests that differences between the retirement patterns of older men and women are due to the fact that fewer women have had career jobs. The career men and the career women appear to behave similarly late in life.

Here is where the Hutchens and Chen paper picks up and asks several interesting questions. If gradual retirement is so widespread, why is there so little of it in career jobs? Why do workers have to switch employers in order to retire in stages? Do they have opportunities to cut back on their current jobs? If so, under what conditions and terms of employment, and are these attractive options?

What is particularly interesting is the authors' answer to the question: do workers have opportunities to cut back on their jobs? It depends on what is meant by an "opportunity." Hutchens and Chen estimate that 84 percent or 50 percent or 30 percent or less than 10 percent of the older, white collar population have this option—take your pick. The answer is 84 percent if you believe the company officials interviewed, and then count all the people who work in these firms in which the interviewee claimed that these options are available, while ignoring the terms and conditions of what might be offered. (About 87 percent of the firms claim that they provide such opportunities to at least some of their employees.) But the answer drops significantly, to 50 percent, if you consider the personal and firm characteristics that are correlated with these options and count only those employees whose predicted values, based on their characteristics, suggest that it is likely or very likely that they would be offered a gradual retirement option. This acknowledges the fact that not all the workers in a firm with this option would actually be offered it.

The answer then drops to 30 percent if you count only those whose predicted values suggest that they are likely or very likely to be offered the option *and* who would not have to retire first *and* who could keep working in their existing jobs with the firm. Finally, the answer drops to less than 10 percent if you take the subset of the 30 percent above who could also maintain their preretirement health insurance coverage during the phased retirement with the firm. Losing health coverage can be a significant problem for those below the age of Medicare eligibility and for some above it, depending on the details of their pension and health insurance coverage. And, although Hutchens and Chen do not address this, the incidence would be lower still if they included only those who could continue to draw a paycheck *and* receive pension benefits from the same firm, which is only allowed in defined benefit (DB) plans at ages above the normal retirement age, typically age 65.

With their econometric estimates on the likelihood of being offered a gradual retirement option, Hutchens and Chen can estimate the probability for an individual with particular personal and firm characteristics, and show how they vary around the averages noted above. Both individual and firm characteristics are important, an interesting finding of the paper. For example, the probability of a gradual retirement option is higher if an individual works in the construction trade or is over 60 or 65 years of age, and lower for a manager (for whom job-splitting might present a problem for the firm), for a union member, or for a worker covered by a DB pension plan.

What I learned from this paper, which is a wonderful melding of establishment data and individual longitudinal data, is that opportunities to withdraw gradually in career jobs appear to be very common (i.e., they exist in many firms), but that they are in fact much less prevalent when one looks more closely. Gradual retirement is not offered to every worker in a firm that does offer it, and opportunities may have some very unattractive features. For example, a worker might have to retire and then return as a contract worker, but only on a full-time basis. Other workers might be offered positions without their prior medical coverage.

Or, a worker might have to find a person for the other half of a job-sharing arrangement. Many part-time workers would not be able to draw a partial pension, as they could do with Social Security benefits if they lower their earnings sufficiently. I believe that the authors' bottom line is correct: the gradual retirement options for career jobs are less prevalent than they seem; and even more importantly, the arrangements that are offered are often unattractive to workers for a variety of reasons.

How might I understand these issues further? What additional research should be done? I think it would be interesting to ask the workers, not just their managers, about their impressions of the prevalence and the nature of these retirement opportunities. The workers' impressions of their options might differ from those of management, who might be trying to make the firm look good by describing the options in their most favorable light. Secondly, it would be enlightening to probe the details of workers' DB pension plans. For example, as Hutchens and Chen point out, under pension rules that base benefits on the last few years' earnings, ending a career with several years as a part-time earner could lower pension benefits for the rest of a worker's life. Some firms have pension plans with these terminal years benefit features, others do not, and I suspect that this feature would be strongly correlated with employees' retirement patterns. Finally, it would be very useful to probe whether, other things being equal, retiring gradually from a career job is, on net, a good idea, and for whom. As mentioned above, there are reasons why it might be beneficial. The worker knows the job and his or her coworkers. Specific human capital is utilized. But other workers might enjoy a new and different job, a change of pace, less strenuous employment, a seasonal job, or employment in another part of the country. We will find, of course, that one size does not fit all. What is attractive to one potential retiree is not to another. The most important characteristic of the elderly is not the average, but the variation around the average. Older workers, firms and the nation will benefit if a variety of gradual or partial retirement options exist—an array that matches the wide variety of preferences among American workers of traditional retirement age.

NOTE

1. When the years required for a career job drops from ten to eight, the extent of bridge-job activity drops by about 5 percent. If the definition drops to five years (on the low side for a "career" job, in my view), bridge-job activity drops by about 20 percent, compared to the ten-year definition (Quinn 2002).

REFERENCES

Altman, Stuart H., and David I. Shactman, eds. 2002. *Policies for an Aging Society.* Baltimore: Johns Hopkins University Press.

Clark, Robert L., Richard V. Burkhauser, Marilyn Moon, Joseph F. Quinn, and Timothy M. Smeeding. 2004. *The Economics of an Aging Society.* Oxford, UK: Blackwell Publishing Ltd. Chapter 5.

Journal of Human Resources dedicated a special issue to the Health and Retirement Study. 1995. *Journal of Human Resources.* University of Wisconsin Press. Vol. 30, no. 1 (Winter).

Quinn, Joseph F. 2002. "Changing Retirement Trends and Their Impact on Elderly Entitlement Programs." In *Policies for an Aging Society.* Ed. Stuart H. Altman and David I. Shactman. Baltimore: Johns Hopkins University Press. 293–315.

CHAPTER FIVE

Letting Older Workers Work

RUDOLPH G. PENNER, PAMELA PERUN,
& C. EUGENE STEUERLE

When the baby boom generation begins retiring and receiving Social Security benefits after 2007, the U.S. economy will rapidly lose productive human capital as skilled and experienced laborers leave the workforce. This loss would not create severe economic problems if there were a large supply of younger workers to replace the retirees, but fertility rates fell rapidly after the peak of the baby boom in the late-1950s. As a result, the labor force will be almost constant between 2010 and 2030 under current policies, and the minute growth that occurs will be largely the result of immigration and high birth rates among recent immigrants.

Many baby boomers will welcome retirement after a career of hard work. Changes in private or public policies may have little or no effect on their decisions. Others may be induced to work longer if given more flexibility. They might be attracted by jobs offering shorter hours or longer vacations. Still others might postpone retirement if offered a different set of economic incentives.

Currently, an employer wishing to offer flexible employment opportunities generally, and to older workers more specifically, faces numerous legal and regulatory barriers as the combined result of our tax laws and regulations, the Employee Retirement Income Security Act (ERISA), and the Age Discrimination in Employment Act (ADEA). These barriers are ladled on top of the important economic disincentive stemming from the higher health insurance costs associated with older workers.

On the employees' side, the design of the traditional defined benefit (DB) pension plan can provide a very strong incentive to retire at a relatively young age. Although such plans are becoming rarer in the private sector, they are still very important for federal, state, and local employees. There are also more subtle institutional pressures to retire at a certain age. There may be social pressures to leave and make room for younger workers, and there may be a widely shared presumption that one's skills and physical stamina decline more rapidly with age than is the case.

Many of the economic and institutional barriers to working longer evolved when there was reason to make room for the giant cohorts of baby boomers working their way up the career ladder. Pressures to downsize were often much stronger than pressures to retain valuable human capital. Early retirement provided a relatively painless way to shed workers. It was also a time when mandatory retirement was legal, life expectancy was shorter, health at any age was more fragile, and many more jobs were physically demanding.

Much has changed since the ERISA and the ADEA were enacted and since most retirement plans were designed. It is clearly time to reassess the legal and institutional arrangements governing the employment of older workers. These arrangements will not be changed easily, but the aging of the baby boomers will force adjustments fairly soon. We need to begin discussing reform immediately so as to ease the transition.

The basic facts underlying this analysis are well known and uncontroversial. We know with certainty that the rate of growth of the labor force will soon be slowing. We know that there are powerful institutional incentives to retire early and that laws and regulations limit the types of partial retirement arrangements that can be offered employees. We know that the welfare of workers can be enhanced by increasing their work options. We do not, however, know how many workers and employers would exploit the opportunity to negotiate new arrangements if barriers were removed. That can only be determined by trying it.

It also must be admitted that policy changes providing more flexibility to employer and employee will provide the flexibility to work less as well as to work more. While this result would conflict with the goal of countering the future slowdown in the growth of the labor force, it would still be beneficial to the employer and employee. The employee would get more leisure time if that is what he or she chose, and presumably the employer would not accept the arrangement unless it resulted in a more efficient labor force.

DEMOGRAPHIC TRENDS

Fertility Rates

The fertility rate[1] hovered around 2.2 during most of the 1930s and then began a somewhat erratic upward trend that peaked at 3.8 in 1957. Soon after, it fell even more precipitously than it had risen and reached a low of 1.7 in 1976. After the late-1970s, the rate rose a bit and remained slightly above 2.0 during the 1990s. It is the speed with which the baby dearth followed the baby boom that will cause the ratio of workers to retirees to fall rapidly between 2010 and 2030. The ratio of payroll taxpayers to Social Security beneficiaries will go from slightly over 3 to only 2 between those twenty years.

Life Expectancy

When Social Security began, life expectancy for a man at age 65 was about 12 years. By 1950, life expectancy at 65 had risen to almost 13 years, and the average age at which a man applied for Social Security was 68.7. Paradoxically, the average age for applying for Social Security benefits fell to less than 64 in 2000 while expected life at age 65 rose to 15.7 years. This suggests that the time a typical man spends in retirement has nearly doubled since 1950. This is despite the fact that people are healthier at every age and the physical demands associated with work have fallen as mechanization has increased and the economy has shifted more toward services.

Health and the Physical Demands Imposed by Work

The health status of the elderly has improved as expected life has increased. Manton, Corder, and Stallard (1997) found that the proportion of those age 65 and over reporting sickness or disability declined from 25 to 21 percent between 1982 and 1994. Steuerle, Spiro, and Johnson (1999), using census and Current Population Survey data, show that it is not until age 75 or older that more than 40 percent of the noninstitutionalized population report being in fair or poor health. The same authors estimate that the portion of the total workforce in physically demanding jobs has steadily declined from 20.3 percent in 1950 to 7.5 percent in 1996.

These findings suggest that over time the ability of those over 65 to work has grown, as has the possibility of finding work that is not physically demanding. Later we shall ask whether the desire to work matches the potential to work.

Retirement Trends

Voluntary retirement is a relatively recent phenomenon in human history. Before the Civil War, most Americans worked as long as they were able. However, Civil War pensions, which were almost as universal as Social Security, and the beginnings of corporate and union pensions made retirement possible in the later part of the nineteenth century. By 1900, about one-third of men age 65 and over were retired. That number had grown to one-half by 1950 and to 84 percent by 1985. Another way of describing the trend is to note that the average age of retirement was 74 in 1910 and 63 in 1998–1999 (Burtless and Quinn 2000). The trend toward earlier and earlier retirement for men appears to have stopped in the mid-1980s.[2] There are a number of possible reasons for this abrupt end to a very long trend: a relatively buoyant economy, the end of mandatory retirement, the end of increases in Social Security benefits relative to average wages, and the replacement of DB pension plans with defined contribution (DC) plans. We shall discuss some of these phenomena in more detail later. The main point to be made here is that the fall in the average retirement age over time, the improvement in health, and the reduced physical demands associated with work suggest that in theory, at least, there is considerable potential for now increasing the retirement age by removing impediments and improving incentives.

Immigration

Many see increased immigration as a possible solution to our nation's demographic problems. Immigrants have contributed significantly to our economic well-being over the years, and increases in the inflow could alter the timing of demographic trends. Immigrants also age, however, and tend to use more public assistance per capita than those born in the United States.

In 1998, there were about 425,000 legal immigrants of working age. By comparison, an average of 1.6 million workers age 51 and over said that they retired in 1999 or 2000. Numerous others reduced their hours of work between 1998 and 2000, even though they may not have described themselves as being retired in 2000.[3] The number of those retiring each year or shifting to part-time status will grow rapidly after 2007. Because immigrants are likely to remain in the labor force longer than a typical older worker who changes his or her mind about retiring, it is difficult to compare how much annual work hours by older workers would have to increase to be equivalent to a certain percentage increase in immigration. However, the question may be moot as the nation may be approaching a limit on the amount of immigration that is politically acceptable.

A View of the Labor Force of the Future

The demographic trends described above explain why labor force growth has been steadily declining since the 1970s, when baby boomers were pouring into the workforce, and will continue to decline until 2030, when most baby boomers will have retired. The annual rate of labor force growth between 1970 and 1980 was 2.60 percent, but by the 1990–2000 period it had more than halved, to 1.13 percent per year. If it is assumed that the labor force participation rate will remain constant for all age groups and both sexes, the labor force annual growth rate will fall to 0.88 percent annually for 2000–2010, 0.34 percent for 2010–2020, and 0.38 percent for 2020–2030 (see Table 1). It will then rise to 0.66 percent for the period 2030–2040, when population trends are projected again to approach a steady state.

Falling growth rates for the labor force and a consequent loss of human capital do not in themselves imply a falling standard of living. A growing capital stock and technological improvements are projected to add to income per capita, but the extremely rapid growth of the retired population in the early part of this century will slow any improvement in living standards for younger workers. The population age 65 and over is expected to grow 1.3 percent per year between 2000 and 2010, 3.1 percent between 2010 and 2020, and 3.5 percent between 2020 and 2040. The problem facing younger workers is exacerbated by the fact that the per-capita resource needs of the elderly are higher than those of the young because of the need for more medical services. Cutler et al. (1990) estimated that

Table 1. Unadjusted and Adjusted Labor Force Projections (Annual Growth Rates)

	Annual Growth Rate (% over Period)				Indexed Relative to 2000 (2000=100)	
	2000–2010	2010–2020	2020–2030	2030–2040	2020	2040
UNADJUSTED						
Total	0.88	0.34	0.38	0.66	112.5	124.5
Male	0.89	0.39	0.38	0.66	113.2	125.3
Female	0.87	0.31	0.38	0.67	112.0	124.0
ADJUSTED						
Total	1.05	0.36	0.14	0.69	114.5	124.1
Male	1.04	0.37	0.14	0.70	114.4	124.2
Female	1.06	0.36	0.14	0.68	114.5	124.1

Source: Toder and Solanki (1999).

the per-capita needs of the population age 65 and older exceed those of the population age 20 to 64 by 27 percent and those of people 19 and under by 76 percent. None of this necessarily implies that the living standards of the labor force will decline absolutely. The aforementioned increase in the capital stock and technological improvements will continue to improve before-tax wages. However, it seems almost certain that the rate of improvement in the after-tax living standards of workers will fall far short of what the nation took for granted over the six decades following World War II.

The labor force projections described above assume that both sexes and all age groups continue to participate in the labor force at today's rates. This is clearly unrealistic for women. Younger women are participating in the labor force at a much higher rate than did today's elderly women, and this implies that they will eventually participate more at older ages as well. If it is assumed that future labor force participation rates among women 50 and older decline at the same rate as men's, the decline in labor force growth rates is somewhat ameliorated, but the difference is surprisingly small. The annual rate of growth rises from 0.88 percent to 1.08 percent for 2000–2010, rises from 0.34 to 0.38 percent for 2010–2020, and remains the same for 2020–2030 and 2030–2040.

Other adjustments can be justified. For example, Toder and Solanki (1999) adjust for changes in the experience and education of the labor force. However, these adjustments make very little difference to the size of the decline in the growth rate of the effective labor force in coming decades. The basic problem remains regardless of how the data are adjusted.

The demographic trends that will slow the growth of the labor force in the coming decades are so powerful that it is implausible to believe that they can be offset completely by increasing the number of hours worked by the older population. Our own estimates, described at length in our complete report (Penner, Perun, and Steuerle 2002), suggest that the participation rate of the 55 to 64 population would have to be increased to only slightly below the levels for the 25 to 49 age group in order to maintain the ratio of the effective labor force to the total population at 2000 levels. Such estimates are extremely sensitive to the time period studied, the choice of population projections, and the adjustments made to the labor force for gender, education and experience. However, our estimates would have to be very wrong to alter our basic conclusion that the economy will have to live with some considerable decline in the rate of growth of the effective labor force regardless of how public and private employment policies are altered. This is obviously not an argument for maintaining the status quo. Demographic trends can be mitigated and the welfare of older workers can be enhanced greatly by expanding their array of employment opportunities.

If We Remove Impediments to Longer Work, Will Retirement Behavior Change?

As noted earlier, many people very much want to retire. Providing some opportunity for more flexible working arrangements would be unlikely to bring them back into the labor force, while others would reduce their hours if given the opportunity to work part time. On the other hand, many people would welcome the opportunity to work longer, as long as they can reduce the hours worked per week or take longer vacations. It is not easy, however, to determine how many fall into this group.

One useful source of clues is the Health and Retirement Study (HRS), which asks detailed questions about why people with different demographic and economic characteristics retire. A problem with HRS data arises, however, because different people have different notions of what it means to be retired. Some who are working a considerable number of hours, but not full-time, consider themselves to be retired.

Table 2 examines the numbers of people age 51 and older who retire each year according to different definitions of retirement. Note that many of these people do work some hours. However, only about 516,000 of the 1.9 million part-time workers aged 51 and above work more than twenty hours per week. Later, when discussing legal impediments to work, we will show that it is legally important whether a worker works more or less than half-time.

Table 3 examines whether retirement is voluntary or involuntary. About 61 percent of workers age 51 through 54 said that they were forced to retire, while 36 percent said that they wanted to retire. The remainder cited a combination of reasons. As the age of retirement increases, the proportion forced to retire declines steadily until it reaches 33 percent for those age 65 through 67, while the proportion wanting to retire steadily rises.

When asked their reasons for retiring, almost 67 percent of men age 51 through 54 said that poor health was very important to their decision. It is interesting to note that this proportion is somewhat greater than the proportion saying that they were forced to retire. The proportion saying that poor health was very important to their retirement decision goes down steadily as the retirement age increases, while the proportion saying that poor health is not at all important goes up. Poor health is somewhat less important to the retirement decisions of women, but it exhibits the same patterns as retirement ages increase. This suggests the somewhat paradoxical result that it may be easier to induce those retiring later to postpone retirement or work more hours than it is to affect the decisions of younger retirees, simply because the former are in better health.

Table 2. Number of Workers Ages 51 and Older Who Retire Per Year, 1998-2000, under Alternative Retirement Definitions

	Work for pay and do not describe self as retired in 1998; report being retired in 2000	Work for pay in 1998; Do not work for pay in 2000	Work full-time in 1998; work less than full-time in 2000	Work full-time in 1998; work less than 20 hours per week in 2000	Work full-time in 1998; do not work in 2000
ALL	1,629,854	2,197,111	1,901,428	1,385,682	1,198,935
GENDER					
Men	925,618	1,087,344	1,014,246	760,167	660,507
Women	704,236	1,109,767	887,182	625,515	538,428
AGE IN 1998					
51 – 54	89,043	275,327	278,307	192,709	180,239
55 – 57	225,885	319,687	385,314	264,178	225,412
58 – 61	297,333	432,723	398,586	302,334	268,175
62 – 64	355,585	370,198	383,000	308,217	254,088
65 – 67	247,834	254,700	206,658	147,782	132,219
68 and older	414,175	544,479	249,564	170,463	138,803
EDUCATION					
Did not complete high school	316,596	520,250	389,345	312,513	272,724
High school graduate	587,165	792,075	632,241	479,934	431,278
Some college	353,669	453,596	420,808	303,861	263,745
College graduate	368,733	425,949	456,044	286,384	231,189
RACE					
Non-Hispanic White	1,386,489	1,812,609	1,557,307	1,113,773	952,301
Non-Hispanic Black	150,473	207,217	174,341	131,804	118,203
Hispanic	53,645	112,397	105,099	85,540	75,875
Other	39,248	64,888	64,682	54,566	52,556

Table 3. Share of Retirees Describing Themselves as Voluntarily or Involuntarily Retired, by Age and Gender

	Age					
	51–54	*55–57*	*58–61*	*62–64*	*65–67*	*51–67*
MEN						
Forced to retire	65.4%	60.3%	49.2%	42.5%	32.4%	47.7%
Part forced, part wanted	3.2	2.8	7.1	8.1	8.8	6.8
Wanted to retire	31.5	36.9	43.6	49.3	58.9	45.6
Number of observations	78	149	396	263	137	1023
WOMEN						
Forced to retire	57.0	56.7	47.0	38.9	33.6	46.6
Part forced, part wanted	2.9	5.0	8.1	5.9	11.1	6.8
Wanted to retire	40.0	38.3	44.9	55.2	55.3	46.6
Number of observations	86	177	379	208	95	945
MEN AND WOMEN COMBINED						
Forced to retire	60.9	58.3	48.2	40.9	32.8	47.2
Part forced, part wanted	3.0	4.0	7.6	7.1	9.6	6.8
Wanted to retire	36.1	37.7	44.2	52.0	57.6	46.0
Number of observations	164	326	775	471	232	1968

Notes: The sample is restricted to men and women who describe themselves as partly or completely retired. Ages were measured the first time respondents described themselves as retired.
Source: Authors' tabulations from the 1992–98 waves of the Health and Retirement Study.

About 46 percent of those describing themselves as retired said they wanted to retire. The key question is how many of these retirees would still have wanted to retire if a greater array of opportunities had been available. About 1.9 million per year reduced their hours of work. With a greater array of opportunities, they may not have reduced hours as much. These numbers reflect the flows of people into total or partial retirement each year. The total population of those describing themselves as retired and age 53 to 70 in 2000 was 9.1 million. About 14.3 million worked fewer than twenty hours per week.

Although the precise implication of these numbers is somewhat murky, the big picture is clear. There does not seem to be a large enough population of older workers capable of working more hours to counter a large portion of the effects of the demographic trends described earlier, but there are hundreds of thousands whose welfare could be potentially improved by offering a wider array of employment choices.

Table 4. Ability to Reduce Hours of Work and Preferences for Reduced Work Schedules, 1998, among Full-Time Wage and Salary Workers Ages 51–65, by Personal and Job Characteristics

	Employer Would Allow Reduction in Hours	Worker Would Work Fewer Hours if Employer Permitted Reduction
ALL	26.4%	18.9%
MEN	27.2	16.0
WOMEN	25.3	22.4
AGE		
51–54	25.5	17.8
55–57	25.8	19.6
58–61	26.7	19.2
62–65	29.6	19.9
EDUCATION		
Did not complete high school	27.5	27.5
High school graduate	26.5	26.5
Some college	27.5	27.5
College graduate	25.2	25.2
PENSION PLAN PARTICIPATION		
No plan	34.3	17.8
Any plan	24.3	17.4
Defined benefit plan	20.5	18.4
Defined contribution plan	25.1	24.8
NUMBER OF OBSERVATIONS	3,944	2,920

Source: Authors' tabulations from the 1998 wave of the Health and Retirement Study.

It is also clear from the HRS that few have the opportunity for flexible arrangements. In 1998, only 26 percent of full-time employees age 51 through 65 worked for employers who would allow a reduction in hours (Table 4). Of all the older workers who left their jobs, including both retirees and those taking other jobs between 1992 and 2000 about 13 percent, or 1.5 million, said that they would have stayed on the job if their employer had permitted them to work fewer hours with correspondingly less pay (Table 5). On the other side, a substantial number (19 percent, or 2.1 million) working full-time in 1998 for employers that did not allow fewer hours said that they would choose to work fewer hours if per-

Table 5. Job Leavers Who Report That They Would Have Stayed on the Job if the Employer Had Permitted Them to Work Fewer Hours with Correspondingly Lower Pay

	Percentage of Job Leavers Who Would Have Stayed	Number of Job Leavers Who Would Have Stayed
ALL	12.6%	1,480,000
GENDER		
Male	12.4	722,000
Female	12.8	757,000
AGE		
53 to 54	10.1	102,000
55 to 57	14.2	300,000
58 to 61	11.5	360,000
62 to 64	12.3	307,000
65 to 67	12.3	196,000
68 to 70	15.1	83,000
71 and older	15.3	132,000

Note: Estimates are based on a sample of 4,054 respondents in the HRS who left their job between 1992 and 2000. Estimates refer to the last separation for those who left more than one job during the period.

mitted. Superficially, it appears as though many more workers would reduce hours than would increase them if given the opportunity. However, the two results reflect responses from very different samples. The latter looks at those working in 1998. The former looks at a sample of those who left work between 1992 and 2000. Moreover, there is no information on how much each group might have changed hours. It is interesting to note that, in general, older job leavers are somewhat more interested in working part time than younger job leavers. This may confirm the earlier conjecture that when younger workers leave a job, they are more likely to do so for health reasons.

A very different picture of older workers' tastes emerges from a Harris Poll survey that suggests that 95 percent of preretirees wish to continue working in some capacity even if they do not get paid very much. It is possible that their enthusiasm will wane as they look at how legal and institutional constraints have restricted the appeal of those opportunities that are available. On the other side, as rising numbers of workers begin retiring in the next decade, it may be in employers' interests to change compensation practices so as to provide a stronger economic incentive to continuing to participate in full-time work while they also encourage part-time work instead of full retirement.

Another crucial question is whether employers not offering reduced hours would do so if legal impediments were removed. It will be shown later that the most severe restraints are imposed on employers offering DB plans. It is interesting to note in Table 4 that only 21 percent of older workers are allowed reduced hours where there are DB plans, whereas 25 percent of workers under DC plans have this opportunity, and the portion rises to 34 percent where there is no plan.

How might these ratios change if barriers and incentives were changed? In the very short run, changes might be modest. However, as noted above, the pressure to allow more flexible arrangements will grow as baby boomers begin retiring. It would be unfortunate if employers were unable to respond to this pressure because of outdated legal and institutional restraints.

Institutional Impediments to Longer Work

Traditional defined benefit pension plans have become an endangered species in the private sector, but enough remain to affect the decisions of millions of workers. Moreover, they remain extremely important in the public sector. The traditional DB plan creates a powerful incentive for the employee to retire at a relatively early age—often younger than the official retirement age stated in the plan and younger than the early retirement age specified by Social Security. It is not absolutely certain why employers and employees have negotiated this design, but one can speculate that such plans were adopted when early retirement was considered to be a good thing in that it made room for younger employees working their way up the career ladder. The design also gives employers more flexibility to downsize during times of economic duress.

A number of research papers since about 1990 have quantified and modeled the incentive effects of the DB plans of large firms on the retirement decisions of older workers. The papers explore the costs and benefits of retiring within a certain age range, as seen by both the older worker and the firm. The findings generally suggest that large (Fortune 500) firms tend to set maximum pension payouts for long-term workers in their fifties and that the pension formulas penalize workers who remain on the job past this age range because the pension is not increased sufficiently to make up for the fact that workers will collect it for a shorter period of time.

Dulitzky (1999) surveys the literature on the effects of early retirement incentives. He examines studies that focus on DB and DC private pension plan rules, employer-provided healthcare, and Medicare provisions and eligibility ages. Kotlikoff and Wise, in a series of papers (1985, 1987, 1989), analyzed the incentive effects of Fortune 500 DB pension plan provisions and found a significant incentive to retire before age 65 on average because benefits for later retirees were not increased by an actuarially fair amount.

Stock and Wise (1990) and Lumsdaine, Stock, and Wise (1994) show further that the early retirement incentive inherent in private DB pension plans will outweigh the incentive to retire later provided by Social Security's scheduled increases in the normal retirement age. A Hewitt Associates study (1997) and William Mercer (2001) each found that firms had increasingly been paring back healthcare coverage for retired workers over age 65 and for early retirees; this type of shift might induce later retirement.

Note that by way of contrast with DB plans, employers in many DC plans now contribute a fairly constant percentage of cash wages to an employee's retirement account. In these cases, there would be little disincentive to retain older workers or for such workers to leave their jobs. These DC plans have grown in relative importance over time. In 1975, DC plans composed only 29 percent of all pension assets, but by 1997 they composed over 50 percent (Munnell, Sundén, and Lidstone 2002). However, workers tend to withdraw savings when moving from job to job: a study by the Employee Benefit Research Institute (1996) noted that of those pension plan participants removing assets from a previous employer's plan, 57 percent took the pension's accumulated value in cash when they changed jobs, while the remainder rolled the assets over into an individual retirement account (IRA) or another qualified plan. Thus, despite their improved work incentive structure, these plans have not yet proven to ensure saving and adequate resources in retirement for many middle-income households. Samwick and Skinner, however, simulated the experiences of workers through a career and concluded that DC plans may still be superior to DB plans simply because job changes often leave many workers without significant DB benefits in retirement (1998).

A more recent phenomenon has been the conversion of traditional DB plans to cash balance (CB) plans, which give a worker what is essentially a deposit into an account that interest or other earnings are credited to. The deposits are often proportional to wages. This particular structure is relatively new, but significant conversions have taken place in a number of firms. In incentive structure for workers, the CB plan is closer to a traditional DC plan even though it technically is a DB plan. The movement toward CB plans may represent, at least in part, a response to the set of incentives we examine below.

The measure of pension benefits that we use to examine retirement incentives in DB plans is the pension accrual, defined here to mean the change in the present value of all future pension benefits earned by staying on the job one more year.[4] We use a standard mortality table for determining life expectancy and, for these purposes, do not distinguish between men and women. To calculate the pension accrual, we also take as a typical worker, someone who starts on the job at age 25, 30, or 35. In many cases, the results are similar, so we do not present all of them. To take a very simple case of what one might expect, assume that a plan offers an employee a pension benefit based upon high salary times 2 percent times years of service, but with a maximum replacement rate of 80 percent (40 years times 2 percent). Suppose also that initial salary is $20,000 at age 25, rising to $44,160 in real terms at age 65, then steady in real terms thereafter. Then at an inflation rate of 4 percent, this worker would get a net additional lifetime benefit of about $1,200 if he or she worked an extra year from age 34 to 35, or about 5 percent of pay. Someone working from age 64 to 65 would receive about $15,000 in real dollars, or over one-third of his or her annual cash compensation, while someone working from age 65 to age 66 would receive a negative benefit equal to minus 80 percent of his or her prior year's salary, or about minus $35,000 in the absence of other provisions that tend to mitigate losses (Steuerle 1988).

In a typical DB plan of this type, there is a long accrual stage during which an additional year on the job not only increases pension benefits by adding an additional percentage of pay (here, 2 percent of final pay) but raises the value of all previous benefit accruals by a combination of real income growth and inflation. The two typically combine to create rapidly growing benefits with each additional year of work up to some maximum. But after one reaches the maximum number of years of service credited or the maximum replacement rate under the plan formula, then one or both of those types of accruals are limited. Moreover, if a worker forgoes annual benefit payments for one year because of staying on the job, then the additional accruals, if any, for the remaining years seldom make up for the fact that the worker receives benefits for one less year of his or her expected life.

Most plans are more complicated than this example. First, the benefit accrual is usually based upon several years of salary, not just one, as is assumed to simplify the example. Second, the percentage factor applied to average salary and years of service sometimes varies with years of service, and plans often provide reduced benefits for those who retire before the plan's normal retirement age. Finally, the plan sometimes contains additional provisions required by law that protect older workers from losing the economic value of their lifetime benefits (although the accrual rate may still be zero, even if no longer negative). The measures of pension accruals in the real plans that we model incorporate all of these details.[5]

We compute pension accruals for DB plans in both the private and public sectors. Data on private-sector plans come from the Pension Insurance Modeling System (PIMS). PIMS is a simulation model developed by the Pension Benefit Guaranty Corporation (PBGC), an agency of the federal government that insures private DB pension plans. It includes information on about six hundred single-employer DB plans. Because the goal of PIMS is to quantify the financial risk and uncertainty facing PBGC, PIMS oversamples large plans and underfunded plans. According to PBGC, the plans modeled in PIMS are somewhat more generous than the average DB pension plan. Although the dataset includes a wide range of plans currently in use, it contains very few plans from small employers and does not include any multi-employer plans.

We also collect information about pension plans provided to federal government workers and to public school teachers in California, Illinois, and New York. Federal workers hired since 1984 participate in the Federal Employees Retirement System (FERS), which provides pension benefits equal to 1 percent of average final pay for each year of government service. Final pay is defined as the highest three-year average salary. For workers who retire at age 62 or later with twenty or more years of service, the percentage factor increases to 1.1 percent of average final pay.[6] Pension benefits for Illinois teachers equal 2.2 percent of final average salary times years of service, while the percentage factor varies with retirement age for California teachers and by years of service for New York teachers. In all cases, we ignore additional benefits that might be provided by another DC plan such as the Thrift Savings Plan, which is available to federal government workers.

Almost regardless of the employer involved, we have found that traditional DB plans entail a strong hill-shaped curve—with the present value of the pension increasing along a slope that becomes increasingly steep and then, after peaking, suddenly falls rather dramatically, almost as if off of a cliff. They sometimes become negative.

Figure 1 shows pension accruals for different types of government plans. It covers the Federal Employee Retirement System and California, Illinois, and New York teachers' plans. In Figure 2, the calculations are for 340 salary-based DB plans in the private sector. For both these figures, we employed a common set of assumptions: that a worker begins at age 25 and that wages grow at some average rate determined for college-educated male workers as reported in Toder et al. (2002). The real interest rate was set at 3 percent and the inflation rate at 3.3 percent. We have also modeled these plans for workers starting at ages 30 and 35; because of many similarities, we briefly discuss, but do not graphically show, these alternative results.

Figure 1. Pension Accruals in Various Federal and State Systems

A. Pension Accruals in the Federal Employee Retirement System

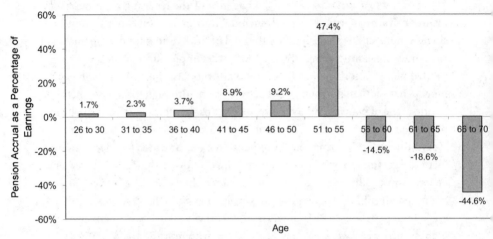

Note: Accrual estimates assume that workers join the plan at age 25 and leave at the age that maximizes the present discounted value of pension benefits (or age 70). The analysis assumes that wages grow at the average age-specific rate for college-educated male workers with DB plans as reported in Toder et al. (2002). The real interest rate is set at 3 percent and the inflation rate at 3.3 percent. Estimates exclude accruals from the Thrift Savings Plan.

B. Average Pension Accruals for California Teachers

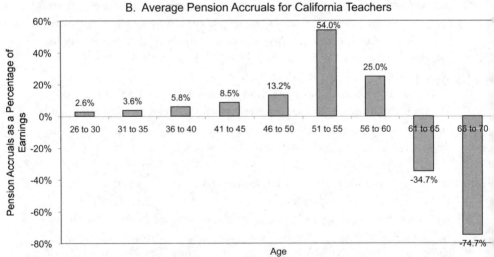

Note: Accrual estimates assume that workers join the plan at age 25 and leave at the age that maximizes the present discounted value of pension benefits (or age 70). The analysis assumes that wages grow at the average age-specific rate for college-educated male workers with DB plans as reported in Toder et al. (2002). The real interest rate is set at 3 percent and the inflation rate at 3.3 percent.

Figure 1. Pension Accruals in Various Federal and State Systems (*cont.*)

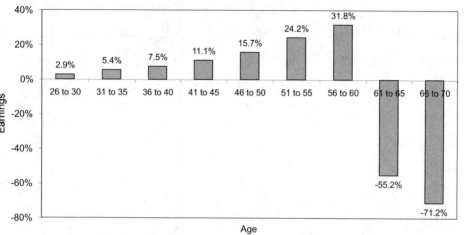

C. Average Pension Accruals for Illinois Teachers

Note: Accrual estimates assume that workers join the plan at age 25 and leave at the age that maximizes the present discounted value of pension benefits (or age 70). The analysis assumes that wages grow at the average age-specific rate for college-educated male workers with DB plans as reported in Toder et al. (2002). The real interest rate is set at 3 percent and the inflation rate at 3.3 percent.

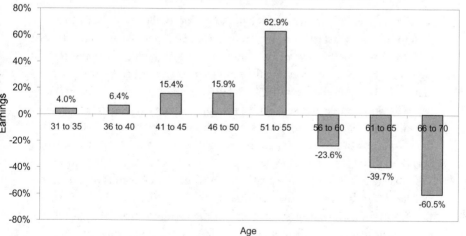

D. Average Pension Accruals for New York State Teachers

Note: Accrual estimates assume that workers join the plan at age 25 and leave at the age that maximizes the present discounted value of pension benefits (or age 70). The analysis assumes that wages grow at the average age-specific rate for college-educated male workers with DB plans as reported in Toder et al. (2002). The real interest rate is set at 3 percent and the inflation rate at 3.3 percent.

Figure 2. Average Accruals in Private DB Plans (For workers starting at age 25)

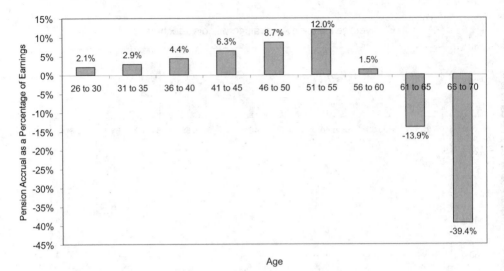

Age

Note: The analysis is based on a sample of 340 salary-based DB plans in the private sector. Accrual estimates assume that workers join the firm at age 25 and leave at the age that maximizes the present discounted value of pension benefits (or age 70). The analysis assumes that wages grow at the average age-specific rate for college-educated male workers with DB plans as reported in Toder et al. (2002). The real interest rate is set at 3 percent and the inflation rate at 3.3 percent. Estimates are weighted by firm size.

These types of plans often show a peaking of accrual rates in the 51 to 55 age span for the worker starting at age 25. In many plans, one can reach this type of peak by providing thirty years of service. Because of the rapidly rising costs of pension accruals, incentives for the employer to shed workers are especially high by this stage and even in the 46 to 50 age span.

Many workers may not start with a firm until a later age. Separate runs show a similar hill shape, but the peak accruals occur from about age 56 to 60 for the worker starting at age 30 and from about 61 to 65 for the worker starting at age 35.

On average in Figure 2, the peak frequently occurs after thirty years of service have been attained. However, this is not always the case. Figure 3 shows the distribution of peak ages of accrual for the various private plans for workers starting at age 25, confirming the overall pattern but showing some modest variations. Underlying these graphs is a set of assumptions that includes an increase in cash wages that reflects a rate of growth in productivity with time (as the economy becomes more productive) and with age. We assumed that real wages grow by about 5 percent per year for workers in their late 20s, by 3 percent for workers in their late 30s, and by less than 2 percent for workers in their

Figure 3. Distribution of the Age at which Pension Accruals Peak, for Private Salary-Based DB Plans

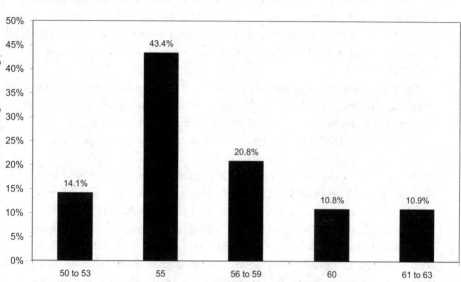

Note: The analysis is based on a sample of 340 salary-based DB plans in the private sector. Accrual estimates assume that workers join the firm at age 25 and leave at the age that maximizes the present discounted value of pension benefits (or age 70). The analysis assumes that wages grow at the average age-specific rate for college-educated male workers with DB plans as reported in Toder et al. (2002). The real interest rate is set at 3 percent and the inflation rate at 3.3 percent. In about 3 percent of plans, pension accruals peak at age 30, when benefits vest. These plans are excluded from the analysis. Estimates are weighted by firm size.

fifties, consistent with observed age-earnings profiles for workers with DB plans (Toder et al. 2002). The value of the accrual rate in a given plan formula in Figures 1 to 3 is measured as a proportion of a cash earnings or wage. For instance, if the cash wage doubles and the pension accrual (in dollars) doubles, then the accrual *rate* would have been a constant proportion of wages—much as a traditional DC plan might have provided. However, when the accrual rate is increasing, it means that the increase in pension benefits is proceeding faster than the increase in cash wages. In a sense, there is a multiplier effect that derives from the nature of the traditional DB formula: in addition to getting an increase in replacement rate, the higher wage in one year raises the base to which years of service and percentage replacement will apply.

We suggest that these descriptions of the traditional DB pension world illustrate that pay in the form of employee benefits is often related to age, independent of productivity. There is, however, one counterargument to address. Economic theory suggests that total compensation should be related to a worker's productivity. As workers gain experience and become more productive, their total compensation should go up. We reflected this in the assumption of different wage growth at different ages. Since DB pension benefits go up much faster than cash wages, one might be tempted to argue that there is a trade-off. The workers are willing to sacrifice some growth in cash wages for a disproportionate increase in pension benefits. Without this pension increase, cash wages would tend to rise faster.

The problem with that argument is that it still does not explain the current structure of incentives and pay. Three examples suffice to prove this point. First, if the goal is to increase pension compensation in precisely the fashion implied by these traditional DB plans, then why would the rate of noncash compensation be so heavily dependent upon the rate of inflation? Productivity and inflation are not directly related. Inflation will not affect the cash wages of, say, a 50-year-old *relative* to a 25-year-old. With the same DB plan, however, the relative accrual rate differs extraordinarily among ages simply because of the rate of inflation. For example, in the simple example provided in the beginning, where a 35-year-old achieved an annual accrual of about $1,200 at a 4 percent inflation rate, the accrual rate would be only about $400 at a rate of 8 percent but over $3,000 if the inflation rate were zero—all for the same given real cash wage (see Steuerle 1988). The extreme sensitivity to inflation can be understood even more easily by imagining a vested 35-year-old switching jobs. At retirement, he or she would get a right to a certain pension from the original employer measured in nominal dollars. The real value of that pension at the time of retirement would depend on the intervening inflation rate.

Second, to believe that the pension compensation scheme exactly matches changes in productivity not reflected in cash wages suggests that this productivity somehow drops off when workers hit some peak, such as thirty years on the job. The negative rate of accrual in many teachers' plans implies that in one year, they have moved from being at peak rates of improvement in productivity to declines of very large magnitudes.

Finally, as we shall show below, the rate of pension accrual differs quite strongly for new employees of different ages who work the same job and gain the same number of years of experience. Moreover, in this case, the age pattern of benefits differs again. Here, accrual rates for pension benefits for, say, five-year workers increase rather consistently with age up to an age like 65 even though for long-term workers we found that accrual rates usually fall toward zero past an age like 55.

In sum, it is indeed possible that some firms might want to pay out a higher proportion of total compensation in the form of pension benefits at later ages. But traditional DB plans operate in such an arbitrary fashion that they would not achieve this result very well, if at all. Again, they might serve the firm well for an average worker, at an average starting age, at an average rate of inflation, at an average rate of wage growth, and with a significant number of years on the job. But few people met such average conditions in the past, and the labor market is so vastly changed today that the plans often don't work even for that illustrative average worker.

Next, we need to consider the cost of health benefits. For our purposes here, we used a national dataset on health expenditures—the 1996 Medical Expenditure Panel Survey (MEPS), as further developed by John Holahan of the Urban Institute. With this dataset, Holahan was able to calculate average private health insurance costs by age for a worker who had year-round, full-time employment. As can be seen in Chart A of Figure 4, *private* insurance health costs rise significantly, from between $500 to $1,000 for workers age 20 to 40 to over $1,500 for workers age 50 to 54 to close to $2,000 for most workers over age 55. Interestingly, these private insurance costs seem to level out by age 55. (The data show a decline for workers age 65 to 69 that may be due to sample size.) Chart B shows *total* health expenditures per worker, reflecting a more pronounced trend of rising health costs with age. Total worker health costs vary between $1,000 and $1,500 for workers age 20 to 44 but shoot up to $2,700 for the 55 to 59 age band and peak at $3,500 for the 70 to 74 age band. There is a slight dip in the 60 to 64 age band, but again sampling issues and other factors may be at work here. The calculations are for the worker only; we do not analyze dependent benefits, in part because of the difficulty of attributing costs for many two-earner couples who are dually insured by both their employers.

Comparing the two parts of Figure 4 suggests that total insured plus uninsured health costs do not level out in the same way as the private insurance costs but continue to rise after individuals are in their mid 50s. After the mid 50s, workers tend to cover a greater share of these expenses through means other than private insurance.

Complicating our health story is a federal law requiring that employers providing health insurance to their workers generally be the primary health insurer for workers 65 and over, thus displacing Medicare benefits to which individuals are otherwise entitled. Making Medicare the primary payer could significantly reduce the cost of employing people 65 and over at modest cost to the government. However, the cost is low partly because so few people work at 65 and above. In 2000, only 24 percent of those age 65 to 74 were in the labor force (Fullerton and Toossi 2001).

Making Medicare the primary payer is equivalent to eliminating an excise tax on workers 65 and older. Employment, wages, and profits would all be expected to increase. Of course, the added cost to the Medicare program would

Figure 4. Per Worker Healthcare Expenditures

A. Per Worker Healthcare Expenditures Paid by Private Insurance

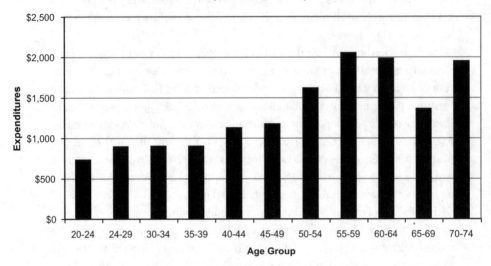

B. Total Per Worker Healthcare Expenditures

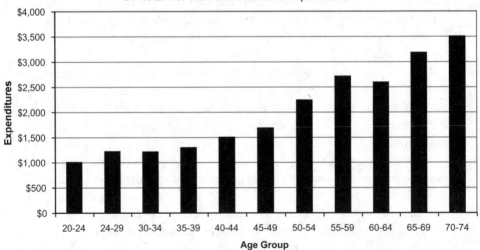

Source: 1996 Medicare Expenditure Panel Survey.

have to be financed with higher taxes, spending cuts in other programs, or an increased deficit. Economists generally believe that a reduction in the cost of fringe benefits results in a wage increase of a similar amount because of a belief that the aggregate labor supply is relatively inelastic. That may not be true, however, for the supply of workers age 65 and above. Without further research, it is not known how the benefits resulting from this proposal would be divided among increased employment, higher wage rates, and increased profits.

A final impediment to working longer is the precedent of Social Security and Medicare eligibility. Private plans build both their normal and early retirement incentives around the ages at which people begin to retire on Social Security, almost independent of individuals' productivity and capacity to work. As public benefits have grown with time, moreover, the incentive to retire has increased (see, e.g., Favreault and Johnson 2002; Johnson 2001).

While the normal retirement age for Social Security is gradually being increased to 67 for those born after 1955, neither the eligibility age of 65 for Medicare nor the early retirement age of 62 has been changed. Today, some 90 percent of workers have filed for Social Security benefits by the time they reach 65. Under Social Security, moreover, if beneficiaries earn more than a fairly low threshold between age 62 and the full retirement age, they are hit quickly with reduced benefits.[7] This remaining earnings test for workers age 62 to the full retirement age sends strong signals to beneficiaries and designers of pension plans. It sets a social norm as to the proper time to retire. The earnings test for workers beyond the "normal" retirement age has recently been eliminated, thus removing an important disincentive to work among those few still working beyond that age.

We have examined the incentives for older workers to leave their jobs and for employers to try to shed them, but we must also discuss barriers to hiring older workers from the outside. One way of examining this issue is to take a group of workers who are assumed to be equal in all respects except age and who apply for the same job paying the same cash wage. We then want to compare the cost of hiring workers who are different ages according to the types of employee benefits offered.

Figure 5 shows the amount of accrued pension benefits for the average worker who works in the pension plans in the PIMS dataset for exactly five years. We use a five-year minimum period to ensure that everyone is at least vested in his or her benefits. Even with vesting, it is quite clear that the younger worker is very cheap relative to the older worker. Someone who works from age 25 to age 30 with a plan accrues very little in the way of pension benefits—an average of

Figure 5. Average DB Pension Accruals in the Private Sector During the First Five Years of Service, by Start Age

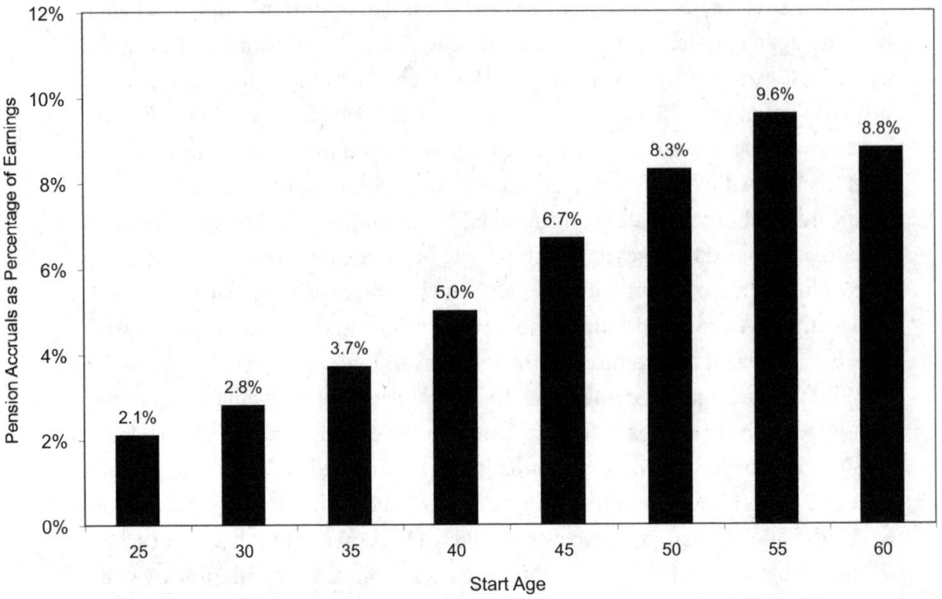

Note: The analysis is based on a sample of 340 salary-based DB plans in the private sector. Accrual estimates assume that workers leave the firm at the age that maximizes the present discounted value of pension benefits, or age 70, whichever comes first. The analysis also assumes that all workers receive a starting annual salary of $35,000 that grows at 5 percent per year. The real interest rate is set at 3 percent and the inflation rate at 3.3 percent. Estimates are weighted by firm size.

2.1 percent of pay in the 340 DB plans examined. When a young worker leaves a firm, the value of any accrued pension benefits must be discounted by the many years until retirement. That is, the "nominal" value of annual benefit to be paid—for example, the additional percentage of some average salary that would be available upon retirement—is the same for the worker who starts at 25 and the one who starts at 55. But the 55-year-old worker might be eligible to receive the benefits immediately at 60, whereas the 25-year-old who leaves the firm at age 30 must wait another 30 years to get that same annual benefit, which increases with neither inflation nor real income growth over that time period. The 65-year-old worker, however, also gets a raw deal: by the time she vests, she has fewer years of life expectancy under which to receive the same annual benefit as the 60-year-old hired at the same job at the same pay. The employer may also be less willing to pay the extra health costs for an older new employee than he would for a long-term employee, because the latter has considerable experience working for the firm (and that experience may offset the effect of rising health costs with age).

Legal and Regulatory Impediments to Phased Retirement

The previous section examined various barriers against keeping older workers employed either on a full- or part-time basis. This section focuses more narrowly on the legal and regulatory impediments limiting the ability of employers and employees to negotiate flexible work arrangements involving less than full-time employment. Such arrangements may require developing a special benefits plan, but such plans are controlled by a complex combination of laws and regulations.

Because they receive special tax benefits, employee benefit plans are subject to special rules in the Internal Revenue Code. In addition, they are generally also subject to federal labor law, much of which arose out of the Employee Retirement Income Security Act (ERISA), whose purpose is to secure the benefits promised employees in employer-sponsored plans. Nothing in ERISA or the tax code requires employers to establish benefit plans or mandates the types of benefits those plans must offer. But both statutes play a critical role in structuring the plans of employers who choose to do so. Not all plans and not all employers are subject to the full array of regulation. The plans sponsored by state and local governments and other public authorities are exempt from ERISA, as well as many important tax-code rules, and are regulated instead by state law (ERISA § 4[b]). A second exception applies to the type of plan. As a general rule, plans that pay health insurance, life insurance, or similar benefits— so-called welfare benefits—are subject to much less regulation and scrutiny than plans that pay retirement benefits. Employers have much more discretion over which employees will be covered and what benefits will be offered in welfare plans.

The opposite is true of retirement plans sponsored by private employers. Their regulatory structure reflects a philosophy that employers should be required to make their plans as uniform as possible and include a broad group of employees. A particular plan must satisfy complicated mathematical nondiscrimination tests. The rationale for these rules originates in the Internal Revenue Code and reflects the sentiment that the tax benefits available through retirement plans should not disproportionately benefit higher-paid employees.[8] Through the passage of ERISA in 1974 and subsequent legislation, benefits law has increasingly required employers to adhere to rules promoting uniformity and standardization in the treatment of employees and types of benefits offered. Therefore, as a general rule, employers find it all but impossible to create benefits specifically for special groups of workers—whether they are older workers, younger workers, or any other category of workers.

The rules also restrict the ability to withdraw pension funds while doing any work for the employer before the plan's normal retirement age. This is understandable since pensions are supposed to be for retirees, but this can limit the ability of a person to work part-time while drawing a partial pension. Profit-sharing plans are somewhat less restrictive with regard to withdrawal rights. This point is elaborated in our complete report.

Phased retirement programs will inevitably be subject to an additional overlay of regulation under the Age Discrimination in Employment Act (ADEA). From a phased retirement perspective, the ADEA is particularly problematic. It is a highly specialized area of labor law within the family of employment discrimination statutes and is both substantively and procedurally quite different from the tax and labor law familiar to benefits professionals. In addition, it is ambiguous and not well tested when compared to its counterparts in the tax code and ERISA. Its application to employee benefit plans is just beginning to be fleshed out by the courts as older employees begin to assert age discrimination claims against perceived benefit cutbacks.

The ADEA forbids employers from discriminating against workers age 40 and older with respect to the "compensation, terms, conditions, or privileges of employment, because of an individual's age" or "to limit, segregate, or classify . . . employees in any way which would deprive or tend to deprive any individual of employment opportunities or otherwise adversely affect his status as an employee because of such individual's age" (ADEA § 4[a]). It applies to public and private employers with at least twenty employees. Under a recent Supreme Court case, however, state governments are immune from suits by individual employees under the ADEA (*Kimel v. Florida Board of Regents* 2000).

The ADEA's primary influence on benefits law to date has been to eliminate rules related to chronological age that used to limit older workers' participation in benefit plans. It does, however, permit a limited number of age distinctions in employee benefits plans.[9] For example, a retirement plan may set a minimum age for early or normal retirement benefits, and DB plans are permitted to pay subsidized early retirement benefits as well as Social Security supplements (ADEA § 4[l][1]). In addition, employers have a defense against age discrimination claims when their actions can be justified by the terms of a bona fide employee benefit plan (ADEA § 4[f][2][B]). This defense is available, provided that the plan satisfies an "equal cost or equal benefit" standard in the benefits paid to older workers participants at the later of age 65 (ADEA § [4][f][2][B][i]). The Equal Employment Opportunity Commission (EEOC), the agency with regulatory authority over the ADEA, however, has taken the position that the equal-cost defense does not apply to retirement plans (EEOC 2000).

The full implications of this EEOC ruling are not clear, and, in general, there continues to be considerable legal uncertainty surrounding the ADEA and its application to employee benefit plans. For example, the ADEA does not elaborate on the meaning of "a bona fide employee benefit plan." It is also silent on when a benefits plan that satisfies all tax-code and ERISA requirements may violate the ADEA's prohibition against age discrimination.

Until there is more guidance on the extent to which benefit plans that satisfy the tax code and ERISA must be changed to comply with the ADEA, employers will be reluctant to adopt phased retirement plans, largely because of their legal exposure. In the first major test of age discrimination in pension plans, the U.S. District Court for the Southern District of Indiana held that the benefit accrual rates in one employer's CB plan did not constitute age discrimination (*Eaton v. Onan Corporation* 2000).[10] The recent adverse ruling regarding the IBM pension plan from the Southern District of Illinois, however, indicates this issue is far from settled (*Cooper v. IBM Personal Pension Plan* 2003). The Pension Protection Act of 2006 helped protect CB plans, but it is not clear how the legislation will eventually be interpreted. Resolving this issue is important because the economic stakes are high for both employees and employers. The potential damages in a case of age discrimination are very significant. In addition to paying employees the benefits they should have received as is required by ERISA, an employer may, under the ADEA, also be required to pay compensatory damages for mental anguish and inconvenience as well as punitive damages for intentional discrimination, attorneys' fees, and court costs.

One way to illustrate the legal difficulties facing phased retirement programs is to look at a precedent involving nearly identical legal issues. During the recession of the early 1990s, employers wanted to offer early retirement incentives to encourage workers to leave voluntarily through retirement rather than involuntarily through layoffs. These incentives were often structured as "windows," or short-term programs; and employers wanted to have the flexibility to decide which employees would be eligible for the programs. The benefits package often included both enhanced retirement benefits and retiree health benefits.

The legal issues confronting these plans were extremely difficult. Under pension law, how could a plan make a short-term program available to a select group of employees? On its face, this seemed to violate long-standing pension rules promoting uniform and standard benefits and preventing employer discretion. In practice, these programs would probably violate nondiscrimination rules as well because older, and presumably higher-paid, employees within the plan population could receive more generous benefits. Under the ADEA, how could an employer offer benefits that could be greater for younger workers than older workers in the targeted group?

In the end, the legal issues were so complex that they could be resolved only through new legislation and regulatory action. The IRS added language to its nondiscrimination regulations setting standards for special early retirement window benefits (Treasury Regulations § 1.401[a][4]-3[f][4] and 1.410[b]-5[d][7]). The ADEA was amended to permit certain early retirement programs and waivers of benefits in those programs (ADEA § 4[f][2][B][ii]). In addition, the ADEA was amended to permit waivers of rights to sue provided they (1) are part of a written agreement specifically listing the claims to be waived; (2) are effective only as to claims available before the waiver is signed; (3) include additional consideration for the employee; and (4) advise the employee to consult with an attorney, give at least 45 days to review the offer, and provide specific information about the program, including eligibility and time limits as well as the job titles and ages of employees covered by the program and the ages of similarly situated employees who are ineligible (ADEA § 7[f]). The compromise resolution of the legal issues surrounding early retirement programs is neither elegant nor simple. It has not completely eliminated litigation because there are sometimes allegations of age discrimination, but the law has generally worked in that early retirement incentive programs are now commonplace and accepted by employers, employees, and courts.

Phased Retirement

As shown earlier and confirmed by surveys, (AARP 1999; Mercer 2001; Rappaport 2001; Watson Wyatt Worldwide 2000a; Watson Wyatt Worldwide 2000b; Huchens and Chen, chapter 4 in this volume) few employers offer phased retirement, although large numbers seem to be interested. The apparent reluctance of employers to craft programs to ease the transition to retirement for current employees has many possible explanations. A large percentage of employers who reported not having a program in the Mercer study felt that phased retirement was not a priority for them (65 percent) or their employees (11 percent). Only 4 percent cited legal complexity as a deterrent. But the numbers alone do not give a true picture. The majority of these same employers do offer phased retirement opportunities—just not through a plan. They prefer to make individual retirement arrangements for selected employees on an ad hoc basis.

From the employer's perspective, this strategy makes a great deal of sense. It achieves the goal of many employers (49 percent in the Watson Wyatt Worldwide survey and 30 percent in the Mercer survey) to retain employees with specialized skills and expertise. It provides an employer with an opportunity to be creative when deciding how the work arrangement should be structured, which employees should be eligible, and how employees will be paid. It is a perfectly legal way to avoid the hassles of a more structured program—but only up to a point. The ADEA, the tax code, and ERISA regulate only employee benefit *plans,* so once an employer arrangement qualifies as a plan it must satisfy all the relevant rules.

Consequently, individual arrangements are stopgap measures at best. If an employer limits phased retirement opportunities to only a few employees, the plan cannot be challenged successfully. Even if the employer chooses only highly-paid executives, individual arrangements are permissible. But if the number of employees grows and the employment arrangements are sufficiently similar, a series of individual arrangements will at some point become a plan. Unfortunately, there are currently no clear legal rules on when a series of informal arrangements becomes a plan. Most employers will not even be aware of their potential exposure until they are sued by an employee.

When individual arrangements are no longer practical, what is the next best strategy for an employer? The survey data indicate that many employers take the first step toward a formal phased retirement program by offering reduced hours or work schedules to current employees. This type of arrangement is unlikely to be termed a "plan" under either ERISA or the tax code because neither law regulates the work hours of employees. But merely offering part-time work would rarely be satisfactory for most employers or most employees. It provides employers nothing extra to offer the employees they most wish to retain and is likely to cause employees to lose some of the welfare and pension benefits they might otherwise receive.

As a practical matter, the only feasible strategy for employers who would like to retain large numbers of employees through phased retirement is to create a broad-based formal program. There are, however, severe limits on the restructuring of existing pension arrangements, and the employer may have to resort to offering more generous cash compensation that is immediately taxable.

While it may be difficult to design a plan that satisfies tax rules, ERISA, and the ADEA, it is not impossible. However, an employer going to the trouble to design such a plan may not have any recruits because of the previously discussed work disincentives inherent in the firm's DB pension plan. It is tempting to consider a shift to a CB plan under these circumstances, but these are under political and legal attack. A firm starting with a DC plan will find it much easier to recruit employees for partial retirement plans, although there are still some restrictions.

Many employers have found (or believe they have found) a satisfactory alternative to the difficulties presented by formal programs for current employees. They just hire retirees—their own and those of other companies. Some 60 percent of employers in the Mercer study, as well as those interviewed by AARP, reported a policy of rehiring retirees. Hiring retirees as consultants—without benefits—is also common. On its face, hiring retirees seems an obvious solution to the problems associated with current retirees. It gives employers an opportunity to attract workers with specialized skills and expertise, usually on a flexible, as-needed basis. It also appears to provide employers with the ability to negotiate employment arrangements that provide flexibility in determining compensation and benefits costs. All in all, it is a win-win situation—but generally only if the retirees are from some other company. For many employers, hiring former employees is hardly trouble-free. The type of arrangement—whether the retiree is hired as an employee or a consultant—largely determines the scope of the difficulties.

When retirees are hired as employees by their former company, the problematic issue is the employer's benefit plans. Again, DB plans are the primary culprits. DB plans may not pay benefits before termination of employment or attainment of normal retirement age. Many employers adopt a popular strategy to satisfy this rule—the "retire-rehire" scenario. In this case, employees who would like to begin receiving retirement benefits while continuing to work "resign" or "retire" but are soon rehired—sometimes the next day—by their former employer. The law is very clear that employees must truly terminate employment to be entitled to retirement benefits from pension plans before the normal retirement age. But the law is very unclear about what constitutes a termination of employment that satisfies the rule.[11] In many cases, employers, particularly small employers, are unaware of this technical legal requirement. Others take advantage of the absence of clear guidelines and bestow retiree status liberally. There is little risk of detection and even less risk of enforcement. On the other hand, the penalty for being caught—possible plan disqualification and loss of tax benefits for all plan participants—is severe. Therefore, many employers are more cautious and require a waiting period before former employees are rehired. In the Mercer study, employers who rehire their own retirees reported requiring a mean waiting period of 5.2 months. Although this is a judgment call, most pension experts would agree that this waiting period would probably satisfy the rule, provided that it was not part of a clearly prearranged agreement.

The retire-rehire problem obviously applies to only an employer's former employees. All retirees hired as employees, however, may pose problems for an employer's benefit plans. Many employers would like to restrict participation by retirees. This is relatively easy to do in welfare plans if employers are careful either to define the category of eligible employees to exclude retirees, where possible, or to keep their hours worked below the minimum required, generally twenty hours a week, for participation. A 1,000-hour-a-year threshold for participation applies in most retirement plans but is generally effective with respect to only "new" retiree employees. Many employers prefer to avoid the retiree benefits eligibility issue entirely by hiring them through consulting contracts. A consultant is an independent contractor, not an employee, and is therefore ineligible for employee benefits programs. This solution works well from a legal perspective, provided that the retiree actually is an independent contractor. The difference between an independent contractor and an employee from a legal perspective is a judgment call; but, under IRS regulations, a very important test is whether the individual sets the conditions—how, when, and where—of his or her work.[12]

Since the early 1980s, public-sector employers such as public colleges and universities and offices of state government have been developing phased retirement programs with innovative benefits features. These employers are not subject to the legal constraints of ERISA and much of tax law affecting private employers so they have much more flexibility in creating retirement arrangements.[13] They have long been aware of the problems posed by an aging workforce because their employees tend to remain employees for a long time. State and local governments provide a wide range of benefits to their employees on a uniform basis. Many of those benefits—such as healthcare—continue for retirees. So, state and local governments already have in place many of the components of a phased retirement program that private employers typically do not. But state and local governments shared one disadvantage with the private sector—the disincentives to continued employment contained in their DB plans. Taking advantage of their exemption as public employers from many of the more complicated tax and ERISA rules governing benefit plans, they developed a plan, typically called a deferred retirement option plan (DROP), which adds pension incentives to their phased retirement programs (Burley and Eichstadt 1998; Calhoun 2000).

A DROP is a DB plan that has a special DC feature for employees who work past the normal retirement age. Employees usually cease accruing benefits under the DB plan on a specified date when their benefit is frozen. While they continue to work, the pension they would otherwise have received (if they had retired) is credited to a special account and earns interest either at an amount stated in the plan or based on the interest earned by the plan as a whole. Many DROPs require employer-employee contributions to the account as well. When the employees retire, they begin receiving annuity payments calculated on the basis of their frozen benefit under the DB plan. They are also entitled to receive their DROP account funds, which can be paid in a lump sum or installments or used to purchase a larger annuity.

A DROP offers several advantages to employees. Most importantly, it provides them an opportunity to earn additional pension credits in the form of interest after they have "maxed out" under the standard DB plan formula. At the same time, they continue to be guaranteed their lifetime monthly income from the DB plan. One drawback to a DROP is that it does not provide any pension income while the employee continues to work.

Tax law and ERISA have a number of provisions that prevent private-sector employers from creating DROPs. For example, DROPs are usually unable to satisfy rules on coverage and discrimination because they are not usually available to a broad group of employees. Various other tax rulings have increased the cost of DROPs to private employers. Because of such factors, DROPs are not available in the private sector as a practical matter.

Institutions of higher education have been leaders in developing phased retirement programs, offering special programs designed for faculty members who have tenure. When the ADEA eliminated mandatory retirement in 1987, it temporarily provided an exemption for tenured faculty members at academic institutions. Prohibitions against mandatory retirement for faculty did not become effective until 1994; until that time, mandatory retirement at age 70 continued to be permissible. When that exemption expired, the academic community became concerned that many faculty would wish to continue working past age 70. If this occurred, it would hamper their ability to hire new faculty and personnel costs would rise. At the same time, many institutions were concerned about the loss of large numbers of faculty that would soon be reaching retirement age. The higher education community became interested in formulating a more orderly transition to retirement for its faculty. At the same time, it felt constrained by legal uncertainties about the scope of the ADEA (and its early retirement exception) and therefore was unwilling to create programs without some protection against age discrimination claims.

The result was the Higher Education Amendments of 1998 to the ADEA, which created a safe harbor for age-based faculty retirement incentive programs. The safe harbor permits additional voluntary benefits to be paid, even though based on age, as a retirement incentive, provided that (1) the employer is an institution of higher education, (2) only employees with unlimited tenure are eligible, (3) the benefits are payable upon voluntary retirement, (4) no other age-based reductions or elimination of benefits occurs, (5) the supplemental benefits are in addition to preexisting retirement or severance benefits, and (6) eligible faculty have 180 days to elect to participate. A recent study by the American Association of University Professors of some 1,400 public and private colleges and universities indicates that the ADEA safe harbor has been extended to phased retirement programs (Ehrenberg and Rizzo 2001). These help faculty make the transition into retirement through part-time work as well as by continuing part-time work after formal retirement. About a quarter of the private institutions in the study reported having phased retirement programs.

Unlike their counterparts among both private and public employers, these plans provide *enhanced* benefits for phased retirement, rather than just a pro rata portion of a standard benefits package or the reduced benefits offered to all part-time employees. In other respects, these programs are similar to those available elsewhere. Some 75 percent establish a minimum age for eligibility, with age 55 being most common, and some 25 percent also establish a maximum age, usually between 65 and 70. Another 75 percent require minimum years of service—between ten and twenty years—for eligibility. Many plans require participants to agree to relinquish tenure and agree to retire fully at specified dates. Institutions with DC plans are twice as likely to offer phased retirement programs as institutions with DB plans. In part, this reflects the difficulties that even these institutions have with providing incentives for continued work through DB plans.

Academic phased retirement programs are quite different from those available in the corporate world. For example, they represent the only phased retirement model explicitly authorized by law, even though they are, legally speaking, just a special case of early retirement programs. In exchange for this legal certainty, academic employers are required to provide enhanced benefits to phased retirees. Employees are required to receive full disclosure about the program's features. The model now in place has many features the corporate employer might find attractive. All in all, it seems to provide a careful balancing of the needs of both employers and employees.

POLICY CONCLUSIONS

In examining institutional barriers to longer work, we noted that traditional DB pension plans are often structured in a way that provides strong incentives to retire before the normal retirement age specified by the plan (usually 65) and, for long-term employees, before the early retirement age specified by Social Security. Traditional DB plans are gradually disappearing in the private sector, but they still affect many workers. It is legally difficult to remove early retirement incentives from traditional DB plans, and there are no clear alternatives for employers. Many convert to a CB format, but this is controversial because some employers have attempted to use conversions to save money. Even in the case of a cost-neutral conversion, such plans tend to be more beneficial to younger and short-term workers than to older, long-time employees. Consequently, it is difficult to structure them in a way that is not vulnerable to accusations of age discrimination, and some confusion has been created by courts that have offered contradictory opinions. As noted earlier, as this volume goes to press, Congress is considering legislation that would clearly allow CB plans, but it is far from certain that the legislation will be enacted. Another alternative could be to encourage employers to add special formulas or accrual rates to existing DB plans for continued work past the normal retirement age. But this raises cost and age-discrimination issues that need to be explored. A third alternative would enable employers to create special plans, such as the DROP plans available in the public sector that reward work beyond retirement while minimizing the regulatory burden of employers.

Another barrier to employment at older ages is health costs. This will continue absent a radical reform in our overall health system, and radical reforms raise controversial issues that go far beyond the scope of this chapter. A minor policy change would, however, be helpful to those 65 and over. We should return to a system in which Medicare is the primary payer for the costs of employees covered by employer health insurance.

Several regulatory changes could be made that would clarify some ambiguities in current policy. We noted that legal barriers to flexible employment arrangements for older employees were greatly reduced when someone was hired from outside the firm, and that could be accomplished by a retire-rehire arrangement where an employee was separated from the firm temporarily. The IRS has never defined what constitutes a true separation, however, and practices vary from firm to firm. It would be helpful to have a clear definition of "separation."

Part-time work is also inhibited by DB pensions where the level is determined by average earnings in the last few years of a person's career. Regulations should be drafted to clarify techniques for computing earnings while working part-time that do not harm a worker by greatly reducing his or her final pension.

The inability to draw anything from a pension fund before the normal retirement age while still working also inhibits arrangements allowing part-time work. (Profit-sharing plans are an exception.) Changing this policy raises a number of complex issues. Allowing partial payment might encourage reductions in hours that leave the employee with inadequate earnings and ultimately with an inadequate pension. The issue involves striking a balance between paternalism and flexibility. We make no recommendation on this point but believe that it should be considered further.

The policy options discussed above would have relatively minor effects. Their main advantage is that most could be accomplished quickly. In the longer run, more fundamental changes are required. Tax law, ERISA, and the ADEA should be amended simultaneously to explicitly authorize phased retirement programs and then to explicitly describe plans that are acceptable, thus providing a safe harbor allowing employers to protect themselves against litigation by employees. The DROP plans in place in the state and local sectors and the partial-retirement plans deemed acceptable for academics could serve as precedents. The new law would require full disclosure to employees regarding the attributes of the new plans.

We believe that changes of this type would benefit both employees and employers without significantly limiting the rights of those employees genuinely suffering age discrimination. It is true that DROP plans and the special arrangements now offered to academics are sometimes used to "buy off" employees who are no longer productive. That is to say, employees are induced to take early retirement and to announce a date certain for full retirement. In most cases, employees enter such arrangements voluntarily. If they were harassed into accepting such a deal, they would still have recourse according to the ADEA.

If more flexible arrangements were made available to the entire labor force, we would hope that the additional opportunities to transition more gradually from full-time work to full retirement would increase the supply of labor hours. As noted earlier, increased flexibility would also allow greater movement from full- to part-time employment. Which effect would predominate is unknowable unless we try it. It seems somewhat more certain that the welfare of both employers and employees would be enhanced.

Notes

1. The fertility rate is defined as births per woman during childbearing years.

2. The labor force participation rate for older women has been on an upward trend, mainly because women of all ages have been seeking work in greater numbers.

3. Some may have described themselves as being retired in both 1998 and 2000, even though they worked some hours in both years.

4. The meaning of the term "pension accrual" as used in this chapter is based upon but different from the term "accrued benefit" found under ERISA. Under ERISA, an accrued benefit is the value of a participant's earned benefit under a defined benefit plan at a particular point in time expressed in nominal dollars as a stream of income beginning at normal retirement age. Once the accrued benefit has been vested, its nominal value

can generally not be lost. In our model, accrued benefits are converted into pension accruals to indicate the difference in the economic value of a particular accrued benefit at different points in time.

5. The model does not take into account the effect of the suspension of benefit rules found in ERISA §203(a)(3)(B) on the benefits of workers who continue to work past normal retirement age.

6. FERS also includes a DC component, the Thrift Savings Plan, which allows workers to make tax-deferred contributions to a retirement savings account, with matching contributions from the government.

7. An actuarial adjustment makes up for benefits lost to the earnings test, but it is not quite fair considering taxes (Steuerle and Bakija 1994).

8. These rules were first enacted in the Revenue Act of 1942 in an effort to ensure that a plan would cover a reasonable proportion (a "good group") of an employer's workforce and would not skew its benefits or contributions to owners, executives, and other highly-paid employees. These rules have been elaborated upon and increasingly tightened in subsequent amendments to the tax code.

9. Many of the changes made by the ADEA to benefit law are incorporated into both the tax code and ERISA. Because the IRS, rather than the Department of Labor, typically has jurisdiction over the ADEA–related rules, they will be discussed as tax code rules.

10. Despite a favorable ruling in litigation, the Onan Corporation agreed to pay plan participants $23 million to settle the lawsuit (Purcell 2003, n. 34).

11. There is little IRS guidance on this point. Its most complete explanation can be found in a relatively obscure document, General Counsel Memorandum 38924 (July 26, 1990). This document discusses the legal difference between the terms "separation from service" for purposes of making pension distributions and "separation from the service," a term used to define a lump sum for purposes of obtaining favorable tax treatment for a distribution.

12. In Revenue Ruling 87–41 (1987), the IRS issued a list of twenty "factors" that are used to determine whether an individual is an employee or an independent contractor.

13. While exempt from much of federal law governing employee benefits, public employers are subject to state statutes that define the benefits they offer. Once implemented, these plans can be difficult to change because it generally requires an act of the legislature to do so.

References

AARP (American Association of Retired Persons). 1999. "Easing the Transition: Phased and Partial Retirement Programs: Highlights." Washington, D.C.: AARP.

Age Discrimination in the Employment Act of 1967 (ADEA). U.S. Public Law 90-202. 90th Congress, 2nd session, 15 December 1967.

Burley, Cindy, and Kent Eichstadt. 1998. "Deferred Retirement Option Programs." *The NAPPA Report.* 12(1).

Burtless, Gary, and Joseph F. Quinn. 2000. "Retirement Trends and Policies to Encourage Work Among Older Americans." Boston College Working Papers in Economics 436. Chestnut Hill, MA: Boston College Department of Economics. http://fmwww.bc. edu/EC-P/WP436.pdf (Accessed April 9, 2002).

Calhoun, Carol V. 2000. "Deferred Retirement Option Plans ('DROP Plans')." *National Council on Teacher Retirement, Sacramento.* http://cvcalhoun.com/affiliate.html. (Accessed May 19, 2002).

Cooper vs. IBM Personal Pension Plan, 274 F. Supp.2d 1010 (S. D. Ill. 2003).

Cutler, D., J. Poterba, L. Sheiner, and L. Summers. 1990. "An Aging Society: Opportunity or Challenge?" *Brookings Papers on Economic Activity.* Washington, DC: The Brookings Institute. 1: 1–73.

Dulitzky, Daniel. 1999. "Incentives for Early Retirement in Private Pension and Health Insurance Plans." The Retirement Project Brief No. 3. Washington, DC: The Urban Institute. http://www.urban.org/retirement/briefs/3/brief_3.html.

Eaton v. Onan Corporation, No. IP 97-814-C H/G, U.S. District Court, Southern District of Indiana, September 29, 2000.

Employee Retirement Income Security Act of 1974 (ERISA). U.S. Public Law 93-406. 93rd Congress, 2nd session, 2 September 1974.

Equal Employment Opportunity Commission (EEOC) Compliance Manual on Employee Benefits, October 3, 2000.

Ehrenberg, Ronald G., and Michael J. Rizzo. 2001. "Faculty Retirement Policies after the End of Mandatory Retirement." *Research Dialogue.* Washington, DC: TIAA-CREF Institute. #69.

Employee Benefit Research Institute. 1996. "Lump-Sum Distributions: Fulfilling the Portability Promise or Eroding Retirement Security." EBRI Issue Brief No. 178. Washington, DC: Employee Benefit Research Institute.

Favreault, Melissa M., and Richard W. Johnson. 2002. "The Family, Social Security, and the Retirement Decision." In *Social Security and the Family.* Melissa M. Favreault, Frank Sammartino, and C. Eugene Steuerle, eds. Washington, DC: The Urban Institute Press.

Fullerton, Howard N., Jr., and Mitra Toossi. 2001. "Labor Force Projections to 2010: Steady Growth and Changing Composition." *Monthly Labor Review.* 124(11): 21–38.

General Counsel Memorandum 38924 (July 26, 1990).

Hewitt Associates. 1997. "Retiree Health Trends and Implications of Possible Medicare Reforms." Report Prepared for the Kaiser Medicare Policy Project. Washington, DC: Hewitt.

Johnson, Richard W. 2001. "Medicare, Retirement Costs, and Labor Supply at Older Ages." Paper presented at the annual meeting of the Gerontological Society of America, Chicago, IL.

Kimel v. Florida Board of Regents, 528 U.S. 62 (2000).

Kotlikoff, Laurence, and David Wise. 1989. "Employee Retirement and a Firm's Pension Plans." In *The Economics of Aging.* David Wise, ed. Chicago: University of Chicago Press. (Also, NBER Working Paper No. 2323).

————. 1987. "The Incentive Effects of Private Pension Plans." In *Issues in Pension Economics.* Zvi Bodie, John Shoven, and David Wise, eds. Chicago: University of Chicago Press.

————. 1985. "Labor Compensation and the Structure of Private Pension Plans: Evidence for Contractual Versus Spot Labor Markets." In *Pensions, Labor, and Individual Choice,* David Wise, ed. Chicago: University of Chicago Press.

Lumsdaine, Robin, James Stock, and David Wise. 1994. "Retirement Incentives: The Interaction between Employer-Provided Pensions, Social Security, and Retiree Health Benefits." NBER Working Paper No. 4613. Cambridge, MA: National Bureau of Economic Research. http://papers.nber.org/papers/W4613.

Manton, Kenneth G., Larry Corder, and Eric Stallard. 1997. "Chronic Disability Trends in Elderly United States Populations: 1982–1994." Proceedings of the National Academy of Sciences 94(6): 2593–9.

Mercer, William M. 2001. "Phased Retirement and the Changing Face of Retirement." William M. Mercer, Inc.

Munnell, Alicia H., Annika Sundén, and Elizabeth Lidstone. 2002. "How Important are Private Pensions?" Issue Brief No. 8. Boston, MA: Center for Retirement Research at Boston College.

Penner, Rudolph G., Pamela Perun, and C. Eugene Steuerle. 2002. "Legal and Institutional Impediments to Partial Retirement and Part-Time Work by Older Workers." Urban Institute.

Purcell, Patrick. 2003. "Pension Issues: Cash Balance Plans." No. RL30196. Washington, DC: The Library of Congress, Congressional Research Service.

Rappaport, Anna. 2001. "Employer Perspective on Retirement Trends and Policies to Encourage Work among Older Americans." William M. Mercer, Inc. White paper.

Samwick, Andrew. 1998. "New Evidence on Pension, Social Security, and the Timing of Retirement." NBER Working Paper No. W6534. Cambridge, MA: National Bureau of Economic Research.

Samwick, Andrew, and Jonathan Skinner. 1998. "How Will Defined Contribution Plans Affect Retirement Income?" NBER Working Paper No. W6645. Cambridge, MA: National Bureau of Economic Research.

Social Security Administration. 2001. *Annual Statistical Supplement to the Social Security Bulletin.* Office of Policy, Office of Research, Evaluation, and Statistics. Washington, DC. (December). Table 6.A4.

Steuerle, Eugene. 1988. Statement before the Subcommittee on Oversight, Committee on Ways and Means, United States House of Representatives. July 12.

Steuerle, Eugene, and Jon M. Bakija. 1994. *Retooling Social Security for the 21st Century: Right and Wrong Approaches to Reform.* Washington, DC: The Urban Institute Press.

Steuerle, Eugene, Christopher Spiro, and Richard W. Johnson. 1999. "Can Americans Work Longer?" *The Retirement Project Straight Talk on Social Security and Retirement Policy Number 5.* Washington, DC: The Urban Institute. http://www.urban.org/Uploaded PDF/Straight5.pdf (Accessed April 9, 2002).

Stock, James, and David Wise. 1990. "The Pension Inducement to Retire: An Option Value Analysis." In *Issues in the Economics of Aging*. David Wise, ed. Chicago: University of Chicago Press.

Toder, Eric, and Sandeep Solanki. 1999. "Effects of Demographic Trends on Labor Supply and Living Standards." *The Retirement Project*. Washington, DC: The Urban Institute. Occasional Paper Number 2.

Toder, Eric, Lawrence Thompson, Melissa Favreault, Richard Johnson, Kevin Perese, Caroline Ratcliffe, Karen Smith, Cori Uccello, Timothy Waidman, Gary Burtless, Claudia Sahm, and Douglas Wolf. 2002. *Modeling Income in the Near Term—Revised Projections of Retirement Income Through 2020 for the 1931–60 Birth Cohorts*. Project Report for the Social Security Administration. Washington, DC: The Urban Institute.

Treasury Regulation § 1.401–1(b)(ii).

Treasury Regulation § 1.401–1(b).

Treasury Regulation § 1.401–1.

Treasury Regulation § 1.410(b)–5(d)(7).

U.S. General Accounting Office. 2001. *Older Workers: Demographic Trends Pose Challenges for Employers and Workers*. GAO-02-85. Washington, DC: General Accounting Office. http://www.gao.gov/new.items/d0285.pdf (Accessed April 9, 2002).

Watson Wyatt Worldwide. 2000a. *Phased Retirement—Reshaping the End of Work*. Watson Wyatt Worldwide. http://www.watsonwyatt.com/us/pubs/insider/showarticle.asp?ArticleID=8376. (last visited June 8, 2002).

Watson Wyatt Worldwide. 2000b. *Phased Retirement: A Work in Progress*. http://www.watsonwyatt.com/us/pubs/insider/showarticle.asp?ArticleID=7610. (last visited June 8, 2002).

Working Group Report on Phased Retirement, submitted to the ERISA Advisory Council of the Department of Labor, November 14, 2000.

Comments on "Letting Older Workers Work"

LANCE R. WESCHER

Many of the chapters in this book predict a sizeable change in the composition of the U.S. labor market. This prediction is based on two readily observable trends. The first is that the percentage of elderly citizens in the population will grow to unprecedented levels due to the well-publicized demographic combination of declining birth rates following the baby boom and increasing longevity. The second is the exacerbation of this labor shortage due to individuals retiring much earlier than they historically have. While this retirement trend has slowed significantly since the middle 1980s, Penner, Perun, and Steuerle provide a detailed picture of the long-term trends that certainly suggests a future labor shortage. Given the improved health of elderly individuals in general, the resolution of this shortage will involve a major change in the bargaining relationship between employers and older employees.

Penner, Perun, and Steuerle carefully examine influences on the labor market from these changes and the regulatory and institutional barriers that may obstruct employers and employees from arriving at mutually beneficial bargaining outcomes. Many of the obstacles are predicted based on careful examination of theory and numerous data sources. Other research—such as chapter 4, by Hutchens and Chen, in this volume—suggests that many companies have not yet perceived these constraints. This may be because the majority of the aforementioned population changes have yet to occur. In a recent survey of Canadian employers, three-quarters of employers indicated that the mass retirement of baby boomers would affect their organization, with 35 percent stating that the impact would be significant (Hewitt Associates 2004). Clearly, it is wise for research such as this chapter to anticipate and prepare in advance for these issues.

Health levels, and thus the ability to continue working, have improved. At the same time, the percentage of workers in less physically demanding occupations has increased. This chapter focuses primarily on institutional aspects of the labor market that make continuing to work an unattractive option for older workers and the obstacles that employers face in changing them. It identifies four primary areas where these barriers emerge: (1) Social Security and Medicare rules, (2) nondiscrimination rules applying to pensions and health insurance, (3) uncertainty surrounding the Age Discrimination in Employment Act (ADEA) legislation, and (4) restrictions contained in the Employee Retirement Income Security Act (ERISA). The principal focus is on how these affect pension and health insurance flexibility for older workers and those desiring partial retirement.

The authors rightly admit that resolution of these issues will neither eliminate the predicted labor shortage nor deliver solvency to the Social Security and Medicare budget. Addressing them does, however, have the potential to increase the welfare of workers and reduce labor shortages for many companies. Increased options for partial retirement are also recommended, but these provide flexibility to work both less and more. To the extent that one of the most valuable assets lost when older workers leave is their knowledge-based human capital, the authors of this and other chapters need not be so hard on this as a weakness. The value of elderly workers' knowledge may be best measured on an issue-to-issue rather than hourly basis. While the net effect of partial retirement on aggregate hours worked is ambiguous, the impact on the number of workers that retain connection with their employers should be positive.

Because the chapter provides a wealth of detail, it may be beneficial to step back to get a broader view of the issues at hand. According to an economist's perspective, workers decide whether to work or retire by maximizing utility based on financial needs and opportunities, and enjoyment from work and leisure. All of these are influenced by multiple factors. For many workers, the enjoyment of work declines and the desire for leisure increases due to health considerations. Medical costs also rise, and ability to perform certain tasks at work may decline. Pension benefits, Social Security, and Medicare also have substantial influences on the financial resources and opportunities of workers. The predicted future labor supply may be insufficient to meet the demand for labor due to demographic trends, retirement norms, and incentives leading a higher portion of the labor force to make the decision to retire. This will have a much stronger downward effect on labor supply than it does on aggregate demand. That is, the drop in an individual's market production is 100 percent when they retire while their market consumption is likely to fall much less.

Employers will be forced to fill the positions left vacant by these retirees while facing an insufficient supply of younger workers. There is reason to believe that it may be possible to lure some of the retirees back into the labor force. As the chapters by Munnell and Wolff in this volume attest, financial needs have increased for many mature workers due to declines in savings and pensions as well as increased longevity. A recent Hewitt Associates (2004) survey of retirees found that more than one-third of respondents indicated that in hindsight they would have postponed retirement. Since a decline in the labor supply will continue to exist, the labor market will be expected to clear at a higher price of labor. Pension, Social Security, and Medicare eligibility for certain workers will likely raise their reservation wage, further increasing the cost of inducing this group back into the labor force.

DEFINED BENEFIT PENSION PLANS

It is a well-researched and reported fact that certain features of defined benefit (DB) employer-provided pension plans offer strong incentives for workers to retire at specific points that may be earlier than they otherwise would. While some of this is due to unintended aspects of pension formulas, much of it is a legacy of a previous labor market response to the same demographic trend now being faced. The population bulge that is now approaching retirement overwhelmed the nation's education system in the late-1950s and 1960s. As the group later entered the job market in an arena of corporate downsizing, pensions gave employers a valuable tool for incenting older workers to leave the labor force and make room for the baby boomers. Two features of pension benefit formulas were used quite commonly for this purpose. The first is a capped level of service in the benefit formula. In the example used in the chapter, a benefit formula multiplied a percentage of pay by years of service capped at forty years. All else being equal, this provides a decrease in the level of annual benefit accrual. The second, far more significant tool, is subsidized early retirement factors. While the influence on pension accrual rates of this type of structure is much greater than that of service caps, these factors are given little attention in this chapter. For example, a pension plan may have a normal retirement age of 65 but allow employees to commence their benefits at age 60 at an actuarially fair reduced rate. This plan may, however, allow employees who meet certain service requirements to receive their benefits early at a subsidized or unreduced rate. This amounts to a rather drastic acceleration of the pension accrual rate. Given such acceleration, the authors' results showing negative accrual rates after certain ages should come as no surprise.

Another important historical point is that pension plans were originally much less formal and less legally binding arrangements. Employers were able to change pension structures relatively easily and thus did not have to take the long-term consequences of aspects of their plans into serious consideration. Also, many companies targeted pension plans solely at their older workers and often excluded younger workers from them prior to age 30 and until they had been with the firm for five or ten years. Participants in the plans often had to work twenty or more years or even be with the employer until retirement before becoming fully vested in their benefits. Such a system provided employers with great flexibility, but it was also ripe for abuse. Employees could be promised benefits and then find themselves ineligible or receiving fewer benefits than they had expected.

Stepping in to protect workers from abuse, regulations such as ERISA's "anti-cutback" rule (discussed in chapter 7 by Muir and Turner) were imposed. In addition, ERISA mandated that all employees who are at least 25 and have one year of service be made participants in the plan. It also provided universal minimum standards for vesting. This legislation had a remarkable effect on the definition of a pension promise. Prior to ERISA, less than 20 percent of DB pensions had vesting standards that accorded to ERISA levels. The expected value of pension benefits to employees thus increased dramatically. Despite this redefinition of employer-provided pensions, the number of employers that dropped their pension plans was minimal. This may be due to the fact that these constraints had no binding effect on employment in the short term, and pension managers were not accustomed to making long-term considerations. Thirty years later, as the baby boomers approach retirement age, the needs of employers have made a complete 180-degree turn, with employers seeking to increase their utilization of older workers. The regulations of ERISA have locked in the aspects of pensions created for the arrival of the baby boomers, however, seriously inhibiting labor-market negotiations from making an equivalent about-face as they leave.

Given the rigidity of traditional DB plans, employers could reasonably attempt to circumnavigate the built-in obstacles. Two general possibilities emerge in this endeavor, each of which is addressed by the authors. First, the employer may partially terminate the DB pension (ERISA protects accrued benefit levels). They could do this by switching to a defined contribution (DC) plan or to a cash balance DB plan. Many companies that have attempted these approaches have experienced strong negative responses from their workers. In particular, the very workers approaching retirement that we are addressing have been the most vocal in their complaints. A second option is to offer some form of an additional pension benefit to elderly workers. This runs into a snag with IRS antidiscrimination regulations that ensure that pension benefits apply equally to higher income and lower income employees. The longer tenured, older employees facing early retirement incentives statistically fall into higher income categories making an additional benefit to them impossible.

If employers will be unable to remove these obstacles associated with traditional DB pensions, how may they most efficiently bargain with elderly workers? Penner, Perun, and Steuerle identify a rational solution to this problem that could take multiple forms. The fundamental principle is to allow workers to begin receiving their benefits prior to retirement. For employees experiencing a negative annual accrual rate, which is common following the achievement of special early retirement status, the effect of this is to eliminate the financial opportunity cost of work. While allowing employees to receive pension benefits prior to retirement violates the Internal Revenue Code principle that pension benefits are solely for retirement, arrangements such as the deferred retirement option plans (DROPs) examined in the chapter may provide a feasible compromise. While these approaches remove some incentive to retire by eliminating the financial opportunity cost of pensions, the scope of their impact should be kept in mind. The nonwage income available to these workers is unaffected by these proposals. The reservation wage of these workers, and thus the cost of inducing them back into the labor force, remains higher than if there were no pension benefits at all.

HEALTH INSURANCE

Health insurance is another piece of the total compensation package that may influence the decision of whether or not to retire. Penner, Perun, and Steuerle provide detailed numbers on the increased costs of insuring elderly workers. The insurance expenditures for workers over age 55 are twice as high as for those under age 40. This clearly demonstrates an area where older employees are more costly to hire or retain. There is no resolution in sight since the gap between costs for older and younger workers continues to grow each year.

For Medicare-eligible workers, employers encounter an obstacle quite similar to that faced with traditional DB pensions. Federal legislation was passed in 1980 requiring that employer-provided health insurance be the first payer over Medicare. This was done to prolong the financial solvency of the Medicare system. Since employer-provided insurance is the first payer, the value of Medicare is an opportunity cost to continued labor force participation. The value of employer-provided health insurance benefits decreases significantly as it crowds out otherwise available Medicare coverage. In fact, it may make an employer's decision to provide health insurance to elderly workers an inefficient allocation.

The authors' proposal to make Medicare the first payer is equivalent to the proposal addressed above to allow employees to receive their pensions while continuing to work. It would eliminate the opportunity cost associated with the existing structure. The existence of Medicare continues to increase workers' available nonwage income, which still raises the reservation wage. Both this proposal and the ability of workers to begin receiving benefits while working should have a non-negative impact on hours worked, though the magnitude is yet unknown. The effect on worker utility is also non-negative. This is an attractive proposal, although it would be helpful to see estimates of the increased burden on the Medicare system. Given the 2004 Medicare Board of Trustees report that recently moved the expected exhaustion date of the Hospital Insurance Trust Fund forward from 2026 to 2019 and the public attention it received, adding to an already overloaded Medicare system may not be politically feasible.

Conclusion

While there is no doubt that the pension-related barriers focused upon in this chapter exist, it is debatable whether they are as important as the chapter might imply. The U.S. Labor Department reports that only 20 percent of workers employed by private companies have DB pensions (Department of Labor 2003). This percentage continues to fall and includes many cash balance plans that do not contain strong early retirement incentives. Employers also have the ability to offer pension benefits from nonqualified plans, though they will not receive tax exemptions on these benefits. While the percentage of workers covered by DB pensions is higher for state and local governments, these plans are regulated by less restrictive laws and have shown some success in accommodating older workers.

Perhaps a more constructive area to examine than private pensions is the public pension system in this country. The current payment structure of the Social Security system is not conducive to partial retirement. A Social Security participant only has the option to select a fixed annuity. People who would like to work part time can commence benefits as early as age 62 but simultaneously agree to receive the reduced benefits for the remainder of their lifetimes. It would suit many individuals to instead have the option to receive a smaller benefit for an initial period when they are more physically capable of work and may still have stronger connections to the workforce, and have benefits increase in older age when needs may increase and the ability to work may decrease. While any proposed changes to the Social Security system are received with great suspicion, a change such as this would more appropriately meet individuals' needs with no necessary cost to the system.

Health insurance benefits may offer more promise than DB pensions in understanding what may dictate retirement decisions over the next decade or more. Penner, Perun, and Steuerle cover this thoroughly, though one may suggest some slightly different conclusions. First, the numbers in Figure 4 show that there remains a gap between the insurance costs and the average healthcare expenditures of elderly workers. That is, even though older workers are receiving more benefits from their employer-provided health insurance, they are also footing a larger bill out-of-pocket than younger workers. Given a potential labor shortage combined with older workers' increased preference for leisure, it is expected to cost more to employ these individuals. Employers may be able to utilize the tax advantages of providing additional health insurance to target this gap between medical expenditures and health insurance to achieve a more efficient compensation package.

Second, the proposal to eliminate the 1980 legislation making Medicare the second payer will face strong political opposition, to say the least, because the system certainly is not in a better financial situation today than it was then. While any mention of adding to what Medicare pays will be met with great distrust, a portion of the recent Medicare prescription drug plan may provide insight into a potentially more feasible and efficient proposal. Fearing that employers who provide retiree health benefits would be inclined to drop the pharmaceutical benefit from their plans in light of Medicare benefits, Medicare offered to subsidize 28 percent of employers' pharmacy claims above a deductible (capped at an indexed $5,000 limit) (Medicare Prescription Drug Act 2003). It may be possible to develop a similar proposal for Medicare-eligible employees in which Medicare helps to subsidize the costs of insuring such workers. To the extent that it prevents employers from dropping coverage, thus shifting these workers' medical expenses fully to Medicare, it may not increase costs to the Medicare system.

All of the discussion of pensions and health insurance thus far dealt with the bargaining relationship between employers and older individuals. One major organization has been neglected in this entire consideration—labor unions. This omission is particularly glaring considering the significance of DB pensions with regard to many of the obstacles. According to the 2000 Labor Department National Compensation Survey, 69 percent of unionized workers are covered by DB pension benefits and 75 percent have medical insurance. This compares to just 14 percent and 49 percent, respectively, for nonunionized workers. A complete discussion must consider the goals of organized labor when analyzing these issues. The notion of how unions' objectives will change according to the demographic trends discussed has yet to be researched to my knowledge.

There is another issue that is not addressed in the chapter. While the authors' proposals eliminate some of the opportunity costs of continued employment for older workers, the benefits costs of older workers remain more expensive relative to those of younger workers. As such, it is necessary to consider the extent to which employers will find older workers the most cost-effective resource. The authors demonstrate that immigration numbers may be insufficient to meet labor demand. There is little to suggest that the emigration of jobs will be insufficient as well. Incentives to outsource labor internationally in numerous industries exist already. As the average cost of domestic labor increases while the benefits portion becomes costlier for the reasons addressed above, the move to outsource will likely increase.

This chapter brings the topic of institutional obstacles to the employment of older workers and partial retirement to the broader discussion in this volume. There is still a great deal that is left unknown. Hutchens and Chen's chapter (4) suggests that many employers are not feeling these constraints, at least not yet. Raskin and Gettas's chapter (3) indicates that there are still informal aspects of many work environments that suggest a bias against older workers. Many of these work arrangements can be addressed by employers, and one would expect them to address these issues prior to more rigid financial ones. Finally, there is a great deal yet to be known regarding how older workers empirically respond to changes in their fringe benefits. Health insurance in particular should be addressed. In addition, as DC pensions such as 401(k)s become far more common than traditional DB pensions, it should be examined how workers utilize, manage, and respond to them.

REFERENCES

Boards of Trustees, Federal Hospital Insurance and Federal Supplementary Medical Insurance Trust Funds. 2004. *2004 Annual Report of the Boards of Trustees of the Federal Hospital Insurance and Federal Supplementary Medical Insurance Trust Funds.* Washington, DC: U.S. Government Printing Office. http://www.treas.gov/offices/economic-policy/reports/medicare.pdf.

Hewitt Associates. 2004. *Trends in Canadian Retirement Programs: 2004.* Lincolnshire, IL: Hewitt Associates.

U.S. Department of Labor, Bureau of Labor Statistics. 2003. Employee Benefits in Private Industry, 2003. (September). http://www.bls.gov/news.release/pdf/ebs2.pdf.

Medicare Prescription Drug, Improvement, and Modernization Act of 2003. Sec. 1860D-22. http://frwebgate.access.gpo.gov/cgi-bin/getdoc.cgi?dbname=108_cong_bills&docid=f:h1enr.txt.pdf.

PART 3

WHAT DO WORKERS WANT?
EMPLOYEE BENEFITS
FOR OLDER AMERICANS

CHAPTER SIX

The Transformation of the American Pension System

EDWARD N. WOLFF

1. INTRODUCTION

While almost all the attention of the media is riveted on the Social Security system, the devolution of the private pension system has received surprisingly little attention. Indeed, one of the most dramatic changes in the economy since the early 1980s has been the substitution of defined contribution (DC) pensions for traditional defined benefit (DB) pension plans. Moreover, pensions are often viewed as an equalizer, offsetting the inequality in standard household net worth. The main focus of this paper is to analyze the effects of this substitution on median wealth holdings and the overall distribution of household wealth.

The work of Poterba, Venti, and Wise (1998) suggests that the transition from DB to DC plans increased pension wealth dramatically. My results, reported below, also confirm that *mean* pension wealth rose strongly between 1983 and 2001. However, *median* pension wealth actually declined, and pension-wealth inequality grew sharply as well.

Section 2 of this paper provides a review of the pertinent literature on this subject. Section 3 describes the data sources, and section 4 develops the accounting framework used in the analysis. Section 5 shows time trends in standard measures of household wealth over the 1983–2001 period. Section 6 investigates changes in pension wealth over this period. Figures are shown for all households, the young (under age 47), the middle-aged (ages 47–64), and the elderly (age 65 and over). Particular attention is focused on age group 47–64 since this group was most affected by the transformation of the pension system. Section 7 presents summary measures on private accumulations, which are defined as the sum of net worth and pension wealth. Section 8 summarizes the major findings of the chapter, while section 9 includes a brief appraisal of the some of the factors behind the transformation of the pension system. Policy recommendations for reforming the pension system are offered in section 10.

2. LITERATURE REVIEW

Previous work has focused on one or a few of the aspects of the adequacy of retirement income or wealth. For instance, a number of papers have presented estimates of Social Security and/or pension wealth. The seminal paper on this topic is by Martin Feldstein (1974), who introduced the concept of Social Security wealth and developed its methodology. His main interest was in the aggregate level of Social Security wealth and its effect on aggregate savings and retirement patterns. In a follow-up paper, Feldstein (1976) considered the effects of Social Security wealth on the overall distribution of wealth on the basis of the 1962 Survey of Financial Characteristics of Consumers (SFCC), a survey performed by the Federal Reserve Board of Washington. The paper found that the inclusion of Social Security wealth had a major effect on lowering the overall inequality of (total) household wealth.

I followed up Feldstein's work (1976) by examining the distributional implications of both Social Security and private pension wealth in several papers, particularly "The Effects of Pensions and Social Security on the Distribution of Wealth in the U.S." (1987), which used the 1969 Measurement of Economic and Social Performance (MESP) database and was the first paper to add estimates of private pension wealth and examine its effects on the overall distribution of wealth. The paper showed that while Social Security wealth had a pronounced equalizing effect on the distribution of augmented wealth (the sum of marketable wealth and retirement wealth), pension wealth actually had a *disequalizing* effect on augmented wealth. The sum of Social Security and pension wealth has, on net, an equalizing effect on the distribution of augmented wealth. My 1988 paper examined the implications of including both Social Security and pension wealth for estimating the life-cycle model of savings. My 1992 paper addressed the methodological issues in estimating both Social Security and pension wealth, and my 1993 papers extended the estimates of Social Security and pension wealth to the 1962 SFCC and the 1983 Survey of Consumer Finances (SCF).

Kennickell and Sunden (1999) used the 1989 and 1992 SCFs to look at the effects of Social Security and pension wealth on the overall distribution of wealth. They also found a net equalizing effect from the inclusion of these two forms of retirement wealth. Interestingly, they found that there is a negative effect of both

DB plan coverage and Social Security wealth on nonpension net worth but that the effects of DC plans, such as 401(k) plans, are insignificant.

Several papers used the Health and Retirement Survey (HRS). Gustman et al. (1997) found that in 1992, pensions, Social Security, and health insurance accounted for 50 percent of the wealth held by all households aged 51 to 61; for 60 percent of total wealth of households who are in the 45th to 55th wealth percentiles; and for 48 percent of those in the 90th to 95th wealth percentiles in the HRS. In a follow-up study, Gustman and Steinmeier (1998) used data from the HRS to examine the composition and distribution of total wealth for a group of 51- to 61-year-olds. They focused on the role of pensions in forming retirement wealth. They found that pensions are widespread, covering two-thirds of households and accounting for one-quarter of accumulated wealth on average. Social Security benefits accounted for another one-quarter of total wealth. They also reported that the ratio of wealth to lifetime earnings was the same for those individuals with pensions and for those without pensions. They concluded that pensions cause very limited displacement of other forms of wealth.

Several studies have documented changes in pension coverage in the United States, particularly the decline in DB pension coverage among workers since the early 1980s. Kotlikoff and Smith (1983) provided one of the most comprehensive treatments of pension coverage and showed that the proportion of U.S. private-sector wage and salary workers covered by pensions more than doubled between 1950 and 1979. Bloom and Freeman (1992), using Current Population Surveys (CPS) for 1979 and 1988, were among the first to call attention to the decline in DB pension coverage. They reported that the percentage of all workers in age group 25–64 covered by these plans fell from 63 to 57 percent over this period. Among male workers in this age group, the share covered dropped from 70 to 61 percent, while among females in the same age group, the share remained almost constant, at 53 percent. Other studies include Even and Macpherson (1994a, 1994b, 1994c, and 1994d). Their 1994c study showed a particularly pronounced drop in DB pension coverage among workers with low levels of education; and their 1994d study showed a convergence in pension coverage rates among female and male workers between 1979 and 1998.

Both Gustman and Steinmeier (1992) and Ippolito (1995) drew attention to the rapid growth of DC plans during the 1980s and early 1990s. Gustman and Steinmeier in particular found that about half of the shift between DB and DC plan coverage is due to shifts in employment mix toward firms with industry, size, and union status that are historically associated with lower DB plan rates and that the other half is due to changes in pension coverage type conditional on industry, size, and union status.

A U.S. Department of Labor report issued in 2000 found that a large proportion of workers, especially low-wage, part-time, and minority workers, were not covered by private pensions. The coverage rate of all private-sector wage and salary workers was 44 percent in 1997. Coverage of part-time, temporary and low-wage workers was especially low. This appears to be ascribable to the proliferation of 401(k) plans and the frequent requirement of employee contributions to such plans. It also found important racial differences, with 47 percent of white workers participating but only 27 percent of Hispanics. Another important finding is that while 70 percent of unionized workers were covered by a pension plan, only 41 percent of nonunionized workers were covered. Moreover, pension participation was found to be highly correlated with wages. While only 6 percent of workers earnings less than $200 per week were involved in a pension plan, 76 percent of workers earning $1,000 per week participated.

A related topic of interest is whether DC pension plans have substituted for DB-type plans. Using employer data (5,500 filings) for 1992, Popke (1999) found that, indeed, 401(k) and other DC plans have been substituted for terminated DB plans and that offering a DC plan raises the chance of a termination in DB coverage. On the other hand, Poterba, Venti, and Wise (1998), using HRS data for 1993, found that the growth of 401(k) plans did not substitute for other forms of household wealth, including DB pensions and that, in fact, it raised household net worth relative to what it would have been without these plans.

Several studies have looked at the overall economic status of the elderly. Hurd (1994) showed that the mean income of households age 65 and over increased sharply between 1970 and 1975 but only moderately from 1975 to 1987. As a fraction of the overall mean household income, average elderly income rose from 54 percent in 1970 to 61 percent in 1975 and then to only 63 percent by 1987. Smith (1997), using 1994 HRS data, found that median nonhome wealth among white households age 70 and over was only $15,600 and that among white households age 51–61 it was only $23,400; and median nonhome wealth for black and Hispanic households in the two age groups was zero! Venti and Wise (1998), using HRS data for 1992, estimated a very high degree of wealth dispersion among persons age 51–61, even after controlling for lifetime earnings.

3. Data Sources and Methods

The main data sources used for this study are the 1983, 1989, 1998, and 2001 SCFs, conducted by the Federal Reserve Board. Each survey consists of a core representative sample combined with a high-income supplement. The supplement is drawn from the Internal Revenue Service's Statistics of Income data file. The presence of a high-income supplement creates some complications because weights must be constructed to meld the high-income supplement with the core sample.[1] The SCF provides considerable detail on pension plans and expected pension benefits for each spouse. For 1983, the Federal Reserve Board did its own calculations of the wealth equivalent value of expected pension benefits and made these available in its Public Use sample. However, this has not been done for the other years.

4. ACCOUNTING FRAMEWORK

The principal wealth concept used here is marketable wealth (or net worth), which is defined as the current value of all marketable, or fungible, assets less the current value of debts. Net worth is thus the difference in value between total assets and total liabilities, or debt (see Table 3 for a listing of assets and liabilities). I use the abbreviation "NW" to refer to standard net worth because it indicates the "disposable" wealth that households have available. It should be stressed that the standard definition of "net worth" includes the market value of DC pension plans. I shall return to this point below.

The imputation of pension wealth involves a large number of steps, and it is summarized below. Greater detail can be found in the appendix to this chapter. Estimates are provided only for 1983, 1989, 1998, and 2001. For retirees (r), the procedure is straightforward. Let PB be the pension benefit currently being received by the retiree. The SCF questionnaire indicates how many pension plans each spouse is involved in and what the expected (or current) pension benefit is. The SCF questionnaire also indicates whether the pension benefits remain fixed in nominal terms over time for a particular beneficiary or are indexed for inflation. In the case of the former, the (gross) DB pension wealth is given by

1a. $DB_r = \int_0 PB(1 - m_t)e^{-\delta t}dt$

where m_t is the mortality rate at time t conditional on age, gender, and race; δ the nominal discount rate, for which the (nominal) ten-year treasury bill rate is used; and the integration runs from the current year to age 109. In the latter case,

1b. $DB_r = \int_0 PB(1 - m_t)e^{-\delta^* t}dt$

and δ^* is the real ten-year treasury bill rate, estimated as the current nominal rate less the Social Security Plan II-B assumption of 4.0 percent annual increase of the Consumer Price Index.

Among current workers (w) the procedure is somewhat more complex. The SCF provides detailed information on pension coverage among current workers, including the type of plan, the formula used to determine the benefit amount (for example, a fixed percentage of the average of the last five year's earnings), the retirement age when the benefits are effective, the likely retirement age of the worker, and vesting requirements. Information is provided not only for the current job (or jobs) of each spouse but for up to five past jobs as well. On the basis of the information provided in the SCF and on projected future earnings (see the appendix for details), future expected pension benefits (EPB_w) are then projected to the year of retirement or the first year of eligibility for the pension. Then the present value of pension wealth for current workers (w) is given by

2. $\quad DB_w = \int_{LR} EPB(1 - m_t)e^{-\delta t}dt$

where RA is the expected age of retirement and LR = A—RA is the number of years to retirement. As above, and the integration runs from the expected age of retirement to age 109.[2]

Estimates are provided for the following components of household wealth:

3. $\quad NW = NWX + DC$

where DC is the current market value of defined contribution pension plans and NWX is marketable household wealth excluding DC. NW corresponds to marketable wealth, or net worth. Total pension wealth, PW, is given by

4. $\quad PW = DC + DB$

Private accumulations (PA) are then defined as the sum of NWX and total pension wealth:

5. $\quad PA = NWX + PW$

The term "private accumulations" is used to distinguish wealth contributed by the private sector of the economy from that by the public sector, notably Social Security.

A few words should be said about methodological issues involved in this accounting framework. Some researchers have criticized my earlier work for treating DB and DC pension wealth as comparable concepts. Their argument is that DC valuation is based on the current market value of DC plans, whereas DB wealth is estimated on the basis of the future stream of pension benefits. This, they argue, is tantamount to comparing apples to oranges. To make the two comparable, it would be necessary to project the future stream of benefits emanating from the DC plans.

However, the main difference between the two types of plans is that the benefit levels in DB plans are already set by the terms of the plans—that is why these are called *defined benefits*. The estimation of DB wealth depends only on future labor force participation and earnings assumptions.[3] According to Farber (2001), job tenure is relatively certain at least for workers in their 50s and early 60s. In comparison, projecting DC wealth to the future would require not only assumptions about future labor force participation and future earnings but also assumptions about future employee contributions, future employer contributions, and future rates of return. Indeed, the stock market experience of 2000–2003 shows how difficult it would have been to project the future value of DC wealth even over this short period. DB benefits are more certain than DC benefits. Indeed, the shifting of the risk from employer to employee is one of the reasons behind the rise of DC plans (see section 9 below).

The concept of private accumulations, moreover, puts DB and DC wealth on an equal footing. The primary interest in this paper is to compare the well-being of two cohorts of workers at the same stage in their life cycle in *different years*. Both net worth and DC plans are valued in terms of current market value, and DB is the present value of the relatively certain stream of future benefits.[4] Thus, by comparing PA values for a given age group in 1983 and 1998, one can ascertain whether the same age group is better off in one year or the other.

If, for example, A had 100 of net worth (including DC) and B had 100 of net worth and 1 of DB, then it seems relatively clear that B is better off. The real issue is to compare A with C, who has 90 of net worth and 10 of DB. It is true that DB is a contingent claim on a future benefit stream. In my calculations, DB is already discounted by conditional mortality rates. If one thinks of securitizing this flow of benefits, one might speculate how much the individual could sell this annuity flow to a financial institution. There would, of course, be some discount factor applied (over and above the uncertainty associated with life expectancy). However, for workers approaching retirement, this discount factor might be relatively small. Moreover, the "security" offered would also be subject to market uncertainties (future interest rates, inflation rates, and stock market movements), so that some discount factor would also have to be applied to the security. Indeed, it is not clear that the risk factor associated with DB wealth would be greater than that associated with stocks, financial securities, or even DC accounts.

If one wanted to project future retirement adequacy, one would have to project both (non-DC) net worth and DC to the year of retirement. Insofar as DC wealth substitutes for non-DC net worth, projecting the net worth of a household that does not have a DC plan may yield a similar result to that for a household that has both DC and non-DC wealth of the same magnitude. This argument further reinforces the comparability of PA values of the same age group in two different years.[5]

5.   Trends in Standard Measures of Household Wealth

Table 1 documents a robust growth in wealth during the 1990s. Median wealth was 16 percent greater in 2001 than in 1989. After rising by 7 percent between 1983 and 1989, median wealth fell by 17 percent from 1989 to 1995 and then rose by 39 percent from 1995 to 2001. As a result, median wealth grew slightly faster between 1989 and 2001, 1.32 percent per year, than between 1983 and 1989, at 1.13 percent per year.

Mean net worth also showed a sharp increase from 1983 to 1989, followed by a rather precipitous decline from 1989 to 1995 and then, buoyed largely by rising stock prices, another surge in 2001. Overall, it was 65 percent higher in 2001 than in 1983 and 44 percent higher than in 1989. In fact mean wealth grew quite a bit faster between 1989 and 2001, at 3.02 percent per year, than from 1983 to 1989, at 2.27 percent per year. Moreover, mean wealth grew almost three times as fast as the median, suggesting widening inequality of wealth over these years.

After surging by 11 percent between 1983 and 1989, median household income (based on CPS data) grew by only 2.3 percent from 1989 to 2001—much slower than median net worth.[6] The net change over the whole period was 14 percent. In contrast, mean income rose by 16 percent from 1983 to 1989 and by another 12 percent from 1989 to 2001, for a total change of 30 percent.

The robust performance of median net worth over the 1990s is particularly surprising in contrast to trends in median income. Indeed, between 1983 and 1998, while median income grew by 13.8 percent, median net worth gained 11.1 percent (and from 1989 to 1998, 2.3 percent and 3.8 percent, respectively). However, between 1998 and 2001 median net worth exploded by 11.5 percent while median income stagnated.

Table 1. Mean and Median Wealth and Income, 1983–2001 (In thousands, 2001 dollars)

	1983	1989	1992	1995	1998	2001	Percent Change 1983–1989	Percent Change 1989–2001	Percent Change 1983–2001
A. Net Worth (NW)									
1. Median	59.3	63.5	54.2	53.0	65.9	73.5	7.0	15.8	23.9
2. Mean	231.0	264.6	257.3	237.7	293.6	380.1	14.6	43.7	64.6
B. Net Worth excluding DC Pension Accounts (NWX)									
1. Median	57.6	60.4	49.3	42.8	50.4	58.0	4.8	−3.9	0.7
2. Mean	247.1	278.5	243.7	208.6	278.8	326.6	12.7	17.3	32.2
C. Income (CPS)[a]									
1. Median	37.1	41.3	38.7	39.6	42.2	42.2	11.2	2.3	13.7
2. Mean	45.2	52.2	49.0	52.2	56.3	58.2	15.5	11.6	28.9

Source: own computations from the 1983, 1989, 1992, 1995, 1998, and 2001 Surveys of Consumer Finances. The 1983 weights are the Full Sample 1983 Composite Weights; and the 1989 weights are the average of the SRC-Design-S1 series (X40131) and the SRC designed based weights (X40125). The 1992 calculations are based on the Designed-Base Weights (X42000), with my adjustments (see Wolff 1996). The 1995 weights are the Designed-Base Weights (X42000). The 1998 and 2001 weights are partially Designed-Based weights (X42001), which account for the systematic deviations from CPS estimates of homeownership by racial/ethnic groups. The 1983, 1989, 1992, and 1995 asset and liability entries are aligned to national balance sheet totals (see footnote 2). The 1998 and 2001 asset and liability entries are based on original, unadjusted survey data.
[a]Source for household income data: U.S. Census of the Bureau, Current Populations Surveys, available on the internet: http://www.census.gov/hhes/income/histinc/ineqtoc.html.

Looking at section B of Table 1, one sees the important role played by DC pension wealth, which forms part of net worth. If DC pension wealth is excluded from net worth, then median wealth actually declined over the 1990s, by 3.9 percent, and mean wealth grew more slowly than standard net worth. The rapid accumulation of DC pension wealth thus helped maintain household savings over the 1990s. I shall return to this point below.

Table 2 shows trends in both wealth and income inequality. It is most useful to begin with the income trends (section C). Household income inequality, based on CPS data, increased between 1983 and 1989, with the share of the top 5 percent rising by 2.5 percentage points, while the share of the next 15 percent and that of the bottom four quintiles all fell.[7] The Gini coefficient rose from 0.414 to 0.431 over this period. Between 1989 and 2001, the share of the top 5 percent rose by another 3.5 percentage points while the next 15 percent and the bottom four quintiles again lost ground, so that the Gini coefficient again

Table 2. Inequality Measures for the Size Distribution of Wealth and Income, 1983–2001

	1983	1989	1992	1995	1998	2001	Percent Change		
							1983–1989	1989–2001	1983–20
A. Net Worth (NW)									
1. Share of Top One Percent (%)	33.8	37.4	37.2	38.5	38.1	33.4	10.7	−10.7	−1.1
2. Gini Coefficient	0.799	0.832	0.823	0.828	0.822	0.826	4.2	−0.7	3.5
B. Net Worth excluding DC Pension Accounts (NWX)									
1. Share of Top One Percent (%)	33.9	35.6	—	—	38.1	36.9	5.0	3.6	8.8
2. Gini Coefficient	0.802	0.835	—	—	0.842	0.845	4.1	1.3	5.4
C. Income (CPS)[a]									
1. Share of Top Five Percent (%)	16.4	18.9	18.6	21.0	21.7	22.4	15.2	18.5	36.6
2. Gini Coefficient	0.414	0.431	0.434	0.450	0.456	0.466	4.1	8.1	12.6

Source: own computations from the 1983, 1989, 1992, 1995, 1998, and 2001 Surveys of Consumer Finances. See note Table 1 for technical details.
[a]Source for household income data: U.S. Census of the Bureau, Current Populations Surveys, available on the intern http://www.census.gov/hhes/income/histinc/ineqtoc.html.

increased, from 0.431 to 0.466. All told, according to the CPS figures, there was no abatement in the growth of inequality in the 1989–2001 period compared to 1983–1989.

The trends are different for wealth. As shown in section A, wealth inequality, after rising steeply between 1983 and 1989, remained virtually unchanged from 1989 to 2001. The share of wealth held by the top 1 percent rose by 3.6 percentage points from 1983 to 1989, and the Gini coefficient increased from 0.800 to 0.830. Between 1989 and 2001, the share of the top percentile actually declined sharply, from 37.4 to 33.4 percent, though this was almost exactly compensated for by an increase in the share of the next four percentiles. As a result, the share of the top 5 percent actually increased slightly, from 58.9 to 59.2 percent, as did the share of the top quintile, from 83.5 to 84.4 percent. The share of the fourth and middle quintiles declined slightly, while that of the bottom 40 percent increased somewhat, so that overall, the Gini coefficient fell very slightly, from 0.832 to 0.826.

However, when one excludes DC pension wealth from net worth, one finds that inequality in wealth actually rose during the 1990s (see section B). The share of the top one percent gained 1.3 percentage points, that of the top 5 percent grew by 3.7 percentage points, and the share of the top quintile increased by 2.6 percentage points between 1989 and 2001, while the Gini coefficient rose by 0.011 points. Here, too, the accumulation of DC pension wealth helped to moderate wealth inequality over the 1990s.

Table 3 shows changes in the overall portfolio composition of household wealth. In 2001, owner-occupied housing was the most important household asset in the breakdown shown in the table, accounting for 28 percent of total assets. However, net home equity amounted to only 19 percent of total assets. Real estate other than owner-occupied housing comprised 10 percent and business equity, another 17 percent. Liquid assets, including bank deposits, money market funds, CDs, and the cash surrender value of life insurance, made up 9 percent, and pension accounts (DC) amounted to 12 percent. Financial securities made up 2 percent; corporate stock and mutual funds, 15 percent; and trust equity, a little less than 5 percent. Debt as a proportion of gross assets was 13 percent, and the debt-equity ratio (the ratio of total household debt to net worth) was 0.14.

There have been some notable trends in the composition of household wealth over the 1983–2001 period. The most important trend from the standpoint of this chapter is that DC pension accounts rose from 1.5 to 12.3 percent of total assets, with almost the entire gain occurring after 1989. This increase almost exactly offset the decline in liquid assets, from 17.4 to 8.8 percent—again, with almost all of the change occurring after 1989. Though there is no direct econometric evidence of substitution here, there is circumstantial evidence that the explosion in the use of various types of pension accounts, like IRAs, 401(k) plans, and other thrift plans, appears to have allowed households to substitute tax-free pension accounts for taxable savings deposits, rather than increasing overall household savings.

A second notable trend is the debt-equity ratio, which leaped from 15.1 to 17.6 percent between 1983 and 1998 but then receded to 14.3 percent in 2001. The principal source of these changes is not from consumer debt, like credit card balances. In fact, nonmortgage debt as a fraction of total assets fell rather continuously, from 6.8 to 3.1 percent, over the period from 1983 to 2001. Rather, the primary source is mortgage debt, including home equity loans and second mortgages, which climbed from 6.3 to 10.7 percent of total assets from 1983 to 1998 but then fell off to 9.4 percent in 2001. Indeed, mortgage debt as a share of the value of homeowner's property increased from 21 to 37 percent from 1983 to 1998 and then dropped off to 33 percent in 2001. Whereas the total market value of homes remained roughly constant as a share of total assets over this period, net home equity plummeted from 24 to 19 percent of total assets.[8]

Table 3. Composition of Total Household Wealth, 1983, 1989 1998, and 2001
(Percent of gross assets)

Component	1983	1989	1998	2001
Principal residence (gross value)	30.1	30.2	29.0	28.2
Other real estate (gross value)	14.9	14.0	10.0	9.8
Unincorporated business equity[a]	18.8	17.2	17.7	17.2
Liquid assets[b]	17.4	17.5	9.6	8.8
Pension accounts[c]	1.5	2.9	11.6	12.3
Financial securities[d]	4.2	3.4	1.8	2.3
Corporate stock and mutual funds	9.0	6.9	14.8	14.8
Net equity in personal trusts	2.6	3.1	3.8	4.8
Miscellaneous assets[e]	1.3	4.9	1.8	1.8
Total	100.0	100.0	100.0	100.0
Debt on principal residence	6.3	8.6	10.7	9.4
All other debt[f]	6.8	6.4	4.2	3.1
Total debt	13.1	15.0	15.0	12.5
Memo:				
Debt / equity ratio	15.1	17.6	17.6	14.3
Net home equity / total assets	23.8	21.6	18.2	18.8
Principal residence debt/ house value	20.9	28.6	37.0	33.4
Stocks, directly or indirectly owned/ total assets[g]	11.3	10.2	22.6	24.5

Note: own computations from the 1983, 1989, 1998 and 2001 Survey of Consumer Finances. See note to Table 1 for technical details.

[a] Net equity in unincorporated farm and non-farm businesses and closely-held corporations.

[b] Checking accounts, savings accounts, time deposits, money market funds, certificates of deposits, and the cash surrender value of life insurance.

[c] IRAs, Keogh plans, 401(k) plans, the accumulated value of defined contribution pension plans, and other retirement accounts.

[d] Corporate bonds, government bonds, open-market paper, and notes.

[e] Gold and other precious metals, royalties, jewelry, antiques, furs, loans to friends and relatives, future contracts, and miscellaneous assets.

[f] Mortgage debt on all real property except principal residence; credit card, installment, and other consumer debt.

[g] Includes direct ownership of stock shares and indirect ownership through mutual funds, trusts, and IRAs, Keogh plans, 401(k) plans, and other retirement accounts.

A third important change is that the share of corporate equities and mutual funds in total assets, after falling from 9.0 to 6.9 percent between 1983 and 1989, grew rather steadily thereafter to 14.8 percent in 2001. This shift, in part, reflects the surge in stock prices during the 1990s. This result, in fact, does not even reflect the full extent of the growth in corporate stock holdings, because stocks are also indirectly held in mutual funds, pension accounts, and trust funds. If these are included, then corporate stocks both directly and indirectly owned by households, after falling slightly from 11.3 percent in 1983 to 10.2 percent in 1989, more than doubled to 24.5 percent of total assets in 2001.[9]

6. Pension Wealth

Table 4 highlights trends in pension holdings during the 1983–2001 period. The share of all households with DC pension accounts skyrocketed, from 11 to 52 percent, or by 41 percentage points. The story is very similar for the three different age groups shown in Table 5—including the elderly. The proportion holding pension accounts advanced by 40 percentage points in the 46 and under group, by 50 percentage points in the 47–64 group, and by 33 percentage points in the 65 and over group. In 2001, about 62 percent of households in the 47–64 group held some form of DC account, compared to 35 percent of elderly households and 54 percent of younger households. Most of the gains occurred after 1989.

Opposite trends are apparent for DB pension wealth. The share of all households with DB pension wealth fell by 18 percentage points between 1983 and 2001, from 53 to 34 percent. Among households in the 47–64 group, the decline was even more precipitous—by 24 percentage points, from 69 to 45 percent—while among elderly households the proportion fell by 20 percentage points and among young households, by 10 percentage points. In 2001, while 47 percent of elderly households held some form of DB pension wealth, only 45 percent of households in the 47–64 group and only 23 percent among young households recorded DB entitlements. Most of the loss in coverage again occurred after 1989.

The percentage of all households covered by either a DC or a DB plan increased from 54 to 66 percent between 1983 and 2001. Among the 47–64 group, the proportion rose by 5.6 percentage points, to 76 percent in 2001, while among the elderly the share fell by 4.3 percentage points, down to 63 percent in 2001. The biggest rise occurred among younger households, whose proportion surged from 36 to 61 percent. The share of households covered by pensions in 2001 was 76 percent in the middle-aged group, compared to 63 percent in the elderly group and 61 percent in the youngest group.

Table 4. Percent of Households with Pension Wealth, 1983–2001

	1983	1989	1998	2001	Percent Point Change 1983–1989	1989–2001	1983–2001
A. All Households							
1. DC Accounts	10.9	24.0	48.8	52.2	13.0	28.2	41.3
2. DB Plans	52.6	45.6	37.1	34.4	(7.0)	(11.2)	(18.2)
3. Pension Wealth	54.4	56.0	64.7	65.6	1.5	9.6	11.2
B. Ages 46 and under							
1. DC Accounts	13.7	31.2	52.0	53.8	17.5	22.6	40.1
2. DB Plans	32.6	37.9	27.4	22.8	5.3	(15.1)	(9.8)
3. Pension Wealth	35.6	52.2	60.4	60.7	16.6	8.6	25.1
C. Ages 47–64							
1. DC Accounts	11.9	28.3	59.7	62.0	16.4	33.7	50.1
2. DB Plans	68.9	56.8	45.9	45.3	(12.1)	(11.5)	(23.7)
3. Pension Wealth	70.2	67.5	74.7	75.9	(2.8)	8.4	5.6
D. Ages 65 and over							
1. DC Accounts	2.1	1.3	32.3	35.0	(0.8)	33.7	32.9
2. DB Plans	66.2	51.3	48.9	46.5	(14.9)	(4.7)	(19.6)
3. Pension Wealth	66.9	51.8	62.2	62.6	(15.1)	10.8	(4.3)

Note: own computations from the 1983, 1989, 1998, and 2001 Surveys of Consumer Finances. Households are classified into age groups by the age of the head of household. Key:
   Pension Wealth PW = DB + DC

As shown in Table 5, there were huge increases in the average holdings of DC pension accounts.[10] Among all households, the average value of these accounts increased tenfold between 1983 and 2001, from $3,900 to $53,700 (both in 2001 dollars). In the 46 and under group, the increase was by a factor of 10.1, and in the 47–64 group the gain was by a factor of 11.1, while among elderly households, the rise was by a factor of 28.4. In 2001, mean DC pension wealth was greatest in the 47–64 group, at $96,600, with the elderly group, at $53,600 and the youngest group at $28,200.

Countervailing trends are again evident for the average value of DB pension wealth. Among all households, the mean value fell by 26 percent between 1983 and 2001, from $55,400 to $41,200 (both in 2001 dollars). Losses were also marked for the 47–64 age group, which saw its mean DB pension wealth decline by 21 percent between 1983 and 2001, and for younger households, whose average DB wealth fell by 27 percent. However, the valuation of pension rights among younger workers has to be interpreted cautiously, since these are based

Table 5. Mean and Median Household Pension Wealth, 1983 and 2001
(In thousands, 2001 dollars)

	1983	2001	% Change 1983–2001
A. All Households			
1. Mean DC Pension Wealth	3.9	53.7	1273.7
2. Mean DB Pension Wealth	55.4	41.2	−25.7
3. Mean Pension Wealth	59.3	94.8	59.8
Memo: Median Pension Wealth among PW Holders Only	64.3	53.7	−16.5
B. Ages 46 and under			
1. Mean DC Pension Wealth	2.6	28.2	1005.6
2. Mean DB Pension Wealth	23.0	16.9	−26.8
3. Mean Pension Wealth	25.6	45.1	76.1
Memo: Median Pension Wealth among PW Holders Only	26.8	30.4	13.6
C. Ages 47–64			
1. Mean DC Pension Wealth	8.0	96.6	1105.8
2. Mean DB Pension Wealth	94.5	74.3	−21.4
3. Mean Pension Wealth	102.5	170.8	66.6
Memo: Median Pension Wealth among PW Holders Only	89.9	98.4	9.4
D. Ages 65 and over			
1. Mean DC Pension Wealth	1.8	53.6	2835.1
2. Mean DB Pension Wealth	60.5	52.1	−14.0
3. Mean Pension Wealth	62.3	105.6	69.5
Memo: Median Pension Wealth among PW Holders Only	66.0	76.7	16.3

Note: own computations from the 1983 and 2001 Surveys of Consumer Finances. Households are classified into age groups by the age of the head of household. Key:
  Pension Wealth PW = DB + DC

on projected benefits in twenty to forty years hence.[11] The average value of DB plans among the elderly fell by somewhat less over this period, 14 percent. In contrast to DC pensions, the average value of DB pension wealth was highest among elderly households—at $105,600 in 2001—compared to $74,300 among middle-aged households and only $16,900 among young households.

I can now consider one of the issues raised in my introduction: has the spread of DC type pension plans adequately compensated for the decline in traditional DB pension coverage? The results indicate that the answer is both yes and no.

Average pension wealth (PW, the sum of DC and DB pensions) increased for all age groups between 1983 and 2001. Among all households, the mean value of total pension wealth climbed by 60 percent. Among those in the 46 and under and 47–64 age groups, the mean value increased by 76 and 66 percent, respectively, while among elderly households the mean value jumped by 70 percent.

The story is not quite as positive when I look at trends in median pension wealth. Among all households, median pension wealth more than doubled between 1983 and 2001, from $4,900 to $10,900 (result not shown). However, much of this gain is a result of increased pension coverage. When the sample is limited to those households with positive pension wealth, the median actually fell by 17 percent, from $64,300 to $53,700, over the period. Among young households who have pension wealth, median pension wealth increased by 14 percent; among middle-aged pension holders, by 9 percent; and among elderly pension holders, by 16 percent. The bottom line is that while mean pension wealth grew strongly over this period, median pension wealth showed much more modest gains.

In Table 6, I investigate trends in the inequality of pension wealth. I use a standard Gini coefficient for this purpose. I look first at the dispersion among pension holders only. Among all households, the inequality of DC pension wealth fell over the period from 1983 to 2001. This was also true among young and middle-aged households but not among elderly DC pension owners.

However, the level of inequality in DC pension wealth was still very high in 2001, even among DC account holders alone. The Gini coefficient among all DC pension account holders was 0.741 in 2001. This compares to a Gini coefficient for net worth of 0.826. Inequality among DC account holders within each age group was almost as great as among all DC account holders.[12]

In contrast, the dispersion in traditional DB pension wealth trended upward over the 1983–2001 period. Among all households who had plans, the Gini coefficient climbed from 0.555 to 0.638. Among middle-aged pension holders, DB pension-wealth inequality also climbed sharply (by 0.088), as it did among elderly pension recipients (0.202). In contrast, DB wealth inequality declined by 0.078 points among young households with DB plans.

In terms of inequality levels, DB pension-wealth inequality was considerably lower among DB pension-wealth holders than among DC pension account holders. Not surprisingly, the switchover from DB pension plans to DC pension plans has resulted in an upsurge in pension-wealth inequality.

This trend is also documented in Table 6. Among all households, the Gini coefficient for total pension wealth rose by 0.051, from 0.749 to 0.800, while among pension-wealth holders, the increase was even more striking—by 0.157,

Table 6. Inequality of Pension Wealth among Pension Holders, 1983 and 2001
(Gini coefficients)

	1983	2001	% Change 1983–2001
A. All Pension Holders			
1. DC Accounts	0.792	0.741	−0.051
2. DB Plans	0.555	0.638	0.084
3. Pension Wealth	0.537	0.695	0.157
Memo: PW among all households in group	0.749	0.800	0.051
B. Pension Holders: Ages 46 and under			
1. DC Accounts	0.778	0.719	−0.059
2. DB Plans	0.646	0.568	−0.078
3. Pension Wealth	0.664	0.677	0.013
Memo: PW among all households in group	0.881	0.804	−0.077
C. Pension Holders: Ages 47–64			
1. DC Accounts	0.732	0.714	−0.018
2. DB Plans	0.530	0.617	0.088
3. Pension Wealth	0.539	0.654	0.115
Memo: PW among all households in group	0.677	0.738	0.061
D. Pension Holders: Ages 65 and over			
1. DC Accounts	0.687	0.703	0.015
2. DB Plans	0.463	0.665	0.202
3. Pension Wealth	0.472	0.666	0.194
Memo: PW among all households in group	0.646	0.791	0.144

Note: own computations from the 1983 and 2001 Surveys of Consumer Finances. Households are classified into age groups by the age of the head of household. Key:
   Pension Wealth PW = DB + DC

from 0.537 to 0.695. The pension-wealth inequality patterns are very similar among both middle-aged and elderly households. However, among the younger households, pension-wealth inequality increased only slightly among all households in this group and declined sharply among young households with pension plans—a reflection of the large increase in the share of young households with such plans.

Figure 1 provides a look at the cumulative distribution of pension wealth among all households in 1983 and 2001. Because the percentage of households

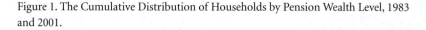

Figure 1. The Cumulative Distribution of Households by Pension Wealth Level, 1983 and 2001.

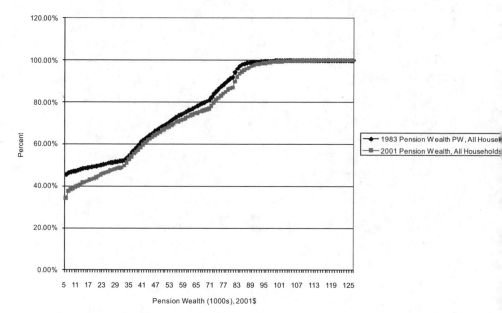

with positive pension wealth expanded over the period, from 54.4 to 65.6, the 1983 cumulative distribution initially lies above the 1998 cumulative distribution. However, what is striking is that though the 1983 cumulative distribution lies above the 2001 cumulative distribution throughout, the two are very close from a pension wealth level of $10,000 through $65,000 (both in 2001 dollars). In other words, despite the gain in the share of households with some pension wealth between 1983 and 2001, a lot of them had very small amounts of pension wealth in 2001 (perhaps an IRA of a few thousand dollars).

Figures 2a and 2b provide further details on the change in the distribution of pension wealth among households in the 47–64 group during the 1983–2001 period. The share with positive pension wealth grew from 70.2 to 75.9 percent over the period, so that percentage gains in pension wealth were very high at lower percentiles. However, pension wealth at the 35th percentile fell by a substantial 14 percent and at the 40th percentile by 7 percent. Pension wealth at the 45th to 60th percentile gained less than 20 percent. In contrast, percentage gains in pension wealth increased from 53 percent at the 80th percentile to a remarkable 123 percent at the 99th percentile.

Figure 2a. Pension Wealth PW in 2001 Dollars by Pension Wealth Percentile, Ages 47–64, 1983 and 2001

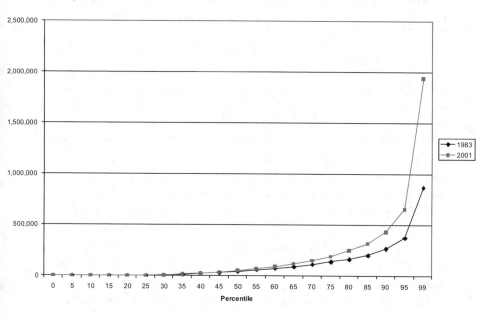

Figure 2b. Percentage Change in Pension Wealth PW in 2001 Dollars by Pension Wealth Percentile, Ages 47–64, 1983 and 2001

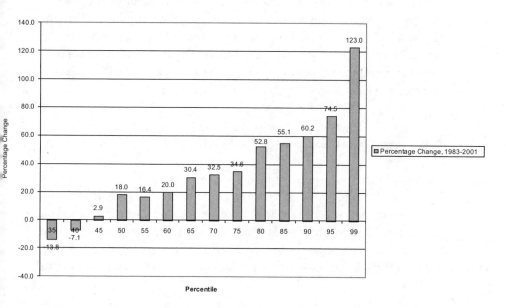

A decomposition of the inequality of pension wealth in 1983 and 2001 reveals the changing contribution of the two forms of pensions to overall pension wealth inequality. As derived in Wolff (1987), for any variable $X = X_1 + X_2$,

$$CV^2(X) = p_1^2 CV^2(X_1) + p_2^2 CV^2(X_2) + 2CC(X_1,X_2)$$

where CV is the coefficient of variation (the ratio of the standard deviation to the mean), CC is the coefficient of covariation, defined as the ratio of the covariance to X^2, $p_1 = X_1/X$, and $p_2 = X_2/X$.[13]

Results are shown in Table 7. As noted above, pension-wealth inequality increased over the 1983–2001 period. In this case, the coefficient of variation of pension wealth among all households rose by 0.60 points, from 2.07 to 2.66. The coefficient of variation of DC wealth fell by over half, from 8.5 to 3.7, while the coefficient of variation of DB pension wealth grew by a little over a half, from 2.0 to 3.2. Much of the change reflected the increasing share of households with DC pension wealth and the corresponding decline in the share of households with DB plans. Still, even in 2001, the inequality of DC pension wealth was greater than that of DB pension wealth.

Despite the decline in DC inequality, the largest contribution to the growth of pension-wealth inequality was the increasing share of DC pension wealth in total pension wealth (rows C1 and D1). Indeed, it more than accounted for more than the total increase in PW inequality over the 1983–2001 period. Moreover, despite the rise in DB inequality over the period, its declining share of total pension wealth helped to reduce overall pension-wealth inequality (lines C2 and D2). The correlation between DC and DB pension wealth was quite small in both 1983 and 2001—0.17 and 0.14, respectively—and it showed a decline over the period. The increase in the coefficient of covariation between the two components also contributed somewhat to the overall rise in pension-wealth inequality over the period. Results for the 47–64 group are quite similar.

7. Private Accumulations

I next look at trends in both mean and median private accumulations (PA) over the 1983 to 2001 period (see Table 8). I begin by recapitulating trends in net worth over the period. Among all households, mean NWX (net worth excluding DC) rose by 32 percent, while the median barely changed. Mean net worth rose by 52 percent, while its median increased by only 14 percent. I next add pension wealth to NWX to obtain PA. Its mean value was up by 38 percent, compared to

Table 7. Contribution of DC and DB Pensions to Overall Pension Wealth (PW) Inequality, 1983 and 2001

Category	All Households				Households, Ages 47–64			
	1983	2001	Change 1983–2001	Contribution to Change 1983–2001[a]	1983	2001	Change 1983–2001	Contribution to Change 1983–2001[a]
A. Coefficient of Variation (CV)								
1) PW	2.07	2.66	0.60		1.63	2.15	0.51	
2) DC	8.52	3.69	−4.83		6.65	2.96	−3.69	
3) DB	2.02	3.20	1.18		1.58	2.67	1.09	
B. Correlation (DC,DB)	0.17	0.14	−0.03		0.19	0.12	−0.07	
C. Decomposition of $CV^2(PW)$								
1) $p_1^2CV^2(DC)$	0.34	4.35	4.01		0.25	2.80	2.55	
2) $p_2^2CV^2(DB)$	3.55	1.93	−1.62		2.15	1.35	−0.80	
3) $2CC(DC,DB)$	0.37	0.80	0.43		0.28	0.46	0.18	
4) $CV^2(PW)$	4.27	7.08	2.82		2.67	4.61	1.94	
D. Percentage Decomposition of $CV^2(PW)$								
1) $p_1^2CV^2(DC)$	8.1	61.4		142.3	9.3	60.8		131.9
2) $p_2^2CV^2(DB)$	83.2	27.3		−57.4	80.4	29.3		−41.2
3) $2CC(DC,DB)$	8.7	11.2		15.1	10.4	9.9		9.3
4) $CV^2(PW)$	100.0	100.0		100.0	100.0	100.0		100.0

Note: own computations from the 1983 and 2001 Survey of Consumer Finances. Key:

CV = Coefficient of variation

CC = Coefficient of covariation

p_1 = DC / PW

p_2 = DB / PW

Note that the 1983 observation is excluded from the calculation if a missing value exists for either DB or DC.

[a] Defined as the change in the component over the 1983–2001 period divided by the change in the CV Squared of PW over the period.

Table 8. Mean, Median, and the Inequality of Private Accumulations, 1983 and 2001 (In thousands, 2001 dollars)

	Mean Values			Median Values			Gini Coefficients		
	1983	2001	% Change, 1983–2001	1983	2001	% Change, 1983–2001	1983	2001	Change, 1983–2001
A. All Households									
1. Net Worth minus DC (NWX)	247.1	326.6	32.2	57.6	58.0	0.7	0.802	0.845	0.043
2. Net Worth (NW)	251.0	380.3	51.5	64.5	73.5	14.0	0.799	0.826	0.028
3. Private Accumulations (PA)	306.4	421.4	37.5	111.6	96.5	–13.5	0.746	0.800	0.054
B. Ages 46 and under									
1. Net Worth minus DC (NWX)	106.8	146.8	37.4	23.1	12.8	–44.8	0.801	0.892	0.091
2. Net Worth (NW)	109.4	175.1	60.0	26.3	20.7	–21.3	0.797	0.859	0.062
3. Private Accumulations (PA)	132.4	191.9	44.9	31.8	31.8	0.0	0.793	0.832	0.039
C. Ages 47–64									
1. Net Worth minus DC (NWX)	365.1	501.7	37.4	108.1	103.5	–4.3	0.762	0.823	0.061
2. Net Worth (NW)	373.1	598.3	60.4	108.3	137.6	27.0	0.761	0.798	0.037
3. Private Accumulations (PA)	467.6	672.6	43.8	204.4	199.9	–2.2	0.681	0.762	0.081
D. Ages 65 and over									
1. Net Worth minus DC (NWX)	370.8	504.0	35.9	101.4	142.0	40.0	0.777	0.766	–0.011
2. Net Worth (NW)	372.7	557.6	49.6	101.9	150.8	47.9	0.778	0.762	–0.016
3. Private Accumulations (PA)	433.2	609.7	40.7	158.5	206.0	30.0	0.715	0.735	0.020

Note: own computations from the 1983 and 2001 Surveys of Consumer Finances.
Households are classified into age groups by the age of the head of household. Key:
Private Accumulations PA = NWX+PW

52 percent for net worth, while its median value was down by a very sizeable 14 percent, compared to a 14 percent increase in median net worth.

Among middle-aged households, the mean value of PA rose by 44 percent, compared to a 60 percent increase in net worth, whereas the median value of PA was down by 2 percent, compared to a 27 percent gain in median net worth. Among elderly households, the mean value of PA rose by 41 percent, compared to a 50 percent rise in net worth, while the median grew by 30 percent, as opposed to a 48 percent increase in net worth. Among younger households, mean PA was up by 45 percent, compared to a 60 percent growth in net worth, while median PA remained completely unchanged, in contrast to a 21 percent decline in median net worth.[14]

Generally speaking, private accumulations fared worse than conventional net worth. Mean PA rose less than mean net worth, while median PA increased far less than median net worth (except for young households). A comparison of trends in PA with those in NWX suggests that households dipped into their private savings to finance their 401(k) and other DC plans.

In Table 8, I also consider the effects of pension wealth on overall wealth inequality. The Gini coefficient for net worth among all households was 0.826 in 2001. If one subtracts DC pensions, then that Gini coefficient rises by 0.019 points to 0.845. Adding DB pension wealth to net worth results in a fall of the Gini coefficient of 0.026 points, to 0.800. This rather modest decline in the Gini coefficient is due to both the high level of pension wealth inequality in the population and the high correlation of pension wealth with marketable net worth (see below).

Looking over time, I also find that the equalizing effect of DB pension wealth has mitigated over the period from 1983 to 2001. Whereas the Gini coefficient for net worth among all households advanced by 0.028 points over the 1983–2001 period, the Gini coefficient for PA gained 0.054 points. Likewise, adding DB pension wealth to net worth results in a decline of 0.053 in the Gini coefficient in 1983 but only a decrease of 0.026 in 2001. However, the joint effect of adding total pension wealth to NWX is more similar in the two years: a 0.056 reduction in the Gini coefficient in 1983 and a 0.045 reduction in 2001.

The results are sharpest for middle-aged households. For this group, the Gini coefficient for net worth increased by 0.037 while that for PA ballooned by 0.081. Likewise, among the elderly, PA inequality increased by 0.020 points, whereas net worth inequality fell by 0.016 points. The exception to this pattern is young households, for whom PA inequality increased less than net worth inequality.

Table 9 provides a decomposition to provide an alternative assessment of the effects of adding private pension wealth to NWX (net worth less DC pension

Table 9. Contribution of Pensions to Inequality in Private Accumulations (PA), 1983 and 2001

Category	All Households				Households, Ages 47–64			
	1983	2001	Change 1983–2001	Contribution to Change 1983–2001[a]	1983	2001	Change 1983–2001	Contribution to Change 1983–2001[a]
A. Coefficient of Variation (CV)								
1) PA	4.89	4.95	0.06		3.89	4.13	0.24	
2) NWX	5.90	6.15	0.25		4.87	5.30	0.43	
3) PW	2.07	2.66	0.60		1.63	2.15	0.51	
B. Correlation (NWX,PW)	0.21	0.26	0.05		0.21	0.26	0.05	
C. Decomposition of CV²(PA)								
1) $P_1^2CV^2(NWX)$	22.97	22.69	−0.27		14.43	15.63	1.20	
2) $P_2^2CV^2(PW)$	0.15	0.36	0.21		0.13	0.30	0.17	
3) $2CC(NWX,PW)$	0.80	1.50	0.70		0.57	1.13	0.56	
4) $CV^2(PA)$	23.91	24.55	0.63		15.12	17.05	1.93	
D. Percentage Decomposition of CV²(PA)								
1) $P_1^2CV^2(NWX)$	96.0	92.4		−43.1	95.4	91.7		62.3
2) $P_2^2CV^2(PW)$	0.6	1.5		33.0	0.9	1.7		8.7
3) $2CC(NWX,PW)$	3.3	6.1		110.1	3.7	6.6		29.0
4) $CV^2(PA)$	100.0	100.0		100.0	100.0	100.0		100.0

Note: own computations from the 1983 and 2001 Survey of Consumer Finances. Key:

CV = Coefficient of variation

CC = Coefficient of covariation

P_1 = NWX / PA

P_2 = PW / PA

Note that the 1983 observation is excluded from the calculation if a missing value exists for either DB or DC.

[a] Defined as the change in the component over the 1983–2001 period divided by the change in the CV Squared Squared of PA over the period.

accounts) on the inequality of PA among all households and those in the 47–64 group. As noted earlier, pension wealth inequality among all households as measured by the coefficient of variation (CV) increased by 0.60 points during the 1983–2001 period. Inequality in NWX increased less over the period—by 0.25 points—and the coefficient of variation of PA grew by only 0.06 (section A). It is of note that the increase in the inequality of PA based on CV is considerably smaller than that based on the Gini coefficient. This reflects the fact that the CV is much more sensitive to changes in the upper tail of the distribution than is the Gini coefficient, and, as shall be seen below, a large portion of the change in the distribution of PA occurs in the middle deciles.

The correlation between NWX and PW increased over the period, from 0.21 to 0.26, and in this decomposition the rising correlation accounted for 110 percent of the rise in the coefficient of variation of PA. The growth in pension wealth inequality together with its rising share in PA also made a positive contribution to the rise in the CV of PA (33 percent), while the declining share of NWX in PA made a negative contribution.

Results are rather different for the 47–64 group. Here the largest contribution is made by the rising inequality in NWX (62 percent), followed by the rising correlation between NWX and PW (29 percent) and then by the rise in PW inequality (9 percent). The results suggest that for this age group, at least lower wealth households substituted DC pension wealth for other components of net worth, accounting for the sharp jump in the inequality of NWX.[15]

Figures 3a and 3b provide a closer look at the size distribution of PA in 1983 and 1998 for households in age group 47 to 64. Here it becomes quite clear that the major gains over the 1983–2001 period were made by households at the high end of the wealth distribution. Indeed, comparing the size distributions in the two years at different percentile levels, I find an almost monotonic relation between percentile level and percentage change in PA over the period. The percentage growth in PA surges from −98 percent at the 10th percentile to 94 percent at the 99th percentile. The crossover point in the two distributions occurs slightly below the median.

8. SUMMARY OF FINDINGS

The 1980s and 1990s witnessed the devolution of the traditional DB pension system in favor of DC pension coverage. In general, middle-aged and elderly Americans have seen marked improvements in both the mean and median levels of their marketable net worth over the period from 1983 to 2001. On the other

Figure 3a. Private Accumulations (PA) in 2001 Dollars by PA Percentile, Ages 47–64, 1983 and 2001

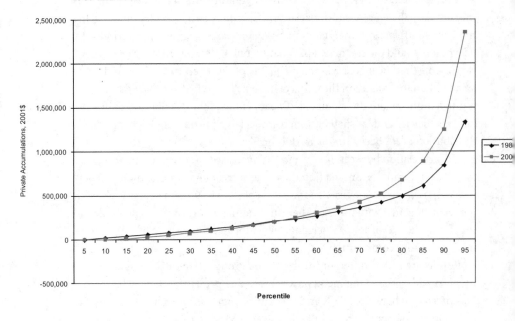

Figure 3b. Percentage Growth of Private Accumulations (in 2001 Dollars), Ages 47–64, By Percentile, 1983 and 2001

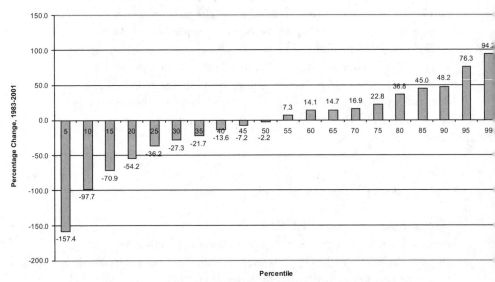

hand, traditional DB pension coverage declined over the same period. The share of households covered by a DB plan fell by 18 percentage points, from 53 percent in 1983 to 34 percent in 2001. Mean DB pension wealth also decreased, from $55,400 to $41,200 (both in 2001 dollars). Average DC pension wealth, on the other hand, skyrocketed. By 2001, over half of all households held some form of DC type pension plan, compared to 11 percent in 1983; and 62 percent of households in the 47–64 group held some form of DC type pension plan in 2001, compared to 12 percent in 1983. Among households in the 65 and older group, 35 percent had a DC account in 2001, while only 2 percent had such an account in 1983.

The rise of DC pensions plans more than fully compensated for the loss of DB type pension plans over the 1983–2001 period in terms of average values. Mean total pension wealth (the sum of DB plus DB wealth) increased by 60 percent in real terms over the period among all households and by 67 percent among households in the 47–64 group. The share of all households covered by either a DB or a DC pension plan also grew over the period, from 54 to 66 percent, while the fraction of households in the 47–64 group with one or the other plan rose from 70 to 76 percent. Moreover, mean private accumulations (the sum of net worth and pension wealth) soared by 37.5 percent.

However, the story looks somewhat different when one looks at trends in median values. Among all households, median pension wealth more than doubled, from $4,900 to $10,900 (both in 2001 dollars). However, in the 47–64 group, median pension wealth increased at a much lower rate, 18 percent, from $42,400 to $50,000. Moreover, among all households, median net worth excluding DC pension plans remained almost unchanged from 1983 to 2001. Indeed, in the 47–64 group it fell by 4 percent, and among young households it was down by 45 percent, though it rose by 40 percent among the elderly. Altogether, median PA fell by a sizeable 14 percent among all households and by 2 percent among households in the 47–64 group. Here, too, results differ greatly between the nonelderly and the elderly. Among households in the 65 and over group, median PA climbed by 30 percent between 1983 and 2001.

The inequality of total pension wealth increased sharply between 1983 and 2001. This trend is traceable to the switchover from DB plans to DC accounts. The inequality of private accumulations rose substantially more than that of net worth during the 1983–2001 period. DB pension wealth has a very modest equalizing effect on overall wealth inequality (particularly in comparison to Social Security wealth). Moreover, DB pension wealth had a weaker offsetting effect on wealth inequality in 2001 than it did in 1983. The results are particularly pronounced for households in the 47–64 group. Within this group, the

Gini coefficient for net worth rose by 0.037 between 1983 and 2001, whereas the Gini coefficient for private accumulations climbed by 0.081.

In sum, I find that despite the proliferation of DC plans, at a time when the stock market experienced one of its longest bull runs in history, the wealth holdings of the nonelderly did not improve. Indeed, median private accumulations actually deteriorated for young and middle-aged households during the 1983–2001 period, though it did improve among the elderly. This is true despite a large shift in the composition of private retirement wealth away from DB plans toward DC plans. Indeed, the devolution of the traditional pension system of the 1980s and 1990s has left many families unprepared to meet challenges of retirement. Despite the hype, the switchover from DB to DC plans has not benefited the average family—it has hurt the average family instead.

One potential consequence of the change to DC plans—and the consequent decline in pension wealth and total private accumulations among the majority of employees—is that many employees may delay their retirement relative to what it would have been under a DB system. In particular, the decline in pension income might reduce the reservation wage of older persons and induce them to increase their labor force participation. It is generally agreed that this type of increase in working life among the elderly due to greater financial need is not socially desirable. The shift to DC plans also makes the retirement decision more subject to the vicissitudes of the financial market. Anecdotal evidence suggests that the sharp drop in the stock market between 2001 and 2003 forced many employees to postpone their retirement plans.

9. Why the Transformation of the Pension System?

One might wonder, why the rapid transformation from DB to DC Plans, particularly if workers are made worse off? I speculate on some of the causes here. There are three reasons why employers might prefer DC plans to DB plans. First, DC plans allow firms to shift the risk to workers. The shift eliminates long-term pension liabilities of firms. Third, employers generally make lower contributions to DC plans than DB plans. Ghilarducci and Sun (2004) estimated that DC plans, on average, cost the employer 50 percent less than traditional DB pension plans.[16]

There were also some pulls and pushes. With regard to the *pull*, the main reason was the availability of DC plans. IRAs were established in 1974. This was quickly followed by 401(k) plans in 1978 for profit-making companies (403[b] plans for nonprofits are much older). Another is the option to convert DB pension plans to so-called cash balance plans (effectively, DC accounts). In 1999, a lawsuit was initiated by older IBM employees when IBM tried to convert its DB pension plan to a cash balance plan. Though the court ruled in favor of the employees, new regulations issued by the IRS since then seem to make such conversions legal. This may further expedite the elimination of DB plans.

With regard to the *push,* the first was the passage of the Employee Retirement Income Security Act (ERISA) in 1975, which increased regulatory burdens on DB plans and made DB plans more costly. ERISA meant that companies are not allowed to "fool around" with their pension assets. Companies must put money into pension funds to meet future liabilities, and they must pay out benefits. ERISA also required companies to pay premiums to the Pension Benefit Guarantee Corporation, which was created in 1974, to insure their pension plans.[17] The second was the Omnibus Budget Reconciliation Act of 1987, which established even tighter funding limits on DB plans. The third push was the decline of unions in the United States. According to CPS data, the unionization rate fell from 20 percent in 1983 to 13 percent in 2001. Unions have been one of the bulwarks supporting the traditional DB pension system.[18]

A 2003 proposal by the Bush administration to establish employer Retirement Savings Accounts (RSAs) as the successor to 401(k) plans might accelerate the growth of DC type plans even more. One provision of RSAs is to eliminate the tax deductibility of both the employer and employee contribution to these new accounts. This would overturn the long-standing ability (since 1942) of firms to deduct pension contributions from their taxes as long as they offer proportional benefits to both executives and rank-and-file workers. Indeed, the new RSAs might hasten the further withdrawal of firms to provide pension support by eliminating the employer contributions to pension plans altogether.

10. What Is to Be Done to Reform the Pension System?

From the point of view of workers, the best solution is to encourage companies to return to the old-fashioned DB plans. This could be accomplished through a combination of tax incentives and tax credits. Also, DB plans should be made portable so that workers would retain credits for their job tenure at one firm if they move to another firm.

Given that it seems politically unlikely that Congress will enact this type of legislation, one must think about how to shore up the DC pension system. Here are six proposals:

1. Make participation universal within a firm so that all workers are covered. Do *not* require employee contributions in order to have funds provided (or matched) by employer. Employer contributions should be *mandatory*. Employee contributions should be *voluntary*.
2. Make provisions *universal* within a firm. No special deals for top management. No sweetheart deals for the CEO. The plans should be the same for rank-and-file workers as they are for top management.
3. To avoid Enron-type disasters, put limits on the amount of company stock invested in the pension plan. Past legislative proposals in Congress impose a cap of 20 percent. Even this may be too high.
4. Have an independent agency administer the pension plan. TIAA-CREF is a good model.
5. Allow investment choices within the pension plan. Mutual funds should be encouraged so as to lessen the risk. A choice should be provided among different mutual funds.
6. Require independent investment advice—perhaps, from TIAA-CREF, Vanguard, or a similar firm.

Appendix. Estimation of Pension Wealth

I follow the methodology (with a few modifications indicated below for subsequent years) laid out in the 1983 Survey of Consumer Finances (SCF) codebook. This allows consistency with the estimates of both pension and Social Security wealth already provided in the 1983 SCF. The computations of retirement wealth in 1983 followed the following steps:

A. Pension Wealth in the 1983 SCF

Total gross pension wealth consists of two main components:[19]

1. Gross present value of pensions from past jobs: the sum of the present value of past job pensions for head and spouse.
2. Gross present value of pensions from current jobs: the sum of the gross present value of current job nonthrift benefits for head and spouse. Expectations data are used for the calculations.

The procedure is as follows. Pension coverage is first ascertained for current jobs. There are five possible categories:

1. covered and vested, anticipates benefits;
2. covered but not vested yet, anticipates benefits;
3. covered but not vested yet, does not anticipate benefits;
4. not covered, anticipates will be—age when expected to be covered is ascertained; and
5. not covered, never will be.

For those who are covered by a pension plan or expect coverage, the person is asked how many distinct pension plans he or she is covered by. For each plan, the age at which the pension benefits are expected to be given is then asked.

The actual expected annual retirement benefit is then determined by the following steps. First, the age at which the respondent will be vested in each plan is determined. Second, the age at which the respondent could retire with full benefits is ascertained. Third, the respondent was asked the nature of the formula used to determine the retirement benefits. There are six possibilities:

1. retirement formula based on age;
2. retirement formula based on years of service;
3. retirement formula based on meeting both age and years of service criteria;
4. retirement formula based on the sum or age and years of service;
5. retirement formula based on meeting either age or years of service criteria; and
6. other combinations or formulas.

Fourth, the age at which the respondent could retire with some benefits was asked. The same six choices of the formula used were then given. Fifth, the age at which the respondent expected benefits to start was then asked.

Seventh, the expected retirement benefit was computed depending on the type of formula. This consists of three possibilities:

1. The annual pay in the final year of the job was computed. This variable, used in pension benefit calculations, is computed by projecting current pay to the year respondents say he or she will leave the job or retire. Wage growth is assumed to have three components: (i) an occupation specific (adjusted for age) term taken from the slopes in the CPS log-wage regressions (for high-income observations this is assumed to be zero); (ii) a Social Security

Plan II-B assumption of 1.5 percent annual economy wide real wage growth; and (iii) a Social Security Plan II-B assumption of 4.0 percent inflation.

2. In some cases, the respondent reported expected retirement benefits. This variable is the expected dollar retirement benefits in the first year of eligibility as answered by the respondent. For some respondents, the dollar amount was reported directly, but for others it was computed by multiplying reported benefits as a percentage times the calculated projected final wage. The variable is given as an annual amount except when a lump sum is expected (in which case the lump sum amount is given).

3. In some cases, the respondent reported expected retirement benefits as a percent of final pay. This variable is the expected retirement benefits in the first year of eligibility as answered by the respondent, expressed as a percent of their projected wages in their final year of work.

Eighth, on the basis of the responses above, the present value of pension benefits from each current and past plan applicable to both spouses was then computed. This variable is measured assuming an annual (or lump-sum) pension benefit as given above, starting in the year of first benefits. Benefits for that and each succeeding year are adjusted for the probability of death and are discounted back to 1983. Sex-based Social Security mortality tables are used to compute the probabilities of death (standard for each year). These are capped at 109 years. Spousal survival benefits are assumed to be opted for 75 percent of the time and are randomly assigned when appropriate. Spousal survival benefits are also adjusted for death probabilities. Benefits are discounted at the 1983 long-term U.S. government bond rate of 10.85 percent.

Ninth, pension wealth was also computed for those individuals currently receiving pension benefits from past jobs. This was based on the following responses:

1. number of years receiving benefits, and
2. amount of pension benefit pay received in 1982.

For pensions already being received, the nominal value of the pension is assumed to be fixed, and is indexed to the year it started by the actual price changes observed as measured by the Consumer Price Index. The present value of pension benefits from each job is then measured assuming an annual pension benefit as given starting in the year of first benefits (or 1983). Benefits for that and each succeeding year (adjusted for probability of receipt) are discounted back to 1983. Sex-based Social Security mortality tables are used to compute the probabilities of dying each year and/or living to receive any benefits. These are capped at 109 years. Spousal survival benefits are assumed to be opted for 75 percent of the time and are randomly assigned when appropriate. Spouse mortality tables are also used. Benefits are discounted at the 1983 long-term U.S. Government bond rate of 10.85 percent. .

B. Modifications for Years after 1983

A few changes were made in the procedures for computing both pension and Social Security wealth. First, the regression equations used to compute future earnings were modified as follows:

Human capital earnings functions are estimated by gender, race, and schooling level. In particular, the sample is divided into sixteen groups by the following characteristics:

1. white and Asian versus African-American and Hispanic;
2. male and female; and
3. less than twelve years of schooling, twelve years of schooling, thirteen to fifteen years of schooling, and sixteen or more years.

For each group, an earnings equation is estimated as follows:

$$\text{Log}(E_i) = b_0 + b_1 \text{Log}(H_i) + b_2 X_i + b_3 X_i^2 + b_4 SE_i + \Sigma_j b_j OCCUP_{ij} + b_{10} MAR_i + b_{11} AS_I + \epsilon_i$$

where log is the natural logarithm; E_i is the current earnings of individual I; H_i is annual hours worked in the current year; X_i is years of experience at current age (estimated as age minus years of schooling minus 5); SE_i is a dummy variable indicating whether the person is self-employed or working for someone else; OCCUP is a set of five dummy variables indicating occupation of employment— (1) professional and managerial; (2) technical, sales, or administrative support,: (3) service; (4) craft, and (5) other blue-collar, with farming the omitted category); MAR is a dummy variable indicating whether the person is married or not married; AS is a dummy variable indicating whether the person is Asian or not (used only for regressions on the first racial category); and ϵ is a stochastic error term. Future earnings are projected on the basis of the regression coefficients.[20]

Second, the ten-year U.S. Treasury bond rate prevailing for each individual year (1989 and 1998) was used as the discount factor. Third, I have used mortality rates by age, gender, and race instead of by age and gender alone in the computation of the present value of both pensions and Social Security wealth.

Fourth, for consistency with 1983, I have continued to employ the Social Security Plan II-B assumption of 1.5 percent annual economy-wide real wage growth, even though this seems too high in comparison with the actual post-1973 growth in annual earnings (which has averaged about 0.2 percent per year). I have also used the Social Security Plan II-B assumption of 4.0 percent annual inflation, even though this seems too high.

NOTES

1. Three studies conducted by the Federal Reserve Board discuss some of the issues involved in developing these weights (see Kennickell and Woodburn [1992] for the 1989 SCF; Kennickell, McManus, and Woodburn [1996] for the 1992 SCF; and Kennickell and Woodburn [1999] for the 1995 SCF). Also, see Wolff (2001) for details on the weights used in this study and other adjustments to the basic SCF data.

2. Technically speaking, the mortality rate m_t associated with the year of retirement is the probability of surviving from the current age to the age of retirement.

3. The establishment of the Pension Benefit Guarantee Corporation in 1974 does, at least, insure the pension benefits in the event of the bankruptcy of a company.

4. Social Security wealth would have the same interpretation as DB wealth (see, for example, Feldstein 1974).

5. A related issue concerns the tax liability attached to pension wealth. DC contributions are tax sheltered when they are made and subject to income tax upon withdrawal. As a result, their current post-tax value is lower than their current market value. In principle, the post-tax value of DC plans should be used when computing current net worth and PA. DB pension income is likewise taxable upon receipt, so that the value of DB pension wealth should also be discounted when computing PA. These adjustments are outside the scope of this paper.

6. I use the CPS income data because I can obtain income statistics for the same years as the SCF wealth data; the SCF income data are for the preceding year.

7. The CPS tabulations provided by the U.S. Bureau of the Census do not include the income shares of the top percentile.

8. This occurred while the homeownership rate rose from 63.4 percent in 1983 to 67.7 percent in 2001.

9. It should be noted that these figures do not include stocks held in pension funds run by corporations, banks, other financial institutions, and labor unions. Technically, these securities are directly owned by the institutions that administer them and therefore are not in the direct control of individuals.

10. Due to space constraints, I show results for only 1983 and 2001. Results for some other key variables are also available for 1989 and 1998.

11. Moreover, there is a large number of missing values for this age group in the 1983 SCF data.

12. This result accords with media accounts of a large divide in the value of 401(k) plans between executives and staff workers in large corporations (see, for example, Leonhardt 2002).

13. The Theil coefficient cannot be used here because of the large number of zero values.

14. Here, again, some caution should be exercised with regard to pension wealth figures for young households, particularly because of a large number of missing values in the 1983 data.

15. Here it should be stressed that a decomposition is not a behavioral model—that is, it does not take into account how other wealth components of NWX change in response to changes in PW.

16. Also see Wolman and Colamosca (2002) for more discussion of this point.

17. However, Gustman and Steinmeier (1992), examining the 1977–1985 period, concluded that regulatory changes could account for no more than half (and perhaps much less) of the shift from DB to DC plans, at least over this period.

18. Another factor that has been mentioned is greater worker mobility in the 1990s than in the 1980s. The argument is that because DB pensions are not portable between employers, workers who switch jobs may prefer DC to DB plans. However, according to Farber (2001), however, there was virtually no change, on average, in the degree of job tenure between the 1980s and 1990s.

19. A third though minor component is also provided: pensions from other non-specified sources.

20. This implicitly assumes that deviations from the regression line in the current year are a result of a transitory component to current income only. This procedure follows the conventions of the 1983 SCF codebook.

References

Bloom, David E., and Richard B. Freeman. 1992. "The Fall in Private Pension Coverage in the United States." *American Economic Review Papers and Proceedings.* Vol. 82, no. 2 (May) 539–58.

Even, William E., and David A. Macpherson. 1994a. "Trends in Individual and Household Pension Coverage." Mimeo. (December).

———. 1994b. "Why Did Male Pension Coverage Decline in the 1980s?" *Industrial and Labor Relations Review.* Vol. 47, no. 3 (April) 429–53.

———. 1994c. "Why Has the Decline in Pension Coverage Accelerated among Less Educated Workers?" Mimeo. (December).

———. 1994d. "Gender Differences in Pensions." *Journal of Human Resources.* Vol. 29, no. 2. 555–87.

Farber, Henry S. 2001. "Job Loss in the United States, 1981–1999." Working Paper No. 453. Princeton, New Jersey: Princeton University, Industrial Relations Section. (June).

Feldstein, Martin S. 1974. "Social Security, Induced Retirement and Aggregate Capital Accumulation." *Journal of Political Economy*. Vol. 82 (October) 905–26.

———. 1976. "Social Security and the Distribution of Wealth." *Journal of the American Statistical Association*. Vol. 71 (December) 800–807.

Ghilarducci, Teresa, and Wei Sun. 2004. "Employer Pension Costs and 401(k)s: 1981–1998." *Industrial Relations*. Vol. 43 (April).

Gustman, Alan L., Olivia S. Mitchell, Andrew A. Samwick, and Thomas L. Steinmeier. 1997. "Pension and Social Security Wealth in the Health and Retirement Study." NBER Working Paper No. W5912 (February).

Gustman, Alan L., and Thomas L. Steinmeier. 1992. "The Stampede toward Defined Contribution Pension Plans: Fact or Fiction?" *Industrial Relations*. Vol. 31, no. 2 (Spring) 361–69.

———. 1998. "Effects of Pensions on Saving: Analysis with Data from the Health and Retirement Study." NBER Working Paper No. W6681 (August).

Hurd, Michael. 1994. "The Economic Status of the Elderly in the United States." In *Aging in the United States and Japan*. Yukio Noguchi and David A. Wise, editors. Chicago: University of Chicago Press. 63–83.

Ippolito, Richard. 1995. "Toward Explaining the Growth in Defined Contributions Plans." *Industrial Relations*. Vol. 34 (January).

Kennickell, Arthur B., Douglas A. McManus, and R. Louise Woodburn. 1996. "Weighting Design for the 1992 Survey of Consumer Finances." Federal Reserve Board of Washington (March). Mimeo.

Kennickell, Arthur B., and R. Louise Woodburn. 1992. "Estimation of Household Net Worth Using Model-Based and Design-Based Weights: Evidence from the 1989 Survey of Consumer Finances." Mimeo, Federal Reserve Board. (April).

Kennickell, Arthur B., and R. Louise Woodburn. 1999. "Consistent Weight Design for the 1989, 1992, and 1995 SCFs, and the Distribution of Wealth." *Review of Income and Wealth*. Vol. 45, no. 2 (June) 193–216.

Kennickell, Arthur B., and Annika E. Sunden. 1999. "Pensions, Social Security, and the Distribution of Wealth." Federal Reserve Board of Washington. Mimeo. (December).

Kotlikoff, Laurence J., and Daniel E. Smith. 1983. *Pensions in the American Economy*. Chicago: University of Chicago Press.

Leonhardt, David. 2002. "For Executives, Nets Egg is Wrapped in a Security Blanket." *New York Times*. (March 5) C1.

Moore, James F., and Olivia S. Mitchell. 2000. "Projected Retirement Wealth and Saving Adequacy." In *Forecasting Retirement Needs and Retirement Wealth*. O. Mitchell, B. Hammond, and A. Rappaport, eds. Philadelphia: University of Pennsylvania Press.

Popke, Leslie E. 1999. "Are 401(k) Plans Replacing Other Employer-Provided Pensions?" *Journal of Human Resources*. Vol. 34, no. 2. 346–68.

Poterba, James M., Steven F. Venti and David A. Wise. 1998. "401(k) Plans and Future Patterns of Retirement Saving." *American Economic Review Papers and Proceedings*. Vol. 88, no. 2 (May) 179–84.

Smith, James P. 1997. "The Changing Economic Circumstances of the Elderly: Income, Wealth, and Social Security." Syracuse University Public Policy Brief No. 8.

Venti, Steven F., and David A. Wise. 1998. "The Cause of Wealth Dispersion at Retirement: Choice or Chance?" *American Economic Review Papers and Proceedings.* Vol. 88, no. 2 (May) 185–91.

U.S. Bureau of the Census Current Population Reports, Series P-60. No. 169-RD. 1990. *Measuring the Effect of Benefits and Taxes on Income and Poverty: 1989.* Washington, DC: U.S. Government Printing Office. (September).

U.S. Department of Labor Pension and Welfare Benefits Administration. 2000. "Coverage Status of Workers under Employer Provided Pension Plans: Findings from the Contingent Work Supplement to the February 1999 Current Population Survey." Washington, DC: Department of Labor.

Wolff, Edward N. 1987. "The Effects of Pensions and Social Security on the Distribution of Wealth in the U.S." In *International Comparisons of Household Wealth Distribution.* E. Wolff, ed. Oxford University Press.

———. 1988. "Social Security, Pensions, and the Life Cycle Accumulation of Wealth: Some Empirical Tests." *Annales d'Economie et de Statistique.* No. 9 (Janvier/Mars).

———. 1990. "Wealth Holdings and Poverty Status in the United States." *Review of Income and Wealth.* Series 36, no. 2 (June) 143–65.

———. 1992. "Methodological Issues in the Estimation of Retirement Wealth." In *Research in Economic Inequality.* Daniel J. Slottje, ed. JAI Press. Vol. 2. 31–56.

———. 1993a. "Social Security Annuities and Transfers: Distributional and Tax Implications." In *Poverty and Prosperity in the USA in the Late Twentieth Century,* Dimitri B. Papadimitriou and Edward N. Wolff eds. Macmillan Publishers. 211–39.

———. 1993b. "The Distributional Implications of Social Security Annuities and Transfers on Household Wealth and Income." In *Research in Economic Inequality,* Edward N. Wolff, ed. JAI Press. Vol. 4. 131–57.

———. 2001. "Recent Trends in Wealth Ownership, from 1983 to 1998." In *Assets for the Poor: The Benefits of Spreading Asset Ownership,* Thomas M. Shapiro and Edward N. Wolff eds. Russell Sage Press. 34–73.

———. 2002. *Top Heavy: The Increasing Inequality of Wealth in America and What Can Be Done about It.* New York: New Press.

Wolman, William, and Anne Colamosca. 2002. *The Great 401(k) Hoax: Why Your Family's Financial Security Is at Risk, and What You Can Do about It.* Perseus Publishing.

CHAPTER SEVEN

Longevity and Retirement Age in Defined Benefit Pension Plans

DANA MUIR & JOHN TURNER

Life expectancy has increased considerably in the United States since 1940. Between 1940 and 2000, life expectancy for males at birth increased by 10.5 years, and for males age 65 it increased by 3.8 years. Because mortality rates are already low until retirement age is reached, future increases in life expectancy will result mainly from mortality reductions after age 65 (Table 1). Unless retirement ages increase, future retirees can expect to spend substantially more years in retirement than do current retirees.

Increasing longevity raises the costs of providing benefits in defined benefit (DB) pension plans as workers survive to receive benefits for more years. Because changes in life expectancy generally occur slowly over time, pension researchers have tended to focus on other issues where short-term change is more dramatic. Over a period of decades, however, the continuous effect on pension costs of the cumulative increases in longevity can be considerable.

This chapter examines the extent to which DB plan sponsors in the United States have raised their early and normal retirement ages due to the increase in their benefit costs caused by increased life expectancy. The terms "early retirement age" (ERA) and "normal retirement age" (NRA) do not refer to when workers actually retire or start collecting benefits but to ages specified in pension-plan documents.

It is difficult to determine which changes in pension plans are responses to increasing life expectancy because changes occur as discrete events that may be substantial, while life-expectancy improvements generally occur gradually over time. This chapter views the evidence in a preliminary manner by examining the changes over a period of time. With large increases in life expectancy, it might be anticipated that managers of DB plans would raise ERAs and NRAs. Employees

Table 1. Cohort Life Expectancies, Intermediate Assumptions, 1940, 2000, and 2080

Year	Males		Females	
	Birth	Age 65	Birth	Age 65
	Life expectancy			
1940	69.4	12.7	75.9	14.7
2000	79.9	16.5	84.4	19.5
2080	85.9	21.1	89.5	24.0
	Life expectancy improvement			
1940–2000	10.5	3.8	8.5	4.8
2000–2080	6.0	4.6	5.1	4.5

Source: Board of Trustees (2003).
Note: Cohort life expectancies are calculated using death rates from the series of years in which the individual will actually reach each succeeding age if he or she survives.

are arguably healthier and more able to work at older ages than in the past, and work is less physically demanding for many workers; these factors make it feasible for workers to retire at later ages.

The large increases in life expectancy have been accompanied by large increases in per-capita wealth. Thus, an alternative hypothesis is that the positive wealth effect on the demand for leisure has caused workers to want more leisure. That may translate into workers wanting no change in retirement age because they want the longer retirement period provided by the growth in life expectancy. Which hypothesis is correct may have important implications for the types of changes that would be politically feasible for Social Security reform. Changes in ERAs and NRAs made voluntarily by employers sponsoring pension plans would indicate the changes that are feasible in the private sector, and thus may provide evidence concerning reforms that would be politically feasible in the context of Social Security reform.

This chapter examines the extent to which U.S. sponsors of DB pension plans have raised the ERAs and NRAs of their plans. To preview the main empirical results, the chapter finds little evidence of increases in the ERA in private-sector DB plans, with the sponsors of some plans decreasing the ERA or reducing the service requirements for retirement at the ERA. By examining evidence for state- and local-government DB plans, this chapter also explores several hypotheses as to why there has been little change in the ERA in private DB plans. The problems private-sector DB plans encounter in raising their ERA may be a factor in the switch from traditional DB plans to cash balance (CB) plans and to defined contribution (DC) plans.

Life Expectancy and Defined Benefit Pension Costs

The Effect of Increases in Life Expectancy on Pension Costs

Life expectancy increased considerably during the last part of the twentieth century. For example, a 40-year-old man was expected to live to 73 in the 1980 population life table, but was expected to live to 78 in 2002 (Oster 2003). This would lengthen his retirement from 11 years to 16 years, assuming he retired at age 62—an increase in retirement years of 45 percent. Thus, it is plausible that life-expectancy increases have had a substantial effect on the cost of DB plans since 1980.

Making a few assumptions, it is possible to calculate a rough estimate of the effect of increasing life expectancy on pension costs. Assuming an average retirement age of 62 in both 1980 and 2002, a 4 percent interest rate, and no inflation-indexing of benefits past retirement, the growth in life expectancy since 1980 has increased the nominal cost of providing a DB plan per male participant by roughly 30 percent. A higher interest rate would yield a lower figure, while partial inflation indexing would yield a higher figure. This number is less than the 45 percent increase in years of retirement because of the effect of interest discounting, which reduces the present value of distant future benefits. Thus, over this period, DB costs have grown more than 1 percent per year, compounded annually, per male participant due to the increase in life expectancy. This number is a rough approximation, but it gives an estimate of the possible magnitude of the effect for a typical DB plan. The "feminization" of some pension plans due to the increased labor force participation of women would further increase cost since that would raise the average life expectancy of the participants in the plan.

Related evidence as to the effect of life expectancy on plan costs is provided by the price changes made by life insurers. Life insurers in the United States have been revising their prices downward from 10 percent to 30 percent because new mortality tables are being used that replace tables established in 1980 (Oster 2003).

In the United Kingdom, the effect of increasing longevity on DB plan costs is thought to be one of the reasons why employers are ending those plans in favor of DC plans (Pensions Policy Institute 2003). According to a British survey, the primary reasons for large numbers of employers terminating DB pension plans are increased costs due to lower real investment returns and greater longevity (White 2003).

The Effects of Uncertainty in Improvements in Life Expectancy

The uncertainty of the cost imposed by unknown future changes in longevity may also affect employers' pension decisions. Future improvements in life expectancy are inherently uncertain, causing employers sponsoring DB plans to bear longevity risk. The obesity epidemic may cause life expectancy to increase less than currently projected, while a revolution in medical science may cause the improvements to be substantially greater than projected. Social Security actuaries projected an increase of 6 years for life expectancy at birth between 2000 and 2080, but the 2003 Technical Panel on Assumptions and Methods, which examined the basis for that projection, recommend projecting an even greater increase in life expectancy, about 7.5 years.

If the improvements in mortality were perfectly foreseen, plan sponsors arguably would have taken them into account in establishing their plans, and would have foreseen the adjustments that they have made to deal with those increased costs. Pension plan sponsors, however, may have poorly anticipated improvements in life expectancy at older ages during the late-1940s and 1950s when many DB plans were established because of the relatively small increases in life expectancy at older ages during the preceding decades. Life expectancy at age 65 rose from 11.7 years in 1900 to 21.2 years in 2000, an 81 percent increase. However, 75 percent of this change occurred after 1950. The improvements in life expectancy at older ages generally accelerated over the century, thanks especially to an unprecedented reduction in mortality from cardiovascular disease that began in the late-1960s (Technical Panel on Assumptions and Methods 2003).

Employer Pension Responses to Increased Worker Longevity

Increasing life expectancy raises pension liabilities based on both future and past work. Employers have a number of options for responding to the increased pension costs. In adjusting the pension plan to offset the benefit cost increase caused by increasing life expectancy, they can either raise the ERA or reduce benefits. They can reduce benefits by cutting benefits received at normal retirement, cutting early retirement benefits, reducing cost-of-living adjustments for benefits being paid, or they can raise the ERAs or NRAs, which are indirect ways of cutting benefits. Since increased life expectancy raises the cost of providing benefits at older ages, a reduction in cost-of-living adjustments may be used as an offset because such a reduction lowers the cost of providing benefits at older ages. Employers can end plan features that provide incentives for early retirement. Some DB plans have started offering lump-sum benefits as an alternative form of benefit payout. To the extent that plans maintain a mortality table without updating it, they are able to shield themselves from increased cost due to increased life expectancy when workers choose lump-sum benefits.

Besides making offsetting adjustments in the DB plan, employers may make other adjustments. Due to compensating differentials in the labor market, employers may reduce the wage they pay, so that the workers themselves absorb the increased cost of providing pension benefits through reduced wages. Alternatively, employers can absorb the costs themselves through higher contributions to the plans. To avoid the higher costs, employers can convert to CB plans or to DC plans, or terminate their DB plans.

For new employees, employers can establish a higher ERA, require more years of service to qualify for early retirement, or provide less generous benefits, but making these changes may be administratively complex. Changes targeted at new employees essentially treat all new employees as though they are new entrants to the labor market, not recognizing that they may be from different birth cohorts with different life expectancies. The approach of basing changes on the date of employment has the further disadvantage that employees with similar jobs are treated differently, which may raise issues of discrimination. Nonetheless, such an approach would be legal under pension law, and may be viewed by employees as fair, since it becomes part of the labor agreement at time of hire.

Employers can reduce future pension accruals for current employees. When they do so, they must distribute an Employee Retirement Income Security Act (ERISA) §204(h) notice to employees advising them of the change and explaining its effect on them. When the reduction is for an early retirement benefit, the notice must provide an explanation of the benefit before and after the change. More information is required if the simple description does not give a reasonable picture of the full extent of the change (Segal Company 2003). Although these notice provisions do not prohibit plan amendments reducing accruals, they do ensure that participants are informed about pending changes. These disclosure requirements may discourage plan sponsors from taking actions that they would prefer not to highlight to their employees, or they may enable employees to exert formal or informal pressure against potential plan amendments.

Alternative adjustments may involve converting traditional DB plans to CB plans and terminating DB plans in favor of 401(k) plans. The cost to employers of CB plans and 401(k) plans is not affected by increases in worker life expectancy because workers in these plans generally receive benefits in the form of an account balance at retirement rather than an annuity.

SURVEY OF CHANGES IN PRIVATE-SECTOR DEFINED BENEFIT PLANS

Changes in the Early and Normal Retirement Ages

Early Retirement Age.   The U.S. Bureau of Labor Statistics collects data on ERAs and NRAs in pension plans for medium and large establishments through its Employee Benefits Survey. In spite of large increases in life expectancy, there has been remarkable stability with respect to the ERA in private-sector DB plans subject to ERISA. In 1982, 9 percent of full-time participants in DB plans in medium and large private-sector establishments could take early retirement before age 55 (Turner and Beller 1989, 403). In 1997, that number was basically unchanged at 8 percent (U.S. Department of Labor 1999) (see Table 2).

Over this period (1982–1997), the percentage of full-time participants in plans that offered early retirement at age 55 increased and then decreased (Table 3). However, in 1997, 64 percent could retire at age 55, virtually unchanged from the 63 percent in 1982.

Using the U.S. Bureau of Labor Statistics data and considering retirement based solely on service, in 1981, 5 percent of participants could retire with thirty years of service at any age, while that had increased to 6 percent by 1997 (Turner and Beller 1989; U.S. Department of Labor 2000).

Mitchell and Dykes (2003), also using the Employee Benefits Survey, noted that within the overall pattern of availability of early retirement at age 55, there was a move toward fewer years of service being required to retire at that age, with the fraction of workers who could retire at age 55 with five years of service

Table 2. Early Retirement Permitted at Less Than Age 55 in Medium and Large Private Establishments for Full-Time Workers Covered by Defined Benefit Pension Plans, Selected Years, 1982–1997

Year	Percent of workers
1982	9
1983	9
1984	7
1985	8
1986	10
1991	8
1997	8

Source: U.S. Department of Labor, selected years.

Table 3. Early Retirement Permitted at Age 55 in Medium and Large Private
Establishments for Full-Time Workers Covered by Defined Benefit Pension Plans,
Selected Years, 1981–1997

Year	Percent of workers
1981	60
1982	63
1983	61
1984	62
1985	67
1986	66
1989	66
1995	67
1997	64

Source: U.S. Department of Labor, selected years.

rising from 3 percent to 20 percent between 1980 and 1997. The percentage of
workers needing ten years of service to retire at age 55 fell, which is consistent
with other studies indicating that some DB plans have encouraged earlier retirement over time (Luzadis and Mitchell 1991). The finding that some plans
reduced the service requirements for early retirement is particularly telling in
providing support for the hypothesis that, in spite of increases in longevity,
workers or employers prefer retirement at early ages.

Gustman and Steinmeier (1998), using data from the Survey of Consumer
Finances for 1983 and 1989, found that over that period the ERA fell by about
one year on average, from 55 to 54.3 years.

In sum, while the statistics vary from year to year, there is little evidence of a
trend toward higher ERAs in DB plans over this period.

Normal Retirement Age. The U.S. Bureau of Labor Statistics data suggest that
for most plans the NRA has been set at least several years later than the ERA. In
1983, 36 percent of full-time employees who were participants in DB plans in
medium and large firms were in plans that had an NRA of 65. By 1991, that had
risen to 45 percent, and by 1997 it had risen to 48 percent (Table 4). All other
workers were in plans with lower NRAs. Thus, there is evidence for some plans
increasing the NRA.

Mitchell and Dykes (2003), also examining the Employee Benefits Survey
data, noted a less pronounced countertrend among some plans toward an NRA

Table 4. Normal Retirement Age at Age 65 in Medium and Large Private
Establishments for Full-Time Workers Covered by Defined Benefit Pension Plans,
Selected Years, 1983–1997

Year	All employees	Professional, technical, and related participants	Clerical and sales participants	Production and service participants
1983	36	31	38	38
1986	36	33	36	38
1991	45	45	47	44
1997	48	54	54	43

Source: U.S. Department of Labor, selected years.

at 62. In 1981, 17 percent of participants faced an NRA of 62, and by 1997 this
figure had risen to 21 percent.

Gustman and Steinmeier (1998), using data from the Survey of Consumer
Finances, found that between 1983 and 1989 the average NRA in their sample
was constant at 61.7 years. When they limited their sample to plans that covered
the same individuals in the same jobs over the six years, they found that the average NRA rose from 61 years in 1983 to 62.3 years in 1989.

It is difficult to unambiguously interpret the U.S. Bureau of Labor Statistics
data on DB plan features because of the large decline in the number of that type
of plan. It is not possible in the aggregated published data to tell whether the
changes in the statistics are due to changes in plan features or to a survivor bias,
with the surviving plans being atypical. The remaining DB plans may be self-
selected plans provided by employers who particularly value the flexibility for
managing labor force withdrawal that is offered by a DB plan with a relatively
early ERA.

Other Changes in Plan Features

Final average pay plans and early retirement subsidies concentrate pension accruals at the end of the work life. Moving from a final-average pay plan to a career average pay plan reduces the cost of older workers. However, over time there
has been little change in the percentage of DB pension participants who are in
terminal-earnings plans. In 1980, 53 percent of full-time participants in DB plans
in medium and large establishments were in plans based on terminal earnings,

compared to 56 percent in 1991 and in 1997 (Turner and Beller 1992; U.S. Department of Labor 1993, 1999). There also has been little change in the integration of DB plans with Social Security. In 1980, 45 percent of participants in
medium and large private-sector plans were in plans that were integrated, and
in 1997 this had increased to 49 percent (Mitchell and Dykes 2003).

Conversions to Cash Balance Plans.   The evidence presented here suggests a plausible hypothesis for a factor causing the decline of traditional DB plans. The apparent rigidity of traditional DB plans with respect to adjustments to the increased liabilities caused by greater longevity may be a factor contributing to the
trend away from them and toward the more flexible CB plans and DC plans. In
DC and CB plans, employers are freed generally from longevity risk, with employees bearing the full effects of increased longevity through reductions in their
annual benefits that are derived from their account balances at retirement.

Based on U.S. Bureau of Labor Statistics surveys of employee benefits, the
percentage of full-time workers in private industry who were covered by DB
plans dropped from 32 percent in 1996–1997 to 22 percent in 2000. Although
they have features of both DB and DC plans, CB plans under U.S. pension law
are considered to be a type of DB plan. Of those covered by DB plans, the incidence of CB plans rose from 4 percent in 1996–1997 to 23 percent in 2000 (U.S.
Department of Labor 2003).

About three hundred large companies have converted their traditional DB
plans to CB plans (Crenshaw 2003). Although the conversion from a traditional
DB plan to a CB plan may raise questions of fairness to older workers, once in
place for new workers the CB plan tends to be neutral with respect to their decision as to retirement age. CB plans are replacing plans that often subsidized,
and thus encouraged, early retirement.

Defined Contribution Plans.   The trend toward DC plans in the United States
has been attributed in part to changes in U.S. pension law, as well as to a number of other factors such as the decline in the percentage of the workforce covered by union contracts, and the increase in worker mobility across jobs. A similar trend toward DC plans has also occurred, however, in the United Kingdom
and a number of other countries. This pattern suggests that there may be common underlying factors causing the trend toward DC plans in different countries. One of those common factors may be the growth in life expectancy, which
has increased the cost of DB plans. Switching to DC plans is a way to control
and reduce pension costs for employers. In the United States, the trend toward
DC plans and the trend toward converting traditional DB plans to CB plans

may be due in part to improvements in life expectancy—both those that have occurred and those projected to occur. These improvements raise the cost of traditional DB plans but do not affect the cost of DC or CB plans.

Why Has the Early Retirement Age Not Been Raised in ERISA Plans?

This section considers four possible explanations for the finding that the ERA has been increased in few ERISA DB plans in spite of large increases in life expectancy: (1) the anti-cutback rule in ERISA, (2) the effect of the increase in worker wealth, (3) the desire of some employers to use DB plans to affect the retirement age of their workforces, and (4) the influence of the Social Security ERA on DB pensions.

The Anti-Cutback Rule

If plan sponsors wish to maintain a constant cost of providing benefits (despite increases in life expectancy) by raising the ERAs or NRAs, they would need to amend their DB plan. ERISA and the Internal Revenue Code (IRC) contain parallel provisions that prohibit a plan sponsor from amending a DB plan if the amendment would decrease accrued benefits (ERISA §204[g]).[1] This prohibition, known as the "anti-cutback rule," applies broadly and makes it difficult for a plan sponsor to increase the NRA and ERA. Other ERISA provisions also may affect a plan sponsor's decision to amend the NRA.

Because the anti-cutback rule prohibits a decrease in accrued benefits, it is important to understand how ERISA defines accrued benefits. According to the statute, an accrued benefit is "determined under the plan and . . . expressed in the form of an annual benefit commencing at normal retirement age" (ERISA §3[23]). ERISA establishes parameters that limit plan flexibility in setting accrual rates (ERISA §204). For employees with at least 5 years of plan participation when they reach age 65, the statute defines "normal retirement age" as the earlier of the date specified by the plan or age 65 (ERISA §3[24]). For employees who do not have five years of plan participation by the time they reach age 65, the NRA is the earlier of either the date specified by the plan or their fifth anniversary of plan participation.

The anti-cutback rule does not refer to the present value of accrued benefits but rather the annual value of accrued benefits at the NRA. Thus, it does not recognize the concept that the present value of accrued benefits based on past service increases with life expectancy, and an offset of that change would not be a cutback measured in terms of expected present value.

The interlocking provisions of ERISA are complex. A plan sponsor may establish a higher ERA for new workers, but if it wishes to increase the plan's NRA to offset increased longevity for current workers, a multipart analysis is required. Consider, for example, a plan sponsor that intends to increase the NRA from age 65 to age 67. This does not require an employee to work additional years. Employees are still able to retire at the ERA, but with reduced benefits, if they have sufficient years of service. Such an amendment might affect: (1) the benefits accrued by a plan participant prior to the plan amendment if the amendment has the effect of delaying receipt of "full" benefits to age 67; (2) the benefits accrued by a plan participant after the plan amendment; and (3) the rate of accrual of benefits after the amendment by establishing a "wear-away" benefit.

First, if the amendment has the effect of reducing the value of a participant's existing accrued benefits calculated at age 65, the amendment will violate the anti-cutback rule. Assume that as of the amendment's effective date, participant X is a high-income worker who has earned an unreduced accrued benefit payable at age 65 of $50,000 per year. Assume also that the amendment has the effect of setting the NRA at 67, providing for actuarially reduced benefits prior to that age, and is applied retroactively to already accrued benefits. The result is that participant X's accrued benefit payable at age 65 would decrease to approximately $43,500 per year, which is $50,000 per year actuarially reduced by 2 years for early distribution, a reduction of approximately 13 percent. ERISA prohibits such an amendment.

Second, assume instead that the plan amendment prospectively raises the NRA for all benefits that accrue after the effective date of the amendment. Such an amendment would not violate ERISA's anti-cutback prohibitions because it does not decrease any existing accrued benefits. It might, however, violate statutory provisions directly and indirectly tied to ERISA's definition of the NRA as age 65. In addition, it makes it difficult for a worker to accurately estimate her or his future benefits, and it adds to the complexity of administering the plan.

In fact, this is exactly the source of the dispute in *Lindsay v. Thiokol Corp.* (1997), where participants alleged that Thiokol Corp. violated ERISA when it amended its DB pension plan to raise the NRA from age 65 to 67. The Tenth Circuit interpreted ERISA as setting the NRA at 65 solely for statutory purposes and not as precluding a plan from setting a higher NRA. The court construed other relevant provisions as only requiring that the plan permit benefit payments to begin at age 65 and protecting whatever benefit the plan provides for at age 65 from forfeiture. Even as amended, the Thiokol plan met those requirements.

Other circuit courts, however, may not follow the Tenth Circuit's reasoning, and the relative dearth of case law on these issues may be a factor that has discouraged plan sponsors from raising the NRA above age 65. The U.S. Bureau of Labor Statistics, which collects data on the NRA in DB plans, does not even provide as a possible category an NRA higher than age 65 (U.S. Department of Labor 2003).

Third, a plan sponsor may amend its plan prospectively in order to avoid violating the anti-cutback provisions but still establish a "wear-away" benefit. A plan may increase the NRA from 65 to 67 and apply the change retroactively. To avoid anti-cutback problems, the plan also would provide that no participant's benefit at age 65 or later can be lower than the participant's vested, accrued benefit as of the effective date of the plan amendment. Return to the case of participant X who, as of the effective date of the plan amendment, has a vested, accrued benefit of $50,000 per year. Under the terms of this amendment, X is entitled to a minimum of $50,000 per year if she or he retires at age 65 or later. But the effect of the increase in the NRA will be that, under the new formula, it may be some period of time before X's accrued benefit exceeds $50,000. And, until X has worked for that additional period of time, she or he does not accrue any additional benefits. This phenomenon is known as a "wear-away." Commentators differ on whether wear-aways constitute illegal age discrimination (compare Forman 2001 with Stein et al. 2001), and there is no authoritative case law on the question in this context. Again, the uncertainty may be a factor in the plan sponsor's decision making.

Prior to the Retirement Equity Act of 1984 (REA), ERISA's anti-cutback provisions did not refer to early retirement benefits. As a result, there was considerable controversy over the ability of plan sponsors to decrease early retirement benefits, particularly in the context of plan terminations. REA amended ERISA to describe the application of the anti-cutback rule to both "early retirement benefit[s]" and to "retirement-type subsid[ies]." Regulations have further elaborated on the law, and in 2003 the IRS announced its intention to "provide guidance on benefits that are treated as early retirement benefits and retirement-type subsidies" for anti-cutback purposes (IRS Notice 2003-10).

Effective with the REA amendments, ERISA specifically states that "eliminating or reducing an early retirement benefit or a retirement-type subsidy" is a plan amendment that constitutes a prohibited cutback to the extent that the amendment would affect benefits associated with service prior to the amendment (ERISA §204[g][2][A]). But, it then states that the cutback prohibition only protects retirement-type subsidies for participants who eventually meet the original plan criteria for the subsidy. This means that early retirement benefits cannot be decreased at all to the extent of a participant's pre-amendment service. And retirement-type subsidies attributable to service before the amendment cannot be decreased if the participant eventually satisfies whatever conditions the original plan placed on the subsidies.

The difference between an early retirement benefit, which is fully protected, and a retirement-type subsidy, which is only partially protected, is not intuitively obvious. According to the legislative history, Congress intended retirement-type subsidies to include those benefits "that continue after retirement" (U.S. Senate No. 98–575, 1984). In contrast, Social Security supplements were not to be defined as retirement-type subsidies.

The statutory and regulatory provisions may appear to be overwhelmingly complex. But the bottom line is that, depending on the type of benefit, one of four rules will apply. First, in some limited situations, the benefit may qualify as an "ancillary benefit," and if so, the amendment is permissible. Second, if the plan sponsor wishes to amend provisions to increase the eligibility date for a retirement-type subsidy that can be accomplished for participants who never meet the pre-amendment plan criteria. But of course if the participants never qualify under the pre-amendment criteria, the plan would not have borne costs for those participants. Third, a plan sponsor may amend a plan prospectively to adjust for increased longevity by decreasing either early retirement benefits or retirement-type subsidies, as otherwise permitted by ERISA—but such an amendment can only be applied to service earned after the effective date of the amendment. Fourth, a plan sponsor cannot increase the NRA associated with benefits accrued before the effective date of the amendment.

Limited case authority holds that a plan sponsor may increase the NRA above age 65. However, this issue has not been extensively litigated.

In sum, these provisions make it difficult for plan sponsors to amend plans to counteract the additional costs associated with increased longevity. And the existence of these limitations may implicitly impose additional limitations on a plan sponsor's options because of employees' perceptions that their benefits are protected from reduction.

Because of the anti-cutback rule, a DB plan amendment would need to affect only the future accrual of annual benefits. This could be done by maintaining different plan features for different periods of work, which would result in bifurcated pension entitlements for a single worker. Alternatively, it could establish a different plan for new employees.

Gustman and Steinmeier (1998), using data from Watson Wyatt Worldwide for thirty-nine of the largest fifty U.S. firms, found that 85 percent treated old and new hires the same way, while 15 percent provided less generous benefits to new hires than to old hires, and the difference for those employees was large. For the annual retirement benefit at 65 years of age and 35 years of service, old hires had benefits that were about twice as high relative to their final wages as new hires.

Either approach is expensive to administer and may be difficult to explain to workers. It also may violate other statutory provisions, such as nondiscrimination provisions. If the ERA were raised for workers already having accrued benefits, there would need to be two ERAs for their different benefits, which would not be a sensible approach. It would make more sense for the employer to establish a new plan or a new ERA for new employees. Reducing the benefit accrual rate, say from 1.75 percent per year of service to 1.5 percent or raising the NRA from an age lower than 65 to 65 is easier than raising the ERA, but employers still would have a public-relations problem of explaining the change to workers. Raising the NRA would mean that benefits accrued before the increase would be calculated based on the old NRA, while benefits accrued after the change would be calculated based on the new NRA. The advantage of CB or DC plan conversions for employers wishing to reduce their benefit obligations is that those changes obfuscate the benefit cutback.

The anti-cutback rule may explain some of the pattern of change and lack of change in ERISA plans. Neither the IRC nor ERISA sets a minimum age for early retirement in pension plans, but once the plan sets a minimum age for early retirement, the anti-cutback rule makes it difficult for employers to adjust their traditional DB plans for this source of increased cost. These restrictions do not apply to non-ERISA plans, such as those of churches and federal, state, and local governments. Thus, the provisions in non-ERISA plans can be instructive as to the changes that would be made in the absence of ERISA.

The Effect of the Increase in Worker Wealth

Due to the increased wealth of workers, many workers want to spend more years of leisure in retirement. Although the workweek has changed relatively little, it appears that many employees have a preference for spending more years in retirement. For this reason, early retirement may appeal to workers, and for this reason changing the ERA could be unpopular. Consider, for example, the negative reaction of unions in France to the proposed change in the benefit formula for government workers. The anti-cutback provisions in ERISA may reinforce the employees' expectations that the ERA will not be changed.

The Ability of Employers to Influence the Retirement Age of Their Workers

One of the reasons that some employers offer DB plans may be so that they can influence the age at which their workers retire. Maintaining a relatively low ERA may appeal to some employers because it preserves the option for encouraging selected older workers to leave, especially in periods of economic downturn. Sometimes, early retirement may be considered as an unemployment benefit for older workers.

DB plans are concentrated to some extent in unionized declining industries such as steel. Those industries have enough problems with unions—with downsizing, wage concerns, and health care pressures—that negotiating an increase in the ERA is not something they are eager to do.

The Influence of the Social Security Early Retirement Age on Defined Benefit Pensions

The Social Security ERA has been 62 for roughly forty years for men and nearly fifty years for women. Congress in 2000 increased Social Security's NRA but not its ERA. By doing so, it reduced the level of benefits available to workers at the ERA. The constancy of the Social Security ERA may influence pension plan sponsors to not increase their ERA.

Non-ERISA Defined Benefit Plans That Have Raised the Early Retirement and Normal Retirement Ages

The role of ERISA in the apparent difficulty of raising the ERA can be evaluated by comparing ERISA plan statistics with data for non-ERISA plans, which are primarily government plans (see Tables 5, 6, and 7). Government plans are not restricted by the ERISA anti-cutback rule, but some may have contractual or state anti-cutback rules.

Early Retirement Age.   Although there is little evidence of an increase in the ERA in ERISA DB plans, there is some evidence of an increase in ERA in non-ERISA plans. Between 1992 and 1998, the percent of teachers in DB plans working for state and local governments who could receive their pension benefits before age 55 declined from 24 percent to 20 percent, while the percent who could receive those benefits at age 55 increased from 39 to 41 percent. The percent of white collar-employees other than teachers who could receive their pension benefits before age 55 declined from 19 percent to 17 percent. By comparison, the percent of blue-collar and service workers who could receive their DB pensions before age 55 was basically unchanged, moving from 19 percent in 1992 to 20 percent in 1998 (see Table 5).

Table 5. Early Retirement Permitted at Less Than Age 55 in State and Local Governments for Full-Time Workers Covered by Defined Benefit Pension Plans, 1992 and 1998

Year	All employees	White-collar employees, except teachers	Teachers	Blue-collar and service employees
1992	21	19	24	19
1998	19	17	20	20

Source: U.S. Department of Labor, 1994, 2000.

Table 6. Early Retirement Permitted at Age 55 in State and Local Governments for Full-Time Workers Covered by Defined Benefit Pension Plans, 1992 and 1998

Year	All employees	White-collar employees, except teachers	Teachers	Blue-collar and service employees
1992	41	43	39	38
1998	40	42	41	35

Source: U.S. Department of Labor, 1994, 2000.

Table 7. Normal Retirement Age at 65 in State and Local Governments for Full-Time Workers Covered by Defined Benefit Pension Plans, 1992 and 1998

Year	All employees	White-collar employees, except teachers	Teachers	Blue-collar and service employees
1992	8	7	9	8
1998	9	8	12	9

Source: U.S. Department of Labor, 1994, 2000.

Normal Retirement Age.   There has been little increase in the NRA in non-ERISA plans (see Table 7). The pension plans for teachers are an exception, however, with the number of participants in plans with an NRA at 65 increasing slightly, from 9 percent to 12 percent between 1992 and 1998. A possible alternative explanation for the increase in ERA and NRA for teachers is the concern over a future teacher shortage due to large numbers of anticipated retirements of teachers.

Selected Non-ERISA Plans That Have Increased their ERA or NRA

This section discusses particular examples of non-ERISA DB plans that have raised their ERA or NRA.

Oregon.   The Oregon Public Employees Retirement System has raised its NRA from 58 to 60 for employees hired after January 1, 1996, while retaining the ERA of 55. In 2003, the NRA was raised from 55 to 60 for police and firefighters, and from 60 to 65 for regular government employees. Long-service employees may retire earlier than the NRA.

Washington, D.C.   Firefighters in 2003 could retire at age 50, but newly hired firefighters cannot retire until age 55.

West Virginia.   State troopers hired after March 12, 1994 are in a West Virginia state pension plan that allows them to retire at age 55. Troopers hired before that date are in a different plan that allows them to retire at age 50 (Herald-Mail 2003).

U.S. Government.   In the Civil Service Retirement System for U.S. government employees hired in 1983 or earlier, the ERA is 55. In the Federal Employees Retirement System, which covers federal government employees hired after 1983, the ERA is 55 for workers born before 1948. For subsequent birth cohorts, the ERA is increased to age 57 and is being phased in over a twenty-two-year period so that workers born in 1970 and later have a minimum retirement age of 57. Workers must have thirty years of service to be eligible to retire at the ERA. When the federal government moved back the ERA, it did that in the context of a complex reform, completely changing the benefit structure in a way so that it was not completely clear whether workers were better or worse off.

The decision by the federal government to move its ERA back by two years, which might have been taken as an example for the private sector, makes especially noteworthy the fact that few private-sector companies have done that.

CONCLUSION

Rough calculations suggest that increases in life expectancy may increase DB pension costs by as much as 1 percent per year. Relatively few sponsors of ERISA DB plans, however, have raised their ERAs in spite of large increases in cost due to large increases in life expectancy. Some private-sector employers have established separate plans with higher ERAs for new employees. In the government sector, the ERA has been increased in the federal government's plan for civil servants and for some state and local government plans, especially for teachers. The evidence from the government sector provides some indication that the anti-cutback rule in ERISA may be making it difficult for private employers to adjust their DB plans for the increased costs due to increasing longevity. Perhaps in part because of the ERISA anti-cutback rule, private-sector employers to a large extent have freed themselves from the costs of increasing longevity by terminating traditional DB plans, switching to DC plans, or converting to CB plans. Even though increased longevity raises costs, an adjustment that would keep benefit costs constant with respect to longevity is considered to be a benefit cutback because accrued benefits for the purpose of that rule are annual benefits, not the present value of benefits. ERISA appears to have limited increases in the NRA by legislative language that may suggest that the NRA cannot be raised higher than 65. Even if ERISA would permit such a change, its substantive and notice provisions may act as an implicit barrier.

The evidence concerning changes in DB plans in the private and government sectors may provide some information as to feasible Social Security reforms. The evidence suggests that some employers may have adjusted their pension plans because of the increased costs imposed by increasing longevity. Some employers have raised their ERA, but this group is a definite minority.

For some employers, the ability to use DB plans to influence the age at which workers retire, including the use of early retirement windows, may continue to be an important factor. Some employers may want to have the ability to encourage workers to retire before the current Social Security ERA of 62. For other employers, the inflexibility of ERISA DB plans with respect to changes in the ERA, combined with the projected increases in life expectancy and the uncertainty as to the amount of future increases, may be a factor causing them to shift away from pension plans that provide annuities.

NOTE

1. Many provisions of ERISA are replicated in the IRC. ERISA §204(g) is replicated in IRC §411(d)(6). For ease of reference in this report, we refer only to the ERISA provisions.

REFERENCES

Board of Trustees, Federal Old-Age and Survivors Insurance and Disability Insurance Trust Funds. 2003. *The 2003 Annual Report of the Board of Trustees of the Federal Old-Age and Survivors Insurance and Disability Insurance Trust Funds.* Washington, DC: U.S. Government Printing Office.

Crenshaw, Albert B. 2003. "Treasury Drops Pension Proposal." Washingtonpost.com. April 8.

Forman, Jonathan Barry. 2001. "Comparing Apples and Oranges: Some Thoughts on the Pension and Social Security Tax Expenditures," *Employee Rights and Employment Policy Journal.* Vol. 5:352–58.

Gustman, Alan L., and Steinmeier, Thomas L. 1998. *Changing Pensions in Cross-Section and Panel Data: Analysis with Employer-Provided Plan Descriptions.* National Bureau of Economic Research Working Paper 6854. (December).

Herald-Mail. 2003. "Troopers' Retirement Issues Sent to High Court." The *Herald-Mail* Online. January 20.

Luzadis, Rebecca, and Mitchell, Olivia S. 1991. "Explaining Pension Dynamics." *Journal of Human Resources.* 26 (Fall): 679–903.

Mitchell, Olivia S., and Erica L. Dykes. 2003. "New Trends in Pension Benefit and Retirement Provisions." In *Benefits for the Workplace of the Future.* Olivia S. Mitchell, David S. Blitzstein, Michael Gordon, and Judith F. Mazo, eds. Philadelphia: University of Pennsylvania Press. 110–33.

Oster, Christopher. 2003. "Good News! Insurers Extend Your Lifespan." *Wall Street Journal.* (June 24) D1.

Pensions Policy Institute. 2003. *The Shift from Defined Benefit to Defined Contribution.* PPI Briefing Note No. 2. (July).

Segal Company. 2003. "IRS Issues Final Regulations on ERISA Section 204(h) Notices of Reductions in Future Pension Benefits." *Bulletin.* (July).

Stein, Norman P., et al. 2001. "Future of Private Pensions," *Employee Rights and Employment Policy Journal.* Vol. 5:360–66.

Technical Panel on Assumptions and Methods. 2003 *Report to the Social Security Advisory Board.* Washington, DC. (October).

Turner, John, and Beller, Daniel J., eds. 1989. *Trends in Pensions.* Washington, DC: U.S. Government Printing Office.

Turner, John, and Beller, Daniel J., eds. 1992. *Trends in Pensions.* Washington, DC: U.S. Government Printing Office.

U.S. Department of Labor, Bureau of Labor Statistics. 1993. *Employee Benefits in Medium and Large Private Establishments, 1991.* Bulletin 2422. (May).

U.S. Department of Labor, Bureau of Labor Statistics. 1999. *Employee Benefits in Medium and Large Private Establishments, 1997.* Bulletin 2517. (September).

U.S. Department of Labor, Bureau of Labor Statistics. 1994. *Employee Benefits in State and Local Governments, 1992.* Bulletin 2444. (July).

U.S. Department of Labor, Bureau of Labor Statistics. 2000. *Employee Benefits in State and Local Governments, 1998.* Bulletin 2531. (December).

U.S. Department of Labor, Bureau of Labor Statistics. 2003. *National Compensation Survey: Employee Benefits in Private Industry in the United States, 2000.* Washington, DC.

U.S. Internal Revenue Service Notice. 2003–10. 2003–5 IRB 369. *Lindsay v. Thiokol Corp.,* 112 F.3d 1068 (10th Cir. 1997).

U.S. Senate Report No. 98-575. 1984.

White, David. 2003. "Employers Support Moves to More Compulsion in Pensions." *Investment & Pensions Europe Ipe.com.* (June 2).

Comments on "Longevity and Retirement Age in Defined Benefit Pension Plans"

JOSEPH S. PIACENTINI

The central theme of this book can be expressed as a simple equation: longer, healthier lives plus looming labor shortages equal longer work lives—that is, later and perhaps more gradual retirements. Longer lives make it too expensive to retire early. Healthier lives and less physically demanding jobs make it possible and potentially desirable to work at more advanced ages. This implies an increased supply of older workers in the future. Aging baby boomers are more numerous than their younger counterparts, so their labor is needed to sustain vigorous economic growth. Demand for older workers' labor, then, is also likely to increase.

Is it possible that labor markets will simply clear, reaching a nice, near optimal equilibrium? Perhaps. But if so, the mechanism by which they clear may be different from the historical norm of wage adjustments. For a variety of reasons, many of which are documented in other chapters in this volume, older workers may prefer reduced and more flexible work schedules to higher wages as an inducement to remain in the labor force.

Among the reasons for this is wealth. Many prospective older workers will possess substantial wealth—often not enough to facilitate an early, complete, and comfortable retirement, but sufficient to fill in for reduced earnings for an extended period preceding complete cessation of work. For many older workers, employment-based pensions account for a large share of wealth, and therein lies one potential obstacle to an optimal equilibrium.

Traditional defined benefit (DB) pension plans were designed around the career-job model. They reward long, even life-long, tenure on a single full-time job, followed by complete retirement at a specified age or after a specified number of years. Certain provisions of pension law, designed to secure workers' rights under these plans, now prohibit or impede various modifications to this basic design that might otherwise accommodate later and/or more gradual retirements. One such provision, as detailed in chapter 5 by Penner, Perun, and Steuerle, all but forces many workers to leave their jobs permanently and totally before drawing any pension from them. Another impedes companies from increasing the age at which early or normal retirement benefits commence. Muir and Turner document stickiness in the retirement age provisions of DB plans and suggest that relevant provisions of pension law are to blame. Their chapter is the primary subject of this comment.

The question Muir and Turner address is an important one. In the face of increasing longevity, have employers raised DB plan retirement ages, and if not, why not?

The Premise

The authors begin from the premise that employers have incentives to increase DB pension retirement ages. They point out that as plan participants' longevity increases, with increasing life expectancy and/or increasing participation of women, employers' pension costs rise. They might also have noted the complementary possibility of growing demand for older workers' labor. Moreover, some workers might willingly trade some pension wealth for the opportunity to work longer and later draw a larger periodic benefit than would otherwise have been possible. Each of these factors might encourage employers to increase retirement ages. The premise that some or many employers would like to do so is therefore persuasive—with one caveat.

The caveat pertains to possible disconnects between the true economic cost of a pension plan and the cost perceived by the sponsoring company and its owners. At least two measures of DB pension cost are likely to be more visible and possibly more important to companies and owners than the true economic cost. One is the level of contributions the company by law must make to the pension plan each year. The other is the pension plan's net annual expense and asset-liability balance reported in the company's financial statements. Both are likely to diverge substantially from the true economic cost, and to be affected differently by changes in mortality.

First, mandatory contributions: federal law sets minimum funding standards for private-sector DB pension plans. The standards are highly complex and, to some extent, flexible. Most relevant to this discussion are the mortality assumptions used in determining the minimum mandatory contribution each year. Plans funded above a certain threshold are subject to a standard that the mortality assumptions be "reasonable." Plans below the threshold must make additional contributions, which must be calculated using mortality assumptions specified in law. These assumptions have been fixed and constant since the provision was added to the law in 1987. Whether plans fall above or below the threshold and become subject to the additional contribution requirement is also determined with reference to these same mandatory mortality assumptions. In practice, then, for many years, plans have not been forced to increase funding contributions to reflect reductions in mortality, and it is possible, or even likely, that many have not done so. And badly underfunded plans, which are likely to face proportionately the largest mandatory contributions, rely on mortality assumptions fixed in law.

Next, financial statements: applicable U.S. accounting rules in practice likewise may permit pension plans to go for many years without revising downward the mortality assumptions that underlie reported pension expenses and asset-liability balances.

All of this suggests that while falling mortality increases the true economic cost of DB pension plans, it may be a long time before these increases show up as mandatory contributions to the plans or as decrements in companies' financial statements. The incentive to increase retirement ages may therefore be muted.

Finally, it is worth noting that in all but the long run, all measures of pension plan costs—funding costs, accounting costs, and true economic costs as well—are probably affected less by reductions in mortality than by other factors. Consider just one factor that was of major importance for many pension plans throughout the 1980s and 1990s: investment performance. Private DB pensions invest heavily in the stock market. At the end of 2003, corporate equities accounted for about one-half of all private DB plan assets, according to the U.S. Federal Reserve Board. Between 1983 and its peak in 2000, the S&P 500 stock index rose more than 800 percent nominally. During many of the intervening years, many pension plans enjoyed holidays from any requirement to contribute, and many companies' financial statements reported net income rather than expense from DB pensions. Again, the incentive to increase retirement ages may have been muted for many.

THE EVIDENCE

Next, the authors examine data on trends in private-sector pension plan design, and generally find that retirement ages have not increased. They also note, however, that participation in traditional DB plans has declined dramatically, while participation in defined contribution (DC) and cash balance (CB) plans ballooned. These latter plans do not specify retirement ages and are generally neutral with respect to the timing of retirement. Perhaps the remaining DB plans reflect a "survivor bias," disproportionately representing employers with unusual preferences for early retirements by workers, the authors note. And perhaps increasing longevity has contributed to the trend away from traditional DB plans.

The authors appear to emphasize the stickiness of DB retirement ages over the trend away from these plans, but the latter phenomenon is probably weightier. The authors quantify the dramatic and abrupt shift toward CB plans in the late-1990s, but not the longer running trend toward DC plans. Yet the numbers are so striking as to demand inclusion: between 1980 and 2002, worker participation in private-sector DB plans declined from 30 million to 22 million, while participation in DC plans increased from 19 million to 53 million.

THE CAUSES

The authors then tackle the question, why have private employers not increased DB pension plan retirement ages? They do an admirable job of explaining highly complex pension rules. As the authors explain, current rules generally make it unlawful to withdraw early or normal retirement rights to previously earned benefits—and these same rules may make it very complicated to similarly revise such rights prospectively. They examine public-sector pensions, where these rules do not apply, and find some evidence of increases in retirement ages. The authors take this finding as suggestive that the rules applicable to private-sector DB plans have been an obstacle to increasing retirement ages in that sector. The authors suggest that these rules have contributed to the trend toward DC and CB plans. It might have been worthwhile to note also that DB plans remain far more common in the public than in the private sector.

Is falling mortality, in combination with legal obstacles to increasing DB plan retirement ages, a cause of the trend away from DB and toward DC plans? In sum, the authors make a compelling case that it is a factor. Is it among the most important causes? The authors consider one competing cause: U.S. tax law changes favoring DC plans. The authors point out that similar trends have occurred in other countries where tax laws were not so amended, and suggest that decreasing mortality may be a common factor behind the trend across countries. But there are many additional factors that may be more important than mortality, some supported in research literature. These include employment shifts away from unionized and goods-producing industries that historically have high propensities to offer DB plans, and increasingly mobile and diverse career patterns, which fit poorly into DB plan designs.

IMPLICATIONS

The authors' conclusions mostly echo their findings. Other than one mention of lessons for Social Security, there is no consideration of policy implications. It is not the intent of this comment to offer policy suggestions, either, but one question comes to mind.

As the authors note, increasing the retirement age for payment of previously earned benefits is prohibited as an unlawful cutback. They do not opine on whether this prohibition should be lifted, nor on whether it is likely to be, nor on what shape any reform in this area might take.

Various chapters in this volume develop the theme that workers increasingly want to work until more advanced ages. This raises the possibility that at least some would willingly pay something for that opportunity—and prompted this comment to ask above whether some workers might willingly trade some pension wealth for the opportunity to work longer and later draw a larger periodic benefit than would otherwise have been possible. If so, one could imagine at least some instances where workers and companies would agree on and jointly advocate a retirement age increase that is impermissible under current law. If such instances became widespread, they might form the basis for a policy reform discussion that has yet to evolve.

NOTE

Any opinions expressed in this comment are my own and should not be attributed to the Department of Labor or the Employee Benefit Security Administration.

CHAPTER EIGHT

How 401(k)s and the Stock Market Crash Explain Increases in Older Workers' Labor Force Participation Rates

SHARON HERMES & TERESA GHILARDUCCI

Older Americans are working more in the early 2000s than in the last five recessions and expansions. The increase can be partly explained by pension income increasingly being tied to financial markets. These defined contribution (DC) accounts replace defined benefit (DB) pensions, which help stabilize economies precisely because their values do not coincide with the business cycle. Since DC account values fall during recessions and cause workers to postpone retirement, unemployment increases. Conversely, when expansions boost DC values, workers retire and intensify labor shortages. Multivariate analysis of cohort averages from the Current Population Survey (CPS) estimates that the 40 percent decline in the S&P 500 from January 2000 to October 2002 caused the labor force participation of older workers ages 55–64 to increase by 2.6 percent for men and 5.4 percent for women. Difference-in-differences analysis of microdata from the Health and Retirement Survey (HRS) indicates the probability of retirement of men and women ages 63–64 with only DC pensions fell by 34.2 and 38.7 percentage points, respectively, from 1998 to 2002

Economic downturns highlight an underappreciated role Social Security and DB pension plans play to stabilize the macroeconomy and moderate fluctuations in unemployment. Social Security and DB pensions stabilize the economy because older workers eligible for them are more likely to leave the labor force and retire rather than be laid off and look for work. This causes unemployment to be lower than it would be otherwise. In addition, the steady guaranteed flow of income from Social Security and DB plans maintains buying power and boosts aggregate demand.

This salubrious macroeconomic effect is lost when workers are increasingly covered by DC pension accounts, such as 401(k)s. DC accounts can be automatic destabilizers. When the economy is in an expansion, DC values increase, making retirement possible and enticing. Yet, precisely when workers are leaving the labor force because of bull financial markets, employers want more workers. On the other hand, when the economy dips, or a regional industry or company fails, the DC and 401(k) plan values can plummet while companies are laying off workers. In other words, the decline in retirement income causes workers to postpone retirement precisely when employers need far fewer employees. Relatively more people stay in the labor force and the unemployment rate is higher than it would be with Social Security and widespread DB pensions. These conclusions flow easily from standard macroeconomic theory; the challenge of this paper is to find support for the argument that the effect exists and that the magnitude is not trivial. Using two different statistical analyses and data sources, we find that older workers are increasing their labor force participation and postponing retirement in response to the stock market crash. First, analysis of aggregate-level data from the CPS shows that the 40 percent decline in the S&P 500 caused older workers ages 55–64 to increase their labor force participation by 2.6 percent for men and 5.4 percent for women. Second, analysis using microdata from the HRS reveals that the probability of retirement for older men and women ages 63–64 with only DC pension wealth fell by 34.2 and 38.7 percentage points, respectively, from 1998 to 2002.

The first part of this study discusses how the value of DC and 401(k) plans fluctuate with the stock market compared to DB pensions and Social Security. Second, we contrast older workers' labor force participation behavior since the beginning of the most recent recession, which was declared over by November 2001, with that of past recessions and expansions. We find older women's labor force participation increased while older men's decreased, especially in contractions since 1948. Yet recently, both older men and older women are looking for work or working more than they had in previous recessions. Third, we show that women are more likely to be working in industries that spend more toward DC plans relative to DB plans, suggesting that women have less generous DB plans than men and are more likely to have DC plans if they are covered at all. In the fourth section, we review studies of how unexpected changes in wealth affect people's work decisions. The fifth section describes the multiple regression analysis that shows how S&P 500 changes affect older workers' labor supply decisions, holding unemployment and wage growth changes constant. In the sixth section, a difference-in-differences analysis concludes that workers with only DC pension plans were dramatically less likely to retire than those with DB plans after the stock market decline of January 2000. We conclude with reflections on how pension systems affect macroeconomic stability.

TRENDS IN RETIREMENT BEHAVIOR AND 401(K) VALUES

It is well known that DC pensions (including 401[k]s) are supplementing and re-placing annuities and DB pension plans (see Wolff's chapter 6 in this volume). The implication is that a growing number of older workers have assets that are more vulnerable to financial-market fluctuations. Between 1981 and 1996, DB wealth fell 39.5 percent while wealth in marketable accounts, including DC plans, increased by 838 percent.

We find evidence that the increase in exposure to the market means that sharp declines in the stock market caused older people to work more. What is the mechanism? Scarcely half of workers have pension accounts likely exposed to the stock market, and the average value is only $15,000. Yet, a drop in the stock market could still influence retirement because over half of workers ages 55–64 have retirement accounts, and the average value is $71,040 (though the median value is only $33,000 [Purcell 2004].) Yet, even at $71,000, common sense suggests that even a large drop in value might not substantially influence such an important decision as retirement. Indeed, small changes in wealth are not as important in work and retirement decisions as are people's expectations of their retirement wealth (Gustman and Steinmeier 2001b). This makes sense because people receive pension benefit statements annually, while they are bom-barded daily with reports on the stock market. Because impressions about the value of financial wealth rely on imperfect knowledge and sensational informa-tion (Schiller 2000), it is reasonable to conclude that workers estimate retire-ment affordability based on easily available, though imperfect, information about the value of their retirement wealth. The level and fluctuations of the S&P 500 became a measure for both the value and the durability of people's retirement wealth.

Disappointed Americans expressed to newspaper journalists how the stock market crash affected their expectations (Greene 2002). "'I thought I would at least be able to take a break and think about what to do with the second half of my life,' Mr. Pringle, 63, said. 'But I didn't have a lot of options when the mar-ket went south.' To many Americans, the sustained slide in the stock market—particularly last week's nose dive—has been something to fret about, a darkening cloud. But to many people at or near retirement age, it has been a colossal jolt" (Zernike 2002).

This view contrasts starkly to a conventional wisdom that 401(k) plans can stabilize economies in two ways. First firms can stabilize their firm's shares by contributing it to employee accounts making bear markets milder.[1] Second, economic models, inspired by the 1990 recession, revived the view that profit-sharing plans would make wages less sticky because they would fluctuate with the financial conditions of the company and layoffs would be avoided. However, Chelius and Smith (1990) found that workers whose compensation packages contain a profit-sharing component no less susceptible to layoffs.

Workers Are Postponing Retirement Because of the Fall in 401(k) Wealth

We hypothesize that women and men worked more in the 2001–2002 recession because their 401(k) pension wealth fell (Cheng and French 2000; Sevak 2001; Eschtruth and Gemus 2002). Anecdotal evidence, labor force participation trends, and regression analysis linking retirement behavior to changes in pension wealth support the claim.

Anecdotal evidence suggests workers did or will postpone their retirement plans because of the unanticipated fall in retirement wealth in the early 2000s. In January 2002, the Gallup Organization reported that nearly one in five investors are considering postponing retirement by four years on average; the figure is higher for older workers, 26 percent for investors aged fifty and older. Four months later, Gallup found that 45 percent of nonretired Americans over age 50 do not expect to have enough money to live comfortably when retired and, on average, predict their retirement at age 63. In 1995, the average estimated age of retirement was 60 (Jones 2002).

The Enron case is a celebrity example of workers with retirement assets concentrated in their employer's stock postponing retirement. Enron's 401(k) has as much as 60 percent of its assets in company stock, which fell from its peak of $90 a share in 2001 to 50 cents a share.[2] Many of Enron's employees saw the value of their 401(k) accounts free-fall and said they would delay retirement as a result.[3] A remarkable correlation between work and the stock market is seen immediately when changes in the labor force participation rates for older workers are put on the same graph as the value of the S&P 500. When men and women's rates are separated, it is clear that the older women, age 55–64 are driving the negative correlation (see Graphs 1 and 2).

Simple two-way correlations reveal that the proportion of the change in older women's labor force participation attributable to the change in the S&P 500 is 0.843 (measured by the square of the Pearson product moment correlation coefficient); the correlation is 0.827 for older men.

Figure 1. LFP of Older Men and the S&P 500 since January 2000

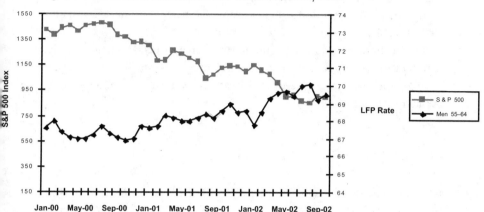

Figure 2. Labor Force Participation of Older Women and the S&P 500 since January 2000

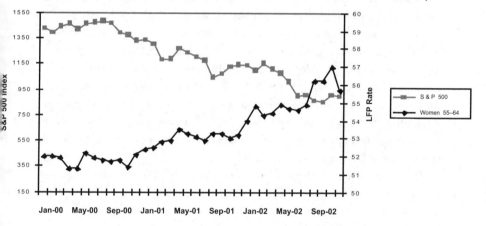

An initial reaction may be that 401(k) plans have nothing to do with the increase in labor force participation rates for older women workers because the rate of labor force participation for all ages of women has increased steadily in the post–World War II period. We have the onus to show that the recent increase is more exaggerated than this long-term trend.

Although it is a well-known fact that the work effort of older men, ages 55–64, has declined since 1970, this trend reversed in the 1990s. Similarly, the decline in women's labor force participation in the 1970s was dramatically reversed in the 1980s and 1990s. The labor force participation rate for older women workers, ages 55–64, was 45.0 percent at the second to the last peak in July 1990 (III) and much larger, 52.6 percent, at the last recorded peak in March 2001 (I). The

increases in older male labor force participation occurred in the late-1990s, although their rate went down slightly from 68.0 percent in the last peak, July
1990 (III), to 67.7 percent in March 2001 (I).[4]

Table 1 shows peak-to-peak trends in labor force participation, the rates that
represent an increase are in bold. Examining trough-to-trough changes in labor
force participation (Table 2) reveals that only older women's work effort increased
in the trough of March 1991.

LABOR FORCE PARTICIPATION IN CONTRACTIONS

In this section, we contrast older people's work efforts in the most recent recession to those of older people in past recessions. Many studies confirm that an increase in the unemployment rate causes more retirements, both voluntary and involuntary (Peracchi and Welch 1994; Hutchens 1988; Burtless 1986) so we would
expect, *ceteris paribus*, that labor force participation would fall in recessions.

Interestingly, this seemingly intuitive assumption does not apply to older
women. Older women have tended to increase their labor force participation in
contractions, whereas older men have withdrawn from the labor market. On
average, since the trough of 1954, older women increased their work effort at
the end of a contraction by 3.0 percent. Men and women over age 65 also have
different patterns. Men age 65 and older withdrew from the labor force in contractions on average by 2.3 percent, whereas women age 65 and older hardly
changed their labor force participation.

These trends suggest that explanations of how 401(k)s affect the retirement
behavior of men and women differ. Men and women face different pension structures and demand for their labor.

Labor Force Participation in Expansions

Economists expect increases in the labor force participation during expansions
as labor markets tighten: wage increases boost the opportunity costs of not working (holding nonlabor income constant, which is a crucial assumption). Indeed,
young workers (age 25–54), have increased their labor force participation in
each of the nine expansions since the one that ended in November 1948. However, it seems the opportunity cost of not working was overwhelmed by other
financial factors in older men's lives because older men decreased their labor
force participation in every expansion since 1954, except the most recent one.
What is interesting for our analysis is that the labor force participation of older

Table 1. Secular Trends: Peak Labor Force Participation* by Sex and Age 1948–2001

PEAK	LFP 25–34		LFP 25–54		LFP 55–64		LFP 65+	
	Men	Women	Men	Women	Men	Women	Men	Women
Nov-48	95.8	34.2	96.5	35.4	89.1	23.9	48.1	9.1
Jul-53	**97.5**	33.4	**97.5**	**37.8**	87.8	**29.5**	41.0	**11.1**
Aug-57	97.0	**35.9**	97.1	**41.7**	86.9	**34.5**	37.3	10.3
Apr-60	**97.4**	**36.1**	97.0	**43.0**	86.7	**36.8**	32.9	**10.7**
Dec-69	96.4	**44.0**	95.9	**49.7**	83.5	**42.7**	27.0	9.6
Nov-73	95.7	**51.7**	95.0	**53.9**	77.8	40.8	22.4	8.7
Jan-80	95.5	**65.5**	94.4	**63.8**	72.5	**41.6**	19.6	8.3
Jul-81	94.8	**66.7**	94.0	**65.1**	70.4	41.2	18.1	8.0
Jul-90	93.9	**73.3**	93.2	**74.0**	68.0	**45.0**	16.3	**8.6**
Mar-01	93.1	**76.1**	91.4	**76.9**	67.7	**52.6**	**17.9**	**9.5**

* These rates are the relevant quarterly rates.
(Bolded numbers in Tables 1–4 indicate the labor force participation was higher than in previous peak.)

Table 2. Secular Trends: Trough Labor Force Participation Rates* by Sex and Age
November 1948–November 2002

TROUGH	25–34		25–54		55–64		65+	
	Men	Women	Men	Women	Men	Women	Men	Women
Oct-49	96.2	33.3	96.9	35.9	87.4	26.8	47.6	10.0
May-54	**97.6**	**35.0**	**97.5**	**38.8**	**88.4**	**30.1**	40.6	9.0
Apr-58	97.2	**35.7**	97.2	**42.1**	88.2	**35.1**	35.9	**10.6**
Feb-61	97.1	**36.4**	96.7	**43.4**	87.7	**38.4**	33.7	**11.5**
Nov-70	96.4	**45.1**	95.8	**50.3**	82.4	**43.4**	26.1	9.6
Mar-75	95.2	**53.9**	94.1	**54.6**	76.3	40.9	22.3	8.1
Jul-80	**95.3**	**65.2**	**94.3**	**63.9**	72.2	**41.4**	18.9	8.1
Nov-82	94.6	**68.5**	94.1	**66.7**	70.1	**41.9**	17.4	7.8
Mar-91	93.7	**73.0**	93.3	**73.8**	67.6	**44.8**	15.6	**8.7**
Nov-02	91.9	**74.9**	90.7	**75.8**	**69.6**	**56.3**	**17.2**	**10.0**

* These rates are the relevant quarterly rates.

Table 3. Men and Women Act Differently in Labor Market Contractions: LFP Changes from Peak to Trough* by Sex and Age November 1948–November 2002

PEAK	TROUGH	25–34		25–54		55–64		65+	
		Men	Women	Men	Women	Men	Women	Men	Women
Nov-48	Oct-49	0.4%	-2.6%	0.4%	1.4%	-1.9%	12.1%	-1.0%	9.9%
Jul-53	May-54	0.1%	4.8%	0.0%	2.6%	0.7%	2.0%	-1.0%	-18.9%
Aug-57	Apr-58	0.2%	-0.6%	0.1%	1.0%	1.5%	1.7%	-3.8%	2.9%
Apr-60	Feb-61	-0.3%	0.8%	-0.3%	0.9%	1.2%	4.3%	2.4%	7.5%
Dec-69	Nov-70	0.0%	2.5%	-0.1%	1.2%	-1.3%	1.6%	-3.3%	0.0%
Nov-73	Mar-75	-0.5%	4.3%	-0.9%	1.3%	-1.9%	0.2%	-0.4%	-6.9%
Jan-80	Jul-80	-0.2%	-0.5%	-0.1%	0.2%	-0.4%	-0.5%	-3.6%	-2.4%
Jul-81	Nov-82	-0.2%	2.7%	0.1%	2.5%	-0.4%	1.7%	-3.9%	-2.5%
Jul-90	Mar-91	-0.2%	-0.4%	0.1%	-0.3%	-0.6%	-0.4%	-4.3%	1.2%
Mar-01	Nov-02	-1.3%	-1.6%	-0.8%	-1.4%	2.8%	7.0%	-3.9%	5.3%
Average change in labor force participation in a trough		-0.2%	0.9%	-0.2%	0.9%	0.0%	3.0%	-2.3%	-0.4%

Table 4. Women Respond More to Expansions: Labor Force Participation Changes from Trough to Peak by Sex and Age July 1953–March 2001

Percentage change in LFP in each expansion	25–34		25–54		55–64		65+	
	Men	Women	Men	Women	Men	Women	Men	Women
Nov-48								
Jul-53	1.4%	0.3%	0.6%	5.3%	0.5%	10.1%	−13.9%	11.0%
Aug-57	−0.6%	**2.6%**	−0.4%	**7.5%**	−1.7%	**14.6%**	−8.1%	**14.4%**
Apr-60	**0.2%**	1.1%	−0.2%	2.1%	−1.7%	4.8%	−8.4%	0.9%
Dec-69	−0.7%	**20.9%**	−0.8%	**14.5%**	−4.8%	**11.2%**	−19.9%	−16.5%
Nov-73	−0.7%	14.6%	−0.8%	7.2%	−5.6%	−6.0%	−14.2%	−9.4%
Jan-80	**0.3%**	**21.5%**	**0.3%**	**16.8%**	−5.0%	1.7%	−12.1%	2.5%
Jul-81	−0.5%	2.3%	−0.3%	1.9%	−2.5%	−0.5%	−4.2%	−1.2%
Jul-90	−0.7%	**7.0%**	−1.0%	**10.9%**	−3.0%	7.4%	−6.3%	**10.3%**
1-Mar	−0.6%	4.2%	−2.0%	4.2%	**0.1%**	**17.4%**	**14.7%**	9.2%
Average percentage change in labor force participation in an expansion	**−0.2%**	**8.3%**	**−0.5%**	**7.8%**	**−2.6%**	**6.8%**	**−8.0%**	**2.4%**

men no longer declined during the last remarkable ten-year expansion from March 1991 to March 2001—there was a slight increase of 0.1 percentage point.

The dramatic reversal in ability and/or propensity to retire prompted older men to increase their labor force participation during the 1990s, which was unprecedented in other recent expansions. The retirement-age (over 65) male labor force participation rate increased from 15.6 percent in March 1991 (a trough) to 17.9 percent in March 2001 (recent peak). Compare this rate to the expansion in the 1960s (February 1961 to December 1969) where retirement-age men were able to decrease their labor force participation by 6.7 percentage points, from 33.7 percent to 27.0 percent. It seems that the relationship of wages offered to older men and their available retirement income was such that the cost of retiring was more than the cost of working. We emphasize: this is a dramatic change in work behavior of men over age 55.

In contrast, older women decreased their labor force participation rate in only two of the last nine expansions. While the labor force participation of older men went up by only 0.1 percent in the expansion from March 1991 to March 2001, the labor force participation rate of older women, age 55–64, went up by

7.8 percentage points over the same time period. In sum, the average decline in labor force participation for older males in the last ten expansions is 2.1 percentage points. Similarly aged women increased their average 2.4 percentage points. The results of our regression analysis, later in the paper, imply that this increase for women during expansion periods was induced by rising wages that were overwhelming the ability to retire as the value of retirement accounts were increasing.

WOMEN HAVE LESS DB PENSION COVERAGE THAN MEN

Most comparisons of men and women's pensions concentrate on coverage rates by type of plan. Data from our sample of the HRS in 1998 and 2002 indicate that older women are more likely not to have any pension coverage at all compared to older men—they have lower coverage rates in both DB and DC plans. In Table 5, we also use actual employer expenditures (for workers in all age groups) to examine not just coverage differences but the differences in how much employers contribute to men's and women's accounts by DB and DC type. The correlation between the DC share of employers' pension contributions and the percentage of females in an industry is positive, though not large at 0.12. Women are at a higher risk of having lower amounts of employer pension contributions and of working in industries that rely relatively more on DC plans. Thus, older people, especially women who are less likely to have a DB pension and whose value of retirement income is sensitive to fluctuations in financial markets, are more likely to delay retirement because their nonlabor income—their pension wealth—has fallen.

ANALYSIS OF LABOR DEMAND AND SUPPLY:
FACTORS CAUSING PEOPLE TO WORK

The literature on the determinants of retirement is rich and attentive to the characteristics of individuals and their labor market experience. One part of our investigation focuses on how changes in the financial market environments— controlling for the opportunity cost of retiring, the wage rate, and the probability of getting a job for both men and women—affect labor force participation. It is possible that any causal relationship between an implied loss of pension income and more work effort is an illusion and mere correlation. In fact, women and men may have faced different wages and job opportunities inducing them to change their labor force participation in different ways. Based on the changes in labor force participation, these opportunities would have had to be much better

Table 5. Work Force and Pension Combination by Share of Female Employment

Pension structure and firm features	Industries with highest third in share of female employment		Industries with average share of female employment		Industries with below average share of female employment	
	1981 n = 690	1998 n = 690	1981 n = 690	1998 n = 690	1981 n = 690	1998 n = 690
DC-share by firm	56%	77%	51%	76%	34%	71%
Percent female	61%	66%	34%	38%	19%	20%
Average salary (in 1998 $)	$14,578	$18,672	$19,950	$25,267	$23,039	$27,192

Definition of variables:
1) Share of all pension contributions spent for DC plans by industry based on a sample of firms that sponsored plans from 1981 to 1998 collected from the Form 5500, Department of Labor, PWBA,
2) Share of Industry employment that is female from the CPS,
3) Average monthly salary by industry, CES national survey, seasonally adjusted, BLS, http://data.bls.gov/cgi-bin/surveymost?

for women than men. The second set of analyses uses a difference-in-differences approach to show that having only a DC plan, rather than a DB plan, decreased the probability of being retired between the ages of 61–64 in 2002. The differences in retirement behavior between these two groups changed significantly from 1998 to 2002.

Below we discuss what may have caused changes in labor force participation since the stock market crashed. Older women's (age 55–64) labor force participation rate increased by 8.1 percent since the bubble burst in the stock market, from 52.0 percent in January 2000 to 56.2 percent in October 2002, while older men's labor force participation rate rose by 3.7 percent. During the same period, unemployment increased more for older men than women—the unemployment rate rose, on average per month, by 2.03 percent for men and 1.31 percent for women. Additionally, weekly earnings rose, on average, 0.23 percent and 0.63 percent for older men and women respectively. This data suggests that labor market opportunities were relatively better for older women than men.

Since the recession started in March 2001, older women's labor force participation rates have continued to increase more than men's, corresponding to faster growth in wages. However, the level of wages for older women is still significantly lower than for men. The likelihood of finding employment has fallen for older

Table 6. Women and Men Face Different Incentives to Retire since the Bubble Burst in the S&P 500 (Average Monthly Change in LFP, Wages, and Unemployment by Sex and Age since the Crash in Financial Markets, January 2000–October 2002)

Sex and Age Group	Average Monthly Change in Labor Force Participation January 2000–October 2002	Average Monthly Change in Earnings January 2000–October 2002	Average Monthly Change in Unemployment January 2000–October 2002
Women 55–64	0.24%	0.63%	1.31%
Men 55–64	0.11%	0.23%	2.03%
Women 65+	0.36%	0.92%	6.19%
Men 65+	0.13%	0.95%	2.98%

women in the recession, as evidenced by their rising average unemployment rate, which is now larger than the growth rate of unemployment for older men. The marginal labor market advantages of older women relative to men have deteriorated in the more recent recessionary period.

Studies show that retirement decisions are affected by changes in nonlabor income, that is, pension wealth. Between 1969 and 1973, Congress unexpectedly boosted Social Security benefits by a significant amount, which spurred more retirements than otherwise would have occurred (Burtless 1986; Anderson, Burkhauser, and Quinn 1986). Gustman and Steinmeier (2002) show that the 1990s stock market boom increased retirement rates by 3 percentage points. Coronado and Perozek (2001) concluded that one-third of the respondents in their HRS sample retired earlier than expected when the stock market boomed, and the youngest retirees had the largest gains in stock-portfolio values—the average increase in the value of stocks was $93,000 for early retirees, compared to an average gain of $58,000 for the entire sample. The greater the share of equities in the portfolio, the earlier the retirement dates.

Using data from the first four waves of the HRS and Survey of Consumer Finances (SCF), Friedberg and Webb (2000) show that the phenomenon of DC plans replacing DB plans since 1983 has raised the median retirement age by 2 to 4 months because the early retirement incentives in DB plans led people to retire almost two years earlier. They predict a further increase in retirement age by 2 to 5 months as more people rely on DC plans. Friedberg and Webb also estimate that a 100 percent increase in financial wealth (using the mean of $37,182) will increase the probability of retirement by about a half percentage point. Munnell, Cahill, and Jivan (2003) also found that DC plans increase the expected retire-

Table 7. Women and Men Face Different Incentives to Retire since the Recession Started in March 2001 (Average Monthly Change in LFP, Wages, and Unemployment by Age and Sex, March 2001–October 2002)

Sex and Age Group	Average Monthly Change in Labor Force Participation March 2001–October 2002	Average Monthly Change in Earnings March 2001–October 2002	Average Monthly Change in Unemployment March 2001–October 2002
Women 55–64	0.34%	0.74%	2.45%
Men 55–64	0.18%	0.48%	1.94%
Women 65+	0.39%	0.67%	9.97%
Men 65+	−0.07%	0.78%	4.36%

ment age and, surprisingly, that workers with DC plans are expected to retire at the same age as workers without any pension coverage.

Cheng and French (2000) investigate the effect of the stock market run-up on labor supply. They find that without the stock market boom, labor force participation would have been 3.2 percent higher for men ages 55–64. Sevak (2000) shows an unexpected 10 percent increase in wealth would have decreased work effort by 3.9 percent for women and 5 percent for men (Sevak 2001).

Further evidence about labor force responses from changes in wealth are gleaned from studies on the effect of unearned income (i.e., lottery winnings) on labor earnings. Imbens, Rubin, and Sacerdote (2001) find that earnings decline when unearned income increases. A survey of lottery players in Massachusetts in the mid-1980s reveals that winners' propensity to consume leisure is positive and larger for older people.

It is important to note that the structure of pensions has helped reduce the effects of industrial retrenchment on unemployment. In the recently shrinking sectors of the economy (manufacturing, mining, etc.) firms have used a combination of voluntary retirements induced by early retirement buyouts of DB plans[5] and layoffs to reduce payroll. Voluntary retirements are a better outcome than layoffs. Layoffs do not change labor force participation at best, and seem to induce older women to seek work (presumably because their spouses lose their jobs) at worst. Services and retail have been the fastest growing industries since the 1980s—employment in retail jumped 23 percent from 1989 to 2001, but the percent of pay going to pensions is the smallest (1.4 percent in 2001) compared to the all industry average of 3.5 percent. Service employment jumped 30 percent, while the share of pay going to pensions was only 2.5 percent in 2001 (Bureau of Labor Statistics, Employment Cost Index, various years). These trends imply that when downturns occur in these industries, layoffs will be the dominant method of downsizing, which will increase labor force participation and exacerbate unemployment for older workers.

Furthermore, health insurance premiums have been growing at a rapid pace—the average growth rate from 2001 to 2005 was almost 12 percent (Henry J. Kaiser Family Foundation 2005). In addition, the provision of retiree health insurance has fallen dramatically since 1995 (Rappaport 2002). This means that workers will also want to remain in the labor force to get health insurance benefits or to supplement Medicare, although the estimates on the effects of retiree health benefit losses on labor force participation range from small to medium (Madarian 1994; Gruber and Madarian 2002). The overall trends in employer expenditures for pensions, a good proxy for quality and coverage, fell by a whopping 22 percent between 1978 and 1998 (Medoff and Calabrese 2001, 134). In 1983, 43 percent of women workers were covered by a pension plan; in 1996 just 39 percent were. The fall is worse for men, and, as we saw earlier, men are more likely to be in industries that have DB plans than women are. More than half of male workers had pensions in 1979; in 2003 only 48 percent did. This decline is affecting all workers at all income levels (Ellwood 2000). The fall in the value of non-labor income, regardless of source, will induce older workers to work longer (*ceteris paribus*) as will cash balance plans that lower benefit accruals for older workers. The Treasury Department lifted the moratorium on DB plans being converted to cash balance plans in 2002.

In sum, we expect that older workers will decrease consumption—shift in aggregate demand—and shift out their labor supply curve when faced with a negative wealth shock, especially in retirement assets. In the regression analysis, we emphasize the effect on labor force participation of being exposed to a retirement plan that depends on the financial market for its value.

REGRESSION STRATEGY AND ANALYSIS

Data

We use two datasets to test the hypothesis that older workers with DC pension wealth will postpone retirement in a recession. The first set of regressions uses average monthly data divided by sex and age group. The variables include labor force participation rates, unemployment rates, average weekly earnings, and the level of the S&P 500. The level of the S&P 500 is used to proxy primarily for changes in the expectations of retirement income security, and secondarily for the value of DC (e.g., 401[k]) pension plans. The unemployment rate and average weekly earnings approximate changes in labor demand. The sample means are presented in Table 9. We ran regressions for each sex and age group for three time periods: from January 1994 to October 2002; from the beginning of the bear stock market, January 2000, to October 2002; and from the peak of the business cycle, March 2001, to October 2002.

In the second set of analyses, we use data from the HRS for 1998 and 2002. The original HRS interviewed individuals born in 1931–1941 who were 61–71 years of age in 2002. We also use data from the RAND Corporation contribution (version C) to the HRS. The data from RAND provide an extensive number of well-defined variables that have been aggregated from various questions throughout the survey. Variables used in the regressions include: age, sex, race, educational attainment, marital status, good or bad health, self-reported retirement status, type of pension plan (DB only or DC only),[6] industry code, health insurance (public, private and/or employer-provided), availability of retiree health insurance,[7] single-year age dummy variables, and an indicator for observations from 2002 (post-treatment period).

Table 12 details the characteristics of the sample in 1998 and 2002. We restrict our sample to respondents ages 61–64 in both waves to create mutually exclusive age cohorts that are near the age of usual retirement. We further restrict our sample to respondents who have only a DB plan or only a DC plan. Including older workers who have both types of pension plans would muddy our results because these plans are likely to differ widely in value and in their effect on the retirement decision. Limiting our sample in this way reduces our observations from 1,415 to 809 in 1998 and from 1,772 to 846 in 2002. We use the HRS respondent-level weights to make our sample nationally representative.

Cohort Regression Analysis

We regressed monthly changes in the labor force participation rate on three independent variables: (1) the average monthly level of the S&P 500, (2) the average monthly unemployment rate, and (3) the average weekly earnings for each month for the relevant age and sex group for three different periods (see Table 8). The longer period between 1994 and 2002 is used as a benchmark for the bear market and recessionary periods. All independent variables are lagged one month in the regressions. The model for the regression equation is:

$$L_s = a + B_1 S\&P500_{(t-1)} + B_2 U_{(t-1)} + B_3 w_{(t-1)} + \epsilon$$

Table 8. Monthly Labor Force Participation Rate by Sex and Age and Time Period since 1994

Women 55–64	January 1994–October 2002 (n = 105) BENCHMARK	January 2000–October 2002 (n = 34) BEAR MARKET	March 2001–October 2002 (n = 20) CONTRACTION
Constant	34.74 (1.523)***	57.843 (2.351)***	56.415 (3.498)***
Weekly earnings[1]	0.029 (0.003)***	0.002 (0.003)	0.002 (0.004)
Unemployment rate	0.179 (0.233)	0.451 (0.263)*	0.66 (0.423)
S&P500	0.002 (.0005)***	−0.006 (0.0008)***	−0.005 (0.002)**
Adjusted R-squared	0.69	0.851	0.623
Men 55–64			
Constant	60.32 (1.997)***	74.511 (2.974)***	81.08 (4.908)***
Weekly earnings	0.005 (0.003)*	−0.003 (0.003)	−0.011 (0.005)*
Unemployment rate	0.264 (0.199)	0.25 (0.191)	0.473 (0.209)
S&P500	0.002 (0.0005)***	−0.004 (0.0009)***	−0.004 (0.001)***
Adjusted R-squared	0.403	0.81	0.738
Women 65+			
Constant	7.246 (0.434)***	11.62 (0.471)***	11.753 (0.748)***
Weekly earnings	0.005 (0.001)***	−0.001 (0.001)	−0.0006 (0.001)
Unemployment rate	−0.013 (0.064)	0.014 (0.049)	0.027 (0.072)
S&P500	0.0004 (0.0001)***	−0.001 (0.0002)***	−0.002 (0.0005)***
Adjusted R-squared	0.217	0.606	0.421
Men 65+			
Constant	14.405 (0.535)***	16.509 (0.821)***	16.355 (1.213)***
Weekly earnings	0.003 (0.001)***	0.002 (0.001)*	0.002 (0.0015)
Unemployment rate	0.136 (0.077)*	0.17 (0.076)**	0.159 (0.092)
S&P500	0.0006 (0.0002)***	−0.0004 (0.0003)	−0.0002 (0.0006)
Adjusted R-squared	0.262	0.261	0.14

1.) The means and definition of variables for the table in Appendix Table A6.

*Statistically significant at the .10 level; **at the .05 level; ***at the .01 level.

The unemployment rate supplements the wage rate as a measure of the marginal benefit from working, which considers the chance of getting work, and the S&P 500 proxies for changes in the value of financial assets.

Results

In the second time period, since the stock market slide began, the coefficient on the S&P 500 level is negative and significant for older workers ages 55–64. From the beginning of the recession in March 2001 to October 2002,[8] older women's labor force participation rose from 52.8 percent to 56.2 percent.

Table 9. Means and Variable Definitions for Regressions in Table 9

Women 55–64	January 1994–October 2002 (n = 105)	January 2000–October 2002 (n = 34)	March 2001–October 2002 (n = 20)
LFP rate	51.10	53.04	53.90
Weekly earnings	493.76	532.99	548.21
Unemployment rate	3.00	2.86	3.09
S&P500	954.10	1222.49	1090.11
Men 55–64			
LFP rate	67.34	68.08	68.63
Weekly earnings	810.75	846.98	856.28
Unemployment rate	3.30	3.29	3.83
S&P500	954.10	1222.49	1090.11
Women 65+			
LFP rate	9.05	9.61	9.76
Weekly earnings	286.64	309.81	314.65
Unemployment rate	3.47	3.21	3.52
S&P500	954.10	1222.49	1090.11
Men 65+			
LFP rate	17.09	17.69	17.78
Weekly earnings	480.26	514.95	528.83
Unemployment rate	3.39	3.26	3.27
S&P 500	954.10	1222.49	1090.11

Definition of variables:
1) Monthly labor force participation rate seasonally adjusted collected from the Current Population Survey (CPS), Department of Labor, http://www.bls.gov/data/home.htm,
2) Average weekly earnings from the CPS's Basic Monthly Survey, calculated (in 2000 $) for each sex and age group of individuals with weekly earnings greater than or equal to 1, http://ferret.bls.census.gov,
3) Monthly unemployment rate seasonally adjusted collected from the CPS, Department of Labor, http://www.bls.gov/data/home.htm,
4) Average monthly level of the S&P 500, http://www.economy.com/freelunch/default.asp.

The results imply that older men and women have been induced to work since the recession began because of real declines in the value of their DC pensions and expectations that their retirement is more insecure because of the fall in the S&P 500. The inducement is larger for women—their elasticity is −0.101 percent vs. −0.064 percent for men.[9] Mean values for all variables are found in Table 9.

The result from the first set of regressions implies that, evaluated at the mean, a 10 percent, or 109.01 point, drop in the S&P 500 would cause older men's labor force participation rate to increase from 68.63 percent to 69.07 percent. Similarly, older women's labor force participation rate would increase from 53.90 percent to 54.44 percent. In the second set of analyses, we will see that the effect of having only a DC plan is even larger for women ages 63–64 from 1998 to 2002.

The S&P 500 had fallen by 630.83 points, or 42.47 percent, since its peak during this time period. Our elasticities indicate that this drop would cause the labor force participation rates of older workers to increase from 67.7 percent to 69.8 percent for men and from 51.8 percent to 54.8 percent for women. The actual values of labor force participation rates for older men and women in October 2002 are 70.1 percent and 56.2 percent respectively, which are slightly higher than predicted. Again, women's labor force participation decisions are more sensitive to levels of the S&P 500, which proxies for the value of their nonlabor income and wealth.

The results for women who are at retirement age (65) reveal similar significant effects, but not so for men in the first period. The S&P 500 significantly boosts the labor force participation rate for women age 65 and older in the bear stock market, January 2000 to October 2002. The elasticity is such that a 10 percent drop in the S&P 500 would cause retirement-age women's labor force participation rate to increase from its mean of 9.6 percent to 9.7 percent. The S&P 500 variable is not significant for retirement-age men in this period.

The results are compared to a benchmark time period, 1994 and 2002, when the elasticities of the S&P 500 movements were much smaller and in the opposite direction. The results suggest that individuals did not increase their labor force participation in response to a fall in the stock market until the last few years when 401(k)s made their ascendancy in the American retirement scene. In 1999, a national magazine dubbed the phenomenon "401(k) Nation" (Smith 1999).

Since the presence of autocorrelation is possible among these variables, we used the Granger causality test (W.H. Greene 2000, 742–43) to find evidence that causality is such that changes in the S&P 500 (lagged) affects labor force participation rates.[10] For men and women ages 55–64 in the 2000–2002 period, the Granger causality test indicates that the S&P 500 level lagged one month has a statistically significant effect on the labor force participation rate and not the reverse. Similarly, the S&P 500 variable is found to granger-cause the labor force participation rate for women age 65 and older.[11] In the other regressions, including those for men 65 and older, the test indicates causality in both directions.

The unemployment rate does not significantly affect older men's or women's labor force participation rates since the decline in the stock market or since the recession began. Unemployment seems to have no greater effect on labor force participation for older or retirement-age men and women in the longer time period (January 1994– October 2002). These conclusions are drawn from changes in averages between cohorts, not from how the same individuals act in different circumstances.

DIFFERENCE-IN-DIFFERENCES

A difference-in-differences approach, using individual-level data from the HRS, compares the change in retirement rates for older workers with only DB or DC pension plans to assess whether DC plans caused retirement rates to fall after the stock market decline. The sample includes workers ages 61–64 in two different time periods, 1998 and 2002, with either a DC plan or a DB plan, but not both. The event that causes the difference, the treatment in the model, is the dramatic fall in the stock market, which began in January 2000. The pre-treatment period is 1998; the post-treatment period is 2002. Retirement rates declined by over 7 percentage points from 1998 to 2002 for workers ages 61–64 with DC pensions (see Table 10).

The difference-in-differences model controls for unobserved, time invariant characteristics. For example, we know the structure of DB plans causes spikes in retirement rates at certain ages of eligibility, whereas DC plans do not (Friedberg and Webb 2000). Because this feature of DB pensions does not change, it is controlled for in our model. We are not emphasizing the difference in retirement rates between individuals with DB and DC pensions but, rather, *how that difference changes when there has been a negative shock to the stock market.* Our probit model is:

$$Ret_{it}^* = \alpha + \beta{}^*DC_{it} + \delta{}^*Y2002_t + \gamma{}^*DC\_2002_{it} + \epsilon_{it}$$

$$Ret_{it} = 1(Ret_{it}^* >= 0)$$

where α is a constant, DC_{it} is a dummy variable indicating DC pension coverage, $Y2002_t$ is a dummy for the year 2002, DC_2002_{it} is an indicator for whether a respondent had a DC plan in 2002, and ϵ_{it} is the error term.[12] The coefficient of interest is γ, which represents the difference-in-differences due to the treatment. A negative and significant coefficient on γ implies that retirement rates of older individuals with DC plans declined when the stock market plunged (see Table 11). The difference-in-difference estimator, γ_{DD}, is defined as

$$\gamma_{DD} = [E(Ret_{it}|DC_{it} = 1, Y2002_t = 1) - E(Ret_{it}|DC_{it} = 1, Y2002_t = 0)] -$$
$$[E(Ret_{it}|DC_{it} = 0, Y2002_t = 1) - E(Ret_{it}|DC_{it} = 0, Y2002_t = 0)]$$

The 1998 and 2002 samples are similar. The average age is 62.43 in 1998 and 62.47 in 2002 and pension coverage rates are consistent. The proportion of women in the sample decreases slightly from 46.2 percent in 1998 to 42.1 percent in 2002. Health insurance coverage also increases, by 4.94 percentage points.

Table 10. Mean Retirement Rates by Age Group, Sex, and Pension Type before and after the Stock Market Decline

| | 1998 | | | 2002 | | |
| | Retirement Rate | | | Retirement Rate | | |
Pension Type	Men	Women	Total	Men	Women	Total
Age 61–64						
DB only	49.57	41.92	45.86	56.91	43.05	50.71
DC only	37.24	29.64	34.11	25.17	28.12	26.43
Difference (DB-DC)	12.33	12.28	11.75	31.74	14.93	24.28
Difference-in-Differences				19.41	2.65	12.53
(1998–2002)				(0.000)	(0.139)	(0.000)
Age 63–64						
DB only	60.77	52.21	56.64	71.05	64.07	68.08
DC only	47.54	54.05	49.78	34.60	31.41	33.40
Difference (DB-DC)	13.23	−1.84	6.86	36.45	32.66	34.68
Difference-in-Differences				23.22	34.50	27.82
(1998–2002)				(0.021)	(0.001)	(0.000)

Notes: P values are in parenthesis. Individuals are coded as retired if they responded in the HRS that their labor force status is "retired." Respondent level weights from the HRS are used to create a nationally representative sample.

Table 11. Expected Value of the Retirement Rate for Pre and Post-Treatment Periods

| | Expected Value of the Retirement Rate | | |
Pension Type	2002	1998	Difference
DC	$\alpha + \beta + \delta + \gamma$	$\alpha + \beta$	$\Delta + \gamma$
DB	$\alpha + \delta$	α	Δ
Difference in Differences			γ

The 61- to 64-year-old group in 2002 has slightly lower educational attainment. The percentage of workers in the mining and construction industry rises from 5.4 percent to 8.7 percent, but other industry density changes are small. Table 12 displays the similarities between the 1998 and 2002 cohorts and suggests that they are good comparison groups.

Results

The coefficient for γ was negative and significant for men but not women in the regressions using the ages 61–64 sample. The results for the 63–64 sample are more significant. The difference-in-differences estimator is negative and significant for both men and women, which suggests that the decline in the stock market was more likely to cause workers ages 63–64 with DC plans to postpone retirement. A robustness check included a set of explanatory variables and a re-estimation to see if the significance of γ changed. The added explanatory variables include dummy variables for the following: single year of age, race (white, black, other), educational attainment level (less than high school, high school, some college, college, and post-college), industry (thirteen different groupings), marital status, health (good or bad), health insurance, and retiree health insurance. The difference-in-differences estimator remained negative and significant for men ages 61–64 and for both sexes ages 63–64 (see Table 13). The marginal effect of having a DC plan in 2002 reduced the retirement probability of men ages 61–64 by 30.8 percentage points. For men and women ages 63–64, this reduction was slightly greater, at 34.2 and 38.7 percentage points, respectively (Table 14). The mean values of the variables used in these regressions are found in Table 15.

Sevak (2001) performed a similar estimation, using a linear probability model (LPM), to assess whether the stock market's boom boosted retirement rates for individuals with DC plans between 1992 and 1998. LPMs are problematic for several reasons, for example, estimated probability results are not constrained to the 0–1 interval, and negative variances are possible (W. H. Greene 2000, 813). However, we also performed the LPM estimation to compare our results. This regression is:

$$\text{Ret}_{it} = \alpha + \beta^* DC_{it} + \delta^* Y2002_t + \gamma^* DC\_2002_{it} + \epsilon_{it}$$

Our results with the LPM are comparable to those with the probit model; however, the significance improves. The difference-in-differences estimator is significant for men ages 61–64 and for both sexes ages 63–64.

Table 12. Characteristics of Age 61–64 Sample with DC-Only or DB-Only Pensions in 1998 and 2002 (in percentages except for age)

Variables	1998	2002
DB only	69.42	71.69
DC only	30.58	28.31
Male	53.76	57.94
Female	46.24	42.06
White	87.71	87.46
Black	9.03	8.99
Other	3.13	3.42
Age	62.43	62.47
Married	74.36	75.99
Good Health	82.62	82.75
Bad Health	17.30	17.18
Retired	42.27	48.94
Health Insurance	80.49	80.63
Retiree Health Insurance	58.47	63.41
High School Degree or Less	51.70	47.25
Agriculture, Forestry, Fishing	1.20	2.20
Mining & Construction	5.40	8.72
Manufacturing—Durable	9.81	10.36
Manufacturing—Nondurable	15.38	14.91
Transportation	11.80	10.99
Wholesale	6.27	6.68
Retail	11.01	12.19
Finance, Insurance, and Real Estate	8.69	6.61
Services—Business and Repair	6.70	8.96
Services—Personal	3.02	2.89
Entertainment and Recreation	1.60	3.18
Professional and Related Services	38.82	39.27
Public Administration	9.71	10.34
	n = 809	n = 846

Notes: Numbers are in percentages, except for age. Respondent-level weights from the HRS are used.

POLICY IMPLICATIONS AND FURTHER RESEARCH

We find that labor force participation rates of older workers have become more sensitive to the value of financial assets. Unfortunately, the sensitivities are such that older workers, especially women, enter or stay in the labor force when financial markets are weak and unemployment is likely growing worse. When compared to similar individuals with DB pensions, men and women ages 63–64 with

Table 13. Regression Results for Probit Model (Difference-in-Differences), Age 61–64

Explanatory Variables	Men 61–64 Coefficient (dF/dx)	Robust Standard Error	Women 61–64 Coefficient (dF/dx)	Robust Standard Error
DC Pension Only	−0.093*	0.056	−0.137**	0.060
Year2002	0.143***	0.042	0.104**	0.043
DC*Year2002	−0.308***	0.063	−0.080	0.086
Age62	0.168***	0.049	0.112**	0.054
Age63	0.277***	0.046	0.264***	0.054
Age64	0.332***	0.045	0.319***	0.052
Black	−0.070	0.057	−0.009	0.050
Other	−0.233***	0.076	−0.078	0.161
Less Than HS	−0.001	0.052	−0.124**	0.056
Some College	−0.027	0.051	−0.023	0.053
College Degree	−0.040	0.062	−0.015	0.071
Post-College	0.001	0.063	0.075	0.062
Agriculture	−0.164*	0.094	−0.117	0.210
Construction	−0.142**	0.061	−0.136	0.149
Manufacturing—Durable	−0.093*	0.056	−0.045	0.074
Manufacturing—Nondurable	−0.080	0.050	−0.159**	0.066
Transportation	−0.035	0.054	−0.188**	0.072
Wholesale	−0.240***	0.057	−0.235**	0.079
Retail	−0.029	0.061	−0.199***	0.056
Finance	−0.128	0.080	−0.115*	0.067
Services—Personal	−0.277**	0.098	−0.124	0.082
Entertainment	−0.022	0.114	−0.199	0.118
Professional	−0.149***	0.055	−0.198***	0.054
Public	−0.163***	0.060	−0.106	0.066
Married	0.023	0.050	0.123***	0.040
Poor Health	0.036	0.047	0.044	0.051
Health Insurance	−0.270***	0.053	−0.179***	0.058
Retiree Health Insurance	0.093**	0.047	0.018	0.049

Notes: Coefficients reported are marginal effects; baseline = Age 61, White, High School, Services-Business. * indicates significance at the .10 level; ** at the .05 level, *** at the .01 level.

only DC pensions are 34 to 38 percent less likely to retire in response to a decline in the stock market.

The destabilizing effect of DC plans on the labor market should only grow worse as more workers are covered by pension plans that are tied to financial markets. Workers ages 25–39 are more likely to have DC plans and less likely to have DB plans than older workers. In 1996, 21.9 percent of younger workers were covered by only 401(k)-type plans, compared to 15 percent for workers over age 55 (Survey of Income and Program Participation 1996).

Table 14. Regression Results for Probit Model (Difference-in-Differences), Age 63–64

Explanatory Variables	Men 63–64 Coefficient (dF/dx)	Robust Standard Error	Women 63–64 Coefficient (dF/dx)	Robust Standard Error
DC Pension Only	−0.085	0.080	0.022	0.100
Year2002	0.146**	0.061	0.151**	0.063
DC*Year2002	−0.342***	0.100	−0.387***	0.105
Age64	0.067	0.051	0.042	0.057
Black	−0.114	0.088	−0.012	0.075
Other	−0.257**	0.122	−0.299	0.252
Less Than HS	0.036	0.076	−0.230***	0.088
Some College	−0.121*	0.071	−0.021	0.076
College Degree	−0.124	0.086	−0.023	0.109
Post-College	−0.077	0.099	0.061	0.093
Agriculture	−0.210*	0.124	n/a	n/a
Construction	−0.196**	0.097	0.063	0.247
Manufacturing—Durable	−0.176**	0.082	−0.013	0.118
Manufacturing—Nondurable	−0.194***	0.073	−0.037	0.111
Transportation	−0.150*	0.081	−0.171	0.126
Wholesale	−0.328***	0.080	−0.253*	0.138
Retail	−0.058	0.100	−0.244**	0.097
Finance	−0.278**	0.112	−0.029	0.108
Services—Personal	−0.354**	0.144	0.043	0.144
Entertainment	0.104	0.148	−0.175	0.186
Professional	−0.201***	0.081	−0.165**	0.084
Public	−0.303***	0.086	−0.082	0.116
Married	−0.045	0.068	0.131**	0.061
Poor Health	0.066	0.067	0.059	0.073
Health Insurance	−0.227***	0.067	−0.199**	0.083
Retiree Health Insurance	0.012	0.068	−0.050	0.074

Notes: Coefficients reported are marginal effects; baseline = Age 63, White, High School, Services-Business. * indicates significance at the .10 level; **at the .05 level; ***at the .01 level.

We expect that industries that are most likely to have 401(k)-type pension plans may experience more volatile labor markets and have more difficulty in retiring workers when times are tough and keeping workers when labor demand is high. We suspect that the implications for non-European Americans are different but in an unexpected way. Since African Americans have far fewer individual-level retirement accounts and rely on Social Security, the destabilizing effects may not affect them, though poverty rates still remain higher than for European Americans. However, the industry effect will dominate any demographic differ-

Table 15. Means for Difference-in-Differences Regressions

Explanatory Variables	Men 61–64	Women 61–64	Men 63–64	Women 63–64
DC Pension Only	0.291	0.254	0.308	0.219
Year2002	0.526	0.498	0.539	0.522
DC*Year2002	0.138	0.124	0.142	0.118
Age62	0.270	0.264	n/a	n/a
Age63	0.254	0.231	n/a	n/a
Age64	0.238	0.241	0.483	0.511
Black	0.114	0.206	0.117	0.202
Other	0.042	0.018	0.038	0.006
Less Than HS	0.189	0.163	0.200	0.169
Some College	0.194	0.209	0.200	0.228
College Degree	0.116	0.097	0.128	0.104
Post-College	0.167	0.161	0.137	0.160
Agriculture	0.029	0.007	0.036	n/a
Construction	0.118	0.009	0.117	0.011
Manufacturing—Durable	0.131	0.080	0.133	0.073
Manufacturing—Nondurable	0.215	0.083	0.216	0.093
Transportation	0.162	0.054	0.157	0.059
Wholesale	0.088	0.032	0.092	0.037
Retail	0.104	0.133	0.079	0.107
Finance	0.061	0.084	0.056	0.096
Services—Personal	0.019	0.046	0.022	0.039
Entertainment	0.027	0.020	0.029	0.020
Professional	0.241	0.576	0.256	0.562
Public	0.107	0.090	0.097	0.081
Married	0.867	0.607	0.856	0.601
Poor Health	0.191	0.190	0.187	0.197
Health Insurance	0.823	0.763	0.793	0.772
Retiree Health Insurance	0.645	0.551	0.607	0.567

ences. Since the United States is the only Organization for Economic Cooperation and Development (OECD) nation that bans mandatory retirement—although other nations are considering age discrimination laws and policies to encourage workers to work longer (see "Part 4: International Policy Lessons for the United States" in this volume)—there should be special attention paid to how the type of pension plan will affect labor supply throughout the business cycle. It makes sense to have policies that encourage DB-type pension plans that provide guaranteed benefits and prevent countercyclical fluctuations in labor supply among older workers.

In the United States, changes in the private pension system that make retirement income more exposed to financial markets may force workers to spend their longer lives in the workforce, which reverses decades of improvements in workers' retirement opportunities.

Notes

1. More than $13 billion in salary deferrals automatically transfer into 401(k)s or similar retirement plans each month. Tom Schlossberg (president of the Purchase) says ". . . And as inflows for retirement savings grow, so will the dampening impact of this pool of money on market fluctuations" (Associated Press 2002).

2. Enron also used an Employee Stock Ownership Plan offset arrangement to permanently cut the value of pensions earned between January 1987 and January 1995 (Francis and Schultz 2002).

3. Thomas O. Padgett, a longtime Enron employee, testified before the Committee on Education and the Workforce in 2002 that he planned to retire that year but now estimates having to work another ten years.

4. Peak and trough labor force participation rates are reported quarterly as denoted by the roman numerals.

5. Employers who are aiming to lay off workers may be wishing they had a way to use the 401(k) plan to manage their labor supply. Pension plans are traditionally used as human resource tools (Lazear 1991). When product demand falls, early retirement programs help shrink payroll. Lucent Technologies used its DB plan to manage one of the biggest corporate layoffs in history. It used the DB plan to offer early-retirement packages to over 15,000 U.S. managers (Associated Press 2001). More recently, in June 2006, 47,600 employees from General Motors Corp. and Delphi accepted early retirement or buyout offers. Generous severance payments have similar effects, but struggling companies often don't have the cash to offer and rely on prefunded pensions to induce the voluntary attrition. Early retirement plans help shrink payroll and are funded by pensions.

6. Pension variables were constructed using data from the current wave and also data carried forward from previous waves, allowing for at least partial vesting in DB plans after five years and rollovers in DC plans after changing employers.

7. This variable is constructed from answers to the question, "could you continue your health insurance coverage up to age 65 if you left your current employer?" This variable may be capturing the presence of retiree health insurance or COBRA coverage, which can also be continued after leaving the employer but at full cost to the individual.

8. The U.S. Bureau of Labor Statistics has seasonally adjusted data only until December 2002, and there are no plans to make the seasonally adjusted data available in the future. We plan to update the analysis by using unseasonally adjusted data.

9. The elasticity is −0.072 percent, or −0.00072, for men and −0.138 percent, or −0.00138, for women in the 55–64 age group in the period from January 2000 to October 2002.

10. "Causality in the sense defined by Granger (1969) and Sims (1972) is inferred when lagged values of a variable, say x_t, have explanatory power in a regression of a variable y_t on lagged values of y_t and x_t." If the test indicates granger-causality, then previous changes in x_t do help explain movements in y_t, even in the presence of the lagged value of y_t (Greene 2000, 742–43).

11. The Granger causality test passes at the 5 percent level for women age 65 and over in the time period from January 2000 to October 2002. The test passes at the 10 percent level for this same group in the time period from March 2001 to October 2002.

12. Probit:

$$\text{Prob}(Y = 1) = \Phi(\beta'x)$$

Where Φ is the distribution function of the standard normal.

The standard normal distribution used in probit models is similar to the logistic distribution used in logit models, although the logistic distribution has fatter tails. To obtain the marginal effects, calculate the partial derivative

$$\partial F(\beta'x)/\partial x = f(\beta'x)\beta$$

which, for the probit, is

$$\phi(\beta'x)\beta$$

where ϕ is the density function of the standard normal.

For the binary independent variables, the marginal effects are given by

$$\text{Prob}[Y = 1|\text{xbar.},d = 1] - \text{Prob}[Y = 1|\text{xbar.},d = 0]$$

where xbar. is the mean of all the other variables in the model. Alternatively, as W. H. Greene points out, "simply taking the derivative with respect to the binary variable as if it were continuous provides an approximation that is often surprisingly accurate" (2000, 817).

The probit model is estimated using the maximum likelihood method. The likelihood equation is

$$L = \Pi[\Phi(\beta'x_i)]^{y_i}[1 - \Phi(\beta'x_i)]^{1-y_i}$$

where the product is taken from i = 1 to n. Taking the natural log of the equation gives

$$\ln L = \Sigma\{y_i \ln \Phi(\beta'x_i) + (1 - y_i) \ln [1 - \Phi(\beta'x_i)]\}$$

where the sum is taken from i = 1 to n. To perform maximization, the first derivative of the log-likelihood function is taken with respect to , and set equal to zero,

$$\partial \ln L/\partial\beta = \Sigma(y_i - \Phi(\beta'x_i)) / [\Phi(\beta'x_i)(1 - \Phi(\beta'x_i))]\phi(\beta'x_i) x_i = 0$$

where the sum is taken from i = 1 to n.

Solving the first derivative for βhat yields the estimated parameters.

REFERENCES

Ameriks, John, and Stephen B. Zeldes. 2001. "How Do Household Portfolio Shares Vary With Age?" Working Paper, TIAA-CREF Institute.

Anderson, Kathryn H., Richard V. Burkhauser, and Joseph F. Quinn. 1986. "Do Retirement Dreams Come True? The Effect of Unanticipated Events on Retirement Plans." *Industrial and Labor Relations Review.* Vol. 39, no. 4 (July): 518–26.

Associated Press. 2001. "Lucent to Offer Early Retirement." *Toronto Star Newspapers.* June 6: E05.

Associated Press. 2002. "401(k) Plans Give Stability to Economy." *Daily Herald Newspapers.* January 2.

Associated Press. 2006. "Report: Most Eligible Ala. Delphi Workers Take Early Retirements." The Associated Press State and Local Wire. 28 June.

Bureau of Labor Statistics. Various years. "Employer Costs for Employee Compensation." http:/stats.bls.goc/news.release/ecec.nws.htm.

Burtless, Gary. 1986. "Social Security, Unanticipated Benefit Increases, and the Timing of Retirement." *The Review of Economic Studies,* Vol. 53, no. 5: 781–805.

———, ed. 1987. "Occupational Effects on the Health and Work Capacity of Older Men." In *Work, Health, and Income among the Elderly.* Studies in Social Economics series. Washington, DC: Brookings Institution. 103–42.

Burtless, Gary, and Robert Moffitt. 1985. "The Joint Choice of Retirement Date and Post-Retirement Hours of Work." *Journal of Labor Economics.* Vol. 3, no. 2 (April): 209–36.

Cerulli Report. 2001. http://www.cerulli.com/report-mu-401k.htm.

Chelius, James, and Robert S. Smith. 1990. "Profit Sharing and Employment Stability." *Industrial and Labor Relations Review.* Vol. 43, no. 3: 256S–273S.

Cheng, Ing-Haw, and Eric French. 2000. "The Effect of the Run-Up in the Stock Market on Labor Supply." *Economic Perspectives—The Federal Reserve Bank of Chicago.* Vol. 24, no. 4: 48–65.

Clark, Robert L., and Joseph F. Quinn. 1999. "Effects of Pensions on Labor Markets and Retirement." Boston College. Unpublished manuscript.

Committee on Education and the Workforce. U.S. House of Representatives. 2002. "The Enron Collapse and Its Implication for Worker Retirement Security." Statement of Thomas O. Padgett, February 7: 104–106. http://frwebgate.access.gpo.gov/cgi-bin/getdoc.cgi?dbname=107_house_hearings&docid=f:81198.pdf.

Coronado, Julia Lynn, and Maria Perozek. 2001. "Wealth Effects and the Consumption of Leisure: Retirement Decisions during the Stock Market Boom of the 1990s." Federal Reserve Board. Unpublished manuscript.

EBRI Background on Company Stock in Retirement Plans. Facts from EBRI, 2002. Available http://www.ebri.org/pdf/publications/facts/1201fact.pdf.

Ellwood, David. 2000. "Winners and Losers in America." In *A Working Nation: Workers, Work, and Government in the New Economy.* David Ellwood and Karen Lynn-Dyson, eds. New York: Russell Sage Foundation.

Eschtruth, Andrew D., and Jonathon Gemus. 2002. "Are Older Workers Responding to the Bear Market?" Just the Facts on Retirement Issues. Center for Retirement Research. (September). www.bc.edu/crr.

Francis, Theo, and Ellen Schultz. 2002. "Enron Pensions Had More Room at the Top." *The Wall Street Journal.* (January 23).

Friedberg, Leora, and Anthony Webb. 2000. "The Impact of 401(k) Plans on Retirement." University of California, San Diego, Discussion Paper No. 30.

Gale, William, Eric Engen, and Cori Uccello. 2000. "The Adequacy of Household Saving." Center for Retirement Research. Boston College.

Granger, Clive W. J. 1969. "Investigating Causal Relations by Econometric Models and Cross-Spectral Methods." *Econometrica* 37, no. 3: 424–38.

Greene, Kelly. 2002. "More Older Investors May Delay Retirement as Portfolios Shrink." *The Wall Street Journal.* (February 14).

Greene, William H. 2000. *Econometric Analysis.* Fourth Edition. New Jersey: Prentice-Hall, Inc.

Gruber, Jonathan, and Brigitte C. Madrian. 2002. "Health Insurance, Labor Supply, and Job Mobility: A Critical Review of the Literature." Working Paper No. w8817, National Bureau of Economic Research. (February).

Gustman, Alan, and Thomas L. Steinmeier. 2002. "Retirement and the Stock Market Bubble." Working Paper No. w9440. National Bureau of Economic Research. (December).

Gustman, Alan, and Thomas L. Steinmeier. 2001a. "Retirement and Wealth." Working Paper No. w8229. National Bureau of Economic Research. (April).

Gustman, Alan, and Thomas L. Steinmeier. 2001b. "Imperfect Knowledge, Retirement, and Saving." Working Paper No. w8406. National Bureau of Economic Research. (August).

HRS Participant Newsletter. 2003. University of Michigan. (Winter): 11–12.

Hutchens, Robert M. 1988. "Do Job Opportunities Decline With Age?" *Industrial and Labor Relations Review.* Vol. 42, no. 1 (October): 89–99.

Imbens, Guido, Donald Rubin, and Bruce Sacerdote. 2001. "Estimating the Effect of Unearned Income on Labor Supply, Earnings, Savings, and Consumption: Evidence from a Survey of Lottery Winners." *American Economic Review.* Vol. 91, no. 4: 778–95.

Jones, Jeffrey M. 2002. "Americans Counting on 401(k)s, Not Social Security: Retirement Savings Tops List of Americans' Financial Worries." *The Wall Street Journal.* (April 25).

The Henry J. Kaiser Family Foundation. 2005. Employee Health Benefits: 2005 Annual Survey. 17.

Lazear, Edward P. 1979. "Why Is There Mandatory Retirement?" *Journal of Political Economy.* Vol. 87, no. 6: 1126–84.

Lazear, Edward P. 1991. "Labor Economics and the Psychology of Organizations." *Journal of Economic Perspectives.* Vol. 5, no. 2: 89–110.

Lo, Andrew, and Dmitry Repin. 2001. "The Psychophysiology of Real-Time Financial Risk Processing." Working Paper No. w8508. National Bureau of Economic Research. (October).

Maddala, G. S. 1999. *Limited-Dependent and Qualitative Variables in Econometrics.* Econometric Society Monographs. Cambridge University Press. 22–27.

Madrian, Brigitte C. 1994. "Employment-Based Health Insurance and Job Mobility: Is There Evidence of Job-Lock?" *Quarterly Journal of Economics.* Vol. 109, no. 1: 27–54.

Medoff, James, and Michael Calabrese. 2001. "The Impact of Labor Market Trends on Health and Benefit Coverage and Inequality." The Pension & Welfare Benefit Agency. U.S. Department of Labor. (February 28).

Munnell, Alicia H., Kevin E. Cahill, and Natalia A. Jivan. 2003. "How Has the Shift to 401(k)s Affected the Retirement Age?" Center for Retirement Research. (September). http://www.bc.edu/crr.

Nesvisky, Matt. 2002. "Measuring the Stress of Financial Traders." *NBER Digest.* (March). http://www.nber.org/digest/mar02/w8508.html.

O'Malley, Chris. 2002. "Economy Devours Nest Eggs; Falling Markets, Failing Companies Halt Plans to Retire." *The Indianapolis Star.* 20 July.

Peracchi, Franco, and Finis Welch. 1994. "Trends in Labor Force Transitions of Older Men and Women." *Journal of Labor Economics.* Vol. 12, no. 2 (April): 210–42.

Purcell, Patrick. 2004. "Retirement Savings and Household Wealth in 2003: Analysis of Census Bureau Data." Congressional Research Service, Library of Congress, order code RL30922. December 2.

Rappaport, Anna M. 2002. "Update on Retiree Health Care Issues and Trends." Mercer Human Resource Consulting.

Samwick, Andrew, and Jonathan Skinner. 1998. "How Will Defined Contribution Pension Plans Affect Retirement Income?" NBER Working Paper #6645.

Schiller, Robert. 2000. *Irrational Exuberance.* Princeton University Press.

Sevak, Purvi. 2001. "Wealth Shocks and Retirement Timing: Evidence from the Nineties." University of Michigan. Unpublished manuscript.

Sims, Christopher A. 1972. "Money, Income, and Causality." *The American Economic Review* 62, no. 4: 540–52.

Smith, Alex Kates. 1999. "Roads to Riches." *U.S. News and World Report.* (June 28): 67.

Survey of Income and Program Participation. 1996. Wave 7. http://ferret.bls.census.gov.

U.S. Department of Labor, Abstract of 1993 Form 5500 Annual Reports (table F5) and http://www.dol.gov/pwba/programs/opr/bulletin/cover.htm.

U.S. Department of Labor, U.S. Bureau of Labor Statistics. *Current Population Survey.* Series ID LFS1603301, LFS21003301, LFS1604901, LFS1604901Q, LFS21004901, LFS1606501, LFS1606501Q, LFS21006501, LFS1603302, LFS21003302, LFS1604902, LFS1604902Q, LFS21004902, LFS1606502, LFS1606502Q, LFS21006502. http://www.bls.gov/data/home.htm.

Wolff, Edward. 2002. *Retirement Insecurity.* Economic Policy Institute. Washington, DC.

Zernike, Kate. 2002. "Stocks' Slide Is Playing Havoc with Older Americans' Dreams." *New York Times.* (July 14): 1.

CHAPTER NINE

The Interaction between Health, Health Insurance, and Retirement

CHRISTIAN E. WELLER & JEFFREY WENGER

As we celebrate our ever-longer lives, we are faced with the fact that this phenomenon has ever-increasing costs associated with it. If a longer life also means more years spent in retirement, workers need to have more lifetime retirement income than previous generations to maintain their standard of living once retired. Planning for how much income is necessary to maintain a standard of living raises questions about the costs of healthcare and about the provision of health insurance for retirees.

Health insurance is an integral part of the retirement decision. Persons age 55 and older are disproportionate users of healthcare. They have more frequent and more severe health problems than younger people. Also, the costs associated with their health problems are typically higher than for younger people with similar health problems, for instance, due to longer recovery periods.

Since the 1980s, rising healthcare costs and increased life expectancy have made health insurance coverage increasingly important by mitigating the financial risks associated with unforeseeable healthcare expenditures in old age. A crucial source of coverage is employer-sponsored health insurance (ESI). However, many employers have reduced access to retiree health insurance for their employees, either by no longer offering this benefit or by reducing the value of this benefit in an effort to contain costs. The declining access to employer-sponsored retiree health insurance poses a problem since there are no realistic substitutes. The near-elderly, those between the ages of 55 and 64, are often not eligible for Medicare, and the elderly (65 and older), who are eligible for Medicare, lack full coverage. And the alternative of private, nongroup health insurance is often prohibitively expensive.

Faced with health problems, climbing healthcare expenditures, and declining access to and affordability of healthcare, workers planning for retirement

267

essentially have three options, assuming that there are no major policy changes: (1) apply for disability insurance, (2) save more during their working years to prepare for the higher costs of retiree health insurance, delay retirement and work longer.

The decision to work longer, though, raises serious concerns, especially if workers in poor health are more likely than workers in good health to extend their labor force participation due to starker declines in access to affordable health insurance. Already, employers will likely face rising healthcare costs since the share of workers in poor health with ESI has grown faster than that of employees in good health. Further, since the labor force participation rate of older persons has risen in recent years, it is possible that the overall health of the labor force is declining, potentially reducing productivity. Moreover, employers may reduce access even faster if they find themselves offering health insurance coverage for a growing share of employees in poor health. Because of the rising cost pressures, older workers in poor health may see the sharpest declines in access to retiree health insurance, which could ultimately result in rising demands on public health-insurance systems.

While the existing research suggests that older workers are working longer in part because of declining access to employer-sponsored retiree health insurance, a number of research questions need to be addressed before conclusive policy recommendations can be made. For example, little is known about the accessibility of health insurance by the type of coverage: is it access to prescription drug coverage instead of hospitalization insurance coverage that keeps workers working longer? Also, it would be helpful to determine the relative effect of wealth and health insurance on the retirement decisions of older workers: could the decline in access to health insurance even be feasibly compensated for by greater savings? In the same vein, innovative forms of health insurance provision have emerged, particularly so-called prefunded health-insurance models, or medical savings accounts. Research on the effectiveness of these initiatives to shore up health insurance coverage has been limited.

Background: What Do We Know about Health, Health Insurance, and Retirement?

Health Status of the Near-Elderly and the Elderly

It is important to keep in mind when studying retirement decisions that health improvements for the near-elderly, those aged 55 to 64 years, and the elderly, aged 65 years and older, appear to be slow or nonexistent. Data from the Department of Health and Human Services (National Center for Health Statistics 2002a) show that the share of near-elderly who reported themselves to be in fair or poor health declined from 26.6 percent in 1982 to 18.5 percent in 1999. This included the recession in the early 1990s, when the share of the near-elderly in fair or poor health rose from 20.3 percent in 1990 to 21.9 percent in 1992. The health status of those age 55 and older appears to have improved or at least remained stable during the recent economic downturn (see Table 1), but at a high level. The share of near-elderly retirees in poor health remained above 20 percent in 2002, and the share of elderly retirees in poor health stabilized at about 35 percent (see Table 1).[1] Also, the share of those age 65 and older with functional limitations has remained stable at around 7 percent from 1983 to 1996 (National Center for Health Statistics 2002b), with about 3 to 3.5 percent of people between the ages of 65 and 74 having functional limitations, and 7.5 to 8 percent of those age 75 and over having functional limitations. Thus, while there may have been some improvements in people's subjective well-being in the 1980s, these improvements may have leveled off in the 1990s, and the objective health status of the elderly appears unchanged.

Older individuals are generally not as healthy as younger ones, and they are more susceptible to chronic, potentially debilitating illnesses. Compared to 35- to 44-year-olds, the near-elderly were twice as likely to report themselves in fair health and four times as likely to report themselves in bad health in 1996. In particular, they were four times as likely to have had a stroke or have cancer, seven times as likely to have had a heart attack, and five times as likely to have had heart disease as the younger comparison group (Gruber and Madrian 1996).

The deterioration of one's health means more medical spending. The near-elderly were twice as likely in 1987 to be admitted to the hospital (with double the length of stay) and 40 percent more likely to need prescription medication,

Table 1. Share of Near-Elderly and Elderly in Poor Health, 1996–2002

	1996	1997	1998	1999	2000	2001	2002	Change 1996 to 2002
Near Elderly Employees	12.4	12.3	12.0	11.2	11.2	11.5	10.8	−1.6
Near Elderly Retirees	23.0	23.0	25.7	21.7	23.6	21.5	20.9	−2.1
Elderly Retirees	35.9	36.0	34.9	35.3	36.5	35.1	35.2	−0.8

Notes: All figures are in percent. Source is the Current Population Survey, various years.

with twice as many medications, than 35- to 44-year-olds. As a result, medical spending for the near-elderly was almost twice as much as for 35- to 44-year-olds (Gruber and Madrian 1996, 2002). Similarly, the near-elderly spent 26 percent more than people ages 45–54 on drugs and medical supplies, but only 1 percent more on medical services in 1999 (Rappaport 2000).

Even holding health status constant, older people appear to have greater healthcare needs than younger ones. Nichols (2001) estimated that men ages 55–64 in good health spent about 2.5 times as much money on healthcare as males between 21 and 29; if the older men were in bad health, they typically spent 4.2 times as much. For females, the ratios were 1.3 and 1.9, respectively.

Health Status and Retirement Decisions

Health status is an important determinant of retirement decisions. Burtless (1987) reported that about 26 percent of respondents in the 1969–1979 Retirement Health Survey (RHS)[2] indicated that they left a job due to health considerations. Several other studies based on the RHS confirmed that workers in poor health were more likely to retire than others (Quinn 1977; Quinn, Burkhauser, and Myers 1990; Rust 1989; Sammartino 1987). Similarly, Packard and Reno (1988) found, using the New Beneficiary Survey, that 24 percent of all newly retired beneficiaries indicated poor health as the primary reason for retirement, and 15 percent of newly retired beneficiaries indicated that their health would not have permitted them to do another job (see also Social Security Administration 1986). Ycas (1987) found that about one fifth of men ages 62–67 and one sixth of men ages 55–70 were retired due to health reasons in 1981, based on the National Health Interview Survey (NHIS).[3] Further, Haveman, Wolfe, and Warlick (1988) found, using the Survey of Disabled and Non-disabled Adults from 1978, that 46 percent of early retirees indicated severe disabilities, and that workers with health problems were more likely to retire early. Leonesio, Vaughan, and Wixon (2000) found that almost half of early beneficiaries had a health problem and that 22 percent reported health problems severe enough to limit their ability to work.

Health Status and Demographics

It is important to note that the likelihood of being in poor health varies with occupation, race, sex, education, and income. Consequently, the probability of being retired early also differs across demographic groups. First, the health status of workers near retirement is linked to occupation. Burtless (1987) reported that workers in professional occupations are one-third less likely to experience work limitations than the average worker and 57 percent less likely than laborers. Moreover, men age 62 have an 82 percent probability of working if they are in good health and 63 percent if they are not. Chirikos and Nestel (1991) found, based on the National Longitudinal Survey that workers in blue-collar and service jobs are more likely to lack the functional capacity to delay retirement. Also, blue-collar workers, who comprise about one third of workers between the ages of 53 and 63 in the Health and Retirement Study (HRS) were found to be 80 percent more likely to experience health problems that affect their ability to work than white-collar workers (U.S. Department of Labor 1994; Bovbjerg 1998). Workers of the same age group in some blue-collar occupations were more than twice as likely as white-collar workers to experience pain that affected their ability to do normal work (Bovbjerg 1998). Also, Leonesio, Vaughan, and Wixon (2000) reported that Old Age and Survivors Insurance (OASI) beneficiaries between 62 and 64 who worked in managerial, professional, technical, sales, or administrative jobs were less likely to have health problems than workers in other occupations.

Second, race also influences the health status of near-retirees. Burtless (1987) found that blacks were more likely than whites to report that health limited their ability to work. Chirikos and Nestel estimated that "black men are significantly less likely than white men to retire functionally capable" (1991, 13). Crimmins, Hayward, and Saito (1996) found, based on the Longitudinal Study on Aging, that blacks may be more likely to experience disabling health limitations than others. While blacks and Hispanics comprised 10 percent of the population in the Survey of Income and Program Participation (SIPP) among those aged 62 to 64 years, they were 13 percent of all early retirees with health problems, and 15 percent of early retirees who reported severe disabilities (Leonesio, Vaughan, and Wixon 2000).

Third, older workers' health differs by sex. Based on the NHIS, men aged 62 to 67 years appear more likely than women to experience health limitations (40.3 percent compared to 34.3 percent), and men are more likely than women to retire early due to poor health (Ycas 1987). Also, Leonesio, Vaughan, and Wixon (2000) report that 63 percent of OASI beneficiaries ages 62–64 without health problems were women.

Fourth, education is a good predictor of health and retirement. Poterba and Summers (1987) found, based on the 1969–1973 RHS, that one additional year of schooling reduces the chance of health limitations by 2 percent and the chance of retirement by 1 percent. Similarly, Burtless (1987) found that more than thirteen years of schooling lowered health limitations of older workers. Crimmins,

Hayward, and Saito (1996) found that less education raises the likelihood of deteriorating health. Also, less educated workers were found, based on the 1969–1973 RHS, to retire earlier than better educated workers (Burtless and Moffitt 1985). Workers with more than thirteen years of schooling were also more likely than workers with less schooling to work full time (Burtless 1987). Blau (1994) found, based on the 1969–1979 RHS, that workers with lower educational attainment are more likely to transition out of the labor force. Finally, Leonesio, Vaughan, and Wixon (2000) reported that workers with less than twelve years of schooling constituted 25 percent of OASI recipients with no health problems and 37 percent with health problems.

Finally, income is a determinant of health and retirement status. Burtless (1987) included a measure for what an older worker could typically hope to earn in 1969 and a measure for pension coverage to control for permanent income. The results indicated that higher income as well as pension coverage lowered the chance of health limitations. Chirikos and Nestel (1991) include pension wealth and found that men with more pension wealth are less likely to be work disabled. Also, men with higher preretirement income and higher expected retirement income are more likely to retire early in better health than others (Burtless 1987; Burtless and Moffitt 1985). Similarly, Samwick (1998) found that the accrual of private pensions increased early retirement.[4] Also, Anderson, Gustman, and Steinmeier (1999) estimated that changes in pension plans together with changes to Social Security account for one fourth of the reduction of full-time work by men in their early 60s based on the 1969–1979 RHS, and the 1983 and 1988 Survey of Consumer Finances. Finally, Leonesio, Vaughan, and Wixon (2000) reported that the median family income of OASI beneficiaries ages 62–64 without health problems was $10,399, whereas it was $7,689 for workers with health problems.

Health Insurance Status and Retirement Decisions

It is not only health status that matters for the decision to retire, it is also access to health insurance. In a 2002 literature review of the influence of health insurance on employment decisions, Gruber and Madrian concluded that "retiree health insurance is a critical determinant of the decision to retire or not" (2002). In particular, the availability of continuation coverage (e.g., COBRA) appeared to increase an individual's propensity to retire (Gruber and Madrian 1995, 1996). Similarly, Hurd and McGarry (1996) argued that retirement health-insurance coverage decreased the probability an individual will work past age 62, but if coverage were conditional on being 65, the effect is smaller. Karoly and Rogowski (1994) found that retiree health insurance increased the probability of retirement by 47 percent. Rust and Phelan (1997) concluded that access to coverage decreased the probability of full-time work by 12 percent at ages 58–59, 29 percent at ages 60–61, and 25 percent at ages 62–63. Furthermore, Headen, Clark, and Ghent (1997) found that retiree health-insurance coverage increased the probability of retirement by 30 percent. Lastly, Rogowski and Karoly (2000) argued that retirement health coverage increases the retirement probability by 62 percent for full-time male workers ages 51–61. Overall, the availability of ESI increases the likelihood of retiring. The effect is especially large for early retirees who are ineligible for Medicare.

The size of the effect of health insurance on retirement decisions appears not to be negligible. Madrian (1994) argued that individuals with ESI would retire five to eighteen months earlier than those without. Likewise, Anderson, Gustman, and Steinmeier (1999) argued that retirement is delayed until eligibility for coverage is reached. Once workers become eligible, they retire four months earlier than workers who are not eligible.

Rising Healthcare Costs

At the same time that the health status of older workers has remained fairly stable, the costs of providing healthcare and health insurance have risen dramatically, raising the importance of health-insurance retirement decisions.

The costs of healthcare rose dramatically in the 1980s and 1990s. While overall prices increased by 110 percent from 1980 to 2002, medical costs rose by 276 percent, prescription drug costs by 327 percent, and the costs of hospital services by 422 percent (see Table 2). Not surprisingly then, the costs of health insurance also rose a lot faster than overall prices, in particular by 200 percent from 1980 to 2001.

Rising prices, however, are only one aspect of changing healthcare expenditures. The money a nation spends on healthcare is determined by a number of other factors, such as changing demographics. In the United States, healthcare expenditures have actually increased faster than prices for medical services. Nominal per-capita spending for healthcare more than quadrupled from $1,067 in 1980 to $5,427 in 2002, a 409 percent increase, compared to a price increase of healthcare of 276 percent over the same period.

As healthcare expenditures rose drastically, largely due to higher prices and changing demographics, the share of GDP spent on medical services also grew

Table 2. Trends in Health Care Costs, Health Insurance Premiums and Health Care Expenditures, 1980 to 2002

Year	Consumer Price Index (% change)	CPI—Medical Care (% change)	CPI—Prescription Drugs (% change)	CPI—Hospital Services (% change)	Prices for Health Insurance (% change)	Health Care Expenditures (% change)	Prescription Drug Expenditures (% change)	Health Care Expenditures (share of GDP)	Prescription Drug Expenditures (share of GDP)
1980	12.4	10.2	9.7	14.5	11.9	11.7	7.8	8.8	0.4
1988	4.4	6.9	7.9	11.0	7.1	10.8	12.4	10.9	0.6
1990	6.3	9.6	10.0	11.4	7.1	11.7	14.7	12.0	0.7
1993	2.8	5.4	3.3	7.6	4.2	8.5	8.4	13.4	0.8
1994	2.6	4.9	3.3	5.5	3.2	5.5	6.6	13.3	0.8
1995	2.5	3.9	2.0	4.5	3.2	5.7	11.2	13.4	0.8
1996	3.4	3.1	3.1	4.2	2.9	5.0	10.5	13.3	0.9
1997	1.7	2.9	2.6	3.2	2.0	5.1	12.8	13.1	0.9
1998	1.6	3.4	4.9	3.2	2.3	5.2	15.2	13.2	1.0
1999	2.7	3.7	6.1	5.2	2.2	6.1	19.7	13.2	1.1
2000	3.4	4.2	3.6	6.2	3.5	7.4	16.4	13.3	1.2
2001	1.5	4.8	6.0	7.1	4.1	8.7	15.7	14.1	1.4
2002	2.4	5.0	4.5	9.8		8.6	14.3	14.8	1.5
Total Change 1980–2002	110.2	275.7	327.0	422.3	199.7	408.6	1239.2	—	—

Notes: All figures are percent annual rate of change, except for totals. The total for health insurance premiums is only through 2001, the latest year for which data are available. The sources for the various consumer price indexes (CPI) is the Bureau of Labor Statistics, Consumer Price Index, the source for the chained price index for health insurance premiums, is the Bureau of Economic Analysis, National Income and Product Accounts, and the source for national health care expenditures are the Centers for Medicare and Medicaid Services, Health Accounts. The expenditure growth for 2002 reflects projections.

quickly. The share of GDP devoted to healthcare rose from 8.8 percent in 1980 to 14.8 percent in 2002, and the share of GDP spent on prescription drugs more than tripled, going from 0.4 percent in 1980 to 1.5 percent in 2002 (see Table 2).

The future is likely to include continuing increases in healthcare expenditures. The Centers for Medicare and Medicaid Services estimate that national healthcare expenditures will continue to grow rapidly over the next decade. National healthcare costs are expected to increase by about 7 percent annually, with prescription drug expenditures forecast to grow between 8.5 percent and 11 percent per year (Centers for Medicare and Medicaid Services 2003).

Declining Access to Affordable Retiree Health Insurance

Retiree access to health insurance depends largely on employers offering this benefit. In 1999, 35 percent of firms with more than five hundred employees and 76 percent of employers with more than one thousand employees offered ESI coverage to their retirees (Fronstin 2000).

But there has been a decline in ESI coverage for some time. In 1988, 66 percent of large firms (with more than two hundred employees) offered health coverage to retirees, compared to 34 percent in 2002. Among small firms (with less than two hundred employees), only 5 percent offered ESI coverage in 2002 (Kaiser 2002). Similarly, the General Accounting Office (2001) reported the percentage of all employers offering ESI coverage for retirees decreased from 70 percent in the early 1980s to 40 percent in 1998.

Many companies that still offer ESI pursue a number of strategies to lower the associated costs. First, eligibility requirements for retiree health insurance are becoming more stringent. In 1984, only one out of ten firms required more than five years of service, compared to three out of four firms in 2000. And for future retirees, 86 percent of employers will require more than five years of service to be eligible (Watson Wyatt Worldwide 2002).

Aside from stricter eligibility requirements, firms are also increasing the share of premiums paid by employees. In 2001, retirees were paying all or part of the costs in eight out of ten company retiree health plans, a dramatic increase from the mid-1980s when about half of all companies paid all of their retirees' premiums (Mercer 2002). In addition, 20 percent of employers with retirement health plans eliminated such plans for new hires, and 17 percent of firms will require future retirees to pay the full premium (Watson Wyatt Worldwide 2002).

Alternatively, firms lowered the costs of ESI for their retirees by reducing prescription drug coverage, lowering early-retirement benefits, or capping their contributions. Only 67 percent of firms included drug coverage, which alone accounts for 40–60 percent of the healthcare costs of Medicare-eligible retirees (Freudenheim 2002; Kaiser 2001b). Also, from 1999 to 2001, 33 percent of firms increased the amount current retirees pay for prescription drugs; 13 percent introduced a three-tiered cost-sharing program for prescription drugs; and 26 percent raised retirees' share of premiums, with further increases indicated for 2002 (Kaiser 2001a, 2002). Also in 1999, 42 percent of employers offering retiree health coverage required early retirees to pay the entire premium, up from 31 percent in 1997 (Mercer 2002). Lastly, in 2002, 45 percent of firms capped contributions for new hires, and 39 percent capped contributions for current employees (Watson Wyatt Worldwide 2002).

The trend towards declining ESI coverage for retirees is likely to continue. In 2002, 31 percent of firms stated they were very or somewhat likely to increase retiree responsibility for prescription drugs; 16 percent said they were likely to introduce a three-tiered cost-sharing program for prescription drugs; and 37 percent said they were very or somewhat likely to increase retirees' shares of premiums by 2004 (Kaiser 2002). Watson Wyatt Worldwide (2002) estimated, based on plan provisions already adopted, that by 2031, employer provided financing will decrease to less than 10 percent of a retiree's total medical expenses.

As access to ESI declines, it is important to keep the link between health status and health insurance coverage in mind. In 2002, ESI coverage declined with age after age 54, and it was lower for those in poor health than for those in good health (see Table 3). In comparison, those in poor health were substantially more likely to rely solely on public health insurance, and they had a somewhat greater chance of having no health insurance coverage than those in good health (see Table 3). Given our previous discussion, one aspect of particular importance to us is whether retiree health insurance coverage for those in poor health has changed in substantially different ways than for those in good health.

Sources of Health Insurance of the Near-Elderly and Elderly in 2001

Declining access to ESI does not necessarily mean that fewer retirees have health insurance. In fact, ESI is still the most important source of coverage for retirees (Schwartz and Stevenson 2001). ESI coverage was the most important source for those who were still employed, with 69.5 percent of this population receiving it. In comparison, 32.0 percent of early retirees had ESI coverage from their former employer, while 18.7 percent received it as dependents (see Table 4). With the exception of the near-elderly who were disabled, of whom 54.2 percent were covered solely by public health insurance, ESI was the most important source of health insurance for the near-elderly. Although ESI was the most important

Table 3. Health Insurance at the Intersection of Health and Age, 2002

Age	Employer, employee		Employer, dependent		Non-group		Public		Non-group and public		Other combinations		None	
	Poor health	Good health	Poor health	Good health	Poor health	Good health	Poor health	Good health	Poor health	Good health	Poor health	Good health	Poor health	Good health
35–44	25.7	45.4	14.4	20.2	1.2	3.9	27.5	3.8	0.9	0.2	3.5	7.1	26.8	19.2
45–54	27.1	49.3	15.8	19.4	2.3	4.7	26.0	2.6	1.1	0.2	4.2	8.7	23.6	15.0
55–64	25.7	48.4	14.2	17.1	4.5	7.3	29.2	4.0	2.5	0.7	3.4	7.6	20.5	15.0
65–74	15.8	26.6	8.6	12.2	0.2	0.8	50.6	30.8	22.7	26.9	0.3	0.7	1.9	2.1
75+	15.2	22.1	5.4	6.5	0.1	0.5	49.1	37.2	29.2	32.6	0.1	0.2	0.7	0.9

Notes: All figures are in percent. Source is the Current Population Survey, various years.

Table 4. Source of Health Insurance for the Near-Elderly, by Labor Force Status, 2002

	Employer, employee	Employer, dependent	Non-Group	Public	Non-group plus public	Multiple coverage	None
Total	43.8	16.5	6.7	9.2	1.1	6.8	16.1
Employed	55.2	14.3	6.2	1.8	0.3	8.7	13.5
Unemployed	22.7	19.0	10.5	12.3	0.0	0.0	35.6
Retired	32.0	18.7	10.0	12.3	2.1	3.9	21.1
Disabled	10.9	12.3	1.5	54.2	4.6	0.9	15.6
Out of the labor force neither retired nor disabled	6.2	42.9	10.5	5.2	0.9	4.0	30.3

Notes: All figures in percent. Source is the Bureau of Labor Statistics' Current Population Survey—March 2003.

source of health insurance for near-elderly employees and early retirees, 30 percent of near-elderly employees and almost 50 percent of early retirees were not covered by it.

Table 5 details the sources of health insurance for near-elderly employees. This group was significantly more likely to have ESI coverage than others in their age group who were not working, and less likely to be covered as dependents through ESI or to have no health insurance. Only 14.3 percent of near-elderly in the labor force were covered as dependents, and 13.5 percent had no health insurance in 2002. Further, the group among near-elderly employees that was least likely to have ESI coverage was people living in families with incomes below $15,000. Moreover, the likelihood of having ESI coverage in their own name was greater for men, blacks, non-Hispanics, those with advanced degrees, those living in families with incomes between $60,000 and $75,000, and those in very good health, compared to their respective counterparts. The fact that blacks were slightly more likely than whites to have their own ESI is compensated for by the fact that whites were almost twice as likely as blacks to be covered as dependents in ESI plans.

Table 6 summarizes the sources of health insurance for near-elderly retirees. Of early retirees, 32.0 percent were covered by ESI in their own name, and another 18.7 percent received it as dependents. In total, 50.7 percent of early retirees had some ESI coverage in 2002. Women, blacks, Hispanics, those with less than a high school education, those in poor health, and those with family incomes of less than $15,000 were more likely than their counterparts not to be covered by ESI.

Table 5. Health Insurance Sources for the Near-Elderly Employed, by Gender, Race, Hispanic Origin, Education, Income, and Health Status, 2002

	Employer, employee	Employer, dependent	Non-Group	Public	Non-group and public	Other combs.	None
Total	55.2	14.3	6.3	1.8	0.3	8.6	13.5
Women	51.7	17.4	6.9	2.1	0.3	8.4	13.2
Men	58.3	11.5	5.6	1.7	0.3	8.9	13.8
White	55.2	15.0	6.6	1.7	0.3	8.7	12.5
Black	59.5	7.8	2.2	3.2	0.2	8.3	18.8
Asian	47.1	13.4	6.8	2.1	0.5	8.4	21.7
Hispanic	48.0	9.0	3.5	3.9	0.3	5.5	30.0
Non-Hispanic	55.7	14.7	6.5	1.7	0.3	8.9	12.3
Less than h.s.	43.7	12.5	5.5	4.9	0.1	5.1	28.3
High school	52.7	16.1	5.9	1.9	0.5	8.4	14.5
Some college	56.9	14.3	6.9	1.5	0.2	8.7	11.7
College grads	57.4	14.2	6.8	1.2	0.2	10.0	10.1
Adv. degree	63.3	11.6	5.6	0.9	0.3	10.2	8.0
Less than $15,000	26.4	4.9	14.7	9.1	1.1	3.8	40.1
$15,000 to $29,999	51.2	6.4	8.5	4.2	0.4	4.4	25.0
$30,000 to $44,999	59.5	11.4	6.5	2.0	0.2	5.5	14.9
$45,000 to $59,999	59.4	15.5	5.2	1.1	0.6	7.3	10.9
$60,000 to $74,999	58.0	18.4	4.5	0.9	0.0	9.7	8.4
$75,000 and over	56.3	17.4	5.1	0.6	0.2	12.1	8.2
Excellent health	57.1	15.0	6.3	1.1	0.2	9.2	11.1
Very good health	57.0	14.6	6.4	1.1	0.2	9.3	11.4
Good health	55.0	13.6	6.1	1.7	0.5	8.3	14.9
Fair health	48.1	13.4	6.0	4.8	0.4	6.9	20.4
Poor health	37.6	15.2	4.8	11.1	0.0	5.7	25.6

Notes: All figures in percent. Source is the Bureau of Labor Statistics' Current Population Survey—March 2003.

Moreover, more early retirees had no health insurance coverage than were covered as dependents in an ESI plan in 2002. Fully 21.1 percent of early retirees had no health insurance coverage, while women, blacks, Hispanics, those with less than a high school degree, those living in families with incomes below $15,000 and those in fair health had an above average likelihood of having no health insurance.

Further, among the elderly, 78 percent were retired. ESI as the sole source of health insurance coverage is irrelevant since this group is eligible for Medicare.

Table 6. Health Insurance Sources for Near-Elderly Retirees, by Gender, Race, Hispanic Origin, Education, Income, and Health Status, 2002

	Employer, employee	Employer, dependent	Non-Group	Public	Non-group and public	Other combs.	None
Total	32.0	18.7	10.0	12.3	2.1	3.9	21.1
Women	22.7	26.0	11.3	12.7	2.1	4.0	21.1
Men	44.4	9.0	8.2	11.8	2.0	3.7	20.9
White	32.6	20.2	10.2	11.0	2.3	4.0	19.8
Black	32.8	8.3	5.7	23.2	1.0	2.1	27.0
Asian	20.4	11.3	14.6	17.3	0.2	5.9	30.2
Hispanic	17.4	13.7	6.4	23.8	1.6	1.8	35.3
Non-Hispanic	32.9	19.0	10.2	11.6	2.1	4.0	20.1
Less than h.s.	19.1	12.5	5.4	29.7	26.5	2.4	29.3
High school	30.0	19.5	9.8	12.4	30.8	4.1	21.3
Some college	31.6	22.4	10.7	7.9	32.6	5.5	21.2
College grads	38.5	18.5	14.9	7.8	30.5	2.0	16.4
Adv. degree	52.5	15.2	8.0	3.7	29.2	4.6	14.3
Less than $15,000	21.4	5.8	12.9	24.6	2.0	1.9	31.5
$15,000 to $29,999	32.9	13.2	10.1	15.3	1.4	4.3	22.9
$30,000 to $44,999	36.0	24.0	8.2	8.2	1.7	3.7	18.1
$45,000 to $59,999	36.5	25.0	11.6	5.5	3.9	4.8	12.8
$60,000 to $74,999	36.8	27.7	9.5	2.9	1.3	5.4	16.5
$75,000 and over	35.6	30.0	6.8	4.8	2.6	5.0	15.1
Excellent health	36.9	21.5	9.9	5.0	1.2	5.6	20.0
Very good health	34.7	22.2	10.9	8.2	1.5	4.2	18.2
Good health	30.6	18.4	10.3	12.3	2.2	3.3	22.8
Fair health	30.5	13.1	7.0	20.5	3.6	4.2	21.2
Poor health	16.6	10.2	11.8	33.0	2.2	0.0	26.2

Notes: All figures in percent. Source is the Bureau of Labor Statistics' Current Population Survey—March 2003.

However, ESI coverage is a substantial supplement to public health insurance. 28.4 percent of elderly retirees had ESI coverage in addition to public health insurance. But, ESI was less important than nongroup health insurance coverage, such as Medigap, in addition to public health insurance, which covered 29.8 percent of elderly retirees in 2002. Women, blacks, Hispanics, those with less than a high school education, those with family incomes of less than $15,000, and those in poor health were less likely than their counterparts to have ESI coverage. In no instance did the majority of a demographic group of elderly retirees receive supplemental health insurance coverage from an employer (see Table 7).

Table 7. Health Insurance Sources for Elderly Retirees, by Gender, Race, Hispanic Origin, Education, Income, and Health Status, 2002

	Employer, employee	Employer, dependent	Non-Group	Public	Non-group and public	Other combs.	None
Total	20.0	8.4	0.3	40.5	29.8	0.1	1.0
Women	14.7	10.5	0.3	42.2	31.0	0.1	1.2
Men	27.5	5.4	0.2	38.2	27.9	0.0	0.8
White	20.5	8.6	0.3	37.9	31.9	0.1	0.7
Black	16.5	5.9	0.2	62.2	12.8	0.4	2.0
Asian	12.4	8.7	0.4	59.3	13.2	0.0	5.9
Hispanic	9.3	5.3	0.0	70.6	11.2	0.0	3.6
Non-Hispanic	20.6	8.6	0.3	38.8	30.8	0.1	0.9
Less than h.s.	12.8	5.6	0.2	53.6	26.5	0.0	1.4
High school	20.0	9.3	0.2	38.7	30.8	0.1	0.9
Some college	22.0	10.1	0.3	34.3	32.6	0.0	0.7
College grads	27.6	9.6	0.2	30.7	30.5	0.2	1.2
Adv. degree	34.0	9.3	0.8	25.9	29.2	0.3	0.5
Less than $15,000	12.2	2.6	0.5	54.8	54.8	28.7	1.3
$15,000 to $29,999	19.9	6.6	0.1	39.2	39.2	33.4	0.6
$30,000 to $44,999	14.7	12.9	0.3	29.5	29.5	31.6	1.0
$45,000 to $59,999	27.0	15.3	0.2	31.0	31.0	25.7	0.9
$60,000 to $74,999	25.2	13.5	0.3	34.6	34.6	24.8	1.5
$75,000 and over	24.8	14.6	0.2	36.1	36.1	22.6	1.7
Excellent health	25.1	8.5	0.3	34.4	29.6	0.1	2.0
Very good health	23.6	9.4	0.3	33.2	32.3	0.1	0.9
Good health	20.7	9.5	0.3	38.7	29.9	0.0	0.9
Fair health	15.8	6.9	0.2	46.1	30.3	0.0	0.8
Poor health	16.3	6.4	0.1	52.5	23.4	0.1	1.2

Notes: All figures in percent. Source is the Bureau of Labor Statistics' Current Population Survey—March 2003.

POSSIBLE RESPONSES TO REDUCED ACCESS TO RETIREE HEALTH INSURANCE

Where health insurance access is declining but the health of retirees is not declining, ESI coverage may be endogenously determined. Workers in poor health may choose to work longer to maintain ESI coverage, thereby slowing the decline in ESI coverage among retirees. Workers may respond in a number of ways to the declining access to ESI for retirees with the possible result that the share of retirees with ESI may actually remain stable. The possible responses include an increased propensity to apply for disability claims in an effort to increase access to public health insurance, greater preretirement savings to cover rising out-of-pocket medical expenditures, and delayed retirement—working longer—in an effort to keep health insurance coverage.

Claiming Disability

Workers faced with losing access to ESI coverage during retirement may increasingly consider applying for disability benefits. Disability claimants under Supplemental Social Insurance are automatically eligible for healthcare, whereas disability claimants under Social Security's disability program are eligible for Medicare two years after the start of receiving disability benefits. Disability insurance has occasionally been criticized for the perceived dramatic drop in the 1960s and 1970s in the labor force participation rates of the near-elderly (Gruber 1999). But the labor force participation rates of the near-elderly actually increased in tandem with the number of disability insurance recipients in later years.

The growth in the availability and generosity of disability benefits, coupled with the decreased demand for older, less-skilled workers, probably provided the impetus for these near-elderly individuals to seek early retirement through disability benefits (Bound and Waidmann 2000). Autor and Duggan (2003) found that increased disability claims could be explained by a declining demand for less-skilled workers, an increase in the earnings replacement rate, and reduced screening stringency after 1984. These factors had a significant effect only on male high-school dropouts, doubling their propensity to seek disability payments.

Applying for disability insurance is one possible response to falling retiree health insurance coverage, but it is an imperfect substitute for longer work or early retirement with retiree health insurance. Gruber and Kubik (1994) found that a 10 percent increase in disability-claim denial rates would lead to a 2.7 percent decrease in nonparticipation among 45- to 64-year old males, implying that most individuals applying for disability would drop out of the labor force rather than continue employment in their conditions. Mitchell and Phillips (2000) found that in the event of early-retirement benefit reductions, individuals would be twice as likely to delay retirement until normal retirement age as to seek disability retirement benefits, implying that disability benefits are not a substitute for retirement benefits. Furthermore, the median male who applies for benefits waits seven years after the onset of disability before submitting an application; the median female waits eight years before applying (Burkhauser, Butler, and Weathers 2001).

Increasing Savings

Workers could also save more for their retiree health insurance while they are still working. Some employers have begun defined contribution health plans for retirees, whereby current workers contribute to a fund that will allow them to pay for some of their retirement healthcare costs (Schmidt 2002). These so-called Voluntary Employee Beneficiary Associations (VEBAs) and Retiree Medical Accounts (RMAs) require employees to assume full responsibility for their own health coverage in exchange for some tax savings, although contributions are made post-tax (Gunsauley 2002; Lee 2002). VEBA funds are placed in a qualified trust and can be used only for their predesignated purpose, thereby offering a certain amount of security, since the money will not be used for other purposes by the company (Gunsauley 2002; Lee 2002).

There have been a few highly visible VEBAs. Perhaps most notable was the steelworkers' use of VEBAs to fund health benefits for the retirees of some bankrupt steel companies and as a means to prefund retiree health benefits outside of bankruptcy (Fleet 2002; Greenwald 2002). Despite provisions to ensure adequate capitalization of VEBA funds, these efforts have been largely unsuccessful due to ultimately insufficient funds. The effects of the inadequate VEBA funding can be devastating. For example, at LTV Corporation, one-fourth of all retirees were not eligible for Medicare, the vast majority of whom could not afford continuing insurance under COBRA and thus had to go without medical coverage when the company went under.

Prefunding of retiree health insurance is a poor substitute for ESI simply because an insurance program is replaced with individual accounts (Lee 2002). The primary concerns associated with prefunding retiree health insurance are similar to those associated with defined contribution (DC) retirement savings plans. All risks are borne by the individual. In the case of defined contribution healthcare plans, in addition to the rising costs of healthcare, these risks include the possibility of an employer's inability to pay promised benefits, the lack of predictability of future health expenditures, and hence the risk of households saving too little for retirement.

Overall, estimates seem to predict, at the most, 20 percent of variation in healthcare costs. Pope et al. (2000) illustrate the expected healthcare expenditure variation using the Principal Inpatient Diagnostic Cost Group model used by the Centers for Medicare and Medicaid Services for people making Medicare capitation payments. In this model, the demographic factors are added to "add-on" factors, which take into consideration mostly serious illness situations requiring hospitalization, to calculate a risk factor for an individual. In an example used by the authors, a 69-year-old male with no disability, not on Medicaid or another health insurance plan, and with no hospitalization, is expected to incur 54.1 percent of the average individual healthcare expenditures for 2000. Van Vliet (1992) found that at least 80 percent of an individual's healthcare costs cannot be predicted, but that the predictability increases with age. For persons age 50 and older, the maximum observed variance that could be explained was 13.4 percent (without taking into consideration prescription drugs and family doctor care, which raises predictability), and for persons age 30 and younger, 11.6 percent of the observed variance was explained. Garber, McCurdy, and McClellan (1997) argued that individuals who incur high medical costs in one year are likely to incur high costs in subsequent years, thus allowing medical expenditures to be more accurately predicted, increasing the accuracy of the prediction by 7 percent. In comparison, Ellis and McGuire (2003), using a sample of Medicare-eligible retirees, suggested that only 1 percent of the observed variance can be explained by age or sex.

Because healthcare expenditures are unpredictable for the individual, the exact savings path remains uncertain. Because large changes in healthcare expenditures can be associated with unexpected changes in health status, and since individuals may be likely to underestimate the probability of these healthcare events occurring, they may save too little. On the other hand, individuals may be prone to save more than they need simply because they are aware that they lack the distributive mechanisms of insurance and hence have to prepare for all eventualities themselves. Although theoretically appealing, the empirical evidence suggests that households are likely to undersave rather than to oversave.

Even if other risks can be mitigated, employees will not save enough. One reason is that savings for health insurance may only substitute for other savings, thus not increasing household savings at all or not enough. For instance, a number of researchers have suggested that the rise of DC plans largely substituted for the decline in DB plans and thus has not contributed much in terms of increased personal savings. The evidence indicates that the decline of DB plans was due to a number of factors, such as sectoral shifts in the economy and the decline of unions, and not necessarily to displacement by DC plans (Gordon 2000; Medoff and Calabrese 2001; Poterba, Venti, and Wise 2002; U.S. Department of Labor 1998), thus possibly resulting in higher savings. However, Engen and Gale (2000) suggested that for most people, DC plans did not lead to more savings, with the exception of low-income households.

Another reason why preretirement savings may be insufficient is that many households already do not save enough for retirement. Increasing their savings needs by shifting the responsibility to save for retiree health insurance from the employer to the employee may only exacerbate the problem.

An integral part of the issue of whether households save enough for retirement is to comprehend the underlying definition of retirement income adequacy. Calculations of retirement income adequacy typically relate retirement consumption to preretirement consumption in three possible ways. First, a household may be considered adequately prepared for retirement if it can maintain a similar real level of consumption as during its working years. Usually, 80 percent of preretirement income is thus considered adequate since the income needs of retirees are likely to be lower than those of workers (Aon Consulting 2001). Households no longer need to save for retirement, taxes are lower, work-related expenses disappear, the family size of retirees is smaller than that of workers, and households eventually pay off their debt (McGill et al. 1996). Second, retirement income adequacy may be defined as a constant nominal level of consumption during retirement as during working years. This means that consumption needs are expected to decline during retirement over time, but in a somewhat arbitrary fashion. Third, real consumption may decline if the marginal utility of consumption is held constant and uncertainty about income and life expectancy are introduced (Engen, Gale, and Uccello 1999). As households must consider an uncertain future, their marginal utility of certain consumption today is higher than the marginal utility of uncertain consumption in the future.

A number of studies have analyzed retirement savings adequacy, with differing results. Gustman and Steinmeier (1999) found, using the HRS, that the average household could replace 60 percent of preretirement income in real terms, and 86 percent of preretirement income in nominal terms, leading the authors to conclude that households are adequately prepared for retirement. Further, Engen, Gale, and Uccello (1999) found, using the SIPP and the Survey of Consumer Finance, that 40 to 50 percent of households fell short of what they needed for adequate retirement income. The average replacement ratio for the median household they calculated is still 72 percent, leading the authors to conclude that households are close to being adequately prepared for retirement.

In comparison, several studies concluded that households were inadequately prepared for retirement. Moore and Mitchell (1997) found, using the 1992 HRS, that the median household would have to save an additional 16 percent annually of earnings if it were to retire at age 62, versus an additional 7 percent annually for retirement at age 65, to finance an adequate real replacement ratio. Their estimate of a savings rate of 7.3 percent for households wishing to retire at age 65 was three times as much as what households actually saved. This meant that households had on average between 75 and 88 percent—depending on marital status—of what they needed when retiring at 65 in 1992. Similarly, Bernheim (1993) calculated that on average, baby boomer households were saving only at 34 percent of their target savings rate. Also, Gustman and Steinmeier's (1999) figures show that, based on real replacement ratios, the average household had 28 percent less than adequate retirement savings. Lastly, Wolff (2002) concluded, based on data from 1998, that 61 percent of households could not replace 75 percent of their preretirement income, which was up from 56 percent of households in 1992.

To make ends meet in retirement when facing an income shortfall, households will have to curtail their retirement consumption. In fact, one of the distinguishing features between studies that conclude that households are adequately prepared for retirement and those that conclude otherwise is the consumption pattern in retirement. For instance, Engen, Gale, and Uccello (1999) and Gustman and Steinmeier (1999) conclude that households are adequately prepared for retirement based on the fact that real retirement consumption declines with age in their models.

Considering the risks involved in preretirement savings for retiree health insurance, defined contribution accounts appear to be inadequate substitutes for ESI. This problem may be aggravated, depending on one's definition of adequate retirement savings.

Working Longer

The third option for employees to address the declining access to employer-sponsored retiree health insurance is to work longer. In particular, do people in poor health work longer or do they retire earlier? People in poor health are substantially less likely to work than those in good health. While typically more than 80 percent of those in good health work, less than 70 percent of those in poor health do. Further, from 1996 to 2000, there appeared to be a trend toward early retirement among those in self-reported poor health. While 67.2 percent of those in poor health were in the labor force in 1996, only 63.0 percent were in the labor force in 2000. However, the share of those in poor health who were still employed rose sharply in 2001 to 67.9 percent, from 63.0 percent in 2000, and declined only slightly to 67.3 percent in 2002 (see Table 8). In comparison, among those in good health, the share of employees grew from 80.5 to 81.8 percent from 2000 to 2002.

Given a fairly stable labor force breakdown between those in good health and poor health among the near-elderly, and given that the share of the near-elderly in poor health has remained steady, it is important to keep in mind that the labor force participation rates of the near-elderly have increased consistently since the mid-1980s. In late 2002, the labor force participation rates of near-elderly men and women reached their highest points, at 69.2 percent for men and 55.1 percent for women (Purcell 2004).[5]

Table 8. Labor Force Status of the Near-Elderly by Self-Reported Health Status, 1996 to 2002

	1996	1997	1998	1999	2000	2001	2002	Change 1996 to 2002
Good Health								
Employed	81.3	81.2	82.1	81.2	80.5	81.6	81.8	0.5
Retired	18.8	18.8	17.9	18.8	19.5	18.4	18.2	−0.6
Poor Health								
Employed	67.2	66.9	64.5	66.3	63.0	67.9	67.3	0.1
Retired	32.8	33.1	35.5	33.7	37.0	32.1	32.7	−0.1

Notes: All figures in percent. Totals do not add to 100% due to rounding. Source is the Current Population Survey, various years.

As discussed earlier, the literature supports the view that increased labor force participation rates may be influenced by access to health insurance. If ESI coverage is an important incentive to remain employed and if ESI access is declining, we should see ESI coverage remain stable or possibly even increase among employees. We should also see ESI coverage among retirees increase less than for employees or possibly even decline. Tables 9 and 10 show that this is the case. The share of near-elderly employees with ESI coverage rose by 3.7 percentage points, from 65.8 percent in 1996 to 69.5 percent in 2002 (see Table 9). In comparison, ESI coverage for early retirees rose only by 0.3 percentage points over the same period (see Table 10). Near-elderly employees became increasingly more likely (compared to near-elderly retirees) to be covered by ESI from 1996 to 2002.

While these figures support the view that the rise in the labor force participation rates of the near-elderly may be due in part to declining ESI access, there is little evidence that those in poor health are more likely than those in good health to stay in the labor force to keep ESI. Among near-elderly employees and early retirees, those in poor health were more likely than those in good health to see an increase in ESI coverage (see Tables 9 and 10).

However, ESI access may be declining for early retirees in poor health. This was the only group for whom there was a noticeable substitution of ESI coverage as dependents by ESI coverage in their own names (see Table 10). This substitution effect held for both men and women, despite differential overall trends in ESI coverage (see Table 11). It is possible that this substitution reflects a difference in out-of-pocket expenditure growth for early retirees. Considering that

Table 9. Trends of Health Insurance Sources for Near-Elderly Employees, 1996–2002

	1996	1997	1998	1999	2000	2001	2002	% change 1996–2002
Employer sponsored health insurance (policy holder)								
Total	53.1	53.8	55.0	56.1	56.8	56.7	55.2	2.1
Women	47.5	48.3	49.7	49.5	51.1	51.9	51.7	4.2
Men	57.9	58.5	59.5	61.8	61.8	60.9	58.3	0.4
Good	54.6	54.9	55.9	56.7	58.0	57.5	56.3	1.7
Poor	43.0	46.1	48.8	50.8	47.5	50.1	46.2	3.2
Employer sponsored health insurance (dependent)								
Total	12.7	13.3	13.4	13.8	12.8	13.5	14.3	1.6
Women	17.0	17.1	17.1	17.2	16.6	17.2	17.4	0.4
Men	9.1	10.0	10.2	10.8	9.6	10.3	11.5	1.4
Good	12.8	13.5	13.5	14.1	13.0	13.7	14.3	1.5
Poor	12.7	11.7	12.4	11.0	11.6	12.2	13.7	1.0
Non-group health insurance only								
Total	8.6	8.2	6.6	6.3	6.1	5.9	6.2	−2.4
Women	8.9	8.7	7.2	7.2	6.4	6.1	6.9	−2.0
Men	8.3	7.7	6.1	5.5	5.9	5.7	5.6	−2.7
Good	8.7	8.3	6.6	6.3	6.2	6.0	6.3	−2.4
Poor	8.1	7.1	6.7	5.9	5.3	5.5	5.8	−2.3
No health insurance								
Total	12.8	13.7	14.1	13.3	13.9	13.4	13.5	0.7
Women	12.9	13.9	14.6	14.2	14.7	13.7	13.2	0.3
Men	12.6	13.6	13.6	12.5	13.1	13.2	13.8	1.2
Good	12.0	12.5	13.1	12.3	12.7	12.6	12.6	0.6
Poor	18.7	22.7	21.1	20.8	22.9	19.9	21.4	2.7

Notes: Health status categories collapsed into two because too few observations were in some self-reported health status categories in earlier years.

employers are reducing ESI access, it seems reasonable to assume that the substitution effect from 1996 to 2002 was merely a temporary phenomenon.

Another aspect that supports the view that declining access to health insurance may have been a cause for the rise in the labor force participation rates of the near-elderly is the fact that the share of early retirees without health insurance has risen substantially more than the share of near-elderly employees without it. From 1996 to 2002, the share of the near-elderly employees without health insurance rose by only 0.7 percentage points to 13.5 percent in 2002 (see

Table 10. Trends of Health Insurance Sources for Near-Elderly Retirees, 1996–2002

	1996	1997	1998	1999	2000	2001	2002	% change 1996–2002
Employer sponsored health insurance (policy holder)								
Total	30.4	30.1	32.4	31.7	29.0	31.6	32.0	1.6
Women	18.9	20.1	21.9	21.3	19.8	22.8	21.1	2.2
Men	46.2	44.6	47.4	46.3	38.6	43.8	44.4	−1.8
Good	33.5	31.5	34.9	34.2	30.9	32.0	33.4	−0.1
Poor	20.1	25.4	25.3	22.6	22.7	29.8	26.8	6.7
Employer sponsored health insurance (dependent)								
Total	20.0	19.0	19.4	20.1	19.9	18.9	18.7	−1.3
Women	26.7	25.6	26.1	27.2	25.3	26.1	26.0	−0.7
Men	10.7	9.5	9.9	10.3	12.0	9.0	9.0	−1.7
Good	20.5	20.4	20.4	21.0	21.7	20.1	20.4	−0.1
Poor	18.0	14.5	16.5	17.1	14.2	14.2	12.3	−5.7
Non-group health insurance								
Total	10.4	11.9	10.0	11.7	12.4	9.4	10.0	−0.4
Women	12.8	14.3	12.0	13.5	13.3	11.0	11.3	−1.5
Men	7.2	8.5	7.1	9.2	10.9	7.3	8.2	1.0
Good	11.4	13.0	10.6	13.2	13.0	9.9	10.4	−1.0
Poor	7.2	8.2	8.2	6.4	10.2	7.5	8.3	1.1
Public insurance only								
Total	10.0	10.1	11.4	10.2	13.6	11.1	12.3	2.3
Women	11.1	10.9	12.1	10.5	13.3	11.3	12.7	1.8
Men	8.4	9.0	10.4	9.7	14.2	10.8	11.8	3.4
Good	6.4	6.7	7.0	6.2	9.4	8.6	9.3	2.9
Poor	22.0	21.5	24.1	24.6	27.2	20.1	23.8	1.8
No health insurance								
Total	18.5	20.4	19.7	19.5	18.6	21.9	21.1	2.6
Women	18.3	20.9	21.6	20.8	19.8	22.8	21.1	2.8
Men	18.8	19.8	17.1	17.7	16.7	20.6	20.9	2.1
Good	17.0	19.7	19.6	19.6	18.2	22.0	20.7	3.7
Poor	23.5	22.9	20.1	19.2	19.8	21.5	22.6	−0.9

Notes: Health status categories collapsed into two because too few observations were in some self-reported health status categories in earlier years.

Table 11. Employer Sponsored Health Insurance Coverage for Near-Elderly Retirees by Health and Gender, 1996 to 2002

	1996	1997	1998	1999	2000	2001	2002	% change 1996–2002
Employer sponsored health insurance (policy holder) for women								
Good health	20.8	20.4	23.9	23.1	24.0	23.7	23.4	2.6
Poor health	12.0	19.3	16.3	14.3	17.8	17.4	19.9	7.9
Employer sponsored health insurance (policy holder) for men								
Good health	51.3	47.8	50.3	50.1	41.3	44.2	47.2	−4.1
Poor health	30.2	34.2	38.6	33.4	30.0	42.7	34.9	4.7
Employer sponsored health insurance (dependents) for women								
Good health	27.9	28.3	28.7	28.8	28.5	27.3	28.3	0.4
Poor health	22.5	16.3	18.7	21.3	15.0	20.9	16.7	−5.5
Employer sponsored health insurance (dependents) for men								
Good health	10.1	8.8	8.8	9.8	11.6	9.6	9.5	−0.6
Poor health	12.5	11.8	13.2	11.9	13.1	7.2	7.1	−5.4

Notes: Health status categories collapsed into two because too few observations were in some self-reported health status categories in earlier years.

Table 9). In comparison, the share of early retirees without health insurance rose by 2.6 percentage points to 21.1 percent (see Table 10). In both cases, the decline in health insurance coverage is partially attributable to a decline in the coverage by nongroup health insurance.

In fact, to some degree, ESI coverage became a substitute for nongroup health insurance for early retirees. As employers covered relatively more early retirees, as a share of early retirees, and as their costs are rising, it is possible that employers will further reduce access to retiree health insurance in the future.

It is not only the near-elderly who seem to be staying in the labor force longer, but also the elderly. Since reaching its low point in 1985, the labor force participation rate of older men had risen from 15.8 percent to almost 18 percent by 2002. The labor force participation rate for elderly women shows the same trend, increasing from 7.3 percent in 1985 to 9.9 percent in 2002 (Purcell 2004).

For the elderly, the changes in labor force participation rates may be a result of the loss of supplemental health insurance. For people over 65 years old in general, nongroup health insurance coverage has declined dramatically. The trends

Table 12. Trends of Health Insurance Sources for Elderly Retirees, 1996–2002

	1996	1997	1998	1999	2000	2001	2002	% change 1996–2002
Public insurance only								
Total	33.7	35.7	38.2	38.4	39.9	39.3	40.5	6.7
Women	35.7	37.7	39.9	39.5	41.2	41.0	42.2	6.5
Men	30.9	33.0	35.7	36.9	38.0	36.8	38.2	7.3
Good	28.5	31.9	35.3	34.9	36.4	34.5	36.5	8.0
Poor	42.9	42.6	43.6	45.0	45.9	48.0	48.1	5.2
Employer sponsored health insurance								
Total	20.5	20.7	20.8	20.9	20.3	20.0	20.0	−0.5
Women	14.7	14.8	15.0	15.8	15.3	15.1	14.7	0.0
Men	28.6	29.0	28.9	28.3	27.3	27.0	27.5	−1.1
Good	22.9	23.1	22.4	22.8	21.8	22.5	22.1	−0.8
Poor	16.2	16.5	17.7	17.4	17.6	15.3	15.9	−0.3
Employer sponsored health insurance (dependents)								
Total	8.7	8.9	8.8	8.1	7.7	9.1	8.4	−0.3
Women	10.7	10.8	11.1	10.4	9.3	10.7	10.5	0.2
Men	5.9	6.4	5.5	4.9	5.4	6.6	5.4	−0.5
Good	9.8	9.5	9.4	8.9	8.2	10.0	9.3	−0.5
Poor	6.7	8.0	7.7	6.7	6.8	7.4	6.7	0.0
Public insurance plus non-group insurance								
Total	36.2	33.6	31.0	31.3	31.0	30.4	29.8	−6.4
Women	38.1	35.8	32.6	33.1	33.1	32.0	31.0	−7.1
Men	33.5	30.6	28.8	28.7	28.1	28.0	27.9	−5.6
Good	37.8	34.6	31.6	32.2	32.3	31.6	30.6	−7.2
Poor	33.3	32.0	29.9	29.6	28.9	28.1	28.2	−5.1

Notes: Health status categories collapsed into two because too few observations were in some self-reported health status categories in earlier years.

from 1996 to 2002 show that a rising share of retirees relied solely on public health insurance as their share rose by 6.8 percentage points, from 33.7 percent in 1996 to 40.5 percent in 2002. At the same time, the share of elderly retirees with supplemental nongroup private insurance declined by 6.4 percentage points, from 36.2 percent to 29.8 percent (see Table 12). This implies that the big changes in elderly retirees' health insurance occurred in the private market, where many older workers have dropped their private plans.

Table 13. Employer Sponsored Health Insurance for Elderly Retirees by Age, 1996 to 2002

	1996	1997	1998	1999	2000	2001	2002	% change 1996–2002
65–74	51.3	50.3	49.3	48.6	47.8	47.0	46.1	−5.2
75+	48.7	49.7	50.7	51.4	52.3	53.0	53.9	5.2
Employed sponsored health insurance (policy holder)								
65–74	22.9	23.1	22.5	22.4	21.5	21.0	20.5	−2.4
75+	17.9	18.3	19.0	19.5	19.2	19.1	19.5	1.6
Employer sponsored health insurance (dependent)								
65–74	11.6	11.6	11.0	10.8	10.2	11.7	11.2	−0.4
75+	5.7	6.3	6.7	5.6	5.4	6.7	6.0	0.3

Notes: Health status categories collapsed into two because too few observations were in some self-reported health status categories in earlier years.

Disaggregating health insurance coverage trends for the over 65 group also suggests that lower ESI access for elderly retirees contributed to the rise in their labor force participation rates. Separating the sources of health insurance by age for the elderly indicates that the elderly between the ages of 65 and 74 have seen their ESI coverage decline, whereas the elderly 75 and over have seen it increase.[6] The share of the younger elderly retirees with ESI in their own names declined by 2.8 percentage points, from 34.5 percent in 1996 to 31.7 percent in 2002. In comparison, the share of older elderly retirees with ESI coverage rose by 1.9 percentage points, from 23.6 percent in 1996 to 25.5 percent in 2002 (see Table 13).

RESEARCH QUESTIONS ON HEALTH, HEALTH INSURANCE, AND RETIREMENT

The near-elderly and elderly have become increasingly more likely to be in the labor force. At the same time, the health status of the near-elderly has remained fairly stable in recent years. Simultaneously, the access to health insurance for early retirees has declined, as has the access of Medicare-eligible retirees to supplemental health insurance. The declining access to ESI may have contributed to the rising labor force participation rates of the near-elderly, as the near elderly in the labor force have become more likely to have ESI coverage. But not every-body appears to have the same options to work longer, since poor health reduces the likelihood of being in the labor force despite the increased provision of ESI for the near-elderly. As a result, near-elderly retirees have become less likely to have ESI coverage, largely due to the loss of dependent coverage. Lastly, although ESI access also declined for elderly retirees, their supplemental health insurance coverage from ESI increased slightly. This may be due, however, to cohort effects because changes to retiree health insurance plans often grandfather in older work-ers and only affect younger employees.

The Role of Prescription Drug Coverage

It is not only necessary to have some form of health insurance for the near-elderly, but also to have health insurance that covers some of the services the near-elderly and elderly are likely to require. For instance, people age 55 and older may require more prescription drugs than younger people, thus prescrip-tion drug benefits are a crucial aspect of retiree health insurance coverage.

The vast majority of the near-elderly, who are still working and who have health insurance through their employer, also appear to have prescription drug coverage under their health insurance plan. Fully 98 percent of workers covered through their jobs had drug benefits in 2001 (Kaiser 2001b). It appears that those without prescription drug benefits under age 65 are mainly those who have no health insurance at all (Alliance for Health Reform 2003).

With respect to early retirees, Finkelstein (2002) concludes, based on data from the HRS, that 85 percent of retirees who are younger than 65 years old who are covered by a private health insurance policy also have a prescription drug benefit.

In comparison, a number of studies have documented access of Medicare beneficiaries to prescription drug benefits. Almost everybody over the age of 65 has access to Medicare. However, until 2004, Medicare did not offer a prescrip-tion drug benefit. Instead, the most important source for prescription drug bene-fits for Medicare beneficiaries continues to be ESI, which provided 28 percent of Medicare beneficiaries with prescription drug coverage in 1999. Medicare HMOs covered 15 percent; Medicaid, 10 percent; Medigap, 7 percent; and other public programs, 2 percent; leaving 38 percent of Medicare beneficiaries with-out prescription drug coverage (Kaiser 2003). These figures reflect a decline in employer-sponsored prescription drug coverage from 1996 to 2004 of 2 per-centage points and an increase in the number of Medicare beneficiaries without prescription drug coverage of 8 percentage points during the same time frame (Kaiser 2003; Walker 2000).

Additional research on prescription drug coverage for the near-elderly and the elderly is needed before solid conclusions on the connection between health insurance and retirement decisions can be drawn. For instance, how has the prescription drug coverage for near-elderly retirees changed over time? Some datasets, such as the HRS, provide some information about the type of health insurance coverage for these age groups. Further, additional research seems appropriate to explore whether Medicare-eligible retirees have continued to lose supplemental prescription drug benefits from their former employers. The Medical Expenditure Panel Survey that is compiled by the Agency for Healthcare Research and Quality, dating back to 1996, appears to be the most promising source of information in this regard.

If there is a documented change in prescription drug coverage for near-elderly and elderly retirees, and if this change diverges from the trends in overall health insurance coverage, the next issue is whether prescription drug coverage has the same or a different effect on the retirement decisions of people who are over 55 years old. Does prescription drug coverage matter more, less, or the same as other health insurance coverage in inducing people to retire? Is the effect of prescription drug coverage on the decision to retire different for different age groups?

Wealth, Health Insurance, and Retirement

Another question is the relative importance of health insurance coverage in determining the retirement decisions of older workers. Research so far has not differentiated between wealth and health insurance coverage in influencing retirement. For instance, some observers attributed the increase in labor force participation rates of the near-elderly in 2001 and 2002 to the declining stock market (Eschtruth and Gemus 2002). But as we documented above, access to affordable retiree health insurance may have played a role in delaying retirement for many near-elderly people.

Labor force participation rates have been rising for some time, even when the stock market rose rapidly. In particular, labor force participation rates for the near-elderly began to rise in the 1980s, coinciding with faster stock market growth as well as with cost increases in prescription drugs, medical supplies, and hospital visits (see Table 14).

The bear market on Wall Street began in early 2000. Households saw their largest wealth declines in the twelve months following the end of the stock mar-

Table 14. Labor Force Participation Rates, the Stock Market and Health Care Costs, 1969 to 2002

	LFPR, 55 to 64		LFPR, 65 and over		Inflation	Drug price inflation	Hospital care inflation	Stock market growth	
	Level	Change	Level	Change				Nominal	Real
Dec. 1969–Nov. 1973	60.44	−1.75	15.87	−3.94	5.02	0.11	N/A	3.51	−1.51
Nov. 1973–Jan. 1980	56.74	−0.51	13.37	−1.66	8.60	6.25	N/A	2.48	−6.12
Jan. 1980–Jul. 1990	54.76	−0.09	11.57	−0.92	4.90	9.22	9.64	9.93	5.03
Jul. 1990–Mar. 1901	57.65	0.70	12.02	0.84	2.81	4.52	5.82	12.70	9.89
Dec. 1995–Mar. 2001	58.91	0.95	12.30	1.54	2.57	4.13	4.42	12.86	10.30
Mar. 2001–Dec. 2002	61.17	2.24	13.17	0.00	1.76	4.81	8.26	−21.25	−23.01

Notes: Sources are the Bureau of Labor Statistics, Labor Force Statistics, Bureau of Labor Statistics, Consumer Price Index, Standard and Poor's, and the National Bureau of Economic Research, Business Cycle Dates. All figures are in percent.

ket boom, at a time when the labor force participation rates of the near-elderly and elderly did not rise much. Household financial wealth declined by $4.4 trillion by March 2001 compared to March 2000. In the year thereafter, households lost an additional $1 trillion. During the year of the largest wealth declines, though, the labor force participation rate of the near-elderly increased by only 0.6 percentage points. But it rose by 0.8 percentage points in the subsequent twelve months.

In comparison, other factors seem to play a more significant role in influencing the labor force participation rates of the near-elderly and elderly. In particular, rising healthcare costs may drive workers to work longer or to reenter the labor force, especially since access to retiree healthcare coverage is declining. As discussed earlier, the near-elderly and elderly demand more prescription drugs and are going to the hospital more often than younger workers, and these medical costs have been rising faster than inflation since the 1980s (see Table 14).

The trend in medical costs has a stronger and more consistent relationship with the labor force participation rates of the elderly and near elderly than stock prices. From 1985 to 2002, there is a strong positive correlation between medical costs and labor force participation rates (see Table 15), especially for non-Medicare-eligible workers. In comparison, the link between the stock market and labor force participation rates is negative only after 2001, when the market crashed (see Table 15). For the entire period after 1985, there is a positive relationship.

Table 15. Correlation between Labor Force Participation Rates, Health Care Costs, and the Stock Market

Correlation with	LFPR, 55 to 64		LFPR, 65 and over	
Period	1985 to 2002	2001 to 2002	1985 to 2002	2001 to 2002
Drug prices	0.95	0.93	0.86	0.53
Hospital care	0.97	0.95	0.87	0.45
Stock prices	0.87	−0.85	0.74	−0.61
Financial wealth	0.93	−0.79	0.80	−0.89
Net worth	0.95	−0.54	0.85	−0.75

Notes: The unemployment rate is the respective unemployment rate for each age group. The period 2001 to 2002 spans the months from March 2001 to December 2002. Financial and net worth data are taken from the Federal Reserve's Flow of Funds Accounts for the United States, and are quarterly data through the third quarter of 2002. Calculations are taken from Weller and Singleton (2003).

·   Given that the evidence may lend support for both hypotheses—that the stock market crash and the declining access to retiree health insurance may have caused workers to stay in the labor force longer—further analysis appears appropriate to disentangle the relative effects of those factors.

Saving for Health Insurance as Part of Retirement

Although it seems unlikely on the surface that preretirement savings will allow employees to adequately prepare for the loss of employer-sponsored retiree health insurance, this issue should not be dismissed out of hand without further analysis.

Health problems of the near-elderly and the elderly are predictable in some ways. Hence, preretirement savings for medical care may be appropriate in some instances. Additional research is necessary to document the predictability of future health problems of the near-elderly and the elderly, and to evaluate already ongoing efforts to encourage preretirement savings for retiree medical care.

CONCLUSION

The research on retirement decisions, health status, and health insurance coverage suggests a number of important trends. For example, the evidence suggests only gradual improvements in the health status of the near-elderly and elderly, suggesting that the need for health insurance coverage among these groups has remained fairly stable. However, access to an important source of health insurance, employer-sponsored health insurance, has declined rapidly in past years. Two of the results of the decline in access are a rise in the labor force participation rate of the near-elderly and less generous early-retirement health insurance benefits, as reflected in a declining dependent coverage by employer sponsored retiree health insurance plans. An indication that this is a fairly recent phenomenon is the fact that the employer-sponsored health insurance coverage for the elderly has remained largely unchanged in contrast to the declining coverage for the near-elderly.

A number of important research questions, however, remain. First, most research on health insurance coverage, especially among the near-elderly, does not differentiate the type of coverage. In particular, little research exists on the access to prescription drug coverage for early retirees. Second, although it is accepted that the loss of retiree health insurance plays a role in the increasing labor force participation rates of the near-elderly, the relative size of this phenomenon is hard to quantify. Other changes, especially the loss of retirement wealth, may play an equally important, or even larger, role. Third, as older workers lose access to retiree health insurance, they may decide to save for retiree health insurance while they are working. The data on so-called defined contribution health insurance accounts, though, have been limited, and the savings decisions of households are still not sufficiently understood.

Notes

1. In Table 1, our category of "poor health" combines those who reported themselves to be in poor or fair health in the Current Population Survey.

2. For a detailed overview of datasets on aging see Hanushek and Maritato (1996) or National Institute on Aging (1998).

3. Ycas (1987) also suggested that the health situation worsened during the early and mid-1970s.

4. Ruhm (1996) found that pension coverage increased the likelihood of continued work. But he also found that the age of entry into pension employment is positively related to retirement. Thus, his results did not contradict the findings that pension wealth accrual matters for early retirement. Workers who entered pension employment later will have to work longer to accrue the same amount of pension wealth.

5. Because the rate of reentrants declined during that period, this increase in labor force participation rates suggests that the near-elderly stayed in the labor force longer and delayed retirement (Weller 2003).

6. This could be a survivor issue, that is, those with health insurance are more likely to live beyond age 75, raising the percentage with health insurance as they age.

REFERENCES

Alliance for Health Reform (AHR). 2003. *A Sourcebook for Journalists, Chapter 7: Prescription Drugs.* Washington, DC: AHR.

Anderson, P.M., A.L. Gustman, and L.T. Steinmeier. 1999. "Trends in Male Labor Force Participation and Retirement: Some Evidence on the Role of Pensions and Social Security in the 1970s and 1980s." *Journal of Labor Economics.* Vol. 17, no. 4: 757–83.

Aon Consulting. 2001. *Replacement Ratio Study.* Chicago, IL: Aon Consulting.

Autor, D.H., and M. Duggan. 2003. "The Rise in the Disability Rolls and the Decline in Unemployment." *Quarterly Journal of Economics.* Vol. 118, no. 1: 157–205.

Bernheim, D.B. 1993. *The Merrill Lynch Baby Boom Retirement Index: Is the Baby Boom Generation Preparing Adequately for Retirement? Summary Report.* New York, NY: Merrill Lynch.

Blau, D.M. 1994. "Labor Force Dynamics of Older Men." *Econometrica.* Vol. 62, no. 1: 117–56.

Bound, J., and T. Waidmann. 2000. "Accounting for Recent Declines in Employment Rates among the Working-Aged Disabled." National Bureau of Economic Research Working Paper 7975, Cambridge, MA: NBER.

Bovbjerg, B. 1998. "Social Security Reform: Raising Retirement Ages Improves Program Solvency but May Cause Hardship for Some." Statement of Barbara Bovbjerg, Associate Director; Income Security Issues; Health, Education, and Human Services Division; General Accounting Office (GAO), before the Special Committee on Aging, United States Senate. Washington DC: GAO. (July 15).

Burkhauser, R.V., J. Butler., and R. Weathers II. 2001. "How Policy Variables Influence the Timing of Social Security Disability Insurance Applications." *Social Security Bulletin.* Vol. 64, no. 1: 52–83.

Burtless, G. 1987. "Occupational Effects on the Health and Work Capacity of Older Men." in *Work, Health, and Income among the Elderly.* G. Burtless, ed. Washington, DC: The Brookings Institution.

Burtless, G., and Moffitt, R.A. 1985. "The Joint Choice of Retirement Age and Postretirement Hours of Work." *Journal of Labor Economics.* Vol. 3, no. 2: 209–36.

Centers for Medicare and Medicaid Services (CMS). 2003. *National Health Accounts: Historical and Current Years.* Baltimore, MD: CMS.

Chirikos, T.N., and G. Nestel. 1991. "Occupational Differences in the Ability of Men to Delay Retirement." *Journal of Human Resources.* Vol. 26, no. 1: 1–26.

Crimmins, E.M., M.D. Hayward, and Y. Saito. 1996. "Differentials in Active Life Expectancy in the Older Population of the United States." *Journal of Gerontology.* Vol. 51, no. 1: 111–20.

Ellis, Randall P., and Thomas G. McGuire. 2003. "Predictability and Predictiveness in Healthcare Spending." Unpublished working paper. Boston University.

Engen, E., and W. Gale. 2000. "The Effects of 401(k) Plans on Household Wealth: Differences across Earnings Groups." NBER Working Paper No. 8032. Cambridge MA: National Bureau of Economic Research.

Engen, E. M., W. G. Gale, and C. E. Uccello. 1999. "The Adequacy of Household Saving." Brookings Papers on Economic Activity. No. 2: 65–165.

Eschtruth, A. D., and J. Gemus. 2002. "Are Older Workers Responding to the Bear Market?" Boston, MA: Center for Retirement Research.

Finkelstein, A. 2002. "The Interaction of Partial Public Insurance Programs and Residual Private Insurance Markets: Evidence from the U.S. Medicare Program." NBER Working Paper No. 9031. Cambridge, MA: National Bureau of Economic Research.

Fleet, S. 2002. "PNC Bank Signs on as Health Plan Principal Trustee for LTV Steel Retirees and Former Employees through Steel Worker Benefits Trust." Business Wire. (May 23).

Freudenheim, M. 2002. "Companies Trim Health Benefits for Many Retirees as Costs Surge." The New York Times. (May 10): A01.

Fronstin, P. 2000. "The Erosion of Retiree Health Benefits and Retirement Behavior: Implications for the Disability Insurance Program." Social Security Bulletin. Vol. 63, no. 4: 38–46.

Garber, A. M., T. E. McCurdy, and M. C. McClellan. 1997. "Persistence of Medicare Expenditures among Elderly Beneficiaries." NBER Working Paper No. 6249. Cambridge, MA: National Bureau of Economic Research.

General Accounting Office (GAO). 2001. "Retiree Health Benefits: Employer-Sponsored Benefits May Be Vulnerable to Further Erosion." Washington, DC: GAO.

Gordon, M. 2000. "ERISA at 25: Has the Law Kept Pace with Evolving Pension and Investment World?" Testimony before the Subcommittee on Employer/Employee Relations, Education, and the Workforce Committee, U.S. House of Representatives, Washington, DC. (February 15).

Greenwald, J. 2002. "Ex-LTV workers form VEBA; Unusual move raises questions, benefit experts say." Business Insurance. (April 22).

Gruber, J. 1999. "Disability Insurance Benefits and Labor Supply." Journal of Political Economy. Vol. 108, no. 6.

Gruber, J., and J. Kubik. 1994. "Disability Insurance Rejection Rate and the Labor Supply of Older Workers." NBER Working Paper No. 4941. Cambridge, MA: NBER.

Gruber, J., and B. Madrian. 1995. "Health Insurance Availability and the Retirement Decision." American Economic Review. Vol. 85, no. 4: 938–48.

———. 1996. "Health Insurance and Early Retirement: Evidence from the Availability of Continuation Coverage." In Advances in the Economics of Aging. D. A. Wise, ed. Chicago: University of Chicago Press. 115–43.

———. 2002. "Health Insurance, Labor Supply, and Job Mobility: A Critical Review of the Literature." NBER Working Paper 8817. Cambridge, MA: NBER.

Gunsauley, C. 2002. "Benefit Liabilities Threaten Retiree Medical Care." *Employee Benefit News.* (November 1).

Gustman, A., and T. L. Steinmeier. 1999. "Effects of Pensions on Savings: Analysis with Data from the Health and Retirement Study." Carnegie-Rochester Conference Series on Public Policy 50, no. 99: 271–324.

Hanushek, E. A., and N. L. Maritato. 1996. "Assessing Knowledge of Retirement Behavior, Panel on Retirement Income Modeling." National Research Council, Washington DC: National Academy Press.

Haveman, R., B. Wolfe, and J. Warlick. 1988. "Labor Market Behavior of Older Men." *Journal of Public Economics.* Vol. 36, no. 2: 153–75.

Headen, A. E., Jr., R. Clark, and L. Shumaker Ghent. 1997. "Effects of Retiree Health Insurance and Pension Coverage on the Retirement Timing of Older Workers: Sensitivity of Estimates." North Carolina State University. Unpublished manuscript.

Hurd, M., and K. McGarry. 1996. "Prospective Retirement: Effects of Job Characteristics, Pension, and Health Insurance." University of California at Los Angeles. Unpublished manuscript.

Kaiser Family Foundation and Health Research and Educational Trust (Kaiser). 2001a. "Retiree Health Benefits." Employer Health Benefits, 2001 Annual Survey, Section 11. Menlo Park, CA: Kaiser. 143–56.

———. 2001b. "Prescription Drug Trends: A Chartbook." Update Publication No. 2112. Menlo Park, CA: Kaiser.

———. 2002. "Retiree Health Benefits." Employer Health Benefits, 2002 Annual Survey, Section 11. Menlo Park, CA: Kaiser. 141–53.

———. 2003. "Medicaid-Medicare and Prescription Drugs." Factsheet. Menlo Park, CA: Kaiser. (April).

Karoly, L. A., and J. Rogowski. 1994. "The Effect of Access to Post-Retirement Health Insurance on the Decision to Retire Early." *Industrial Labor Relations Review.* Vol. 48, no. 1: 103–23.

Lee, K. 2002. "Education the best option: Funding mechanisms for retiree healthcare deemed insufficient." *Employee Benefit News.* (December 1).

Leonesio, M. V., D. R. Vaughan, and B. Wixon. 2000. "Early Retirees under Social Security: Health Status and Economic Resources." ORES Working Paper Series No. 86. Washington, DC: Social Security Administration, Office of Policy, Office of Research, Evaluation and Statistics.

Madrian, B. C. 1994. "The Effect of Health Insurance on Retirement." Brookings Papers on Economic Activity 1:181–252.

McGill, D. M., K. N. Brown, J. J. Haley, and Sylvester Schieber. 1996. *Fundamentals of Private Pensions.* 7th Edition, Philadelphia: University of Pennsylvania Press.

Medoff, J., and M. Calabrese. 2001. *The Impact of Labor Market Trends on Health and Pension Benefit Coverage and Inequality.* Washington, DC: U.S. Department of Labor.

Mercer Human Relations Consulting and Foster Higgens (Mercer). 2002. *Employer Sponsored Health Plans—Key Findings.* Washington, DC: Mercer Human Relations Consulting.

Mitchell, O. S., and J. F. Moore. 1998. "Can Americans Afford to Retire? New Evidence on Retirement Saving Adequacy." *Journal of Risk and Insurance.* Vol. 65, no. 3: 371–400.

Mitchell, O., and J. Phillips. 2000. "Retirement Responses to Early Social Security Benefit Reductions." NBER Working Paper 7963. Cambridge, MA: NBER.

Moore, J. F., and O. S. Mitchell. 1997. "Projected Retirement Wealth and Savings Adequacy in the Health and Retirement Study." NBER Working Paper No. 6240. Cambridge, MA: NBER.

National Center for Health Statistics (NCHS). 2002a. *Self-Reported Health by Age, Sex, and Race: United States, 1982–1999.* Hyattsville, MD: NCHS. http://www.cdc.gov/nchs/about/otheract/aging/trenddata.htm#Health Status.

———. 2002b. *Functional Limitation by Age, Sex, and Race (National), 1983–1996.* Hyattsville, MD: NCHS. http://www.cdc.gov/nchs/about/otheract/aging/trenddata.htm#Functional Status.

National Institute on Aging (NIA). 1998. *Databases on Aging: Survey Summaries.* Washington, DC: NIA.

Nichols, L. 2001. "Policy Options for Filling Gaps in the Health Insurance Coverage of Older Workers and Early Retirees." *Ensuring Health and Income Security for an Aging Workforce.* P. Budetti, R. Burkhauser, J. Gregory, and H. A. Hunt, eds. Kalamazoo, MI: W. E. Upjohn Institute for Employment Research.

Packard, M. D., and V. P. Reno. 1988. "A Look at Very Early Retirees." In *Issues in Contemporary Retirement.* R. Ricardo-Campbell and E. P. Lazear, eds. Stanford, CA: Hoover Institution Press. 243–65.

Pope, Gregory C., Randall P. Ellis, Arlene S. Ash, Chuan-Fen Liu, John Z. Ayanian, David W. Bates, Helen Burstin, Lisa I. Iezzoni, and Melvin J. Ingber. 2000. "Principal Inpatient Diagnostic Cost Group Model for Medicare Risk Adjustment." *Healthcare Financing Review.* Vol. 21, no. 3: 93–118.

Poterba, J., and L. Summers. 1987. "Public Policy Implications of Declining Old-Age Mortality." In *Work, Health, and Income among the Elderly.* Gary Burtless, ed. Washington, DC: The Brookings Institution.

Poterba, J., S. Venti, and D. Wise. 2002. "The Transition to Personal Accounts and Increasing Retirement Wealth: Macro and Micro Evidence." Presented at the annual meetings of the American Economic Association, Atlanta. (January).

Purcell, Patrick. 2004. Pension Sponsorship and Participation: Summary of Recent Trends. Congressional Research Service Report RL 301 22. Washington, D.C.: Library of Congress.

Quinn, J. F. 1977. "Microeconomic Determinants of Early Retirement: A Cross-Sectional View of White Married Men." *Journal of Human Resources.* Vol. 12, no. 3: 329–46.

Quinn, J. F., R. V. Burkhauser, D. A. Myers. 1990. *Passing the Torch: The Influence of Financial Incentives on Work and Retirement.* Kalamazoo, MI: The W. E. Upjohn Institute on Employment Research.

Rappaport, A. 2000. "Variation of Employee Benefit Costs by Age." *Social Security Bulletin.* Vol. 63, no. 4: 47–56.

Rogowski, J., and L. A. Karoly. 2000. "Health Insurance and Retirement Behavior: Evidence from the Health and Retirement Survey." *Journal of Health Economics.* Vol. 19, no. 4: 529–39.

Ruhm, C. J. 1996. "Do Pensions Increase the Labor Supply of Older Men?" *Journal of Public Economics.* Vol. 59, no. 2: 157–75.

Rust, J. 1989. "A Dynamic Programming Model of Retirement Behavior." In *The Economics of Aging.* D. Wise, ed. Chicago, IL: The University of Chicago Press.

Rust, J., and C. Phelan. 1997. "How Social Security and Medicare Affect Retirement Behavior in a World of Incomplete Markets." *Econometrica.* Vol. 65, no. 4: 781–831.

Sammartino, F. 1987. "The Effect of Health on Retirement." *Social Security Bulletin.* Vol. 50, no. 2: 31–47.

Samwick, A. 1998. "New Evidence on Pensions, Social Security, and the Timing of Retirement." NBER Working Paper No. 6534. Cambridge, MA: NBER.

Schmidt, R. L. 2002. "Strategies for Dealing with Retiree Medical." *Employee Benefit News.* (August 1).

Schwartz, K., and B. Stevenson. 2001. "Health Insurance Coverage of People in the Ten Years before Medicare Eligibility." In *Ensuring Health and Income Security for an Aging Workforce.* Budetti, P., R. Burkhauser, J. Gregory, and H. A. Hunt, eds. Kalamazoo, MI: W. E. Upjohn Institute for Employment Research.

Social Security Administration (SSA). 1986. "Increasing the Social Security Retirement Age: Older Workers in Physically Demanding Occupations or Ill Health." *Social Security Bulletin.* Vol. 49, no. 1: 5–23.

Van Vliet, René C. J. A. 1992. "Predictability of Individual Healthcare Expenditures." *Journal of Risk and Insurance.* Vol. 59, no. 3: 443–61.

Walker, D. M. 2000. "Prescription Drugs: Increasing Medicare Beneficiary Access and Related Implications." Testimony before the Subcommittee on Health, Committee on Ways and Means, U.S. House of Representatives. Washington, D.C.: U.S. Congress. (February 15).

Watson Wyatt Worldwide. 2002. *Retiree Health Benefits: Time to Resuscitate?* Washington, DC: Watson Wyatt Worldwide.

Weller, C. 2003. "Older Workers Staying in the Labor Force." *Economic Snapshot.* Washington, DC: Economic Policy Institute. (July 16).

Weller, C., and L. Singleton, L. 2003. "Between a Rock and a Hard Place: How the Loss of Healthcare Coverage Puts Older Workers in a Bind." *Indicators.* Vol. 2, no. 4: 79–96.

Wolff, E. 2002. "Is the Equalizing Effect of Retirement Wealth Wearing Off?" New York University. Unpublished manuscript.

U.S. Department of Labor (DOL), Bureau of Labor Statistics. 1998. *Employment Cost Indexes 1975–1997.* Washington, DC: Department of Labor.

U.S. Department of Labor (DOL), Bureau of Labor Statistics. 1994. *Report on the American Workforce.* Washington, DC: Bureau of Labor Statistics.

Ycas, M. 1987. "Recent Trends in Health near the Age of Retirement: New Findings from the Health Interview Survey." *Social Security Bulletin.* Vol. 50, no. 2: 5–30.

Comments on "How 401(k)s and the Stock Market Crash Explain Increases in Older Workers' Labor Force Participation Rates" and "The Interaction between Health, Health Insurance, and Retirement"

STEPHEN A. WOODBURY

The chapters in part 3, "What Do Workers Want?" have addressed the three central aspects of work and aging: availability of work opportunities, access to health care, and adequacy of retirement income. Christian Weller and Jeffrey Wenger describe the decline in older workers' access to health insurance. Sharon Hermes and Teresa Ghilarducci raise a novel problem, increased macroeconomic instability, which may result from the move from defined benefit (DB) to defined contribution (DC) pensions. These comments discuss, in a critical light, each of the papers and some of the issues they address.

"How 401(k)s and the Stock Market Crash Explain Increases in Older Workers' Labor Force Participation Rates"

Hermes and Ghilarducci make two key points in their paper. First, DC pension plans place more risk on workers than do traditional DB plans and place more retirees' means of support at risk. Second, the increasing reliance on DC plans has had a destabilizing effect on the economy, in that workers' retirement decisions are likely to be affected by relatively short-term swings in financial markets.

Specifically, the value to a worker of a DC pension plan depends on the value of the financial assets held by the plan. Because asset values fall during a recession, workers who are covered by DC plans tend to avoid retirement and remain in the labor force during a recession. So the cyclical influence of DC plans tends to be perverse, causing labor force participation to rise in recession and fall during recovery. In contrast, the value to workers of DB plans bears little relation to the state of financial markets, so the retirement decisions of workers who are covered by DB plans are far less sensitive to cyclical swings.

Hermes and Ghilarducci's second point is novel and important, although it needs to be understood in context. A generation ago, DB pensions were a source of great concern because they were unregulated and subject to abuse. Congress's response was to adopt the Employee Retirement Income Security Act of 1974 (ERISA), which subjected DB pension plans to rules and regulations that made them more secure for workers and more costly for employers to implement and maintain. The result, which was predictable, has been for employers to move away from DB plans (which now are regulated and relatively costly) and toward DC plans (which are less regulated and hence less costly).

That DC plans have a perverse influence on macroeconomic stability is important and must be chalked up against DC plans. The point is connected to the fact that DC plans place the financial market risks of accumulating pension assets largely on the worker (although it is a distinct point). The destabilizing influence of DC plans ranks with the fact that DC plans place much financial risk on workers as a key drawback of DC plans.

But DC plans have three important characteristics that can be chalked up in their favor (Clark and Schieber 1998; Turner 1993). First, benefit accrual under DC plans is usually front loaded, whereas benefit accrual under DB plans tends to be back loaded. In general, then, a worker gains more pension benefit rights earlier in his or her job tenure under a DC plan than under a DB plan. Second, and as a result, DC plans do not impose an early departure penalty on a worker. A worker who is covered by a DB plan and leaves a company before the early retirement age will likely suffer a large loss of pension wealth. In contrast, a worker who is covered by a DC plan and leaves a company will have his or her pension wealth preserved. Third, DC benefit plans are easily portable, whereas DB plans generally are not. A DC pension accumulation is held in a worker's name and is unrelated to an employer. When a worker moves, the accumulation goes with him or her. All three of these points suggest that mobile workers (or workers who experience one or more dislocations during their work lives) are likely to fare better under DC plans than under DB plans. To the extent that the labor force is becoming more mobile and dislocation becoming more common, DC plans may be preferred by workers and yield higher pension benefits.

The point is that a comprehensive comparison of DC and DB plans needs to take account of a wide array of plan attributes. The purpose of Hermes and Ghilarducci's paper is not to make such a comprehensive comparison, but rather to contribute a new consideration to that comparison: whether pension plans contribute to macroeconomic stability. This consideration will need to be given appropriate weight in any future appraisal of the relative merits of DB and DC plans.

"The Interaction between Health, Health Insurance, and Retirement"

Weller and Wenger provide a wealth of data and information on the relationships among health, health insurance, and retirement behavior. The story told in the main section of their paper is that rising healthcare costs have resulted in a decline in older workers' access to health insurance. They go on to describe the possible responses of workers to reduced availability of retiree health insurance. The three possibilities considered are to apply for disability insurance under Supplemental Security Insurance, to save more during working years, and to work longer.

But what about policies to address the problem? The implicit recommendation is to leave the existing systems alone and let workers adjust. That is a policy response, of course, and it may even be the right one, but other possibilities exist. To understand what those policies might be, it is first necessary to understand why healthcare costs are high and rising.

Perhaps the primary reason for high and rising healthcare costs is that employer contributions to workers' health plans have been tax free for over sixty years. The result has been a continuing disconnect between the recipients of healthcare (workers and their families) and the payers (employers). Workers increasingly have been called upon to contribute to the health insurance premium and to pay higher deductibles and copayments, but these still fall far short of the full cost of the healthcare received. Healthcare consumers have little incentive to economize on the amount of healthcare they receive, so they receive an inefficiently large amount, and costs become inflated.

The underlying problem is the tax system. Indeed, the existing tax treatment of both health insurance and pensions in the United States lacks consistency under either an accrual income tax system or a consumption tax system. Under an accrual income tax, employer-provided health insurance represents a current benefit that should be taxed annually as current income.[1] Similarly, employer contributions to pension plans represent an addition to wealth that would be taxed at the time they are made.[2]

The idea of a consumption tax is to tax what an individual takes out of the economic system. So under a consumption tax, health-insurance expenditures would be considered current consumption, and the same tax that applied to any other consumption would apply to employer contributions to health insurance. Because pension contributions represent saving, they would not be taxed when they are made under a consumption tax (neither would the interest earned on pension contributions be taxed under a consumption tax, because it is reinvested). Only when the worker retires and draws retirement income would pension contributions be taxed.

Nominally, the United States has an income tax under which employer contributions to both health insurance and pensions could be taxed as income. But both receive favorable tax treatment; health insurance contributions are tax free, and pensions are tax favored in that current pension contributions and interest on previous contributions go untaxed. The tax treatment of health insurance is consistent with neither a consumption tax nor an income tax, and the tax treatment of pensions is consistent with a consumption tax. This is the system that is responsible for many of the problems that face aging workers.

Following the first Clinton administration's failed attempt to reform healthcare in 1993–1994, numerous tax reforms were proposed that promised to eliminate the favorable tax treatment of health insurance either by taxing health contributions under the current system or by adopting a consumption tax (Woodbury 1997). Employers and workers alike objected stridently to these proposals, and the strength of their objections suggests how difficult it would be to change the tax treatment of health insurance.

Nevertheless, proposals to eliminate the tax-favored treatment of heath insurance still have force. For example, Cogan, Hubbard, and Kessler (2004) have suggested making health insurance purchased by individuals, as well as that purchased by employers, tax deductible. This would eliminate the incentive for workers to receive compensation in the form of health insurance, make individuals conscious of the cost of health insurance and healthcare, and bring a degree of discipline to the markets for health insurance and healthcare. Some such reform will be necessary if healthcare costs are to be brought under control, and reducing healthcare costs (by uncoupling health insurance from the employment relationship so that employers no longer bear responsibility for healthcare) would go a long way toward creating job opportunities for Americans in their 50s and early 60s.

CONCLUSION

What do older workers want? They want what any individual of any age wants: adequate income to live with dignity, and a standard of living that does not place them in an underclass. This means they want housing, food, entertainment, transportation, and healthcare (among other things) comparable to a social norm or to a standard to which they are accustomed.

Aging Americans face a daunting array of problems: unattractive work opportunities and low earnings, uncertainty over the adequacy and affordability of health care, and inadequate retirement savings. Solving these problems and satisfying the wants of aging Americans will be a tall order, and the papers in this section show clearly how these problems are starting to manifest themselves and how they will unfold in coming years. Market solutions may be adequate, and probably are all that can be expected, to create labor-market opportunities for aging Americans. Tax reform or draconian regulation of the healthcare system may be needed to make healthcare accessible to workers as they age. But solving these problems, whether by market or other means, is one of the main challenges facing this country as the baby-boom generation ages.

NOTES

1. Bradford (1986, 20) has noted that there may be a case for excluding medical expenditures from the definition of accrual income if we believe that medical expenditures are unfortunate and do not contribute to utility. However, Feldstein (1973) uses efficiency considerations to argue for including employer contributions to health insurance in the income-tax base.

2. The interest earned on pension contributions also represents an addition to wealth that would be taxed annually. When a worker retires, all applicable taxes would already have been paid on the benefit, and the flow of retirement income received by the worker would not be taxed.

REFERENCES

Bradford, David F. 1986. *Untangling the Income Tax.* Cambridge: Harvard University Press.
Clark, Robert, and Sylvester Schieber. 1998. "Factors Affecting Participation Rates and Contribution Levels in 401(k) Plans." Olivia S. Mitchell, Sylvester J. Schieber, eds. *Living with Defined Contribution Pensions: Remaking Responsibility for Retirement.* Philadelphia: University of Pennsylvania Press.

Cogan, John F., R. Glenn Hubbard, and Daniel P. Kessler. 2004. "Healthy, Wealthy, and Wise." *The Wall Street Journal.* (May 4).

Feldstein, Martin S. 1973. "The Welfare Loss of Excess Health Insurance." *Journal of Political Economy.* Vol. 81: 251–80.

Turner, John A. 1993. *Pension Policy for a Mobile Labor Force.* Kalamazoo: W.E. Upjohn Institute.

Woodbury, Stephen A. 1997. "Employee Benefits and Tax Reform." In *Tax Reform: Implications for Economic Security and Employee Benefits.* Dallas L. Salisbury, ed. Washington, DC: Employee Benefit Research Institute. 27–34.

Comments on "The Interaction between Health, Health Insurance, and Retirement"

TODD ELDER

Christian Weller and Jeffrey Wenger provide an enlightening synthesis of literatures related to the health and economic status of the elderly and near-elderly, the interaction between health and retirement, the effects of health insurance on labor-market behavior, and the inadequacy of retirement savings. Their principal findings suggest that the decline in employer-provided retiree health insurance (EPRHI) coverage in recent years may be inducing older workers to postpone retirement. If health insurance coverage plays a primary role in retirement decisions, any effort to increase labor force participation of the near elderly will require that they have the means to obtain health insurance, a particularly difficult challenge given that the contraction of EPRHI plans suggests that employers may not be willing to bear the large expense that older workers generate.

Of the multitude of issues at the forefront of current debate about retirement and the economic status of the elderly and near-elderly, arguably none is more important than the role of health insurance and medical expenses in individual retirement decisions. The mantra that "retirement policy is health policy" gains credence when one considers that health costs have been consistently outpacing inflation in recent years, with reports from Watson Wyatt Worldwide and other sources indicating that employers' health insurance costs, in particular, have been rising at double-digit annual rates in the past decade. The demographic changes resulting from the retirement of the baby boomers in coming years will dramatically affect costs of employer-provided pension plans and Social Security obligations, but the effect on the healthcare system and Medicare will likely be far more dramatic, given that per-person medical expenditures have risen so sharply. As a result, health and health insurance policy presents an urgent need for attention among all retirement issues.

Much of Weller and Wenger's analysis is concerned with possible employee responses to the decline in the availability of EPRHI. They offer three possible avenues through which an employee might respond: delaying retirement and working longer, applying for federal disability programs that carry insurance coverage, or saving more (or better) during work years in anticipation of post-retirement medical costs.

WILL THE NEAR-ELDERLY WORK MORE IN RESPONSE TO DECLINING ACCESS TO EMPLOYER-PROVIDED RETIREE HEALTH INSURANCE?

The central theme of this book is concerned with increasing the labor force participation rates of older Americans. The desirability of that presumption is debatable, as a characteristic of an advanced society is having more leisure time over the entire life cycle, that is, more years spent in retirement, particularly years in which to enjoy leisure before health deteriorates. If the goal were simply to increase labor supply/participation of near-elderly individuals, Weller and Wenger's research, along with that of others such as Gruber and Madrian (2002) and Blau and Gilleskie (2001), seems to imply that the solution is simple: decreased employer provision of retiree health insurance will cause labor force participation rates to "take care of themselves," as the near-elderly will delay retirement in response to declining access to retiree health insurance.

Abstracting from whether delaying retirement as a response to declining health insurance options is beneficial or not, there is still some question as to whether it will actually happen on a large scale. A significant body of research suggests that firms' responses to increasing medical costs have been to change the nature of EPRHI. Cutler (2003) finds that much of the reduction in employee health coverage in the past twenty years was not due to employers reducing access to coverage, but instead, due to employers shifting the responsibility of paying for coverage to employees. The effect of EPRHI on retirement decisions is therefore a moving target. Plans in which the employer pays the full cost, as was the case for most plans in the 1980s and early 1990s, will likely have significant influences on retirement, but plans in which the employee pays much or all of the premium will have much smaller effects. Although it should be noted that changing EPRHI coverage will affect future participation rates much more than current ones—so we haven't seen the full effects yet—one would still expect some of the labor market impact to have happened already.

Regardless of who ultimately pays for employer-provided retiree health insurance plans, the decline in the number of firms offering these plans began long ago. As Weller and Wenger note, the General Accounting Office estimates that slightly more than half as many firms offered EPRHI in 1998 as in 1983. Again, this fact suggests that at least some of the labor market impact of employers changing the provisions of health insurance plans should already have happened. According to the U.S. Bureau of Labor Statistics (Purcell 2006), labor force participation rates among near-elderly men (ages 55 to 64) increased from 67.9 percent to 69.2 percent from 1985 to 2002. Although this is a relatively modest increase, it may be evidence of an effect. Compelling evidence to the contrary emerges when considering the labor force participation of elderly men age 65 and over, whose participation rates increased from 15.8 percent to 17.8 percent over the same time period. Relative to baseline rates, participation increased by roughly 1.9 percent for those ages 55–64 and by 12.7 percent among those over 65.

While there are many possible causes of the relatively dramatic increase in elderly labor supply, this phenomenon illuminates the difficulties in pointing to rising near-elderly labor supply as prima facie evidence of an impact of EPRHI on work decisions, since those over 65 are arguably less influenced by health insurance issues due to the near-universal coverage of Medicare for this age group. Of course, one should exercise caution in interpreting these patterns as evidence of no EPRHI effect since many elderly people may desire additional coverage to supplement Medicare. Due to the fact that the elderly have substantially higher health expenses than the near-elderly, declining access to EPRHI may affect this group more profoundly even in the presence of Medicare, so the relatively larger labor force participation increase of the over-65 group may still be consistent with an effect of EPRHI on labor market behavior.

Weller and Wenger's Table 12 illuminates another dramatic fact about the extent of insurance coverage among the elderly that may have implications for the role EPRHI plays in retirement decisions. From 1996 to 2002, elderly retirees became 6.7 percentage points more likely to be covered *only* by public insurance, that is, Medicare. While the rate of coverage by employer-sponsored plans remained relatively stable over this time (due in part to cohort effects), nearly all of this increase was accounted for by a decline in the proportion of the elderly who were covered by private nongroup insurance. Apparently, retirees are increasingly steering clear of individual accounts in the private market, since this 6.4 percentage point fall represents a striking 17.7 percent decline. The root cause of this decline may lie in the increased cost associated with private non-group plans, although this is an open research question. If so, does this imply that declining access to EPRHI is affecting the retirement decisions of those over 65 since alternative forms of insurance are becoming increasingly more expensive? Again, this is an open research question, but the age pattern of EPRHI's influence, and recent patterns in elderly labor supply more generally, represent one of the biggest puzzles in the study of health and retirement policy. These puzzles provide a clear agenda for future research.

A final issue of note in considering whether workers will work longer in response to declining retiree coverage options relates to whether the elderly and near-elderly are able to work longer. In related work, Weller (2003) studies the extent to which health problems limit the work options for older Americans, finding that health limitations play a significant role in the retirement decisions of the near-elderly. Given that those in poor health are likely to value EPRHI the most, Weller's findings suggest that those who would most want to change their labor market behavior in response to the erosion of EPRHI coverage are unable to do so. The role of hours constraints is likely to be of primary importance here, since many would like to continue working in some capacity in order to continue coverage through their employer but are unable to do so unless they work full time.

Hutchens (2003), in an innovative look at the extent to which employers accommodate workers who would like to phase into retirement, finds that 51 percent of surveyed establishments would provide health insurance to a rehired retiree who worked part-time. However, most of these firms are simply those that offer retiree health insurance, and therefore continue the insurance after the retirees are rehired. Thirty-one percent of employers answered that rehires would receive no health insurance benefits, and another 8 percent indicated that the answer depends on how many hours the rehired retiree worked, with coverage in the plan being subject to minimum hours requirements. Commonly, employees are only covered if they work more than thirty hours per week, which is not that much different from a "true" full-time worker. Hutchens's findings imply that the dual roles of health limitations and employers' unwillingness to cover part-time workers will lead to a great deal of workers who want to continue receiving health insurance through their employer being unable to do so. Among those who are able to work full time but prefer to work part time, the lack of accommodation of employers to their wishes causes workers to either go uninsured or to work more than they otherwise would, with either outcome leading to a decrease in employee well being.

Will the Near-Elderly Increasingly Use Federal Disability Programs?

Although a number of authors have studied the determinants of dramatic increases in the rolls of the Social Security Disability Insurance (SSDI) and Supplemental Security Income (SSI) programs since the 1970s, none have investigated the extent to which the increasing cost and declining coverage of EPRHI could play a role. Weller and Wenger suggest that this may be one avenue by which employees will cope with declining affordable retiree health insurance options in the future, and some recent research hints that this hypothesis may be true.

Yelowitz (2000) argues that the expansion of the Qualified Medicare Beneficiary (QMB) program, which offers a substitute for Medicaid for the elderly poor and also expands eligibility to higher income and asset levels than Medicaid, can explain the decrease in SSI recipients among those over age 65 since the mid-1980s (in many states, SSI eligibility guarantees Medicaid eligibility). In contrast, the SSI rolls among those under age 65, who must be both disabled and poor to qualify for the program, expanded dramatically during the same time period. Yelowitz's results imply that insurance considerations rather than cash benefits, which are meant to supplement the income of elderly poor, are dominating the SSI take-up decision. To this author's knowledge, there is no research regarding the extent to which increased SSDI applications can be traced to insurance considerations as opposed to cash benefits, but given that SSI applications seem very sensitive to an individual's insurance status, it would not be surprising to find a similar result for SSDI. There is also some evidence (Elder and Powers 2003) that the sensitivity of SSI participation to cash benefit level is declining over time, while the guarantee of affordable health insurance coverage through Medicaid is gaining in importance, perhaps because of rising medical costs.

If near-elderly and elderly individuals substitute disability applications for EPRHI, then overall costs would not decline, but simply shift from employers to the government. Again, the extent to which this is currently happening and will happen in the future is an unresolved question that should be the focus of future research.

Self-Insurance and Individual Retiree Medical Accounts

The final avenue that Weller and Wenger discuss for employee responses to the decline in EPRHI availability involves workers increasingly using voluntary self-insurance plans such as Retiree Medical Accounts (RMAs) or by saving more during the working years in order to self-insure without the need for any additional apparatus. Economic theory predicts that as firms eliminate retiree health insurance (or, equivalently, shift the cost of these plans fully onto workers), they will pay higher wages in order to keep total compensation constant. As a result, earnings will be higher during preretirement years so workers can increase savings for retirement and basically self-insure. The authors make a compelling case that self-insurance is unlikely to work in practice, with the fundamental point being that workers already do not save enough for retirement. Influential work by Bernheim et al. (2000) and other authors suggests that individuals do not accurately predict their postretirement expenses along several dimensions, and medical expenses do not appear to be an exception. Although the adequacy of preretirement savings, on average, is still a somewhat open question, there is general agreement that a sizeable fraction of Americans do not save enough for retirement. If savings are not adequate now, introducing another individual component that people have to save for (shifting responsibility from the firm to employees) would likely exacerbate these issues.

Why people do not save enough for retirement is yet another open question, and the answers to it will fundamentally affect whether self-insurance will be a successful strategy. Authors have suggested that people may not be able to accurately forecast their probability of survival into old age, and even if they can, perhaps they discount the future too heavily or use hyperbolic discount rates to make apparently "irrational" decisions. It's clear that people cannot accurately predict their retirement health expenditures during the preretirement years, mainly because they are unable to accurately assess low-probability, high-cost medical events.

One of the most compelling lines of reasoning in Weller and Wenger's article is related to the inability of individuals to accurately predict their healthcare expenditures even in the very near future. When the authors model healthcare expenditures as a function of a host of observable characteristics, including lagged spending, they can only explain roughly 12–14 percent of the total variation in expenditures in a regression framework. Obviously, an individual will be better able to explain his or her healthcare expenditures than an applied researcher because the individual knows many of the "unobservables," but this caveat only refers to the ability of an individual to explain medical costs that are one period ahead. The variation of retirement medical costs that can be explained by variables known to an individual planning a retirement many years in the future would likely be even less. Bernheim et al. (2000) suggest that when individuals cannot predict future spending adequately, the costs of oversaving may be roughly equivalent to the costs of undersaving; therefore, the likelihood of an individual undersaving is likely to be far greater in the context of medical self-insurance than for other expenditures not related to healthcare.

Individual self-insurance for medical expenses, whether it is through personal savings or RMAs that are given preferential tax treatment, would generate another substantial disadvantage related to the shifting of risk away from employers to workers. In chapter 8 in this volume, Ghilarducci and Hermes argue that the shift from defined benefit to defined contribution pension plans has not only transferred much of the risk for retirement savings from employers to workers, it has also destabilized the U.S. economy. An analogous, but arguably much larger, effect could happen if the responsibility for saving for medical expenses shifts from employers to workers since there is substantially more risk involved in the sense of low-probability but financially catastrophic events. Put another way, medical expenses are more uncertain than other retirement expenses, especially from the point of view of a young worker who is planning for a retirement many years in the future. The shifting of risk will lead to a large loss in worker well-being, and the likelihood of undersaving is substantial, even more so than in the case of pension saving.

Some authors and policy makers have suggested an alternative means of self-insurance that involves voluntary pooled-risk plans in which groups of employees pool together in order to buy into a group health insurance plan. This risk pooling will reduce the cost of private insurance plans by reducing the per-unit risk an insurance company must bear relative to individual private plans. However, these arrangements are not likely to substantially reduce the cost of insurance in the private market because of adverse selection, which is the same reason that individual plans are often prohibitively expensive. Since the pooled plans are voluntary, the types of retirees who enter into these plans instead of simply remaining uninsured are those who expect to incur large medical expenses in the future, those who have strong distaste for risk, or both. The second group doesn't affect prices, but the former does. The advantage of employer-provided health insurance consists in its ability to ameliorate the adverse selection problem because people choose employers for a variety of reasons, not only those related to health insurance. In voluntary pooled plans, the individuals who will be entering into these agreements are doing so solely to gain access to health insurance, so the advantage of having a group plan is largely eliminated. In sum, these plans would not appreciably reduce the market failures associated with current individual private plans, and therefore are not viable alternatives for the future health insurance coverage of those who wish to retire prior to age 65.

The Known, the Unknown, and the Unknowable

In order to quantify the extent to which rising healthcare costs and the contraction of EPRHI plans will affect the labor market decisions and well-being of near-elderly and elderly Americans, future research must endeavor to answer many currently unanswered questions while leveraging what we currently know. For example, it is generally accepted that employees respond to health insurance provisions when making retirement and work decisions, but the extent to which these responses will change in the future, as the nature of the EPRHI plans change, is still largely unknown. Similarly, we know that employers have shifted much of the burden of paying for health insurance, both retiree and otherwise, onto employees, but the extent to which this shifting responds to possible future increases in medical costs is largely unknown.

Demographic trends suggest that the share of the elderly and near-elderly in the workforce will increase into the future as the baby boomers retire. The effect of this shift toward older workers in the labor force is "known" (in the sense that social scientists can agree about anything), but what is not known is how employers will respond to increasing cost pressures on their insurance plans. It is likely that costs will be further shifted to individual workers and that plans will be scaled back even more than they currently are, but the extent to which this will happen is unknown.

An important "unknown" in the context of health insurance and retirement involves the extent to which known average effects vary across the distribution of workers. As an illustration, the effect of EPRHI on retirement decisions is known to be substantial, which suggests that the effect of EPRHI on workers' welfare is also substantial. What is not known is how the contraction of EPRHI plans will affect the entire distribution of workers. Weller and Wenger's Table 5 shows that the proportion of near-elderly workers who are uninsured varies strikingly by race, education, and income level; and Table 6 shows a similar relationship among near-elderly retirees. Currently, the poor are much more likely to be uninsured than middle-income and wealthy individuals but not much less likely to be covered by EPRHI. If employers continue to shift more of the cost of EPRHI onto employees, it is likely that uninsured rates will rise even further among the poor and that sharp income differences in EPRHI coverage will emerge. Merely looking at average effects will miss the larger issue of who is affected the most. Much future research will likely be devoted to this issue.

Finally, the future impacts of declining access to affordable retiree health insurance depends most crucially on the unknowable: the extent to which the current rapid increase in medical costs will continue into the future. The answers to all the questions posed in Weller and Wenger's chapter are difficult to determine because of this issue, which fundamentally underlies the recent changes in the provision of EPRHI. Will future medical technological advances prove to be cost saving, rather than cost inflating, or will the current double-digit inflation rates continue into the future? The answer to this question, while unfortunately unknowable, will ultimately affect the labor force participation decisions and well-being of future generations of older workers.

References

Bernheim, Douglas, Lorenzo Forni, Jagadeesh Gokhale, and Laurence J. Kotlikoff. 2000. "How Much Should Americans Be Saving For Retirement?" *American Economic Review*. Papers and Proceedings. Vol. 90, no. 2: 288–92.

Blau, David, and Donna B. Gilleskie. 2001. "Retiree Health Insurance and the Labor Force Behavior of Older Men in the 1990s." *Review of Economics and Statistics*. Vol. 83, no. 1: 64–80.

Cutler, David. 2003. "Employee Costs and the Decline in Health Insurance Coverage." In *Frontiers in Health Policy Research, Volume 6*. Cambridge, MA: MIT Press.

Elder, Todd, and Elizabeth Powers. 2003. "SSI for the Aged and the Problem of 'Take-Up.'" Unpublished manuscript. University of Illinois.

Ghilarducci, Teresa, and Sharon Hermes. 2006. "How 401(k)s and the Stock Market Crash Explain Increases in Older Workers' Labor Force Participation Rates." In *Work Options for Older Americans* (this volume).

Gruber, J., and B. Madrian. 2002. "Health Insurance, Labor Supply, and Job Mobility: A Critical Review of the Literature." National Bureau of Economic Research Working Paper 8817. Cambridge, MA: NBER.

Hutchens, Robert. 2003. "The Cornell Study of Employer-Phased Retirement Policies: A Report on Key Findings." Cornell University, School of Industrial and Labor Relations. (October).

Purcell, Patrick. 2006. "Older Workers: Employment and Retirement Trends." In *Work Options for Older Americans* (this volume).

Weller, C. 2003. "Older Workers Staying in the Labor Force." Economic Policy Institute Economic Snapshots. Washington, DC: Economic Policy Institute. (July 16).

Yelowitz, Aaron S. 2000. "Public Policy and Health Insurance Choices of the Elderly: Evidence from the Medicare Buy-In Program." *Journal of Public Economics*. Vol. 78, no. 3: 301–24.

PART 4

INTERNATIONAL POLICY LESSONS
FOR THE UNITED STATES

CHAPTER TEN

International Responses to an Aging Labor Force

Lessons for U.S. Policy

CHARLES JESZECK, TONY DeFRANK,
KATHARINE LEAVITT, JEFFREY S. PETERSEN,
JANICE PETERSON, YUNSIAN TAI,
& HOWARD WIAL

As is the case in developed nations around the world, the aging of the U.S. population will pose challenges to U.S. national economy and retirement income programs. Organizations as diverse as the World Bank, the Organization for Economic Cooperation and Development (OECD), the U.S. Federal Reserve, and others have studied these challenges, which range from the growing fiscal pressures in national pension systems[1] caused by fewer workers having to provide benefits for greater numbers of retirees, to potential economic strains due to shortages of skilled workers as they exit the labor force. Most of these organizations believe that greater labor force participation by older workers can be part of the solution to mitigate the adverse effects of aging populations. Drawing upon the experience of other high-income industrialized nations, we then examine the following questions: (1) How does the United States compare with other high-income nations with regard to recent and projected trends in key demographic and labor force characteristics? (2) How are recently enacted retirement policy reforms in high-income nations expected to affect the labor force participation rate of older workers?[2] and (3) What did these nations learn from enacting policies that may increase the labor force participation of older workers? We conclude with some observations on the implication of these developments for U.S. labor and retirement policy.

To answer these questions, we compiled and analyzed demographic and labor force data from the OECD, the United Nations Population Division, and the International Labour Organization (ILO), highlighting data from the United States and seven other comparison OECD nations. We identified three nations—Japan, Sweden, and the United Kingdom—that had displayed high levels of older worker labor force participation in the past and were implementing policy reforms that continued to emphasize the importance of older worker labor force participation.[3]

AGED WORKERS IN THE UNITED STATES

Aging Trends in the Domestic Labor Market

The number of older workers will grow rapidly into the 2020s. According to the U.S. Bureau of Labor Statistics (BLS), in 2000, 17.6 million persons over age 55, or about one-third of the over-55 population, were in the labor force.[4] BLS estimates that there will be 31.8 million older labor force participants in 2015, an average annual increase of 4.0 percent from 2000. However, this rapid growth is expected to level off by the mid-2020s. BLS estimates that 33.2 million older persons will be in the labor force in 2025, an average annual increase of only 0.4 percent from 2015.

This expected increase is a result of the aging of the baby-boom generation and a general trend in greater labor force participation among older persons. The oldest baby boomers turned 55 years old in 2001, and the youngest will turn 55 in 2019. The percentage of older persons who participate in the labor force has been growing since the mid-1980s, a trend that is expected to continue. Currently, 31 percent of all persons age 55 and older participate in the labor force, a number that is expected to grow to 38 percent by 2015, according to projections by BLS.

This increase in labor force participation among older workers is primarily driven by the growth in the number of older women and their labor force participation rates. Labor force participation rates of women between the ages of 55 and 64 have been steadily increasing from 42 percent in the mid-1980s to 52 percent in 2000. A further increase in the participation rate, to 61 percent, is expected to occur by 2015, according to BLS. The labor force participation rate of women age 65 and older is currently 9 percent. This is up from the low point of just under 7 percent in the mid-1980s but is lower than the 10 percent levels of the 1950s. BLS projects the participation rate in this age group to grow to 10 percent by 2015.[5]

The labor force participation rates of males age 55 and older have been falling for many years, but are projected to increase in the future. Older male labor force participation hit a low point in the mid-1990s that was part of a downward trend that had been occurring for several decades. Since then, the labor force participation rate of males between the ages of 55 and 64 has held steady at approximately 65 percent; BLS projects an increase to 69 percent in 2015. The labor force participation rate of males 65 and older also held steady at about 17 percent during the 1990s and is projected to rise to nearly 20 percent by 2015.[6]

As the number of older workers grows, older workers will also become a larger percentage of all workers. In 1950 and 1960, older workers comprised 17 percent and 18 percent of the labor force, respectively. As the relatively large baby-boom generation entered the workforce between 1960 and 1990, the proportion of older workers fell to 12 percent of the total because the number of workers under age 55 swelled. Older workers now represent 13 percent of the total workforce, and BLS estimates that by 2015 they will be 20 percent of the total workforce.

What Do Aged Workers in the Domestic Labor Market Do?

Older workers hold jobs in a wide range of occupations that are somewhat reflective of the occupations of younger workers (Table 1). Nearly the same percentage of workers in the age categories of 40–54, 55–64, and 65–74 are employed in white-collar occupations (approximately 62 percent). The slight difference in the employment distribution among these age groups is found in blue-collar and service occupations. Nearly 15 percent of workers ages 65 to 74 are employed in service occupations compared to 11 percent of workers ages 40–54. Blue-collar work accounts for 26 percent of employment among workers ages 40–54 and 23 percent of workers ages 65–74. The general shift in the economy away from physically demanding jobs is present among workers of all ages, but it is far more pronounced among older workers as they age.

Workers ages 55–64 constitute a significant proportion of many occupations as they are nearly 13.8 million members (11 percent) of the total workforce (Table 2). The highest numbers of older workers ages 55–64 are in executive or manager occupations (2.4 million, or 12 percent of the total occupation) and professional occupations (2.3 million, or 11 percent of the total occupation). Workers ages 65–74 comprise much smaller percentages of occupations since most persons in this age group have exited the labor force. They constitute less than 4 percent of the major occupational categories with the exception of farming, fishing, and forestry.

Between 2000 and 2008, the number and percentage of workers over age 55 will increase in all major occupational categories, according to our projections.[7] The largest change should occur in white-collar occupations. Among executives and managers, the percentage of workers in this occupation who are over 55 is

Table 1. Comparison of Distribution of Occupations among Selected Age Groups, 2000

| Occupation | Distribution of Occupations | | | |
	Age 30–39	Age 40–54	Age 55–64	Age 65–74
Executive, administrator, manager	15.5%	18.0%	17.2%	16.1%
Sales	10.6	10.7	11.6	15.5
Administrative support	12.8	13.7	13.9	15.4
Professional	15.7	17.4	16.6	14.5
Technicians	3.9	3.4	2.4	0.9
White Collar[a]	58.5	63.2	61.7	62.4
Production, craft, repair	12.5	11.7	9.9	6.5
Farming, forest, fishing	2.1	2.1	2.8	5.8
Transportation	4.6	4.0	4.7	5.6
Machine operator, assembler	6.2	5.6	5.0	3.1
Laborers, handlers	3.7	2.8	2.7	2.2
Blue Collar[b]	29.1	26.2	25.1	23.2
Services[c]	12.5	10.8	13.2	14.5

Source: March 2000 CPS.
Notes: [a]For the purposes of this report we grouped white-collar, blue-collar and service occupations together. White-collar occupations were defined as: executive, administrator, manager; sales; administrative support; professional; and technical.
[b]Blue-collar occupations were defined as: production, craft, repair; farming, forestry, fishing; transportation; machine operator, assembler; laborers, handlers.
[c]Services were separated from blue-collar and white-collar occupations since there was a significant amount of overlap between these two categories within the service category. Services occupations were defined as private household, protective services, food preparation, health services, cleaning and building services, and personal services.

projected to grow from 15 percent to 23 percent. The percentage of the workforce that is over age 55 in professional occupations should also grow substantially, from 14 percent to 19 percent. The smallest change should occur in employment in service occupations as the percentage of the workforce older than age 55 employed in the service sector grows from 13 percent to 14 percent. In line with these major occupational changes, certain specific occupations will increasingly rely on older workers. For example, from 2000 to 2008, the percent of teachers older than age 55 will increase from 13 percent to 19 percent, and the percent of nurses and other health professionals older than age 55 will increase from 12 percent to 18 percent.

Table 2. Occupations of Workers Age 55–64 and 65–74, 2000

	Number of workers		Proportion of all workers in the occupation that are:	
Occupation	Age 55–64	Age 65–74	Age 55–64	Age 65–74
Executive, administrator, manager	2,376,268	553,003	12.0%	2.8%
Professional	2,296,711	498,714	11.3%	2.4%
Administrative support	1,927,958	529,227	10.5%	2.9%
Sales	1,610,556	533,841	11.6%	3.5%
Technicians	331,563	32,138	7.4%	0.7%
Production, craft, repair	1,367,729	223,508	9.4%	1.5%
Machine operator, assembly	695,672	105,748	9.3%	1.4%
Transportation	653,316	193,120	11.9%	3.5%
Farm, forest, fishing	391,057	197,984	12.5%	6.3%
Laborers, handlers	374,737	74,724	7.2%	1.4%
Services	1,829,659	499,328	13.2%	2.9%
All occupations	13,855,226	3,441,334	10.6%	2.6%

Source: March 2000 CPS.

As workers age, their occupational composition moves toward white-collar and service occupations and away from physically demanding occupations. According to our projections, the composition of the older workforce will shift further from blue-collar to white-collar occupations in the near future. Between 2000 and 2008, the proportion of workers ages 55–74 in managerial or administrative, and professional or technical occupations will increase by 2.9 percent and 1.6 percent, respectively, while the proportion in blue-collar and service occupations will decrease.

The change in the occupational composition of older workers into less physically demanding occupations is supported by an analysis of changes in occupations of related age groups, as shown in Table 3. Group I consists of individuals between the ages of 45 and 54 in 1990 and individuals between 55 and 64 in 2000. Group II consists of individuals between the ages of 55 and 64 in 1990 and between 65 and 74 in 2000. In 2000, both groups had fewer individuals in the more physically demanding occupations of production, craft, and repair, machine operation and assembly; they also had a greater number of older workers in white-collar and service occupations in 2000. Part of this shift likely occurred

Table 3. Changes in the Occupational Distribution of Older Workers, 1990–2000

	Group I			Group II		
Occupation	Age 45–54 Year 1990	Age 55–64 Year 2000	Percentage Change	Age 55–64 Year 1990	Age 65–74 Year 2000	Percentage Change
Exec., administrator, manager	15.9%	17.2%	+8.1%	14.4%	16.1%	+11.8%
Professional	14.6	16.6	+13.6	14.0	14.5	+3.6
Administrative support	15.8	13.9	–12.0	15.3	15.4	+1.0
Sales	11.4	11.6	+1.8	12.4	15.5	+25.0
Technicians	2.9	2.4	–17.2	1.8	0.9	–50.0
Production, craft, repair	12.4	9.9	–20.2	11.2	6.5	–42.0
Machine operator, assembly	6.5	5.0	–23.0	6.8	3.1	–51.5
Transportation	4.6	4.7	+2.2	4.5	5.6	+24.4
Farm, forest, fishing	2.4	2.8	+16.7	3.9	5.8	+74.4
Laborers, handlers	2.6	2.7	+3.7	2.7	2.2	–18.5
Services	10.9	13.2	+21.0	13.0	14.5	+11.5
Total	100.0	100.0		100.0	100.0	

Source: March 1990 and 2000 CPS.

because as workers age they can experience health problems that make their jobs more difficult to perform and therefore they choose to move into less physically demanding jobs or out of the labor force entirely.[8]

The shift toward white-collar occupations is partially explained by differences in educational attainment within the baby-boom generation and the cohort preceding it. Fifty-seven percent of persons who are ages 40–54[9] have some college education (28 percent have a college degree), compared to 42 percent of individuals ages 55–74 (21 percent have a college degree). Moreover, only 11 percent of individuals ages 40–54 lack a high school diploma, compared to 22 percent of persons ages 55–74. The greater level of educational attainment among the baby boomers may lead to more employment opportunities as they age. They may have a broader diversification of jobs available to them, compared to the current generation of older workers.

Earnings Trends among the Aged in the United States

Between 1989 and 1999, older workers experienced larger percentage gains in median earnings than younger workers. Adjusted for inflation, workers between the ages of 55 and 64 and workers between 65 and 74 had median earnings increases of 10 percent and 21 percent, respectively, for the ten-year period, compared to increases of 3 percent and 6 percent for workers ages 40–54 and 30–39, respectively. These earnings increases were primarily driven by a greater number of older workers working full time instead of part time (57 percent in 1989 versus 63 percent in 1999) and a movement in the occupational composition toward higher paying white-collar jobs (see Table 3). Average hours worked increased by 5 percent and 9 percent for workers ages 55–64 and 65–74, respectively, compared to a 3 percent increase among workers ages 40–54. Improvements in the economy likely offered older workers the opportunity to move into full-time employment as labor shortages increased the demand for their services. During the economic expansion of the mid- to late-1980s, the unemployment rate declined from 7 percent in 1985 to 5 percent in 1989; by comparison, in the mid- to late-1990s, the unemployment rate declined from 6 percent to 4 percent.

According to our projections, workers between the ages of 55 and 74 will continue to make gains in their earnings that exceed those of their counterparts who fall between the ages of 40 and 54. Currently, workers ages 55–64 and workers ages 65–74 earn 95 percent and 59 percent, respectively, of what workers ages 40–54 earn. We project these numbers to rise to 111 percent and 67 percent, respectively, by 2008. These relative gains are tied to the change in the composition of the older workforce to higher paid white-collar occupations; younger workers' occupational composition is changing to more blue-collar and service occupations.

AGED WORKERS OUTSIDE THE UNITED STATES

Aging Trends in Labor Markets outside the United States

The recent and projected labor force participation and population aging trends for most other high-income nations[10] will be less pronounced in the United States, but the aging of the population will nevertheless pose a challenge to retirement income programs. ILO data for 2000 show that the labor force participation rates for older U.S. workers, though not as high as in previous decades, will be higher than in most other high-income nations. It is expected that, because of higher fertility and immigration rates, the U.S. population will also age more slowly than other high-income nations. However, even though the population of the United States is not aging as rapidly as other countries, the old-age dependency ratio—the number of people over the age of 60 for every one hundred working-age people (ages 15–59)—is projected to rise from 19 in 2000 to 35 in 2050.[11] This near doubling of the old-age dependency ratio will strain the resources of programs that pay for retirement.

Although the labor force participation of workers ages 50–64 is expected to decline in most high-income nations, including the United States, between 2000 and 2010, the United States has and will continue to have higher rates of labor force participation for older workers than most other high-income nations (see Figure 1).[12] In some high-income nations, such as France, Germany, and Italy, about 2 to 4 percent of persons age 65 and older participated in the labor force. In contrast, the labor force participation rate in 2000 among U.S. workers age 65 and over was 10 percent, the second highest labor force participation rate among selected high-income nations and 1.4 percentage points higher than the aggregate for all twenty-three nations the World Bank has designated as high-income (see Figure 1). Labor force participation among U.S. workers ages 50–64 was 66 percent (see Figure 2). This trails only Sweden's (79 percent) and Japan's (73 percent) rates for this age group.

The relatively high rate of labor force participation by older U.S. workers is being sustained by an increasing percentage of older women working. In the United States, as in other high-income nations, labor force participation among older men has declined since 1950 and, for the most part, is projected to continue declining through 2010 (see Figure 3). During that same period, however, labor force participation among older women is projected generally to rise (see Figure 4). In the United States, labor force participation among women ages 50–64 will nearly double from 1950 to 2010, increasing from 31 percent to 58 percent.[13]

The size of the-baby boom generation, rising life expectancy, and declining fertility are expected to contribute to a rising median age in high-income nations. Because the baby-boom generation is large in number, a growing proportion of the populations in high-income nations will be over 60 years old. In the United States, for example, this will be the case for about one-quarter of the population. Moreover, as this generation has grown older, life expectancy has increased in all high-income nations. From 1955 to 2000, life expectancy in the United States increased from 70 to 77 years and is projected to increase to 80 by 2040.

As a result of these trends, the median age of the U.S. population, like that of other high-income nations, is projected to increase steadily in the coming decades, but it will still be lower than that of most high-income nations. Specifically, the median age of the U.S. population in 2030 is expected to be comparable to the current median ages in some high-income nations. For example, the median age of the U.S. population rose from 30 to 36 years from 1980 to 2000 and is projected to increase to 40 in 2030 (see Figure 5). In contrast, the median

Figure 1. Labor Force Participation Rates for Persons Age 65+ in High-Income
Nations, 2000 and 2010

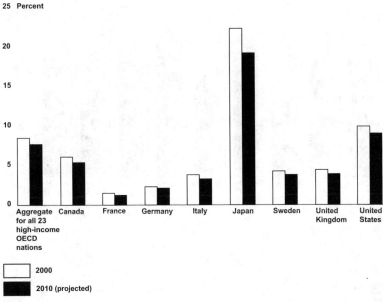

Source: Economically Active Population 1950-2010, 4th Edition, Rev. 2, International Labour Organization, Geneva, 2002.

Figure 2. Labor Force Participation Rates for Persons Age 50 to 64 in High-Income
Nations, 2000 and 2010

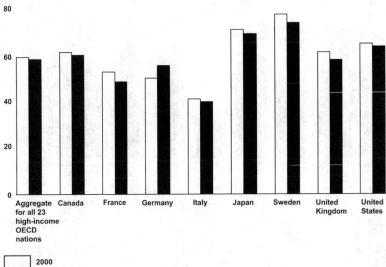

Source: Economically Active Population 1950-2010, 4th Edition, Rev. 2, International Labour Organization, Geneva, 2002.

Figure 3. Labor Force Participation Rates for Men Age 50–64 in High-Income
Nations, 1950–2010

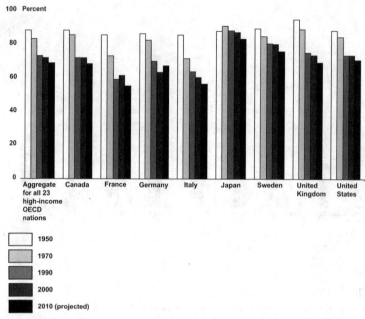

Source: Economically Active Population 1950-2010, 4th Edition, Rev. 2, International Labour Organization, Geneva, 2002.

Figure 4. Labor Force Participation Rates for Women Age 50 to 64 in High-Income
Nations, 1950–2010

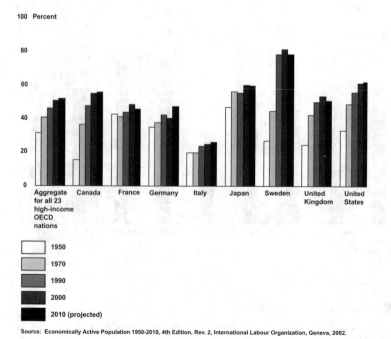

Source: Economically Active Population 1950-2010, 4th Edition, Rev. 2, International Labour Organization, Geneva, 2002.

Figure 5. Median Age of the Population in High-Income Nations, 1980–2050

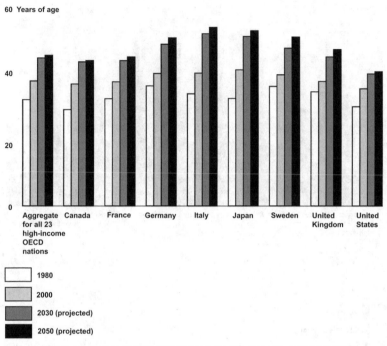

Source: Economically Active Population 1950-2010, 4th Edition, Rev. 2, International Labour Organization, Geneva, 2002.
Prospects: 2000 Revision and World Urbanization Prospects: 2001 Revision.

age of the populations of high-income countries, as designated by the World Bank, was 38 in 2000 and is projected to rise to 45 in 2030. Germany, Italy, Japan, and Sweden have the current and projected oldest populations, with median ages ranging from 40 to 41 in 2000 and projected increases to 51 to 54 in 2050.

Two factors will slow the trend toward an older population in the United States compared with most other OECD nations: fertility and immigration rates. Although fertility rates in high-income nations have declined overall since 1980, during the same time they have increased from 1.8 to 2.0 in the United States. The United States also has an immigration rate more than four times as high as Sweden and Japan, almost three times as high as the United Kingdom, and higher than that of most high-income nations.[14]

The consequences of these demographic trends are most evident in the old-age dependency ratio. In most high-income nations, this ratio has been rising since World War II and is projected to grow at a faster rate in the next half century (see Figure 6). The ratio in the United States is relatively low compared with other

Figure 6. Elderly Dependency Ratio in High-Income Nations, 1950–2050

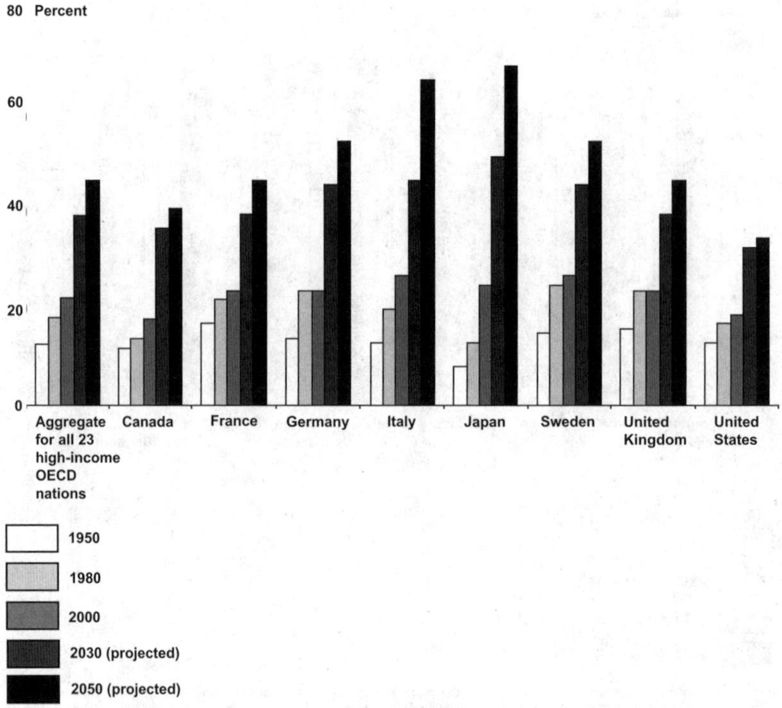

Source: Population Division of the Department of Economic and Social Affairs of the United Nations Secretariat, World Population Prospects: 2000 Revision and World Urbanization Prospects: 2001 Revision.

high-income nations. For every one hundred people of working age (15–59) in the United States, approximately 19 people were in or nearing retirement age (60 or above) in 2000 compared with a ratio of 22 for the aggregate of the twenty-three nations the World Bank has designated as high-income. This difference is projected to grow. By 2050, this ratio for all high-income countries is projected to be 47, in comparison with 35 for the United States. Even though the United States ratio will be smaller than that of other high-income nations in 2050, it represents an increase of over 75 percent from the 2000 ratio.

Attempts to Increase Work Opportunities for the Aged outside the United States

Recently enacted retirement-policy reforms in the United Kingdom, Japan, and Sweden are expected to lead to higher labor force participation of older workers. Reforms adjusting benefits in the national pension systems of each of these nations provide incentives for older workers to extend their working lives. National and employer-provided pension reforms that introduce defined contribution (DC) features that do not link benefits to a specific age are also expected to encourage greater labor force participation of older workers. Other reforms that seek to limit the use of disability benefits as a route to early retirement will also influence older worker labor force participation. Acknowledging that improving the employment opportunities of older workers is an important consideration, each of these nations is studying or has enacted reforms that address the issues of older workers' employment more generally. Such reforms include loosening or eliminating mandatory retirement age standards, encouraging the elimination of age discrimination in employment, improving older worker training, providing employment earnings incentives, and exploring quality-of-work-life issues such as the flexibility of work arrangements.

Reforms in the United Kingdom, Japan, and Sweden that increase the age at which workers are eligible for benefits or allow flexibility in when and how pension benefits can be taken are some of the policy changes that may encourage older workers to stay in the workforce. The United Kingdom will phase in an increase in the age at which women become eligible for national pension benefits so that, beginning in 2020, men and women will no longer be able to draw benefits before age 65. Japan has also enacted reforms that will gradually increase the full eligibility age for its earnings-based national pension system. In Japan, by 2025 for men and 2030 for women, the earliest age when this pension can be claimed will have risen from 60 to 65. Rather than increasing the age for benefit eligibility, pension reforms in Sweden allow older workers to take a full or partial national pension (i.e., one-fourth, one-half, or three-fourths of a full pension) at age 61 or later with no upper age limit and continue working.[15] This flexibility may make it easier to retire gradually with a mix of pension benefits and earnings.

Pension reforms that change benefit calculations so they reward continued work or discourage early retirement may also promote continued labor force participation by older workers. Sweden changed its benefit calculation to reward those who work longer. Under the new pension system in Sweden,[16] pensions are based on lifetime earnings, instead of the highest fifteen out of thirty years of earnings as they were under the old system. The United Kingdom adjusted its benefit calculation formula to increase the reward for those who defer drawing benefits from the national pension system. For example, by 2010, individuals who defer drawing their pension benefits will receive benefits that are 10.4 percent, rather than 7.5 percent, larger for each year deferred.[17] In Japan, reforms have changed how pensions are calculated, reducing the level of benefits for future retirees through lower accrual rates. The expected effect of these changes is a 20-percent reduction in lifetime benefits by 2020, thereby making early retirement less affordable.

Finally, reforms in Sweden and the United Kingdom, in changing how pension benefits are indexed, may discourage early retirement. The new pension system in Sweden indexes pension benefits to life expectancy.[18] With increasing life expectancy, different generations of individuals with similar work and earnings histories will have to work longer to maintain a comparable standard of living in retirement. This benefit adjustment provides incentives for increased labor force participation by requiring individuals to bear the cost of increased life expectancy, either through additional work or lower benefits. The United Kingdom also revised the index it used to adjust benefits in the portion of its pension that provides flat-rate benefits. Prior to the reform, the United Kingdom adjusted benefits using either the higher of increases in average prices or average wages as an index. Now the United Kingdom uses only average price increases.[19] Since prices tend to increase more slowly than wages, this reform has effectively reduced benefits relative to earnings.[20]

Each of the nations we studied implemented reforms that included DC features in their national and employer-provided pension systems, although this shift was more pronounced in Sweden and the United Kingdom than in Japan. DC pensions are more retirement-age neutral than traditional defined benefit (DB) pension plans. As part of its recent national pension reform, Sweden instituted a pay-as-you-go pension system with DC features, including among other things a fixed contribution rate and notional individual accounts (the "notional defined contribution pension").[21] The new Swedish pension system also includes a smaller, funded DC plan with an account for each individual worker (the premium pension). Reforms introduced in the United Kingdom in 1988 and 2001 permitted individuals to opt out of part of the national pension plan by participating either in employer-sponsored DC plans or defined contribution individual pension plans called "personal pensions."[22] To participate in the individual plans, workers obtain an account from a financial institution and make contributions into their account or are provided access to a pension by their employer.[23] Japan implemented legislation permitting employer-provided and personal DC pension plans in 2002.[24]

In Sweden and the United Kingdom, the inclusion of DC features in the national pension system has prompted complementary changes among the employer-provided pensions. In Sweden, three of the four major employer-provided pension plans converted from DB plans to pure DC plans or plans with a mix of both features following the national pension reform.[25] In the United Kingdom, many employers have closed their DB plans to new workers and replaced them with DC plans. For Japan, where DC pensions were only recently introduced, there is currently little data on the number of individual or employer-provided plans being formed or on the degree to which employers are substituting DC plans for existing DB plans.

The inclusion of DC features in national and employer-provided pension systems is expected to encourage greater labor force participation of older workers. Because workers will have a greater responsibility for ensuring retirement through contributions and the returns they can earn on them, it will be in their best interest to make contributions for as long as they can. In addition, because DC plans often have greater portability than DB plans, older workers may have a greater ability to shift to jobs that suit their leisure and health needs rather than retiring.[26]

Both Sweden and the United Kingdom, where disability insurance has traditionally been an avenue to early withdrawal from the labor force, have introduced reforms in recent years that will tighten eligibility for disability benefits.[27] In efforts to reduce the amount of early retirement financed through disability pensions, throughout the last decade Sweden has implemented successive reforms to tighten the eligibility requirements for disability insurance. This has included eliminating the ability of older workers to take a disability pension solely on the basis of long-term unemployment or a combination of unemployment and medical reasons. Medical reasons now provide the only valid criteria for granting a disability pension in Sweden. As part of its efforts, the United Kingdom, since the mid-1990s, has tightened eligibility requirements, reduced paid benefits, and provided more support for returning to the workforce after an absence. For example, the government now reviews claims of incapacity to work every three years, compared to the previous policy of not reviewing claims after the initial application; reduces or offsets disability benefits if the recipient also receives an employer-provided pension over a certain minimum level; provides services such as job-search assistance to the disabled as a way to enable their return to work; and will test a policy allowing recipients to keep a portion of their wages if they return to work.[28]

Each nation we studied has enacted, or is considering, policies that address barriers to older workers' continued employment, such as mandatory retirement and age discrimination. In conjunction with its national pension reform, Sweden has already passed legislation giving employees the right to remain in employment until the age of 67, prohibiting the widespread practice of collective bargaining agreements prescribing mandatory retirement at age 65.[29] As members of the European Union, both Sweden and the United Kingdom must legislatively prohibit employment discrimination based on age by 2006. It is unknown how the European Union requirement will affect mandatory retirement ages in specific industries or occupations in the United Kingdom.

In the absence of legislation, both the United Kingdom and Japan have encouraged employers to end age discrimination voluntarily. The United Kingdom, for example, has publicized the benefits of an age-diverse workforce and issued best practices for eliminating age discrimination. Like the United Kingdom, Japan has also encouraged firms to modify employment practices and retirement policies voluntarily. The government has programs that subsidize the wages of workers who take jobs at reduced pay after mandatory retirement and subsidizes companies that modify their employment practices to accommodate older workers.

Each of the nations we studied has also made some efforts to provide older workers with access to training, job-search assistance, and workplace flexibility. In the United Kingdom, for example, one government program provides job-search assistance for people age 50 and older when they have been out of work six months or longer and also offers training opportunities and a wage enhancement.[30] As part of its efforts, Japan has employment assistance centers (called "Silver Human Resource Centers") that provide older workers with temporary jobs or volunteer opportunities. The Japanese government has also promoted a program to match older workers with suitable employers. In Sweden, efforts include the creation of a commission to explore policies to promote increased flexibility in working arrangements, such as granting older people a legal right to work part time and adjusting the public financing of education to promote skill development among older workers.

Institutional Reforms outside the United States that Encourage the Aged to Work

The experiences of other nations suggest that the scope and comprehensiveness of reforms, the transparency and availability of information, and the strength of the economy play important roles in encouraging labor force participation by older workers. According to government officials in Japan, Sweden, and the United Kingdom, reforms have a better chance of succeeding if they are comprehensive and complementary. In addition, they said that education and information are important for helping workers understand what the reforms will mean for their retirement income. Officials also agreed that a strong economy was important for success.

Officials from each of the nations we studied said that the success of national pension reform, including those elements that influence older workers' labor force participation, depends, in part, on the scope and purpose of the reforms.

Officials from all three nations noted that reforms are most successful when they are comprehensive in scope. Both Sweden and the United Kingdom, for example, in reforming their pension systems also made changes to both their disability insurance programs and their labor market policies. Some officials also stressed that reforms should be designed so that the intent of a particular reform is not thwarted by countervailing policies in other areas. For example, Swedish pension experts and other officials have acknowledged that the continued presence of mandatory retirement ages in collective bargaining agreements and labor regulations can work at cross-purposes with features in the new national pension system that now relate benefit levels to retiree life expectancy and that essentially have no upper retirement age. They noted that to increase the effectiveness of the work incentives in their national pension reforms, these impediments will have to be resolved, and complementary reform policies that foster alternative work arrangements and quality-of-work-life issues generally will need to be established. Other nations also acknowledged the importance of complementary reforms. Japan has supplemented its national pension reforms with wage subsidies to encourage older employees to continue to work. Japan and the United Kingdom also support their national pension reforms by committing additional resources to organizations and services that provide job-search assistance to older workers.

Officials in each nation that we studied emphasized that access to information and public education about how the reforms will affect retirement income would also be needed if the reforms were to have their intended effect. There is concern in these nations that many workers are currently unaware of the implications of the reforms. For example, surveys conducted by the Swedish government and advocates for senior citizens indicate that many individuals do not yet have a detailed understanding of the new pension system. Similarly, U.K. government officials expressed concern that their citizens could have comparable difficulties understanding recent pension reforms. To help their citizens understand that they may need to work longer or save more in order to ensure an adequate retirement income, each of the nations we studied has taken steps to educate workers. In Sweden, the government has launched several large information campaigns since the new pension system's implementation. In addition, participants receive annual statements of their account balances in both the notional DC and premium pensions. To help educate its workers, the U.K. government has created a pension forecast tool that will present workers with estimates of pension income from both government and nongovernment sources. In Japan, because DC pensions are very new and offer both advantages and disadvantages to participants, employers are required to provide information to employees about DC plan features and management.

In addition to the importance of information and education, government officials and pension experts agreed that a strong national economy is necessary for the success of pension and labor market reforms that may contribute to higher labor force participation by older workers. A strong economy eases the implementation of pension reform by offering increased employment opportunities for older workers. High unemployment and low economic growth will limit older workers' ability to remain employed, forcing them into complete retirement. Experts we spoke with believe that the low growth of the Japanese economy during the last decade has been a factor limiting the scope of pension and labor market reform, for example, in the area of mandatory retirement ages. Fiscal constraints also preclude more fundamental reform of pension-system financing and structure. In contrast, the currently strong U.K. economy acts as an incentive for employers to retain their older workers and there will likely be an increased need for older workers in the long term, particularly as the workforce ages between now and 2020. The current tight labor market also makes it easier for job-search assistance programs to find jobs for clients.

Lessons to Be Learned by the United States from these Global Responses

Adverse financial and/or demographic projections have led to efforts to reform national pension systems in each of the nations we studied. Yet despite their obvious differences, officials from each of the three nations emphasized the importance of increasing the labor force participation of older workers in their own nation's reform efforts. Encouraging workers to stay in the labor force longer can help alleviate the fiscal and budgetary stress induced by rising national pension expenditures and can potentially enhance economic growth. In those nations where national pension reform has included benefit reductions, working longer might also help to mitigate serious reductions in retiree living standards.

In some ways, the United States is ahead of many nations in fostering the labor force participation of older workers. Among private U.S. employers, for example, the 25-year-old shift away from traditional DB retirement plans toward plans with DC features continues. This shift not only includes an increase in the number of pure DC plans, such as 401(k) plans, it also includes a conversion of traditional DB plans to hybrids with DC features.[31] Even within the U.S. public sector, where the dominant retirement plan continues to have a traditional DB structure, employers have responded to current or incipient labor shortages among teachers and public safety workers by creating incentives within these retirement plans for near retirees to extend their employment.[32] The United States is also increasing its normal retirement age for Social Security benefits to 67, an age higher than in many other nations. The U.S. has already forged ahead in labor-market flexibility, leading the world in prohibiting age discrimination and mandatory retirement ages and in its public discussion of bridge employment, phased retirement, and other alternative employment arrangements.

However, the United States still has room to strengthen its policies affecting older workers and has much to learn from others. A key finding of our work is that the scope and comprehensiveness of the reforms themselves play important roles in encouraging labor force participation by older workers. At this time, there has been little effort to develop comprehensive national employment policy for older workers in the United States, and what has been done has largely focused on ensuring employer flexibility in hiring older workers by minimizing any regulatory burden or potential for litigation.[33]

While employer flexibility is clearly an important issue on its own, current policy efforts have failed to focus on other issues central to the living standards and quality of life of older workers. First, a major impetus for the Social Security program itself and indeed a major policy consideration in its own right would be to minimize the extent to which policies seeking to foster increased elderly and near-elderly labor force participation result in additional employment that becomes necessary for many persons simply to avoid poverty or near-poverty standards of living in retirement. Yet isolated or narrowly focused policies to foster work that fail to recognize their interaction with adverse trends in other sources of retirement income could result in precisely the generation of such activity.

The trends in sources of retirement income other than work suggest that the potential for the growth of employment among some older persons to avoid a poverty level of income in retirement is significant. For example, economists have lamented the United States's chronically low savings rates, including saving for retirement. Regarding pensions, only about 50 percent of the labor force is covered by any pension plan at any one time. In addition, the decline in equity prices and the reduced willingness of some employers to continue to match employee contributions has resulted not only in a diminution of many 401(k) accounts but also in the reduced participation of workers in those DC plans.[34] Finally, the backstop of retirement income, the Social Security program, already has a much lower replacement rate than the national pension systems of many other nations and is facing insolvency during the next several decades. The extent to which current efforts to reform Social Security result in benefit reductions could create additional pressures on retirement incomes. All of these developments imply that policies to encourage the labor force participation of older workers, if not carefully crafted, could unduly sharpen the tradeoff between work and an adequate retirement income: for too many of our nation's elderly, work may become more of a necessity to avoid poverty rather than a choice.

A balanced national policy on older worker labor force participation would also be sensitive to any distributional consequences that could occur within the unique context of U.S. history, society, and institutions. For example, reforms that more closely link benefits to life expectancy, as have been suggested and implemented in other nations, could have significantly different and more adverse distributional effects in the United States than in these other nations. American subpopulations with lower average life expectancies, such as African Americans, would be more adversely affected by such policy changes since they would collect benefits for shorter time periods relative to other demographic groups. African American men, for example, have shorter life expectancies at birth and at age 65 compared to men of other ethnicities.

The focus on extending the labor force participation of older workers internationally has also led to reconsideration by other nations of changing the traditional binary definition of retirement where a person is either considered to be working or retired to a definition that is more flexible or continuous in nature. The long-term trend of improved health and longevity of older persons throughout the high-income nations now permits a range of options beyond the tradeoff between traditional full-time career employment and complete out-of-the-workforce retirement and also makes the notion of life-long learning an increasingly realistic possibility for a much greater number of workers. These developments also have implications for reforming existing U.S. employment programs in ways to more effectively encourage the elderly to work. On one hand, the U.S. labor market, with its considerable flexibility in terms of part-time employment, scheduling, and other alternative employment arrangements, is very congenial to these concepts.[35] Yet, on the other hand, some basic U.S. employment programs remain anchored on the past notion of a binary retirement choice. For example, today, few state Unemployment Insurance (UI) programs have implemented work-sharing benefit provisions or pay benefits to claimants looking exclusively for part-time work.[36] In addition, key national job-training programs have built-in performance incentives that discourage the training and job placement of older workers.[37]

Finally, consideration must be given to the effects of policies to foster older labor force participation on the level of community service and unpaid family work performed to assist the household members who might need care. Community service remains a strongly rooted tradition in the United States, particularly among senior citizens. It is unclear what the effects on cities and towns, nonprofit organizations and other entities would be if the elderly substituted paid market work for community service on a significant level. To the extent that policies to foster older workers to the point that their labor force participation contains an "involuntary" element, the tension between providing "unpaid care" and ensuring an adequate standard of living will only be intensified. Given the employer community's historical opposition to mandated family- and elder-care leave at the federal and state levels, it is likely that legislative efforts to balance these two competing needs would be controversial and difficult to negotiate. Yet the division between paid and unpaid work, between community or family and the market, will forcefully shape future American society. The challenge that the United States now faces is to develop policies to extend the worklives of older employees, policies that recognize the demographic and fiscal realities of the twenty-first century, respond to the imperatives of economic growth, and ensure employers a supply of experienced skilled labor, without requiring "Senior America" to work simply to evade the specter of twilight poverty.

Notes

1. For this paper, the term "national pension system" will be used when referring to "universal" government programs that provide retirement benefits to persons in nations other than the United States.

2. In this chapter, we define older workers as persons 50 years of age and older. In some cases, because of the limitations of available data, we analyze subgroups of older workers, for example, those 55 years of age and older.

3. Besides the United States, the seven other nations highlighted are the other six of the "G-7"—Canada, France, Germany, Italy, Japan, and the United Kingdom—and Sweden. For more details on our scope and methodology and on the national and occupational pension systems and labor market policies of the three nations we studied (Sweden, Japan, and the United Kingdom), see *Older Workers: Policies of Other Nations to Increase Labor Force Participation,* (GAO-03-307, February 13, 2003).

4. The labor force consists of persons who are employed and unemployed persons who are actively seeking work.

5. The increases in the labor force participation rates of older women have been primarily attributable to the aging of women who have been working since earlier ages.

6. For opposing viewpoints on this trend see D. Costa, "Has the Trend toward Earlier Retirement Reversed?" and J. Quinn, "Has the Early Retirement Trend Reversed?" Costa questions the prediction that workers will work later into life, citing the increasing attractiveness of, and ability to pay for, retirement. Quinn counters with evidence that earlier retirement has come to an end due to a new attitude toward working later in life. Both

papers prepared for presentation at the First Annual Joint Conference for Retirement Research Consortium "New Developments in Retirement Research," May 20–21, 1999.

7. We used a methodology developed by BLS to make our projections. We estimate the replacement needs for occupations based upon five-year age cohorts from 1988–1993 and 1994–1998 and project forward to 2003 and 2008. Thus, the accuracy of these projections relies on recent historical trends continuing into the future.

8. The percent changes in the distribution of occupations for all workers from 1990 to 2000 was as follows: managers and administrators (12.3–14.6 percent); professional (13.0–15.1 percent); technical (3.2–3.3 percent); sales (12.4–12.2 percent); administrative support (15.7–13.8 percent); services (13.3–13.9 percent); production, craft, and repair (11.8–10.7 percent); machine operation and assembly (6.8–5.6 percent); transportation (4.2–4.1 percent); labor and handling (4.5–4.2 percent); agriculture, forest, and fishing (2.8–2.5 percent).

9. The baby-boom generation actually encompasses persons ages 36–54 since we are using data from 2000. However, the age group was presented as 40–54 for consistency with other numbers in the report.

10. "High-income nations" are the twenty-three nations that the World Bank has designated as "high income." This group includes the eight comparison nations highlighted earlier, as well as Australia, Austria, Belgium, Denmark, Finland, Greece, Iceland, Ireland, Luxembourg, the Netherlands, New Zealand, Norway, Portugal, Spain, and Switzerland.

11. In the United States, the old-age dependency ratio is typically measured by comparing persons over age 65 with persons 16–64. We presented data for persons over age 60 compared with persons age 15–59 because ILO makes these data available in these age ranges.

12. We present ILO data because they are the only comparable available data on the high-income nations. However, ILO projections differ from those conducted by BLS that actually project increases in the labor force participation for older U.S. workers between 2000 and 2025. However, in both cases, the labor force participation for older workers in the United States remains comparatively higher than many, though not all, other high-income nations.

13. Sweden has experienced the most dramatic rise in labor force participation among women ages 50–64, with rates tripling from 25 percent to 76 percent since 1950.

14. The net immigration rate in the United States from 1995 to 2000 was 4.53 persons per 1,000 residents. Source: *World Population Prospects: The 2000 Revision,* United Nations Population Division. Found in S. Nyce and S. Schieber. 2001. "Our Assumptions about Aging and What We Are Doing about It," draft manuscript.

15. For example, if a worker "retires" from his or her full-time job at age 61 and continues to work part-time while drawing 50 percent of his or her national pension, these earnings will continue to add to the value of his or her pension account. When the worker retires completely, the pension will be recalculated to take into account these additional earnings. See *Older Workers: Policies of Other Nations to Increase Labor Force Participation,* (GAO-03-307, February 13, 2003).

16. Sweden switched from a traditional pay-as-you-go defined benefit plan to a system that combines a fully funded defined contribution plan and a pay-as-you-go "notional" defined contribution plan with automatic adjustments to preserve financial stability. The notional defined contribution is the larger of the two plans, accounting for 86 percent of all national pension contributions. See GAO-03-307, 13 February 2003.

17. Experts we spoke with disagreed about the effectiveness of this reform in increasing older worker labor force participation. The government has considered changes to this reform. For example, it is considering allowing people a choice between taking the benefit increase as a lump-sum payment or as increases in each benefit payment. It is also considering pushing up the implementation of the benefit increase so that it will take effect in 2006 rather than 2010. This could increase the incentive for older worker labor force participation.

18. For example, workers' pensions in the notional defined contribution plan are calculated by dividing their pension account (the value of their accumulated pension rights) by an annuity factor. Estimated cohort life expectancy is the key element in the determination of the annuity factor, which is also determined by the "norm" real rate of return (a 1.6-percent increase in average real wages) and age at retirement. A higher average life expectancy for a cohort will increase the size of the annuity factor for that cohort compared to preceding cohorts. Consequently, individuals in later cohorts retiring at the same age and with the same pension account as those in earlier cohorts will receive a lower pension. See GAO 03-307.

19. The U.K. government announced in December 2002 that it will increase flat-rate pension benefits in future years by at least 2.5 percent per year, even if this is larger than the increase in average prices.

20. This change was introduced in 1980. Experts believe that the flat-rate basic portion of the U.K. national pension, which currently amounts to about 15 percent of average male earnings, will drop to 7 percent of average male earnings by 2050. However, means-tested benefits indexed to earnings growth are available to low-income individuals starting at age 60. See GAO 03-307.

21. This plan is called a notional defined contribution plan because pension rights (i.e., claims on future pension income), not actual financial assets, are credited to the individual's notional accounts. In the U.S. context, this component of the Swedish national pension could be considered analogous to a "cash balance" plan, a type of DB plan.

22. Prior to 1988, the United Kingdom's national pension system had allowed individuals to opt out of the earnings-related part of the national pension system for employer-provided DB plans only. See GAO-03-307, 13 February 2003.

23. Workers opting out of the earnings-related portion of the national pension system for individual pension plans continue to pay contributions to the national pension system, but the government transfers a portion of contributions to the workers' individual pension accounts to compensate them for foregoing earnings-related national pension benefits. See GAO-03-307, 13 February 2003.

24. The law specifies the earliest age of withdrawal of pension funds from these DC plans as 60 if enrolled for ten or more years, or 65 if enrolled for less than ten years.

25. Employer-provided pensions, which are negotiated through collective bargaining, cover close to 90 percent of Swedish workers. See GAO-03-307, 13 February 2003.

26. DC plans likely increased the portability of benefits for many United Kingdom workers previously covered by DB plans. In Sweden, workers' pension benefits were more portable under the old employer-provided pension plans than under the DB plans in many other nations. However, some Swedish pension experts noted that because pension premiums are generally higher for older workers, and a worker's final employer has typically been responsible for paying his or her pension benefits, it has been difficult for older workers to change jobs later in their careers. These experts argued that with the recent negotiated pension plan changes the cost burden on the final employer is reduced.

27. In contrast, statistics provided by a Japanese official indicate that workers have not used disability insurance as a major means of withdrawing early from the labor force.

28. The policy that will allow disability recipients to keep a portion of their wages if they return to work is subject to means testing and a one-year time limit.

29. It should be noted that reaching an agreement on changing the mandatory retirement age in Sweden was difficult, and the legislation that implemented this change has been controversial.

30. All clients are eligible to receive services to help them find employment; clients are also eligible for up to £60 per week wage enhancement if they meet certain criteria. See GAO-03-307.

31. See *Private Pensions: Implications of Conversions to Cash Balance Plans* (GAO/HEHS-00-185) September 29, 2000, and *Cash Balance Plans: Implications for Retirement Income* (GAO/HEHS-00-207) September 29, 2000.

32. For example, some state and local government employers have implemented Deferred Retirement Option Plan (DROP) features into their DB plans. DROPs allow a pension participant, at an eligible retirement age, to have pension benefits start even though he or she continues to work. Under a DROP, instead of paying a pension benefit directly to the participant, it is placed into a separate account in the individual's name. When the participant retires, he or she receives the accumulated balance with interest in addition to the ongoing pension benefit. DROP features are very common in plans covering teachers, firefighters, and law enforcement personnel. See *Older Workers: Demographic Trends Pose Challenges for Workers and Employers* (GAO-02-85), 16 November 2001.

33. For example, the Department of Labor's ERISA (Employee Retirement Income Security Act) Advisory Council, after receiving testimony from employers and other interested parties on federal policy with regard to phased retirement and the older worker issue, made recommendations to the Secretary of Labor, most of which had this general orientation. See GAO-02-85.

34. See "Bailing Out of the Retirement Plan," *The Wall Street Journal*, March 11, 2003, p. D1.

35. It is interesting to note that in actuality, few U.S. employers have so far focused on making such options available to their older employees on any widespread basis. This is partially because few private employers have yet felt any necessity to do so and there are other regulatory obstacles that might discourage such employers from initiating such efforts. For a discussion of these and related issues, see GAO-02-85.

36. The Unemployment Insurance program provides income to workers who are unemployed through no fault of their own and are actively seeking work. Work sharing is a plan under which an employer, faced with the need for layoffs because of reduced workload, might spread out the hours of work required to produce a given product of goods or services, avoiding layoffs by reducing the number of regularly scheduled hours of work for all employees in an establishment. UI benefits would be payable to workers for the hours of work lost by this action, as a proportion of the benefit amount for a full week of unemployment. As of August 2002, eighteen states had work-sharing features in their UI programs. See http://ows.doleta.gov/unemploy/uilawstable.asp.

37. For example of such incentives in training programs under the Workforce Investment Act, see *Older Workers: Employment Assistance Focuses on Subsidized Jobs and Job Search, but Revised Performance Measures Could Improve Access to Other Services,* GAO-03-350, January 24, 2003. The Workforce Investment Act provides job search assistance and training to adults, youth, and individuals who have lost their jobs because of layoffs or plant closings. It is the largest federal employment-training program.

REFERENCES

Costa, D. 1999. *"Has the Trend toward Earlier Retirement Reversed?"* Paper prepared for presentation at the First Annual Joint Conference for Retirement Research Consortium "New Developments in Retirement Research" (May 20–21).

Diamond, P., and J. Gruber. 1999. "Social Security and Retirement in the United States." *Social Security and Retirement around the World.* Chicago: University of Chicago Press.

Eschtruth, Andrew D., and Jonathan Gemus. 2002. *Are Older Workers Responding to the Bear Market?* JTF No. 5. Boston: Center for Retirement Research, Boston College (September).

Nyce, Steven A., and Sylvester J. Schieber. 2001. "World Population Prospects: The 2000 Revision. United Nations Population Division." *The Economic Implications of Aging Societies: The Costs of Living Happily Ever After.* Cambridge University Press.

Quinn, J. 1999. *"Has the Early Retirement Trend Reversed?"* Paper prepared for presentation at the First Annual Joint Conference for Retirement Research Consortium "New Developments in Retirement Research" (May 20–21).

U.S. Government Accountability Office. 2003. *Older Workers: Policies of Other Nations to Increase Labor Force Participation.* Washington, DC: GAO-03-307 (February 13).

U.S. Government Accountability Office. 2003. *Older Workers: Employment Assistance Focuses on Subsidized Jobs and Job Search, but Revised Performance Measures Could Improve Access to Other Services.* Washington, DC: GAO-03-350 (January 24).

U.S. Government Accountability Office. 2001. *Older Workers: Demographic Trends Pose Challenges for Workers and Employers.* Washington, DC: GAO-02-85 (November 16).

U.S. Government Accountability Office. 2001. *Retiree Health Insurance: Gaps in Coverage and Availability.* Washington, DC: GAO-02-178T (November 1).

U.S. Government Accountability Office. 2000. *Private Pensions: Implications of Conversions to Cash Balance Plans.* Washington, DC: GAO/HEHS-00-185 (September 29).

U.S. Government Accountability Office. 2000. *Cash Balance Plans: Implications for Retirement Income.* Washington, DC: GAO/HEHS-00-207 (September 29).

U.S. Government Accountability Office. 2000. *Pension Plans: Characteristics of Persons in the Labor Force without Pension Coverage.* Washington, DC: GAO/HEHS00131 (August 22).

———. 2003. "Bailing Out of the Retirement Plan." *The Wall Street Journal.* (March 11): D1.

Comments on "International Responses to an Aging Labor Force: Lessons for U.S. Policy"

SARA E. RIX

For the economy as a whole the increase in participation and employment

rates of older workers [is] crucial for using the full potential of labour supply

to sustain economic growth, tax revenues and social protection systems, in-

cluding adequate pensions, in the face of expected reductions in the popula-

tion of working age.

—European Commission 2004, 3

Advocates for the aged in the United States have long looked with envy across the Atlantic to public pension systems that have provided millions of European workers with the opportunity to retire in comfort at early ages, an opportunity for the most part taken advantage of by those workers. In the pre-accession countries of the European Union (EU)[1] as a whole, for example, the average age of exit from the labor force is about 61. As of 2005, the employment-to-population ratio for the 55–64 age group hovered around 44, in contrast to almost 61 for the United States (European Commission 2006, 173; U.S. Department of Labor

2006, 205). In only a handful of EU countries does the labor force participation rate for the 65-and-over population exceed that of the United States, which stood at 15.1 percent in 2005. Indeed, hardly anyone in France or Germany remains in the labor force after the age of 65. That, however, may be set to change.

Concern about the sustainability of pension systems, viewed by some as a fiscal time bomb, is mounting in many European countries as well as in Japan, as low fertility, rising life expectancy, and, in Europe, often very early retirement cause the ratio of workers to retirees to shrink. Generous retirement benefits are being whittled away as governments seek to contain the escalating costs of supporting their aging populations. Many policymakers are looking to higher employment rates and delayed retirement as a means of shoring up their public pension systems. Although the affected parties, namely workers, are not always in accord, halting or perhaps reversing the trend toward early retirement is broadly regarded by policymakers as a partial solution to the so-called pension crisis and a desirable end in itself. Getting older people to work and keeping them at it longer have been placed high on the agenda of the European Union. Expanding employment opportunities for older persons is a major issue in Japan as well.

A feature distinguishing Europe and Japan from the United States is the extent and nature of the debate on older workers and where debate is occurring. Significantly more attention is being paid to older worker issues in Europe and Japan than in the United States, and discussion abroad about what to do about those workers occurs far more frequently at the government level, with the active involvement of the social partners—labor and employer associations. In contrast, in the United States, where the demographic picture is more favorable than it is in Europe or Japan and where the need for Social Security reform is perceived as less urgent, older worker employment has not been singled out for much congressional attention. Rather, efforts to expand employment opportunities for older workers have tended to rest largely with organizations for older persons and other older worker advocates, whose efforts have been buttressed by a sizable body of scholarly research and policy analyses on the aging workforce.[2]

Countries in Europe, along with Japan, have implemented various reforms designed to keep people working longer. These include raising the early and/or full retirement ages, increasing the contribution period required to qualify for full pension benefits, linking pension benefits to increases in life expectancy, and introducing defined contribution plans that reward participants for working longer. In addition, the European Council[3] has set ambitious employment goals for the European Union. Agreed to in 2001, its Stockholm target calls for increasing the employment level of persons ages 55–64 to 50 percent by 2010, while the 2002 Barcelona target seeks a progressive increase of about five years in the average age of labor force withdrawal by 2010. In addition, the member states of the EU have until 2006 to enact legislation banning age discrimination.

Six pre-accession member states—Denmark, Finland, Ireland, Portugal, Sweden, and the United Kingdom—had labor force participation rates above the 50 percent threshold of the Stockholm target as of 2005. At just over 69 percent (European Commission 2006), the rate for Sweden is, in fact, substantially above the target, but a number of countries have employment rates of less than 40 percent for the 55–64 age group.

According to the European Commission (2003), for the 50-percent Stockholm target to be realized by 2010, employment in the 55–64 age group must increase by about 7.5 million over what it was in 2001. Meeting the Barcelona target of a five-year increase in the effective retirement age would require an increase in employment of 7 to 9 million, or some 900,000 additional workers per year. This compares to recent annual employment increases in the neighborhood of 250,000.

Achieving these goals over such a short period of time seems problematic. Nonetheless, at least one country, the Netherlands, has experienced a 10-percentage point increase in the labor force participation rate of persons ages 55–64 over a comparable number of years, 1991–2000 (International Labor Office, 2006). While this dramatic increase warrants scrutiny, the Netherlands is still far from the Stockholm target; participation rose from a very low 29 percent in 1991 to 38.9 percent in 2000.[4]

The European Council recognizes that the Stockholm and the Barcelona targets are not going to materialize as a result of the passage of time alone. Rather, they will require substantive effort on the part of the public and private sectors to ensure that work becomes a real option for everyone and that there are more jobs and better quality work, appropriate financial incentives to make work pay, higher and adaptable work skills, and a partnership approach to expanding employment opportunities involving the social partners. The Organization for Economic Cooperation and Development (OECD) calls for a "comprehensive range of coordinated measures to influence both labour supply and demand," including raising the normal retirement age in light of increases in life expectancy, reducing early-retirement incentives, reforming programs (e.g., disability, sickness, and unemployment) that offer alternative early-retirement options, training, flexible work arrangements, improving work conditions appropriate for older workers, and dealing with age discrimination (Organization for Economic Cooperation and Development 2003, 116).

NIBBLING AWAY AT RETIREMENT BENEFITS

The chapter by Charles Jeszeck et al. is a somewhat revised version of a report published by the U.S. General Accounting Office (now the Government Accountability Office) (Jeszeck et al. 2003) that focuses largely on pension reform and its role in increasing the labor force participation rate of older persons.[5] Unless specifically noted, this commentary refers to the authors simply as GAO.

GAO was asked by a member of the Senate Special Committee on Aging to do the following: (1) compare the United States to other high-income industrialized nations with respect to key demographic and labor force characteristics; (2) look into the anticipated impact of retirement policy reforms on the labor force participation rate of older workers; and (3) determine what the countries have learned that might increase the participation of older workers. The report provides an overview of the labor force and demographic situation in eight high-income countries, discusses the pension systems of, and examines retirement policy reforms in Japan, Sweden, and the United Kingdom, where pension systems have been reformed in ways that may make retirement, especially at very young ages, less feasible financially.

GAO is particularly successful in clearly and very concisely describing the main characteristics of the public pension systems of the three countries. Given the complexities of the systems, especially the United Kingdom's, these summaries are welcome. Discussion of recent retirement policy reforms is similarly informative. Just what the United States has to learn from these countries is less clear. Many of the reforms are too recent or only partially implemented for the countries themselves to be able to assess their impact on participation rates.

Like the OECD, the country experts with whom GAO consulted contend that if labor force participation rates are to be increased, reform must be comprehensive in scope, requiring, for instance, that changes to public pension systems be accompanied by reforms to employer-provided pension systems and related social insurance programs (such as disability insurance), and in labor market policies. Recent reforms, however, seemed to have focused more on public pension systems than on labor market policies that might expand employment opportunities for older workers. With the notable exception of Sweden's new pension system, which allows workers to combine earnings with a full or partial pension, the reforms also seem somewhat more stick than carrot.[6]

From a U.S. perspective, what is striking about some of the systems is how frequently and/or substantially they have been reformed. Understanding the U.K. pension system is a challenge, in large part because of the difficulty of keeping up with the reforms. The frequency and scope of some of the changes must make it rather hard for workers to estimate what they will receive in the way of retirement benefits. As a result, one might have expected higher labor force participation rates for the older population in the United Kingdom, since employment, at least until the mandatory retirement age, is something over which workers have some control. Perhaps the barriers to prolonged employment are too daunting. Or perhaps the reforms have been less unsettling to plan participants themselves than they appear to this outsider.

Similarly, Japan's public pension system has been subjected to frequent reform; GAO points out that it undergoes actuarial reevaluation every five years. Some of the resultant far-reaching changes are probably politically untenable in the United States. The magnitude of recent retirement-age increases is an example. The age of eligibility for full Social Security benefits in the United States is being increased by two years. The amendments legislating the increase, however, provided for a seventeen-year lead-in before the increase would begin phasing in over the following twenty-two years.

Japan, in contrast, is raising its pension-eligibility age by five years over a shorter period of time. The law phasing in the higher eligibility age for the flat-rate portion of Japan's employee pension was enacted in 1994, with implementation beginning in 2001 (Iwamura 1995) and becoming fully in effect by 2013 for men. Legislation introduced in 1999 provides for a five-year increase in the age of eligibility for the earnings-related portion of the employee pension.[7] Japanese workers, in other words, have had to get used to significantly greater change much more rapidly than their American counterparts.

One of the arguments given for the lengthy lead-in to the eligibility-age increase in the United States was that it would give workers time to adjust to the change. GAO's international experts had emphasized the importance of transparency in whatever reforms are introduced, stressing the need for workers "to receive information about the changes that is understandable and can be used to make knowledgeable decisions" (U.S. General Accounting Office 2003, 4). Over the seventeen years, American workers apparently failed to receive or process information about the age increase, for by 2000, when the phase-in went into effect, some 85 percent of U.S. workers were unaware of the increase (Salisbury, Turyn, and Helman 2001). So much for the preparation time to make knowledgeable decisions!

A FOCUS ON THE WORKER

Raising the retirement age and otherwise cutting benefits, indexing benefits to life expectancy, and placing a greater burden on workers for their retirement income may indeed keep people working longer because they can no longer afford to retire so early, not because they are eager to remain at work. There was less discussion by GAO of reforms that might make people *want* to work longer, perhaps because countries have been less successful in identifying and implementing changes (e.g., phased retirement and the creation of good part-time jobs and other flexible work options) designed to foster voluntary increases in the effective retirement age.

Though not included in the GAO chapter, Finland has attempted a comprehensive approach to increasing older worker employment through the Finnish National Program on Aging Workers (FINPAW). This multiyear undertaking involved the Ministries of Social Affairs and Health, Labor, and Education, as well as the Finnish Institute of Occupational Health, trade unions, and employers' associations in efforts to (1) strengthen the status of older persons in the labor market; (2) improve older persons' prospects of continuing to work; and (3) assist them in finding employment. Specific labor-market interventions, such as training projects and activities to help workers maintain their work ability, efforts to change attitudes about aging and older persons, research and development projects, and legislative proposals, were initiated as part of the program.

The proportion of older persons with jobs and enrolled in training programs rose in Finland, as did the retirement age. However, it is not known how much of the improvement can be attributed to FINPAW's efforts as opposed to a favorable economic climate (Organization for Economic Cooperation and Development 2004). Still, the program would seem to warrant greater scrutiny in an effort to understand what might facilitate the continued employment of older workers. An examination of the sharp rise in the labor force participation rate of persons ages 55–64 in the Netherlands might also prove instructive.

The employment prospects of older workers in the EU may improve as a result of age discrimination legislation that member states, in response to an EU directive, must pass by 2006.[8] Were it not for this directive, however, there is no certainty that such legislation would have been enacted anytime soon, at least in the United Kingdom, where the government had been urging a voluntary approach to eliminating age discrimination. Like the United Kingdom, Japan has encouraged a voluntary approach to increasing the mandatory retirement age and succeeded in getting businesses to raise it from 55 to 60. However, firms and unions balked at a further voluntary rise to 65.

Significantly in the GAO chapter, older workers were defined as age 50 and older, although data limitations at times required looking at subgroups, such as age 55 and older. But in fact, the 50 or 55 and older population is a heterogeneous group, which older worker advocates might do well to keep in mind. Policies and programs that are appropriate for and appeal to workers between the ages of 55 and 60 may be inappropriate for or of little interest to most workers above the age of 70. Employers who might be receptive to retaining more workers on the young end of the older worker spectrum might well resist if faced with accommodating many workers in their 70s and beyond.

Greater attention to the heterogeneity of the potential older workforce seems warranted, as do the job performance issues that are sure to be placed on the table if a sizable older workforce becomes the reality. The recently released *Health and Safety Needs of Older Workers* by the National Research Council notes that despite improvements in the health status of the aged population, normative and pathologic age-related differences have implications for performance and productivity; as the workforce ages, addressing the health and safety needs of older workers will become increasingly important to employers, policy makers, and workers themselves (Wegman and McGee 2004). The GAO chapter would have been even more useful had it included a discussion of how European and Japanese policy makers, employers, unions, and others are dealing with these issues.

Lessons Anyone?

Book-review critic Jonathan Yardley has written that "one of the cardinal rules of reviewing books (or anything else, for that matter) is that one must review the book that the author actually wrote rather than complaining that he or she didn't write the book you wanted to read" (Yardley 2004, BW02). GAO appears to have accomplished what it was charged with, so it is perhaps churlish to imply that it should have done more or done something else. Nonetheless, there are many topics about which discussion might have provided a fuller and more rounded picture of how successful other countries have been or are likely to be in halting and even reversing early-retirement trends.

What specifically, for example, are the various EU countries doing to achieve the Stockholm and Barcelona targets? (Some of the pension and other reforms examined by GAO might have been implemented with an eye toward those targets, although no connection between them was made in the chapter.) How likely is it that sufficient jobs will be created over a very few number of years? Thus, how likely is it that the countries will reach their targets? What happens if they do not? How are the National Action Plans—required to show how member states will meet their objectives—monitored and enforced? What explains the high rates of participation in countries that already exceed the targets?[9] What does the job creation picture look like for older workers in Japan? Will the movement away from lifetime employment and toward greater flexibility in hiring and terminating undermine efforts of the Japanese government to keep more older persons at work longer?

It is too early to know whether recent pension reforms will entice many workers to postpone retirement, but some certainly seem likely to do so. What are the implications of delayed retirement for younger workers? While there is very little historical evidence to suggest that older workers take jobs from younger workers or block their promotion opportunities, will that be as true in the future if large numbers of older workers remain on the job? How well will the labor force accommodate aging baby boomers who indicate they want more flexibility at work?

U.S. newspaper readers suffer no shortage of information on public opinions about work and retirement and how workers view their retirement years. Comparable data for Europe and Japan might provide insights into the difficulty or ease with which countries will meet their employment goals. Anecdotal evidence in the form of widespread public protest in reaction to pension reform in some countries and comments like that of the middle-aged French worker who observed that "Americans can work until they are 85," but retirement in Europe "is a sacred right" (Miller 2004, A16) suggest that the task ahead will be formidable.

Judging from public-opinion polls, Americans are not enthusiastic about increases in the age of eligibility for Social Security benefits.[10] Yet, very high proportions of workers say they expect to work in retirement or never retire, many because they will need the money but more because they want to (AARP 2002, 2003, 2004). What about workers in Europe and Japan? Do preretirees expect to work longer as a result of pension cutbacks? Would European workers be more receptive to working longer if alternative work options and phased retirement options were more readily available? Or would such options actually reduce their work efforts?[11]

A key question that probably did deserve more attention in the GAO chapter involves how much there really is to learn from an examination of reforms in other countries. Just how relevant are the experiences in countries as different from the United States as, say, Japan?

Cultural context, of course, plays a role in all of this. It is especially important in understanding the higher labor force participation rate of older Japanese, with their presumably stronger work ethic. The "preference for leisure" that Costa (1998) suggests has come to characterize older Americans has yet to take hold in Japan, which undoubtedly helps explain those higher participation rates. However, employment in Japan is facilitated by specific policies that would be unpalatable at best and illegal at worst in the United States. So, for example, Japanese employers can discriminate against workers on the basis of age, reduce the wages and salaries of older workers, mandatorily retire workers, and rehire retired workers in their previous jobs but at lower wages or (more commonly) in different jobs at lower wages.

Japan's Silver Human Resource Centers, mentioned in an appendix to the GAO report, have been touted by some older worker experts as potential models for other countries (Bass and Oka 1995). Unless the centers have been transformed in recent years, they are more akin to the U.S. Senior Community Service Employment Program (SCSEP),[12] a subsidized job placement program for low-income older persons, than to an employment program that would meet the training and employment needs of the general older worker population. In fact, some of the Silver Human Resource Centers jobs have involved weeding city parks, sweeping up cigarette butts, or otherwise cleaning streets, activities that Americans might like to see here, although not necessarily engaged in by their grandparents. Nonetheless, the Silver Human Resource Centers program, like SCSEP, does provide employment for many people who would have a difficult time finding it otherwise.

CONCLUSION

What lessons are there to be learned from cross-national examinations such as GAO's? And if there are lessons, are we ready to learn them? Should older workers and expanded employment be placed on the agenda for public debate and discussion, as it is in so many other countries? And if so, what is the compelling argument that will get them there? The situation in the United States, after all, is by no means as bleak as that in many European countries and Japan. The United States's fertility rate is higher, as is its immigration rate; the U.S. population is projected to continue growing, and the Social Security system is in less dire straits than the public pension systems of so many European countries and Japan. The Congressional Budget Office has reported that the trust funds will not become exhausted until 2052, twelve years later than projected by the Social Security Administration in 2006 (Congress of the United States, 2004; Board of Trustees 2006). Hence, the United States faces less pressure for reform than do many other high-income industrialized countries. Moreover, as suggested in the first paragraph of this commentary, when it comes to employment, the United States perhaps deserves a pat on the back, that is, if a higher labor force participation rate is a good thing, and for those voluntarily in the labor force at older ages, it undoubtedly is.

Jeszeck et al. observe in chapter 10 of this volume that "in some ways, the United States is ahead of many nations in fostering the labor force participation of older workers," even without such active intervention on the part of policy makers. Perhaps, therefore, older worker advocates and others in some of the countries studied by GAO have reason to look to the United States, not necessarily in envy but because there may be something of value to be learned from the United States with its relatively high labor force participation rate for older persons.

Notes

The views expressed in this commentary are those of the author and do not necessarily represent the views of AARP.

1. These fifteen countries are Austria, Belgium, Denmark, Finland, France, Germany, Greece, Ireland, Italy, Luxembourg, the Netherlands, Portugal, Spain, Sweden, and the United Kingdom.

2. This is not to say that policy makers have completely ignored older workers, for that has not been the case. After liberalizing the Social Security earnings test, for example, Congress enacted in 2000 P.L. 106-182, which eliminated the test for workers at or over the full retirement age; many had argued that this test served as a work disincentive. The 1983 amendments to the Social Security Act introduced a phased-in increase in the age of eligibility for full Social Security benefits and increased the delayed retirement credit paid to workers who remain employed beyond the normal retirement age. The Age Discrimination in Employment Act was passed in 1967; amendments to this act eliminated mandatory retirement for most occupations in 1986. To date, however, there has been no focus on older workers and increasing their attachment to the labor force comparable to that evident in Europe or Japan.

3. The European Council, consisting of heads of state or government, foreign ministers of the member states, and the president of the European Commission, sets general EU policy.

4. The above figures for the Netherlands are from the International Labor Organization (ILO), which standardizes data to permit comparability across countries. Figures from the Netherlands itself reveal a somewhat lower labor force participation rate than do the ILO figures. Nonetheless, they also show an increase of about the same amount over about the same period: from 25 percent in 1990 to 34 percent in 2001 (The Geneva Association May 2003: 63).

5. U.S. General Accounting Office. 2003. *Older Workers: Policies of Other Nations to Increase Labor Force Participation,* Washington, DC: U.S. General Accounting Office. Differences between the two documents can be found in the conclusions and some of the footnotes. Not included in the version of the paper prepared for workshop on Work Options for Mature Americans, appendices in *Older Workers: Policies of Other Nations to Increase Labor Force Participation* offer greater detail on the reforms in Sweden, Japan, and the United Kingdom than appears in the body of the report. The title of the paper delivered at the workshop does not accurately capture what the paper is about, which is pen-

sion reform in response to *population* aging. There is considerably less on changes that have been or may be introduced as a result of *workforce* aging.

6. However, Sweden's new notional defined contribution plan links a worker's annuity at retirement to estimated life expectancy at the age of retirement. With increasing life expectancy over time, workers will have to plan on working longer or opting for lower benefits.

7. Both increases will be fully implemented five years later for women than for men.

8. The directive calls for legislation prohibiting discrimination at work based on age, sexual orientation, religious beliefs, and disability.

9. GAO notes that experts in Sweden suggest that the traditionally high labor force participation rates for older workers in that country may be a reflection of low unemployment rates through the early 1990s, the same retirement age for men and women, and the inclusion of older workers in reemployment programs.

10. See Rix (1999) for an overview of opinion poll research on proposals to raise the retirement age.

11. Finland's experience with a partial-pension scheme suggests that it may reduce effective labor supply because a large share of part-time pensioners would apparently have continued in full-time work had the part-time option not been available (Organization for Economic Cooperation and Development 2004, 72).

12. SCSEP now stresses non-subsidized job placement.

REFERENCES

AARP. 2002. *Staying Ahead of the Curve: The AARP Work and Career Study.* Washington, DC: AARP.

AARP. 2003. *Staying Ahead of the Curve 2003: The AARP Working in Retirement Study.* Washington, DC: AARP.

AARP. 2004. *Baby Boomers Envision Retirement II.* Washington, DC: AARP.

Bass, Scott A., and Masato Oka. 1995. "An Older-Worker Employment Model: Japan's Silver Human Resource Centers." *The Gerontologist.* Vol. 35, no. 5: 679–82.

Board of Trustees, Federal Old-Age and Survivors Insurance and Disability Insurance Trust Funds. 2006. *The 2006 Annual Report of the Board of Trustees of the Federal Old-Age and Survivors Insurance and Federal Disability Insurance Trust Funds.* Washington, DC: Board of Trustees.

Congress of the United States, Congressional Budget Office. 2004. *The Outlook for Social Security.* Washington, DC: Congressional Budget Office.

Costa, Dora L. 1998. *The Evolution of Retirement.* Chicago: University of Chicago Press.

European Commission. 2002. *Employment in Europe 2002: Recent Trends and Prospects.* Luxembourg: Office for Official Publications of the European Communities.

European Commission, Directorate-General for Employment and Social Affairs. 2003. *Employment in Europe 2003.* http://europa.eu.int/comm/employment_social/employment_analysis/employ_2003_en.htm [6/20/04].

European Commission. 2004. "Increasing the Employment of Older Workers and Delaying the Exit from the Labour Market." Communication from the Commission to the Council, the European Parliament, the European Economic and Social Committee and the Committee of the Regions, COM(2004) 146 final. Brussels: Commission of the European Communities.

European Commission. 2006. Eurostat. Employment. http://epp.eurostat.ec.europa.eu/portal/page?_pageid=1090,1&_dad=portal&_schema=PORTAL [7/22/06].

Geneva Association. 2003. "Public Policy, Ageing Études and Work: An International Symposium at St. Catherine's College, Cambridge, 17–19 December 2002." Études et Dossiers No. 270. Geneva: The Geneva Association.

International labor Office. 2006. LABORSTA Internet, Yearly Data: Total and Economically Active Population, by Age Group. http://laborsta.ilo.org [7/22/06].

Iwamura, Masahiko. 1995. "1994 Revision of Pension System." Japan Labor Bulletin. Vol. 34, no. 3. Special Topic. http://www.jil.go.jp/bulletin/year/1995/vol34-03/06.htm.

Jeszeck, Charles, Tony DeFrank, Katharine Leavitt, Jeffrey S. Petersen, Janice Peterson, Yunsian Tai, and Howard Wial. 2003. International Responses to an Aging Labor Force: Lessons for U.S. Policy. Washington, DC: U.S. General Accounting Office.

Miller, John W. 2004. "Pension Systems Strain Europe—Early Retirement Culture Has Become a Public-Policy Headache." Wall Street Journal. (June 17): A16.

Organization for Economic Cooperation and Development (OECD). 2003. OECD Employment Outlook 2003: Towards More and Better Jobs. Paris: OECD.

Organization for Economic Cooperation and Development (OECD). 2004. Ageing and Employment Policies: Finland. Paris: OECD.

Rix, Sara E. 1999. "Social Security Reform: Rethinking Retirement-Age Policy—A Look at Raising Social Security's Retirement Age." Issue Brief No. 40. Washington, DC: AARP Public Policy Institute.

Salisbury, Dallas, Teresa Turyn, and Ruth Helman. 2001. "EBRI 2001 Retirement Surveys: Retirement Confidence Survey (RCS), Minority RCS, and Small Employer Retirement Survey (SERS)." EBRI Issue Brief No. 234. Washington, DC: Employee Benefit Research Institute. (June).

U.S. Department of Labor, Bureau of Labor Statistics. 2006. Employment and Earnings. Vol. 53, no. 1. Washington, DC: U.S. Government Printing Office.

U.S. General Accounting Office. 2003. Older Workers: Policies of Other Nations to Increase Labor Force Participation. GAO Report #GAO-03-307. Washington, DC: GAO.

Wegman, David H., and James P. McGee, editors. 2004. Health and Safety Needs of Older Workers. Washington, DC: The National Academies Press.

Yardley, Jonathan. 2004. "A World War II Tale of Quietly Heroic Resistance." The Washington Post. (March 21).

CHAPTER ELEVEN

Raising the Retirement Age
in OECD Countries

YUNG-PING CHEN & JOHN TURNER

Life expectancy is increasing in most countries. Worldwide, the average life expectancy is expected to increase ten years between 2000 and 2050 (Centers for Disease Control and Prevention 2003). In the European Union (EU), life expectancy at age 65 has increased by more than one year per decade since 1950. Demographers expect this trend to continue. By 2050, demographic projections suggest that 65-year-old Europeans will live at least four to five years longer than they were expected to in 2000 (Commission of the European Communities 2002).

How should retirement policy react to increased life expectancy at older ages? A possible option to encourage greater work at older ages is the postponement of the eligibility age for retirement benefits, notably under national pension plans.

Policy arguments both support and oppose raising the retirement age in a national pension plan. Increasing life expectancy and an aging population raise the ratio of retirees to workers. Raising the retirement age, if done so that workers will receive the benefits at an older retirement age which they would have received at a younger age, lowers the cost of a national pension system. It also has the potential for encouraging later retirement, offsetting to some extent the rising ratio of retirees to workers. However, raising the retirement age reduces workers' options for leaving the labor force. It is especially disadvantageous for older workers with shorter life expectancy, who tend to be lower-income, less-educated workers. For some workers who have physically demanding jobs, it is hard to continue working at older ages. Older workers who are laid off often have a difficult time finding another job, which may be due in part to age discrimination.

This chapter investigates public policy toward retirement age among the high-income Organization for Economic Cooperation and Development (OECD) countries. It indicates that a number of OECD countries have instituted retirement age policies that in the U.S. context would appear to be politically infeasible, and considers policies that have been used to permit or encourage the postponement of retirement age. First, it surveys countries that have raised the early retirement age in a national pension plan. Second, it surveys countries that have passed legislation raising the retirement age at which occupational pension benefits can be received or that have companies that have raised the retirement age. Third, it considers countries that have outlawed mandatory retirement. The extent to which these policies to encourage work at older ages are due to increasing longevity is probably unknowable, though it is plausible to assume that increasing longevity has played a major role.

Policies that encourage postponement of the retirement age have their own problems. These policies raise legitimate concerns about effects on workers in different categories of jobs and personal circumstances that make additional full-time work difficult. Thus, the chapter concludes with a discussion of the role phased retirement may have in facilitating postponed retirement.

RETIREMENT AGE POLICY

Employment and retirement policies have occupied the attention of policy-setting bodies in the EU at least since 1982 (Reday-Mulvey 2000). In 1982, the Council of the European Communities recommended the following principles for formulating policy on the age of retirement: (1) loosening the rules on the age of retirement, for example, by providing greater flexibility by making it possible to bring forward or defer the age of retirement; (2) gradually reducing work time during the years preceding retirement; (3) increasing the freedom to perform paid work for those drawing an old-age pension.

In 1999, with the help of member states, the European Commission planned "to bring ways and means of reversing the trend towards early retirement, to study new patterns of gradual retirement, and to increase the viability and flexibility of pension schemes." In addition, the Commission invited member states "to promote life-long training and flexible work patterns" (Reday-Mulvey 2000, 51).

National Pension Retirement Age Legislation in the OECD

When the OECD was founded in 1961, it had twenty member countries. Of those, only two were outside of Western Europe—Canada and the United States. Since then, Finland and three Asian-Pacific nations have joined—Australia,

Japan, and New Zealand. More recently South Korea, Poland, Hungary, the Czech Republic, the Slovak Republic, and Mexico have joined, raising the total to thirty (Organization for Economic Cooperation and Development 2004). This chapter considers retirement age policy in twenty-two countries—eighteen of the original twenty countries (excluding the United States and Turkey) plus Finland and the three from Asia and the Pacific.

Countries That Have Raised the Retirement Age for Both Sexes

Because it is politically difficult to do so, it is remarkable that a number of countries in the traditional OECD have raised the retirement age in their national pension programs for both men and women. The following section considers countries that have raised the retirement age only for women because it had been lower than that for men. Some countries have effectively raised the retirement age by eliminating special early retirement for some occupations. This survey indicates that changes in national pension eligibility age have often been made with little advance notice, with the full extent of the change phased in over time. Those countries are not considered here.

Austria.   Up to the year 2000, the retirement age for the national pension plan in Austria was 60 for men and 55 for women. In May 2000, Austria legislated a stepwise increase in the retirement age. Starting in October 2000 and ending in September 2002, in quarterly steps, the retirement age has increased to 61.5 for men and 56.5 for women. In 2003, Austria passed a reform bill that will increase the retirement age from 61.5 to 65 for men and from 56.5 to 60 for women. The increases are occurring gradually from July 2004 to 2013 (Avery 2003).

Denmark.   Denmark had a national pension plan that provided a transitional benefit for people ages 50–59 who had become unemployed and had contributed to the unemployment benefit program for at least thirty years. That plan was closed to new entrants in 1996, and will be fully phased out by 2006 (Commission of the European Communities 2002).

Finland.   In 2002, Finland legislated changes that took effect in 2005. The retirement age in the earnings-related national pension system was raised from 60 to 62, and the individual early retirement pension, which was available at age 58 to long-service workers, was abolished (The Geneva Association 2003).

Germany.   In the 1980s in West Germany, workers could retire at ages 60, 63, or 65, depending on meeting certain qualifying conditions. Legislation passed in

1989 and effective in 1992 stipulated a phased increase of both the age 60 and age 63 retirement options, starting in 2001 and ending in 2012. At that time, the age-60 limit will have been increased to 62. Temporary transition rules will allow retirement at age 60 for some birth cohorts.

Greece.   Greece has established a national pension retirement age of 65 for men and women who first start working after 1993. In 2000, the retirement age was 58 for men and women with long careers of work.

Italy.   Italy has a national pension that retirees can receive at any age so long as they have worked a minimum number of years. Having started in 1999, the required number of years is increasing, being thirty-seven years in 2002 and rising to forty years in 2008 (Social Security Administration 2002).

Japan.   Having begun in 2000, Japan is gradually raising its retirement age in its Employees' Pension Insurance program from 60 to 65 for both men and women, with it reaching age 65 for men in 2025 and women in 2030.

New Zealand.   New Zealand raised the national pension retirement age from 60 in 1991 to 65 in 2001. Those who turned 60 before April 1992 were eligible for a national pension benefit at age 60. The legislation putting into effect the change was passed in August 1991 and took effect on April 1, 1992. From April 1992, the eligibility age was increased from 60 to 61. The initial one-year increase reflected a general acceptance that age 60 was too low. From July 1993, the eligibility age rose by 3 months for each 6-month period until April 2001, when the retirement age reached age 65. Effectively, a 5-year increase in the retirement age took effect within nine years. A Transitional Retirement Benefit was paid over this period to those affected by the changes, with the age of eligibility for this benefit also rising until it was phased out on April 1, 2001.

Sweden.   When Sweden reformed its national pension system in 1999, it raised the retirement age for the old-age pension from 60 to 61 (Social Security Administration 1999). This change was not politically difficult because most workers already retired at age 61 or later.

Increases in the Retirement Age for Women to Equalize It for Men and Women
Most OECD countries have, at some point, permitted women to receive national pension old-age benefits at younger ages than men. For a number of years, in the United States, women could receive Social Security benefits at age 62, while men could not receive them until age 65. Most of the countries for which the

differential persists, however, are moving to equalize retirement ages for men and women. For some countries, this change is occurring because the EU requires its member countries to equalize the national pension retirement age for men and women. Equalizing the retirement age for the sexes does not necessarily imply an increase for women, but in practice it generally has occurred that way.

Australia.   Australia is raising the minimum age at which a woman can receive its means-tested pension, called the "age pension," which is received by the majority of retirees, by 6 months every two years, from age 60 in 1995 to age 65 in 2013. The legislation making this change was enacted in 1994. The retirement age for the means-tested program has been 65 for men for a number of years. However, disability benefits are often used as a bridge to the age pension.

Austria.   Legislated in 1992, but taking effect in 2018, the retirement age for women in Austria, which is 56.5, will be increased to that of men, which is age 61.5. The change will occur stepwise until it is completed in 2034.

Japan.   Japan's national pension system has several parts for most workers. National pension reform in 1985 raised the retirement age for women for the national Employee's Pension Insurance from 55 to 60 over a fifteen-year period. It reached age 60 in 2000, the same age for men (Liu 1987). Beginning in 2000, the retirement age for both men and women started increasing to 65, which is the retirement age for the National Pension Insurance program.

Portugal.   Portugal raised the retirement age for women from 62 to 65, equaling that of men, over the period from 1994 to 1999.

Switzerland.   Switzerland, by contrast, initially decided not to equalize the retirement age treatment of the sexes, raising the retirement age for women from 62 to 64. It raised the retirement age for women from 62 to 63 in January 2001 and to 64 in January 2005. The retirement age for men is 65. In 2003, however, the Swiss Parliament passed a bill further raising the retirement age for women to 65 in 2009. In 2004, Swiss voters rejected that bill by a large majority in a referendum. Workers can receive early-retirement benefits from their mandatory occupational pension plans, if their plan rules allow it, at age 60 for men and age 57 for women (International Social Security Association 2003).

United Kingdom.   The national pension retirement age in the United Kingdom is 65 for men and 60 for women. As a result of legislation passed in 1995, it will be raised gradually for women over a ten-year period, starting in 2010 for

women who reach age 60 that year, until it reaches 65 in 2020. The increase occurs at the rate of 1 month in the retirement age for every 2 months in birth
date (O'Connell 2002).

Countries That Have a Retirement Age of 65 or Higher

Some countries in the OECD have not legislated increases in the age at which
workers can receive national pension benefits because they have had a long-
standing eligibility age of 65 or older.

Denmark.   In Denmark, the universal flat-rate old-age pension benefit, which
is financed from general tax revenue, is available at age 65. The minimum age for
receipt of tax-favored employer-provided pension benefits is age 67, but other
programs facilitate early retirement.

Iceland.   In Iceland, the universal pension is available at age 65.

Ireland.   In Ireland, the national retirement pension is available at age 65, and
the old-age contributory pension is available at age 66.

Netherlands.   In the Netherlands, the basic national old-age pension is available
at age 65. However, the early retirement program was developed in the early 1980s
as a way to allow earlier retirement. With at least ten years of uninterrupted
employment, a worker could retire at age 60 with a replacement rate of at least
80 percent. The government plans to phase out the present system.

Norway.   In Norway, the retirement age is 67 for both the universal and the
earnings-related national old-age benefit (Social Security Administration 1999).
Nearly all workers are covered by occupational pensions, however, that permit
retirement at age 62.

   In summary, a number of traditional OECD countries have legislated an increase in the retirement age in their national pension programs. Others have
had a long-standing policy of having a retirement age of 65 or higher.

Countries That Have Raised the Earliest Age at Which Employer-Provided Pension Benefits Can Be Received

Some countries have raised the earliest age at which benefits from employer-
provided pensions can be received. This survey indicates international experience
with respect to the age at which workers can receive benefits in occupational pension plans.

Australia.   In 1992, the Australian government announced that it would increase the early retirement age for the mandatory employer-provided program providing old-age benefits, called the "superannuation benefit," from 55 to 60. The new rules took effect in July 1999. The minimum retirement age is 55 for both men and women born before July 1, 1960. For those born after that date but before July 1961, the minimum age is 56. In similar fashion, the minimum age rises by 1 year for every subsequent annual birth cohort until it reaches 60 for persons born after June 30, 1964 (Kehl 2002).

Belgium.   In 2003, Belgium passed a law stipulating that occupational pension benefits cannot be paid before age 60. Previously, benefits could be received at age 58 or earlier. For all existing plans, current rules are applicable until January 1, 2010 (Watson Wyatt Worldwide 2003).

Switzerland.   To harmonize the retirement age for national pensions and occupational pensions, Switzerland increased the retirement age for occupational pension plans from 62 to 64 in 2001, with the increase from 62 to 63 taking place in that year and the increase from 63 to 64 taking place in 2005.

United Kingdom.   The United Kingdom has raised the minimum age at which occupational pensions can be received from 50 to 55. The British government has proposed raising the minimum retirement age for members of the armed forces, police, firefighters, nurses, and teachers. Currently, members of the armed forces can receive pension benefits at age 40 after eighteen years of work. The change would require eligible members to wait until age 55 for a reduced pension, beginning in 2005. Teachers, nurses, police, and firefighters would be required to work five years longer, from 50 to 55 (Winnett and Carr-Brown 2003). Civil servants will have a new retirement age of 65 for all new employees starting in 2006. This is an increase from the current retirement age of 60 (O'Connell 2003).

In the United Kingdom in 2003, Honda Motor Company announced that it was raising the retirement age in its pension plan from 60 to 62. All employees under age 55 would have to work to the new retirement age. It is thought that Honda is the first major U.K. employer to do this, but that the precedent may cause other employers to follow suit.

European Union.   The retirement age policy of the EU for its civil servants provides further evidence of a trend of raising the retirement age. Proposed in 1999 and taking effect in 2004, EU civil servants have had an increase in the retirement age from 60 to 63 (Spiteri 2003).

Mandatory Retirement and Age Discrimination

Laws outlawing mandatory retirement and age discrimination can also be used to permit or encourage workers to delay retirement.

European Union.   In January 1996, the EU raised to 65 the mandatory retirement age for airline pilots. By comparison, the mandatory retirement age for airline pilots in the United States is 60. Countries have until 2006 to implement legislation banning age discrimination and mandatory retirement ages.

New Zealand.   New Zealand has passed human rights legislation that bans mandatory retirement ages. Before that legislation, the police departments had set a mandatory retirement age of 55 (Nzoom.com 2003). Few countries have laws banning mandatory retirement.

Phased Retirement and Its Relevance to Raising the Retirement Age

Some older workers may experience poor health or develop some degree of physical disability that limits their ability to work full time. Other people may have their ability to work full-time curtailed by their need to provide caregiving services to family members. These workplace concerns may be ameliorated by employment and pension arrangements that allow workers to retire gradually through phasing out of work over a period of time.

Phased retirement may help workers in other contexts. Some people may need to work in order to supplement their retirement benefits; others may wish to work to enhance their standard of living or for nonfinancial reasons. For these purposes, most people presumably would prefer not to work full time. However, under current U.S. employment and pension regulations, full retirement is generally the only viable choice for those near retirement age. Such a lack of options deprives the society of the contributions of these individuals, as it diminishes their opportunity to work. This dilemma could be resolved by arrangements that would allow workers to retire gradually.

The above is not just a theoretical notion. That some people prefer retiring from work gradually rather than abruptly has been observed anecdotally and reported in surveys conducted in the United States. For example, according to the 2001 Retirement Risk Survey, sponsored by the Society of Actuaries, two-thirds of preretirees (66 percent) and almost half of retirees (47 percent) said they were or would have been very or somewhat interested in being able to cut back gradually on the hours they worked at their current job, rather than stopping work all at once when they got closer to retirement. Moreover, almost two in ten retirees (19 percent) described their retirement process as closest to "gradually reduced the number of hours you worked before stopping completely" (Society of Actuaries 2001).

There is also evidence of preference for work during retirement, an apparent oxymoron notwithstanding. In a 2003 survey, 70 percent of workers intended to work in retirement and 28 percent of retirees had worked at some time during retirement, according to the Retirement Confidence Survey, reported by the Employee Benefit Research Institute, Mathew Greenwald & Associates, and the American Savings Education Council (Employee Benefit Research Institute 2003).

Phased retirement may benefit both workers and society. For many individuals, a life-stage transition that is less abrupt is often better than one that is sudden. For society, such an arrangement could offset some of the expected labor force shortage, while helping to contain the costs of pensions. From a business perspective, it is important to retain and use long-service employees to mentor and train younger workers.

Despite their salubrious effects, formal phased retirement arrangements are rare, at least in part because a number of barriers to their implementation, including legal barriers, barriers relating to pension plan objectives, and others (See chapter 5, by Penner, Perun, and Steuerle, in this volume; Penner et al. 2002; Chen and Scott 2003).

In Europe, while there are reports of growing receptivity on the part of workers and employers to phased retirement, actual practice still lags, as is to be expected with any innovation. For example, one report on Germany indicated that experiences were mainly negative because older workers were unwilling to change to part-time work and employers did not provide attractive part-time work opportunities (Naegele 1999).

Conclusion

People are living longer, and the aging of the population is further advanced in some European countries than in the United States. Retirement systems in OECD countries increasingly recognize that people are living longer. Possible policy prescriptions in recognition of increasingly long lives include: reducing the barriers to continued work by older workers; encouraging older workers to work longer; and promoting higher rates of economic growth, thereby creating demand for more workers. A number of countries have addressed the challenges arising from increased longevity by enacting policies that permit or encourage older workers to continue working. Some OECD countries have enacted policies raising the retirement age in their national pension programs, while some have long-standing national pension eligibility ages of 65 or higher, policies that appear at present to be politically infeasible in the United States. In addition, some countries have raised the earliest age at which employer-provided pension benefits can be received. Policies that raise the early retirement age need to take into account workers who have difficulty continuing full-time work at older ages. Phased retirement is one possible policy to help those workers.

NOTES

The views, opinions, and judgments expressed here are solely the responsibility of the authors and do not represent the position of AARP. Chen expresses thanks to Sara Rix, John Scott, and Anna Rappaport for discussions on phased retirement.

REFERENCES

Avery, Helen. 2003. "Austrian MPs Pass Pension Reform Bill." Investment & Pensions Europe—IPE.com. June 12. http://www.ipe.com/article_default.asp?article=14835.
Centers for Disease Control and Prevention. 2003. "Trends in Aging—United States and Worldwide." Morbidity and Mortality Weekly Report. Vol. 52 (February 14): 101–9.
Chen, Y. P., and J. C. Scott. 2003. "Gradual Retirement: An Additional Option in Work and Retirement." North American Actuarial Journal. Vol. 7, no. 3: 62–74.
Commission of the European Communities. 2002. "Joint Report to the Commission and the Council on Adequate and Sustainable Pensions." Communication from the Commission to the Council, the European Parliament, the European Economic and Social Committee and the Committee of the Regions. (December).
Employee Benefit Research Institute, American Savings Education Council, and Mathew Greenwald and Associates. Executive Summary. 2003 Retirement Confidence Survey. www.ebri.org/rcs/2003/03rcssof.pdf.
The Geneva Association. 2003. The Four Pillars. Vol. 32 (February).
International Social Security Association (ISSA). 2003. "Complementary & Private Pensions throughout the World 2003." Geneva, Switzerland.
Kehl, David. 2002. "Superannuation Preservation Rules: A Summary." Research Note. No. 22. Information and Research Services, Department of the Parliamentary Library-Australia. (February 19).
Liu, Lillian. 1987. "Social Security Reforms in Japan." Social Security Bulletin. Vol. 50 (August): 29–37.
Naegele, Gerhard. 1999. "Gradual Retirement in Germany." Journal of Aging and Social Policy. Vol. 10, no. 3: 83–102.

Nzoom.com. 2003. "Retirement Age Chewed Over." (May 27). http://onebusiness.nzoom/onebusinnes.

O'Connell, Alison. 2002. "Raising State Pension Age: Are We Ready?" London, England: Pensions Policy Institute.

Organization for Economic Cooperation and Development (OECD). 2004. "Ratification of the Convention on the OECD." Downloaded February 6, 2004 from http://www.oecd.org/document/58/0,2340,en_2649_201185_1889402_1_1_1_1,00.html.

Penner, Rudolf, Pamela Perun, and Eugene Steuerle. 2002. *Legal and Institutional Impediments to Partial Retirement and Part-Time Work by Older Workers.* Washington, DC: The Urban Institute.

Reday-Mulvey, Genevieve. 2000. "Gradual Retirement in Europe." *Journal of Aging & Social Policy.* Vol 11, no. 2/3: 49–60.

Social Security Administration (SSA). 1999 and other years. *Social Security Programs throughout the World.* SSA Publication No. 13-11805.

Society of Actuaries. Key Findings and Issues. *2001 Retirement Risk Survey.* http://www.soa.org/sections/rrs_findings.pdf.

Spiteri, Sharon. 2003. "EU Civil Servants Pension Reform Gets Go-Ahead." Euobserver.com. http://www.euobserver/com/index.phtml?aid=12862. Downloaded September 30.

Watson Wyatt Worldwide. 2003. "New Pension Law in Belgium." *Global News Briefs.* May.

Winnett, Robert, and Jonathan Carr-Brown. 2003. "Army and Police Face Loss of Early Retirement Rights." *The Sunday Times.* United Kingdom. (June 22).

Contributors

Jennjou Chen, National Chengchi University, Taipei City, Taiwan

Yung-Ping Chen, University of Massachusetts

Tony DeFrank, U.S. Government Accountability Office

Todd Elder, University of Illinois

Gregory Gettas, Columbia University

Teresa Ghilarducci, University of Notre Dame

Sharon Hermes, U.S. Government Accountability Office

Robert M. Hutchens, Cornell University, School of Industrial and Labor Relations

Charles Jeszeck, U.S. Government Accountability Office

Katharine Leavitt, U.S. Government Accountability Office

Dana Muir, University of Michigan Business School

Alicia H. Munnell, Boston College, Carroll School of Management

Kevin Neuman, University of Wisconsin, Stevens Point

Rudolph G. Penner, Urban Institute

Pamela Perun, Urban Institute

Jeffrey S. Petersen, U.S. Government Accountability Office

Janice Peterson, U.S. Government Accountability Office

Joseph S. Piacentini, U.S. Department of Labor, Employee Benefit Security Administration

Patrick J. Purcell, Congressional Research Service, Library of Congress

Joseph Quinn, Boston College

Patricia M. Raskin, Columbia University

Sara E. Rix, AARP Public Policy Institute

C. Eugene Steuerle, Urban Institute

Yunsian Tai, U.S. Government Accountability Office

John Turner, Washington, DC

Christian E. Weller, Center for American Progress

Jeffrey Wenger, University of Georgia, School of Public and International Affairs

Lance R. Wescher, University of Notre Dame

Howard Wial, U.S. Government Accountability Office

Edward N. Wolff, New York University

Stephen A. Woodbury, Michigan State University and W. E. Upjohn Institute

Index